Application of Mathematics for Modeling Industrial Innovative Systems and Processes

Application of Mathematics for Modeling Industrial Innovative Systems and Processes

Editor

Aleksey I. Shinkevich

Basel • Beijing • Wuhan • Barcelona • Belgrade • Novi Sad • Cluj • Manchester

Editor
Aleksey I. Shinkevich
Kazan National Research
Technological University
Kazan
Russia

Editorial Office
MDPI
St. Alban-Anlage 66
4052 Basel, Switzerland

This is a reprint of articles from the Special Issue published online in the open access journal *Mathematics* (ISSN 2227-7390) (available at: https://www.mdpi.com/journal/mathematics/special-issues/Model_Ind_Innov_Syst).

For citation purposes, cite each article independently as indicated on the article page online and as indicated below:

Lastname, A.A.; Lastname, B.B. Article Title. *Journal Name* **Year**, *Volume Number*, Page Range.

ISBN 978-3-7258-0737-6 (Hbk)
ISBN 978-3-7258-0738-3 (PDF)
doi.org/10.3390/books978-3-7258-0738-3

© 2024 by the authors. Articles in this book are Open Access and distributed under the Creative Commons Attribution (CC BY) license. The book as a whole is distributed by MDPI under the terms and conditions of the Creative Commons Attribution-NonCommercial-NoDerivs (CC BY-NC-ND) license.

Contents

About the Editor vii

Aleksey I. Shinkevich, Irina G. Ershova, Farida F. Galimulina and Alla A. Yarlychenko
Innovative Mesosystems Algorithm for Sustainable Development Priority Areas Identification in Industry Based on Decision Trees Construction
Reprinted from: *Mathematics* 2021, *9*, 3055, doi:10.3390/math9233055 1

Aleksey I. Shinkevich, Alsu R. Akhmetshina and Ruslan R. Khalilov
Development of a Methodology for Forecasting the Sustainable Development of Industry in Russia Based on the Tools of Factor and Discriminant Analysis
Reprinted from: *Mathematics* 2022, *10*, 859, doi:10.3390/math10060859 19

Oleg M. Flisyuk, Nicolay A. Martsulevich, Valery P. Meshalkin and Alexandr V. Garabadzhiu
Mathematical Modeling of Changes in the Dispersed Composition of Solid Phase Particles in Technological Apparatuses of Periodic and Continuous Action
Reprinted from: *Mathematics* 2022, *10*, 994, doi:10.3390/math10060994 35

Maha A. Omair, Yusra A. Tashkandy, Sameh Askar and Abdulhamid A. Alzaid
Family of Distributions Derived from Whittaker Function
Reprinted from: *Mathematics* 2022, *10*, 1058, doi:10.3390/math10071058 47

Aleksey I. Shinkevich, Nadezhda Yu. Psareva and Tatyana V. Malysheva
Choosing Industrial Zones Multi-Criteria Problem Solution for Chemical Industries Development Using the Additive Global Criterion Method
Reprinted from: *Mathematics* 2022, *10*, 1434, doi:10.3390/math10091434 70

Jian Chen, Jiajun Tian, Shuheng Jiang, Yunsheng Zhou, Hai Li and Jing Xu
The Allocation of Base Stations with Region Clustering and Single-Objective Nonlinear Optimization
Reprinted from: *Mathematics* 2022, *10*, 2257, doi:10.3390/math10132257 86

Aleksey I. Shinkevich, Irina G. Ershova and Farida F. Galimulina
Forecasting the Efficiency of Innovative Industrial Systems Based on Neural Networks
Reprinted from: *Mathematics* 2023, *11*, 164, doi:10.3390/math11010164 105

Lotfi Ben Said, Alia Khanfir Chabchoub and Mondher Wali
Mathematical Model Describing the Hardening and Failure Behaviour of Aluminium Alloys: Application in Metal Shear Cutting Process
Reprinted from: *Mathematics* 2023, *11*, 1980, doi:10.3390/math11091980 130

You-Shyang Chen, Jieh-Ren Chang, Ying-Hsun Hung and Jia-Hsien Lai
Oversampling Application of Identifying 3D Selective Laser Sintering Yield by Hybrid Mathematical Classification Models
Reprinted from: *Mathematics* 2023, *11*, 3204, doi:10.3390/math11143204 148

Farida F. Galimulina and Naira V. Barsegyan
Application of Mass Service Theory to Economic Systems Optimization Problems—A Review
Reprinted from: *Mathematics* 2024, *12*, 403, doi:10.3390/math12030403 178

About the Editor

Aleksey I. Shinkevich

Alexey I. Shinkevich is a Doctor of Economics, Doctor of Technical Sciences, and Professor at Kazan National Research Technological University. He was awarded the honorary titles of "Honorary Worker of Education of the Russian Federation", "Academician of the Russian Academy of Sciences", "Corresponding Member of the Russian Academy of Sciences", "Honored Worker of Science and Education", and "Founder of a scientific school". He completed internships in the world's leading scientific and educational centers, including Tempe, Arizona, USA (2011); Dusseldorf, Germany (2017); Eskisehir, Turkey (2022); and Yerevan, Armenia (2023). He is the chairman of the Dissertation Council for the defense of dissertations for the degree of Candidate of Sciences, for the degree of Doctor of Sciences 24.2.312.08 in the specialties 1.2.2. Mathematical modeling, numerical methods, and software packages (technical sciences); and 2.5.22. Product quality management, standardization, and organization of production (technical sciences).

He has authored 35 books and more than 700 scientific articles, including those published on Scopus and Web of Science; he has also registered 25 programs for electronic computers.

His research interests include the organization of resource-saving industries in petrochemistry, circular economy, supply chain management, logistics, research on innovative economic development using a neo-institutional approach and mathematical modeling methods, digitalization of industry, and sustainable development of industrial enterprises.

Article

Innovative Mesosystems Algorithm for Sustainable Development Priority Areas Identification in Industry Based on Decision Trees Construction

Aleksey I. Shinkevich [1,*], Irina G. Ershova [2], Farida F. Galimulina [1] and Alla A. Yarlychenko [1]

1 Logistics and Management Department, Kazan National Research Technological University, 420015 Kazan, Russia; dlogscm@kstu.ru (F.F.G.); yarlychenkoaa@kazan.psbank.ru (A.A.Y.)
2 Department of Finance and Credit, Southwest State University, 305040 Kursk, Russia; ershovairgen@yandex.ru
* Correspondence: ShinkevichAI@corp.knrtu.ru

Citation: Shinkevich, A.I.; Ershova, I.G.; Galimulina, F.F.; Yarlychenko, A.A. Innovative Mesosystems Algorithm for Sustainable Development Priority Areas Identification in Industry Based on Decision Trees Construction. *Mathematics* **2021**, *9*, 3055. https://doi.org/10.3390/math9233055

Academic Editor: Antonella Basso

Received: 13 November 2021
Accepted: 26 November 2021
Published: 28 November 2021

Publisher's Note: MDPI stays neutral with regard to jurisdictional claims in published maps and institutional affiliations.

Copyright: © 2021 by the authors. Licensee MDPI, Basel, Switzerland. This article is an open access article distributed under the terms and conditions of the Creative Commons Attribution (CC BY) license (https://creativecommons.org/licenses/by/4.0/).

Abstract: Globally, assessing sustainable development methodology is kept in sustainable society index (SSI) format, but at the level of meso- and microsystems it remains undeveloped. The aim of the study is to typologize innovative mesosystems in Russian industry in the context of sustainable development based on the CART algorithm and to develop an algorithm for identifying priority areas of sustainable development. The research methods applied included formalization, a systematic approach, and the CART algorithm (calculation of the Gini index, training sample segmentation, the use of a recursive function and regression assessment). As a result of the study, the algorithm for the differentiated identification of innovative mesosystems sustainable development priority directions in industry based on the unique author's methodology (ISDI) is proposed. The predominance of mesosystems with weak level of sustainable development requiring state support in favor of such mesosystems restructure is revealed. The novelty of the research lies in the development of new science-based solutions to ensure an accelerated transition of industry to the path of sustainable development. The difference of the author's approach from the provisions known in science is the inclusion of environmental innovations in the mechanism for managing the sustainable development of innovative mesosystems and subsequent accounting in the process of mathematical processing of an array of data, which determines the uniqueness of the constructed decision trees.

Keywords: sustainable development; innovative mesosystems; manufacturing; profitability; environmental innovations; decision trees; integral indicator of sustainable development

1. Introduction

Modern trends in industrial development—the concept of sustainable development, ESG initiative, green industry, carbon neutrality, etc.—are implemented to different degrees at the micro, meso and macro levels. Cross-country comparisons of sustainable society index (SSI) level indicate the lag of Russian industry compared to other countries: at the end of 2019, the consolidated indicator of human wellbeing in Russia was 7.6 points (the top position was taken by Bermuda—9.7), environmental wellbeing—2.6 points (the top position was taken by the Northern Mariana Islands—9.6), "economic wellbeing"—4.9 points (the top position was taken by the Cayman Islands and Liechtenstein—10) [1]. The reasons for rating low positions are the differences existing between mesosystems in industry specialization, resource base availability, innovation activity, investment attractiveness, etc., that affects the state of macro environment as a whole. The existing heterogeneity of mesosystems in industry dictates the need to form a flexible approach to management based on the methodology for their sustainable development assessment.

The foregoing actualizes the problems highlighted in this study and determines its purpose—innovative mesosystems typologization in industry in the context of sustainable development based on the CART algorithm and the development of an algorithm for identifying sustainable development priority areas adequate to the identified type of mesosystems. The study is important for reducing the polarization of mesosystems at the national level and at aligning mesosystems position relative to the average level in Russia.

In this study, a systematic approach is implemented: the author contributed to the development of the methodology for sustainable industry development in Russia and applied mathematical tools, in total, allowing to obtain reliable results, the practical value of which lies in the development of recommendations flexible system.

The theoretical and methodological study basis has an extensive array of research works. Our research focuses on the concept of sustainable development and its implementation in industry. A number of works contain the results of a study of general issues of industrial enterprises transition to sustainable development [2–8]. Chen's work emphasizes that the competitiveness of modern industrial enterprises is due precisely to their focus on sustainable development, taking into account environmental performance [9]. Holden et al. introduces the concept of "space for sustainable development", defining threshold boundaries within which the state of the system is stable [10].

Innovative aspects of industrial development at mesosystems level are considered by scientists in the context of ensuring competitiveness [11], a differentiated approach to the management of mesosystems innovative development in Russian industry [12], the efficiency increase of organizational and economic processes of implementing an innovative strategy of microsystems [13], the ratio of costs and benefits of innovation activity [14], diffusion of innovations [15], etc.

An extensive number of scientific works are mainly devoted to the environmental aspects of mesosystems sustainable development in industry [16–20]. In particular, Zhao et al. investigates the specifics of carbon trading mechanism implementation and the subsequent effect in relation to 3E (economy, energy, and environment) [21].

Socio-economic systems are described by a nonlinear function of behavior, which determines the use of a wide range of mathematical tools. These include cluster analysis, factor analysis, decision trees, and other data processing methods. A contribution to sustainable development methodology progress is made by Koh et al., whose methodological solution is based on a systematic approach that integrates the efficiency of natural and social resources use; the "integrated resource efficiency index" (IRE-index) and the "integrated resource efficiency view" (IREV) are being proposed [22]. In the works of Lubnina et al. a method for calculating an aggregated indicator based on the summation of subindicators (economic, environmental, and social reliability of production), is adjusted by a relative weighting factor [23–25]. A capacious technique using factor analysis is proposed [26] in relation to agriculture; the authors considered factor loadings of particular indicators for assessing sustainable development without aggregation into a complex indicator. The approach of Miola and Schiltz is based on the absolute dependence of the country's position at the world level on the chosen method for sustainable development assessment and is also based on a comparative analysis of various methods for measuring the achievement of sustainable development goals [27]. In addition, the study touches on the issue of managing mesosystems in the context of resource cycles closure, that is relevant for the global economy, namely, a closed cycle of water use. This benchmark is set by the UN Sustainable Development Goals (Goal 12: Ensure Sustainable Consumption and Production Patterns) [28].

The use of mathematical tools for calculating the integral indicator of sustainable development is reflected in numerous works of scientists. Therefore, in the work of Galal and Moneim, a mathematical model of nonlinear programming is built, the objective function of which is to maximize the manufacturing enterprise sustainability index, depending on three fundamental factors of sustainable development. The model is developed in order to determine promising directions for ensuring sustainable development of a manufacturing enterprise [29].

Pieloch-Babiarz et al. when studying the influence of macroeconomic indicators on enterprises sustainable development, determines the indicator of microsystem sustainable development by summing three particular standardized indicators corresponding to its factors [30]. At the same time, the authors do not take into account enterprises innovative activities nature, which, in our opinion, is an integral element of industry greening (in particular, through production facilities modernization).

As for cluster analysis as a classification tool, it does not reflect the sequence of distribution of observations into groups, which limits the researcher's ability to visually select the number of iterations.

The decision tree tool used for mesosystems typology is disclosed in the works of Rutkowski et al. [31], Kuswanto and Mubarok [32], Xu et al. [33], Breiman et al. [34], Apté and Weiss [35], who consistently describe observations segmentation method, based on mathematical functions, in particular, on the calculation of the Gini index. A common modelling tool is the CART algorithm, which is primary in our study [36–38]. This method, in comparison with other mathematical tools, allows not only to take into account the influence of several variables on an independent variable in the classification process, but also to observe the sequence, the logic of classification, as well as to fix the intervals of values for each of the selected groups of observations.

Nevertheless, despite the extensive scientific groundwork in the field of sustainable development, in our opinion, there are also methodological gaps such as no standardized methodology for assessing the innovative mesosystems sustainable development (there is only for a macrosystem in the sustainable society index (SSI) format [1]); environmental innovations are not taken into account when assessing the sustainable development of different levels systems; the clustering method prevails to identify the typology of mesosystems, the CART algorithm is poorly applied, allowing clear and consistent observations classification; there is no complex differentiated mechanism for managing innovative mesosystems, that is in turn simultaneously takes into account different classification algorithms. The aforementioned dictates the need to solve the identified shortcomings and to develop methodological tools in the field of ensuring innovative mesosystems sustainable development in industry based on the construction of decision trees.

In addition, the conceptual apparatus needs to be clarified within the semantic aspects of this work. In the scientific literature, the allocation of systems of different levels is presented in the social plane, where microsystems are understood as the closest environment of children, mesosystems are an interconnected set of micro-systems, macrosystems unite larger systems [39]; in the medical plane [40]. From the point of view of economics, we associate systems with the level of management: microsystem—the management system of an individual organization, mesosystem—the management system of the development of a region or an industrial complex, macrosystem—the level of management of the economy of the whole country. By "innovative mesosystem" we mean a set of interconnected microsystems, united on a territorial basis, characterized by socio-economic development level, industry specifics, resource base availability, innovative activity, and investment attractiveness.

2. Materials and Methods

In order to form a representative sample and to develop well-grounded organizational decisions in the framework of industrial development management in Russia, an array of data characterizing the innovative development of mesosystems in industry [41,42] has been collected. The data set includes mesosystems that are distinguished by industrial sector activity, patent activity, innovative activity in environmental safety field, and, in general, meeting the principles of sustainable development (66 observations).

Measures development to ensure industry sustainable development is due to the limitations of mesosystems (strengths and weaknesses), that determined the stages of the study:

1. Innovative mesosystems comparative analysis in industry according to the level of an integral indicator of sustainable development;

2. Innovative mesosystems typology identification in industry in Russia based on sustainable development factors and the author's system of key performance indicators;
3. Algorithm formation for differentiated priority areas identification for industry innovative mesosystems sustainable development.

The set of indicators relies on the author's approach specificity, focused on innovative and sustainable development comprehensive assessment of Russian industry mesosystems. The methodology is based on the geometric mean calculation, that is influenced by different factors dimensionality and the greater clarity of sustainable development factors comparison.

The integral indicator of innovative mesosystems sustainable development in industry (ISDI) is adopted as a dependent variable (target), the calculation method of which is based on the geometric mean and is described by the Formula (1):

$$ISDI = \sqrt[3]{I_{econ} \times I_{soc} \times I_{ecol}}, \qquad (1)$$

where I_{econ} is an economic factor for innovative mesosystems sustainable development in industry, I_{soc} is a social factor, I_{ecol} is an environmental factor:

$$\begin{aligned} I_{econ} &= \sqrt[3]{V_{ent} \times V_{ROA} \times V_{pat}}, \\ I_{soc} &= \sqrt[2]{V_{InPers} \times V_{Pers}}, \\ I_{ecol} &= \sqrt[3]{V_{EnvIn} \times V_{rec} \times V_{neutr}}, \end{aligned} \qquad (2)$$

where V_{ent} is the share of manufacturing enterprises with a high carbon footprint,%; V_{ROA} is return of manufacturing industries assets in the mesosystem,%; V_{pat} is the patent applications quality index; V_{InPers} is the personnel number index engaged in research and development, referred to the average personnel number in Russia (the absolute N_{InPers} personnel indicator number, thousand people, is used to construct classification trees); V_{Pers} is the share of people employed in manufacturing from the total number of people employed,%; V_{EnvIn} is share of organizations implementing environmental innovations,%; V_{rec} is volume of circulating and consistently index of used water in the mesosystem, referred to the average volume in Russia; V_{neutr} is the share of captured and neutralized air pollutants in the total amount of waste pollutants from stationary sources in the mesosystem,%.

The V_{ent} indicator covers the manufacturing industries with environment highest negative impact and reflects the share of regional enterprises operating in the production of coke and petroleum products (720.6 thousand tons of pollutant emissions into the atmosphere), chemicals and medicines (364.7 thousand tons), metallurgical production (3696.1 thousand tons) and the production of non-metallic mineral products (382.4 thousand tons).

Patent applications V_{pat} quality index is defined as the ratio of issued patents number to the number of filed patent applications, Formula (3):

$$V_{pat} = \frac{N_{claims}}{N_{pat.is.}}, \qquad (3)$$

where N_{claims} is the number of claims for patents, units; $N_{pat.is.}$—patents issued, units.

When calculating organizations share that carried out environmental innovations, V_{EnvIn} method of calculating the average harmonic is applied, the choice of which is due to mesosystem specifics in terms of all or some types of environmental innovations implementation. In this regard, the Formula (4) is applied:

$$V_{EnvIn} = \frac{n}{\sum_{i=1}^{n} \frac{1}{d}}, \qquad (4)$$

where n is the innovations type that improve environmental safety in production of goods, works, services (reduction of material costs, energy consumption for production, carbon dioxide emissions, transition to safe or less hazardous types of raw materials and materials, environmental pollution reduction, recycling of waste production and resources, conservation and reproduction of natural resources used by agriculture); d is the share of organizations in mesosystem that carried out the n-th type of environmental innovation.

In order to identify the specifics of innovative mesosystems sustainable development in Russian industrial production, a simple two-dimensional histogram of the ISDI frequency distribution is used, and a normal distribution density law is set.

The regression construction and classification trees are based on the CART algorithm, applied for classification tree construction, based on the Gini index [31–34] and the data array t that is determined by the Formula (5):

$$Gini(t) = 1 - \sum_{i=1}^{n} p_i^2, \qquad (5)$$

where n is the number of classes, p is the probability that observations belong to the i-th class.

When dividing the data array t into two classes (t_1 and t_2) with the corresponding set of observations (N_1 and N_2), the Gini index represents the data set t uncertainty degree and is determined by the Formula (6):

$$Gini_{split}(t) = \frac{N_1}{N} Gini(t_1) + \frac{N_2}{N} Gini(t_2). \qquad (6)$$

The higher the Gini index $Gini_{split}(t)$ value, the higher the degree of uncertainty in data selection. In this regard, the minimum value of the Gini index $Gini_{split}(t)$ determines the choice of partitioning the array into t_1 and t_2.

When constructing a regression tree, mathematical data processing is based on identifying the correlation between the dependent continuous variable Y and the independent variables X, i.e., dataset (training sample) t has the form (7):

$$t = \{(Y_1, X_1), (Y_2, X_2) \ldots (Y_N, X_N)\}. \qquad (7)$$

The input data set is training, it is recursively divided into two groups, and then the output value is determined for each of regression tree two branches. Regression estimation is carried out according to the Formula (8):

$$\hat{f} = \left(\frac{1}{N} \times \sum_{i=1}^{N} Y_i \right) \times I_t(X), \qquad (8)$$

where N is the number of observations (the number of innovative mesosystems), I_t is a function of space that describes the entry of observation X_i into the space t_i, belonging to a particular class and that is described by Expression (9):

$$\begin{aligned} t_1 &= \{X_i \in t : X_i \leq a\}, \\ t_2 &= \{X_i \in t : X_i > a\}, \end{aligned} \qquad (9)$$

where a is the segmentation point for the X_i variable.

As a result of dividing the input data array into two classes, the regression estimate will take the form (10):

$$\hat{f}(X) = \left(\frac{1}{N_1} \times \sum_{I_1} Y_i \right) \times I_{t_1}(X) + \left(\frac{1}{N_2} \times \sum_{I_2} Y_i \right) \times I_{t_2}(X), \qquad (10)$$

where I_1 and I_2 are t_1 and t_2 spaces functions, respectively; N_1 and N_2 are the observations numbers in the space t_1 and t_2, respectively.

The estimation of the distribution quality of observations is carried out by minimizing squares sum of the differences method, and the choice of the tree branch is based on the calculation of the root-mean-square error σ^2, which has the form (11):

$$\sigma^2 = \frac{1}{N} \times \sum_{i=1}^{N} \left(Y_i - \hat{f}(X_i)\right)^2 \to min. \tag{11}$$

When constructing classification and regression trees, the tools of the Statistica software package are used: data mining—general classification/regression tree models and data mining—interactive trees (C&RT, CHAID). The calculations of sustainable development indicators, as well as specific indicators, are carried out in the Microsoft Excel environment.

3. Results

3.1. Patterns of Innovative Mesosystems Development in Industry in Russia

The author's use of methodology makes it possible to give a numerical assessment of industry factors innovative mesosystems sustainable development (Table 1). A number of values are negative due to negative return on assets. We deliberately do not resort to transforming negative values in order to focus on the most problematic mesosystems with their innovative and industrial activity.

Table 1. Factors and integral indicator of innovative mesosystems sustainable development (calculated according to the author's method).

Innovative Mesosystem	I_{econ}	I_{ecol}	I_{soc}	ISDI	Innovative Mesosystem	I_{econ}	I_{ecol}	I_{soc}	ISDI
Belgorod Region	6.55	16.74	1.57	5.56	Sevastopol city	3.56	5.16	0.96	2.60
Bryansk Region	3.52	3.76	0.95	2.33	Republic of Daghestan	−1.45	2.94	0.98	−1.61
Vladimir Region	5.12	3.75	3.44	4.04	Republic of North Ossetia—Alania	3.05	0.01	0.81	0.01
Voronezh Region	3.95	16.39	3.78	6.25	Stavropol Territory	7.55	10.08	1.62	4.98
Ivanovo Region	1.15	5.31	1.15	1.91	Republic of Bashkortostan	8.91	15.53	3.37	7.75
Kaluga Region	7.43	5.96	4.24	5.73	Republic of Mari El	−4.45	0.01	0.63	0.01
Kostroma Region	5.78	6.73	0.46	2.62	Republic of Mordovia	4.47	7.21	1.15	3.33
Kursk Region	3.84	13.74	1.83	4.59	Republic of Tatarstan	5.63	18.95	4.77	7.98
Lipetsk Region	9.94	16.66	1.01	5.51	Udmurtian Republic	5.66	4.77	2.03	3.80
Moscow Region	7.12	16.80	11.76	11.20	Chuvash Republic	7.89	4.42	1.70	3.90
Orel Region	5.10	8.32	1.12	3.62	Perm Territory	9.41	12.16	4.45	7.99
Ryazan Region	9.04	9.00	2.19	5.63	Kirov Region	4.94	11.14	1.72	4.56
Smolensk Region	5.02	17.49	1.25	4.79	Nizhny Novgorod Region	9.41	11.65	9.06	9.98
Tambov Region	3.79	0.01	1.10	0.01	Penza Region	4.40	4.52	3.14	3.97
Tver Region	3.46	14.45	2.57	5.05	Samara Region	−4.48	15.82	4.27	−6.71
Tula Region	5.12	15.80	3.11	6.31	Saratov Region	6.76	19.36	2.68	7.05
Yaroslavl Region	3.78	3.75	3.51	3.68	Ulyanovsk Region	3.62	7.70	3.20	4.47
Moscow city	6.23	18.92	13.07	11.55	Sverdlovsk Region	8.89	25.39	6.41	11.31
Republic of Karelia	2.86	9.11	1.14	3.10	Tyumen Region	5.89	12.31	2.34	5.54
Komi Republic	7.75	10.08	1.07	4.37	Chelyabinsk Region	9.10	22.17	5.82	10.55
Arkhangelsk Region	1.40	8.59	1.30	2.50	Republic of Khakassia	10.11	9.74	0.34	3.22
Kaliningrad Region	3.40	7.28	1.27	3.16	Altay Territory	9.96	9.76	1.77	5.56
Leningrad Region	5.05	17.87	3.47	6.79	Krasnoyarsk Territory	12.84	13.92	3.20	8.30
Murmansk Region	−3.77	10.27	1.50	−3.87	Irkutsk Region	10.97	15.12	2.12	7.06
Novgorod Region	6.97	11.97	1.78	5.30	Kemerovo Region	6.10	17.14	1.16	4.95
Pskov Region	2.46	1.28	0.49	1.16	Novosibirsk Region	5.77	11.03	5.35	6.98
Sankt-Petersburg city	5.51	11.55	10.26	8.68	Omsk Region	11.26	11.22	2.50	6.81
Republic of Adygeya	6.81	3.73	0.62	2.51	Tomsk Region	4.66	9.59	3.48	5.38
Republic of Crimea	4.99	5.14	1.33	3.24	Republic of Buryatia	4.41	8.25	1.01	3.32
Krasnodar Territory	2.73	15.28	2.65	4.80	Republic of Sakha (Yakutia)	−2.76	10.69	0.85	−2.93
Astrakhan Region	−5.16	4.88	0.89	−2.82	Trans-Baikal Territory	4.97	12.28	0.54	3.21
Volgograd Region	8.92	12.47	2.18	6.24	Primorye Territory	2.31	15.96	2.50	4.52
Rostov Region	7.12	20.56	4.01	8.37	Khabarovsk Territory	4.54	13.36	1.36	4.35

The presented data set is characterized by the following statistical indicators:
- The maximum value is 11.55 (Moscow city);
- Minimum value—−6.71 (Samara Region);
- Sample variance—11.76;
- Standard error—3.43;
- Arithmetic middling is 4.7;
- Asymmetric property—−0.75;
- Mode—5.56;
- Median—4.79.

An analytical study of innovative mesosystems sustainable development data array factors in industry in Russia and the integral indicator of their sustainable development at the first stage is carried out by constructing a simple two-dimensional histogram of the ISDI frequency distribution (Figure 1). Indicator uniform intervals are set with a step equal to 2. A total 10 ranges are obtained, indicating high spread of the indicator and uneven innovative mesosystems sustainable development. The resulting distribution often makes it possible to identify the following patterns of development:

- In total, 19 mesosystems or 29% of observations (ISDI $\in (6; 12)$) have high ISDI values, mainly due to high number of researchers or good environmental conditions, allowing us to judge the environmental and social responsibility of industrial enterprises and industrial regions of Russia.
- Further, 37 mesosystems or 56% of observations (ISDI $\in (2; 6)$) prevail in terms of innovations development in industry from the standpoint of environmental safety; this category prevails in terms of observations share;
- In addition, 10 mesosystems or 15% of observations (ISDI $\in (-8; 2)$) are characterized by a low or even negative index value, which is primarily due to ineffective asset management, which in the case of high wear and tear of equipment has negative impact not only on industrial products quality, but also on the environment quality.

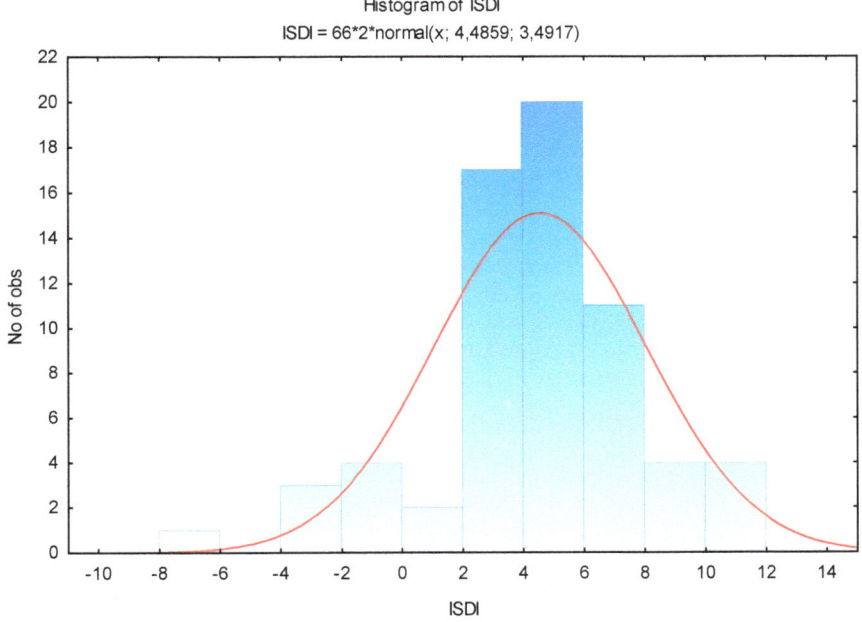

Figure 1. Frequency distribution diagram for the ISDI variable.

The proposed methodology has no analogues in the "arsenal" of the Federal State Statistics Service. At the same time, within the framework of the study, the quality of the proposed methodological solution was assessed by comparing the calculated values with the values of the indicator reflecting the share of organizations that carried out technological innovations in the mesosystem (the choice in favor of this indicator as a base for comparison is due to the object of the study—innovative mesosystems). The indicators are normalized by the minimax method according to Formula (12):

$$x_{norm} = \frac{x_i - x_{min}}{x_{max} - x_{min}}. \tag{12}$$

As a result of assessing the quality of the author's methodology, a graph of deviations of the obtained values of the integral indicator of the sustainable development of innovative mesosystems in industry from the values of the share of organizations implementing technological innovations in the mesosystem (Figure 2) is constructed. The graph shows a certain coincidence of patterns, as evidenced by the accuracy estimate of the model, based on the calculation of the standard deviation and equal to 61%. We emphasize that the proposed author's methodology is unique, and currently there is no statistical basis for an integrated assessment of the sustainable development of systems at different levels.

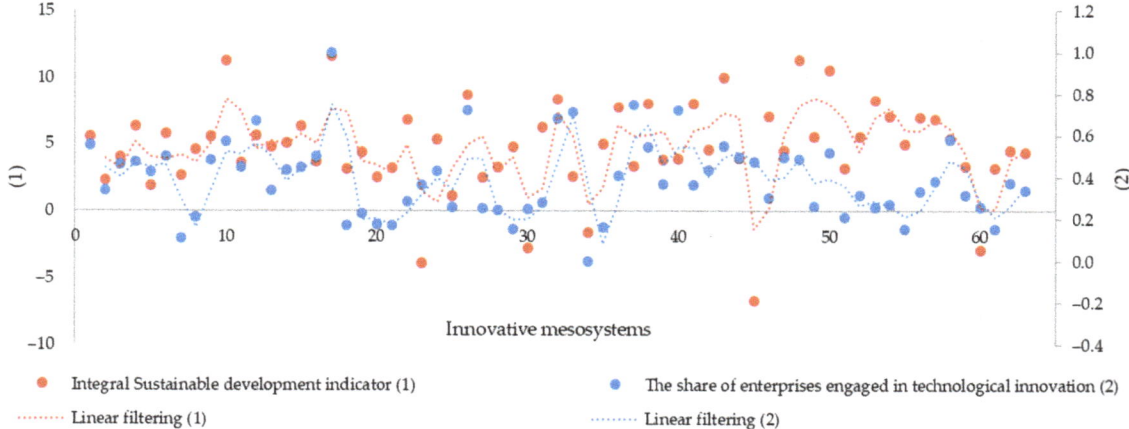

Figure 2. Deviation schedule.

The identified patterns of development confirm the need to develop a differentiated approach for ensuring and supporting the innovative mesosystems sustainable development, in particular, taking into account their industry specifics, since regions with a high volume of metallurgical production, oil, gas and metal ore production experience the greatest pressure on the environment (Tyumen Region, Kemerovo Region, Krasnoyarsk Territory, Sverdlovsk Region, etc.).

3.2. Multi-Criteria and Variable Typology of Innovative Mesosystems in Industry in Russia

The level of sustainable development (ISDI) integral indicator is selected as a dependent variable.

The mesosystem decision tree method is applied in two variations such as classification and regression trees, the fundamental difference of which is that in the first case, discrete forecasting takes place (a terminal node (leaf) is a class of observations corresponding to a node), in the second case, continuous forecasting (terminal node is the modal interval of the dependent variable).

For the purpose of constructing a classification tree, the ISDI dependent variable is reflected as a categorical one, having the values "high" or "low" level of sustainable development integral indicator of the innovative mesosystem:

$$\begin{array}{l} \text{«high», if Integral SDI} \geq 5, \\ \text{«low», if Integral SDI} < 5. \end{array} \qquad (13)$$

The classification tree is built in two versions. At the first stage, aggregated factors of sustainable development were used as classification criteria, and at the second stage, private indicators of innovative mesosystems were used. Such a dual approach allows a comprehensive approach to the development of strategic solutions that ensure the transition of the studied objects to sustainable development.

1. In the first version, the categorical independent variables are the factors of sustainable development calculated by the author's method—economic, social, environmental (Figure 3). Out of the four alternatives, a tree with the lowest cross-validation cost of 0.12 is selected, with five terminal nodes (red blocks), four decision nodes (blue blocks), and nine nodes (ID). Terminal vertices imply the absence of further decision-making, which was taken as the final version of the mesosystem classification in this version. Each node is characterized by the number of innovative mesosystems covered. The evaluation of the significance of the input independent variables calculated in the Statistica program allows us to summarize the greatest importance of the economic factor in the classification of observations (significance is 1), and the lesser importance of the environmental (significance is 0.9) and social (significance is 0.57) factors of the sustainable development of innovative mesosystems.

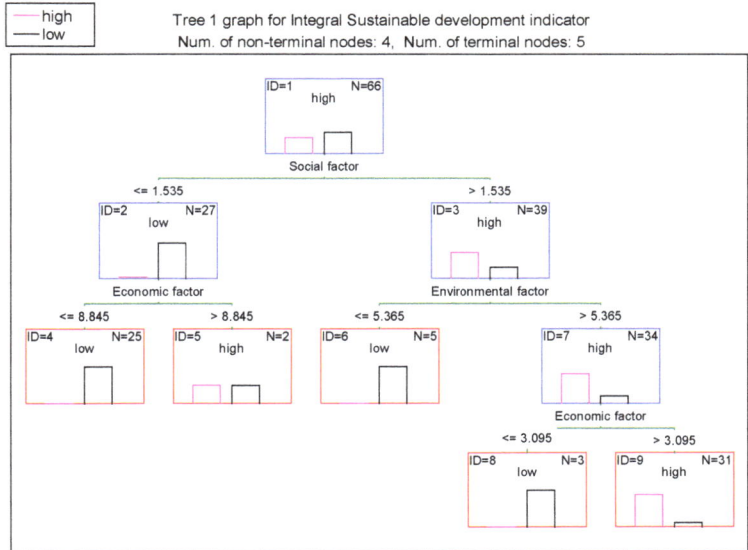

Figure 3. Classification tree for identifying patterns of innovative mesosystems sustainable development in industry (based on sustainable development factors).

The algorithm and segmentation rules in mathematical expression for observations t have the form (14):

$$\begin{aligned} t_{ID=2} &= \{X_i \in t : I_{soc} \leq 1.535\}, \\ t_{ID=3} &= \{X_i \in t : I_{soc} > 1.535\}, \\ t_{ID=4} &= \{X_i \in t : I_{econ} \leq 8.845\}, \\ t_{ID=5} &= \{X_i \in t : I_{econ} > 8.845\}, \\ t_{ID=6} &= \{X_i \in t : I_{ecol} \leq 5.365\}, \\ t_{ID=7} &= \{X_i \in t : I_{ecol} > 5.365\}, \\ t_{ID=8} &= \{X_i \in t : I_{econ} \leq 3.095\}, \\ t_{ID=9} &= \{X_i \in t : I_{econ} > 3.095\}. \end{aligned} \qquad (14)$$

The root of the tree (ID = 1) reflects the predominance of mesosystems with high level of sustainable development integral indicator. As a result of the first iteration, 66 studied mesosystems are classified according to the level of the social factor of sustainable development into two classes—below and above 1.535, respectively; 59% of mesosystems (39 regions) have relatively high level of innovation system social development. Sustainable development and ESG initiatives are based on the principle of environmental friendliness, and, according to node ID = 7, the industry of more than half of the mesosystems is actively developing in the environmental plane (34 regions). The most important predictor, the economic factor, contributed to innovative mesosystems differentiation:

- Category F-1 (three mesosystems: Krasnodar Territory, Samara Region and Primorsky Territory)—relatively low level of sustainable development, ecological bias of industrial development, high social factor influence, but low economic development—$I_{econ} \leq 3.095$ (ID = 8);
- Category F-2 (31 mesosystems: Moscow and the Moscow region, St. Petersburg, the Republic of Tatarstan, the Republic of Bashkortostan, the Novosibirsk region, etc.)—relatively high level of sustainable development, greening of industry, high influence of the social factor, moderate economic development—$I_{econ} > 3.095$ (ID = 9);
- Category F-3 (25 mesosystems: Bryansk Region, Arkhangelsk Region, Kaliningrad Region, etc.)—relatively low level of sustainable development, mostly weak environmentalization of industry, low influence of the social factor, notable economic development—$I_{econ} \leq 8.845$ (ID = 4);
- Category F-4 (two mesosystems: the Republic of Khakassia and Lipetsk region)—relatively high level of sustainable development, ecologization of industry, low influence of the social factor, high economic development—$I_{econ} \geq 8.845$ (ID = 5);
- Category F-5 (five mesosystems: Vladimir region, Yaroslavl region, Udmurt Republic, Chuvash Republic, Penza region)—relatively low level of sustainable development, weak emphasis on greening industry, high influence of social factor, noticeable economic development—$I_{econ} \leq 8.845$ (ID = 6).

2. The second version of the classification tree included in the array of independent variables private indicators of innovative mesosystems development, which are most highly correlated with the dependent variable ISDI (Figure 4).

In this case, the key classification criterion is the social factor, namely, the number of researchers of the innovative mesosystem (the predictor value is 1), followed by the return on assets (the significance was 0.93) and the share of manufacturing enterprises with a high carbon footprint (the significance was 0.87). This tree is characterized by the same number of nodes.

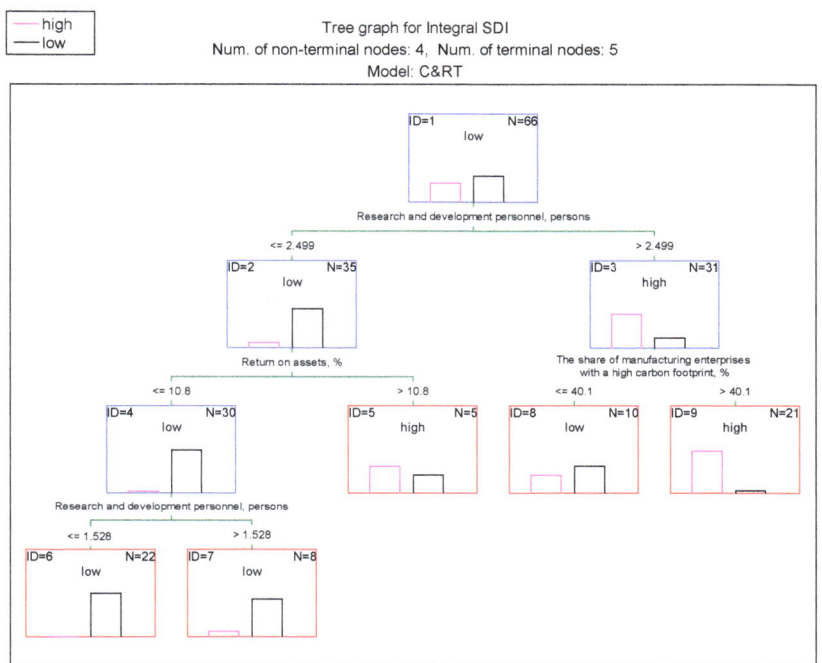

Figure 4. Classification tree to identify patterns of sustainable development of innovation mesosystems in industry (based on private indicators of mesosystem development).

The segmentation algorithm for observations t has the form (15):

$$\begin{aligned}
t_{ID=2} &= \{X_i \in t : N_{InPers} \leq 2.499\}, \\
t_{ID=3} &= \{X_i \in t : N_{InPers} > 2.499\}, \\
t_{ID=4} &= \{X_i \in t : V_{ROA} \leq 10.8\}, \\
t_{ID=5} &= \{X_i \in t : V_{ROA} > 10.8\}, \\
t_{ID=6} &= \{X_i \in t : N_{InPers} \leq 1.528\}, \\
t_{ID=7} &= \{X_i \in t : N_{InPers} > 1.528\}, \\
t_{ID=8} &= \{X_i \in t : V_{ent} \leq 40.1\}, \\
t_{ID=9} &= \{X_i \in t : V_{ent} > 40.1\}.
\end{aligned} \quad (15)$$

In the first step, 66 mesosystems are classified by the number of R&D personnel; at the second step, depending on the size of the population, the monitored objects are subdivided into groups with high and moderate return on assets or into groups with a high and moderate share of enterprises that pollute the environment most intensively. According to the resulting decision tree, there are five types of innovative mesosystems in Russian industry:

- Category V-1 (22 mesosystems)—relatively low level of sustainable development, moderate return on assets ($V_{ROA} \leq 10.8\%$), the number of researchers—$V_{InPers} \leq 1.528$ thousand people (ID = 6);
- Category V-2 (eight mesosystems)—relatively low level of sustainable development, moderate return on assets ($V_{ROA} \leq 10.8\%$), the number of researchers—$1.528 < V_{InPers} \leq 2.499$ thousand people (ID = 7);
- Category V-3 (five mesosystems)—relatively high level of sustainable development, high return on assets ($V_{ROA} > 10.8\%$), the number of researchers $V_{InPers} \leq 2.499$ thousand people (ID = 5);

- Category V-4 (10 mesosystems)—relatively low level of sustainable development, moderate environmental pollution by manufacturing industries ($V_{ent} \leq 40.1\%$), the number of researchers $V_{InPers} > 2.499$ thousand people (ID = 8);
- Category V-5 (21 mesosystems)—relatively high level of sustainable development, intensive environmental pollution by manufacturing industries ($V_{ent} > 40.1\%$), the number of researchers $V_{InPers} > 2.499$ thousand people (ID = 9).

In general, the results of this classification indicate the prevalence of mesosystems with a low level of sustainable development—40 observed objects (61%).

The results obtained in the form of decision trees and the revealed patterns formed the basis for the formation of an algorithm for the differentiated identification of priority areas for sustainable development of innovative mesosystems in the Russian industry (Figure 5). The proposed algorithm is an integrated approach to the formation of an effective toolkit for managing the development of industrial mesosystems: on the one hand, it is a multifactorial (multicomponent) approach; on the other hand, it covers key management subsystems—asset management, human resources, R&D, resource consumption, and environmental safety. The developed methodology is characterized by the potential to optimize resources, their concentration on problem areas of the industrial system, and to reduce the risks of irrational planning within a single mesosystem.

The implementation of an alternative method of mesosystem typology is based on continuous forecasting. If, in the case of the classification tree, we ranged between the two states of the objective function—the integral indicator of sustainable development low and high levels, in the case of the regression tree, the leaves (red blocks) contain information about the interval of specific values of the objective function (Figure 6). Obviously, the most significant criterion for mesosystems classification is the number of researchers (importance equal to one), approximately equal importance is revealed according to the criteria of return on assets (0.73) and the share of enterprises that intensively pollute the environment as a result of production activity (0.7).

According to the results of the fourth iteration, four classes of innovative mesosystems in industry are identified on the regression tree—blocks ID = 6, 7, 12, 13 (Table 2):

- Mesosystems of the R-1 class (17 objects) are characterized by relatively low level of sustainable development, the average ISDI value for the class is 2.69; low number of personnel engaged in research and development (less than 1.15 thousand people);
- Mesosystems of the R-2 class (26 objects)—the most numerous groups of observations, with moderate level of sustainable development; the number of researchers is limited by the interval $V_{InPers} \in (1.15; 6.95]$;
- Mesosystems of Class R-3 (10 objects: Voronezh Region, Kaluga Region, Leningrad Region, Rostov Region, Republic of Bashkortostan, Republic of Tatarstan, Perm Territory, Tyumen Region, Krasnoyarsk Territory, Tomsk Region)—a small group of observations, noticeable level sustainable development; the number of researchers is limited by the interval $V_{InPers} \in (6.95; 14.41]$;
- Mesosystems of Class R-4 (seven objects: Moscow Region, Moscow city, Sankt-Petersburg city, Nizhny Novgorod Region, Sverdlovsk Region, Chelyabinsk Region, Novosibirsk Region)—a small group with high level of sustainable development and high number of research personnel (more 14.41 thousand people).

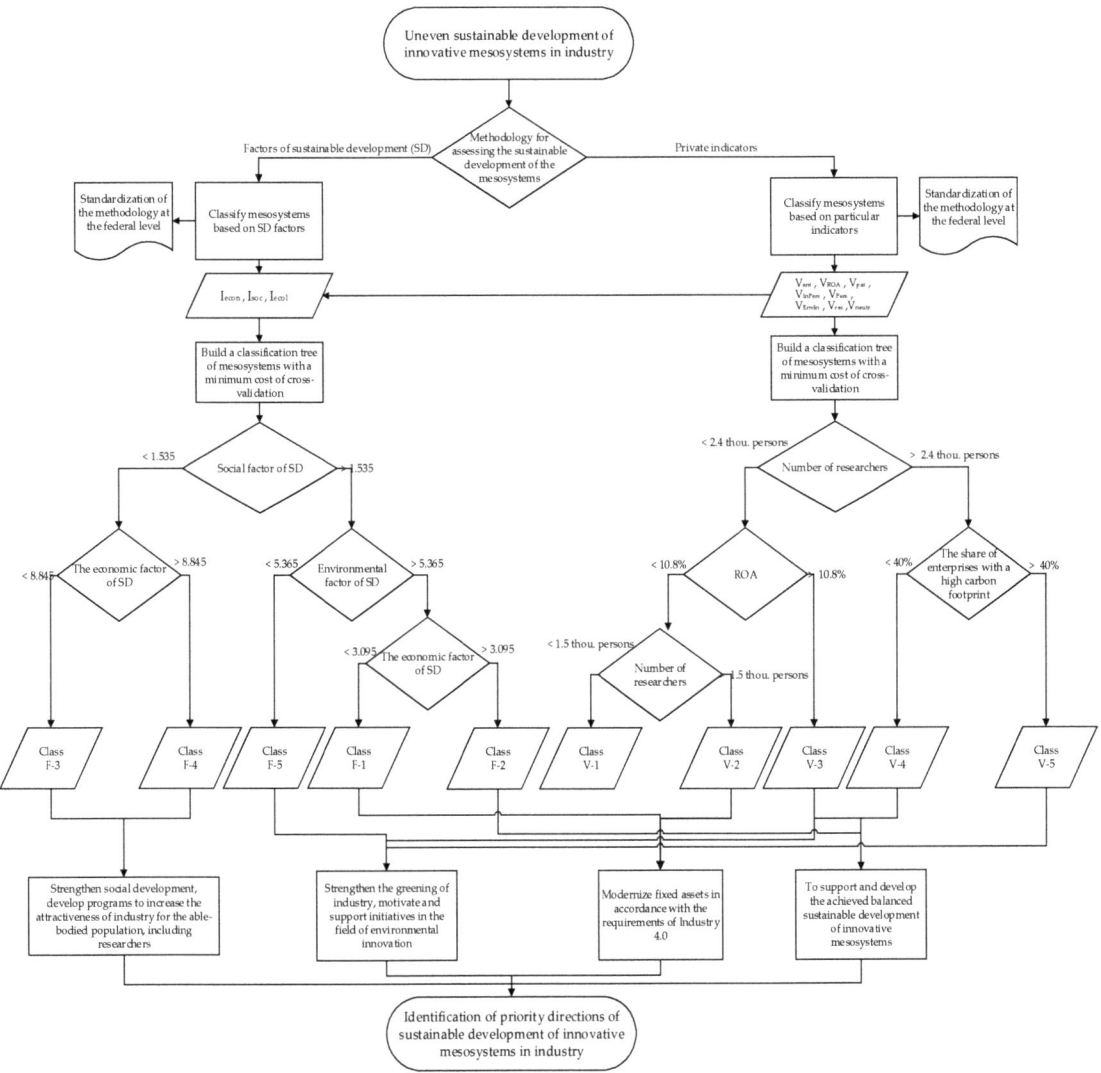

Figure 5. Algorithm for differentiated identification of priority areas for sustainable development of innovative mesosystems in industry.

Table 2. Typology of innovative mesosystems based on a regression tree.

Criterion	Class 1	Class 2	Class 3	Class 4
Average value of the dependent variable "integral indicator of sustainable development" (ISDI)	2693	4919	7008	10.036
The nature of sustainable development of innovative mesosystems	weak	moderate	perceptible	high
Number of innovative mesosystems	17	26	10	7
Classification criterion: number of personnel engaged in research (thousand people)	[0; 1149]	[1149; 6949]	[6949; 14.406]	[14.406; +∞)

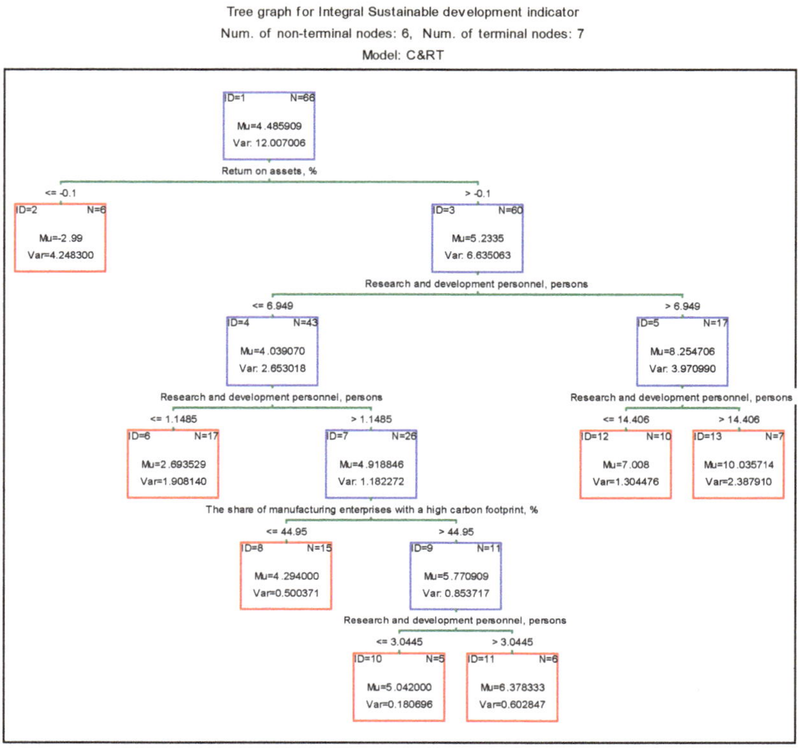

Figure 6. Regression tree for identifying patterns of sustainable development of innovative mesosystems in industry (based on continuous forecasting).

Thus, mesosystems of Classes 1 and 2 are more in need of the development of a set of measures capable of reducing the separation from mesosystems of Class 4. These measures include:

- Stimulation of scientific research in the field of ensuring environmental safety (primarily material);
- Stimulation of production facilities modernization, financial support, easing of the taxation system, acceptable terms of lending to industrial enterprises;
- Increasing the investment attractiveness of mesosystems, etc.

In general, the presented approaches to the typology of innovative mesosystems in industry make it possible to summarize the prevalence of objects with a low level of sustainable development integral indicator, which determines the importance of a differentiated approach to stimulating the mesosystems sustainable development.

4. Discussion

As noted earlier, the issue of sustainable development is particularly relevant, as evidenced by the vast array of research projects. In particular, the methodology for assessing the sustainable development systems level, fixed for assessing macrosystems [1], has been widely developed, but there is no standardized methodology for micro- and mesosystems. We believe that the existing methodological solutions [22–27] are highly specialized. A capacious methodology with the use of factor analysis is presented in [26], nevertheless, particular indicators factor loads for assessing sustainable development are calculated without aggregation into a complex indicator.

The solutions we offer are distinguished by taking into account the synergy of innovation and environmental components in the format of environmental innovations, since only in this case a breakthrough in ensuring country's sustainable development of industry is possible. In this work, we develop a methodology for assessing sustainable development in the mathematical plane, using the toolkit of decision trees for the typology of innovative mesosystems in industry, which is also based on calculating the integral indicator of sustainable development using the geometric mean method.

The use of the CART algorithm in order to build classification and regression trees is based on the calculation of the Gini index, segmentation of the original data set (training sample) into two sets of observations, the use of a recursive function and regression estimation. The choice in favor of this mathematical tool is due to the possibility of simultaneously, taking into account a number of the most important indicators and visibility in the sequential classification of observations, which fundamentally distinguishes it from cluster analysis.

As a result of the research, the following scientific results are obtained.

1. A unique methodology for assessing the innovative mesosystems sustainable development (ISDI), that takes into account all three factors of sustainable development (economic, social and environmental) and includes an important element of environmental innovation, which allows a comparative assessment of mesosystems in industry, taking into account their level of load on the environment, innovative activity in the field of environmental safety, asset use efficiency and motivated researchers, has been developed. The methodology implementation is aimed at overcoming methodological difficulties determined by the lack of standardized solutions in this area. In addition, the proposed approach is superior to other methodological solutions due to the use of calculating the geometric mean, which makes it possible to take into account the absolute values and differing dimensions of the factors.

2. Revealed patterns of innovative mesosystems sustainable development in industrial production in Russia on the basis of constructing a simple two-dimensional histogram of frequency distribution ISDI (normal distribution density law). Three categories of mesosystems have been identified, differing in the level of sustainable development integral indicator (with high, medium, and low ISDI levels). The first category includes mesosystems characterized by a balance of sustainable development factors and active innovation, which can serve as an example of successful experience in greening industry and compliance with ESG principles, as well as broadcast this experience to regions of the second and third categories.

3. A multicriteria and variable typology of innovative mesosystems in industry in Russia based on the use of mathematical tools—the construction of classification and regression trees are proposed. As a result, three variants of innovative mesosystems classification have been developed:
   - Mesosystem classification tree (dependent variable has discrete values—high and low ISDI levels) based on three factors of sustainable development;
   - Classification tree of mesosystems (discrete) based on particular indicators of the development of innovative mesosystems, most correlated with the dependent variable ISDI;
   - Regression tree (dependent variable ISDI has continuous values) based on particular indicators—the number of researchers, return on assets and the share of enterprises that intensively pollute the environment as a result of production activity.

4. On the basis of the first two types of classification, an algorithm for differentiated identification of sustainable development priority areas of innovative mesosystems in industry is proposed, which allows improving key management subsystems (asset management, human resources, R&D, resource consumption, environmental safety) and focusing resources on solving acute problems facing innovative mesosystems. The third type of classification makes it possible to categorize innovative mesosystems

in industry according to the ISDI level and to propose a set of measures to reduce their polarization.
5. It is determined that the economic factor prevailing over environmental and social factors (modernization of petrochemical and metallurgical industry enterprises, increasing the profitability of assets and patent activity of mesosystems), and secondly, the number of personnel realizing their potential in the field of R&D, have the greatest impact on decision-making that stimulate the transition of innovative mesosystems to sustainable development. Accordingly, the program for the development of innovative mesosystems in Russia should stimulate the sustainable development of industry, primarily by regulating these parameters.

In general, the nonlinear behavior of innovative mesosystems has been revealed, which is confirmed by their disproportionality in economic development, innovation activity and environmental responsibility. The predominance of objects with a low level of sustainable development integral indicator is revealed, which actualizes a differentiated approach to stimulating the sustainable development of innovative mesosystems in Russian industry. The provision of the country's development advanced rates should be conditioned by the resources concentration and support not only on investment-attractive mesosystems. This thesis correlates with the conclusions of the team of scientists Larissa B. et al., who give reasonable arguments in favor of improving the policy of sustainable development, taking into account the differences in cultural capital between countries [43] (adapting to our study—between innovative mesosystems).

The proposed solutions may be taken into account in order to develop a standardized methodology for assessing the innovative mesosystems sustainable development in industry, by government bodies when developing strategies and programs for territorial development in order to prioritize support for mesosystems that are weak in terms of sustainable development.

The study of this problem is planned to be continued within the framework of computer programs applicable for meso- and microsystems development.

Author Contributions: Conceptualization, A.I.S. and F.F.G.; methodology, F.F.G.; formal analysis, I.G.E.; investigation, A.I.S. and A.A.Y.; data curation, I.G.E.; writing—original draft preparation, A.I.S. and F.F.G.; writing—review and editing, A.A.Y.; visualization, F.F.G. All authors have read and agreed to the published version of the manuscript.

Funding: This research received no external funding.

Institutional Review Board Statement: Not applicable.

Informed Consent Statement: Not applicable.

Data Availability Statement: Not applicable.

Acknowledgments: The research was carried out within the framework of the grant of the President of the Russian Federation for state support of leading scientific schools of the Russian Federation, Project Number NSh-2600.2020.6.

Conflicts of Interest: The authors declare no conflict of interest.

References

1. SSI. Sustainable Society Index. Available online: https://ssi.wi.th-koeln.de/history.html (accessed on 23 October 2021).
2. Dyrdonova, A.N.; Lin'kova, T.S. Principles of petrochemical cluster' sustainability assessment based on its members' energy efficiency performance. *E3S Web Conf.* **2019**, *124*, 04013. [CrossRef]
3. Samarina, V.P.; Skufina, T.P.; Savon, D.Y.; Shinkevich, A.I. Management of externalities in the context of sustainable development of the russian arctic zone. *Sustainability* **2021**, *13*, 7549. [CrossRef]
4. Samarina, V.P.; Skufina, T.P.; Savon, D.Y.U. Comprehensive assessment of sustainable development of mining and metallurgical holdings: Problems and mechanisms of their resolution. *Ugology* **2021**, *7*, 20–24. [CrossRef]
5. Shinkevich, M.V.; Shinkevich, A.I.; Ponkratova, L.A.; Klimova, N.V.; Yusupova, G.F.; Lushchik, I.V.; Zhuravleva, T.A. Models and Technologies to Manage the Institutionalization of Sustainable Innovative Development of Meso-Systems. *Mediterr. J. Soc. Sci.* **2015**, *6*, 32–39. [CrossRef]

6. Linnerud, K.; Holden, E.; Simonsen, M. Closing the sustainable development gap: A global study of goal interactions. *Sustain. Dev.* **2021**, *29*, 738–753. [CrossRef]
7. Vertakova, Y.V.; Plotnikov, V.A. The Integrated Approach to Sustainable Development: The Case of Energy Efficiency and Solid Waste Management. *Int. J. Energy Econ. Policy* **2019**, *9*, 194–201. [CrossRef]
8. Shinkevich, A.I. Sustainable development of territories in the zone of industrial facilities. *IOP Conf. Ser. Mater. Sci. Eng.* **2020**, *890*, 012190. [CrossRef]
9. Chen, T. Competitive and sustainable manufacturing in the age of globalization. *Sustainability* **2017**, *9*, 26. [CrossRef]
10. Holden, E.; Linnerud, K.; Banister, D. Sustainable development: Our Common Future revisited. *Glob. Environ. Chang.* **2014**, *26*, 130–139. [CrossRef]
11. Malysheva, T.V.; Shinkevich, A.I.; Kharisova, G.M.; Nuretdinova, Y.V.; Khasyanov, O.R.; Nuretdinov, I.G.; Zaitseva, N.A.; Kudryavtseva, S.S. The Sustainable Development of Competitive Enterprises through the Implementation of Innovative Development Strategy. *Int. J. Econ. Financ. Issues* **2016**, *6*, 185–191.
12. Rajskaya, M.V.; Sagdeeva, A.A.; Panteleeva, Y.V.; Malysheva, T.V.; Ershova, I.G. Differentiated approach problems to innovative development management in Russian regions. *Humanit. Soc. Sci. Rev.* **2019**, *7*, 1262–1268. [CrossRef]
13. Barsegyan, N.V.; Salimyanova, I.G.; Kushaeva, E.R. Typology of innovation strategies for petrochemical enterprises. *J. Phys. Conf. Ser.* **2020**, *1515*, 042090. [CrossRef]
14. Shinkevich, A.I.; Kudryavtseva, S.S.; Rajskaya, M.V.; Zimina, I.V.; Dyrdonova, A.N.; Misbakhova, C.A. Integral technique for analyzing of national innovation systems development. *Espacios* **2018**, *39*, 6.
15. Shinkevich, M.V.; Shinkevich, A.I.; Chudnovskiy, A.D.; Lushchik, I.V.; Kaigorodova, G.N.; Ishmuradova, I.I.; Bashkirtseva, S.A.; Marfina, L.V.; Zhuravleva, T.A. Formalization of sustainable innovative development process in the model of innovations diffusion. *Int. J. Econ. Financ. Issues* **2016**, *6*, 179–184.
16. Ratner, S.; Lychev, A.; Rozhnov, A.; Lobanov, I. Efficiency Evaluation of Regional Environmental Management Systems in Russia Using Data Envelopment Analysis. *Mathematics* **2021**, *9*, 2210. [CrossRef]
17. Li, D.; Lv, H. Investment in environmental innovation with environmental regulation and consumers' environmental awareness: A dynamic analysis. *Sustain. Prod. Consum.* **2021**, *28*, 1366–1380. [CrossRef]
18. Ren, S.; Sun, H.; Zhang, T. Do environmental subsidies spur environmental innovation? Empirical evidence from Chinese listed firms. *Technol. Forecast. Soc. Chang.* **2021**, *173*, 121123. [CrossRef]
19. Ullah, S.; Nasim, A. Do firm-level sustainability targets drive environmental innovation? Insights from BRICS Economies. *J. Environ. Manag.* **2021**, *294*, 112754. [CrossRef]
20. Mongo, M.; Belaïd, F.; Ramdani, B. The effects of environmental innovations on CO_2 emissions: Empirical evidence from Europe. *Environ. Sci. Policy* **2021**, *118*, 1–9. [CrossRef]
21. Zhao, X.; Zhang, Y.; Liang, J.; Li, Y.; Jia, R.; Wang, L. The sustainable development of the economic-energy-environment (3E) system under the carbon trading (CT) mechanism: A Chinese case. *Sustainability* **2018**, *10*, 98. [CrossRef]
22. Koh, S.C.L.; Morris, J.; Ebrahimi, S.M.; Obayi, R. Integrated Resource Efficiency: Measurement and Management. *Int. J. Oper. Prod. Manag.* **2016**, *36*, 1576–1600. [CrossRef]
23. Lubnina, A.A.; Melnik, A.N.; Smolyagina, M.V. On modelling of different sectors of economy in terms of sustainable development. *Int. Bus. Manag.* **2016**, *10*, 5592–5595. [CrossRef]
24. Smolyagina, M.V.; Lubnina, A.A. Concerning the environmental marketing of waste management in the context of sustainable development. *Int. J. Pharm. Technol.* **2016**, *8*, 11257–11264.
25. Shinkevich, A.I.; Lubnina, A.A.; Chikisheva, N.M.; Simonova, L.M.; Alenina, E.E.; Khrustalev, B.B.; Sadykova, R.S.; Kharisova, R.R. Innovative forms of production organization in the context of high-tech Meso-economic systems sustainable development. *Int. Rev. Manag. Mark.* **2016**, *6*, 219–224.
26. Laurett, R.; Paço, A.; Mainardes, E.W. Measuring sustainable development, its antecedents, barriers and consequences in agriculture: An exploratory factor analysis. *Environ. Dev.* **2021**, *37*, 100583. [CrossRef]
27. Miola, A.; Schiltz, F. Measuring sustainable development goals performance: How to monitor policy action in the 2030 Agenda implementation? *Ecol. Econ.* **2019**, *164*, 106373. [CrossRef]
28. United Nations. Sustainable Development Goals. Available online: https://www.un.org/sustainabledevelopment/ (accessed on 23 October 2021).
29. Galal, N.M.; Moneim, A.F.A. A mathematical programming approach to the optimal sustainable product mix for the process industry. *Sustainability* **2015**, *7*, 13085–13103. [CrossRef]
30. Pieloch-Babiarz, A.; Misztal, A.; Kowalska, M. An impact of macroeconomic stabilization on the sustainable development of manufacturing enterprises: The case of Central and Eastern European Countries. *Environ. Dev. Sustain.* **2020**, *23*, 8669–8698. [CrossRef]
31. Rutkowski, L.; Jaworski, M.; Pietruczuk, L.; Duda, P. The CART decision tree for mining data streams. *Inf. Sci.* **2014**, *266*, 1–15. [CrossRef]
32. Kuswanto, H.; Mubarok, R. Classification of Cancer Drug Compounds for Radiation Protection Optimization Using CART. *Procedia Comput. Sci.* **2019**, *161*, 458–465. [CrossRef]
33. Xu, L.; Du, H.; Zhang, X. A classification approach for urban metabolism using the CART model and its application in China. *Ecol. Indic.* **2021**, *123*, 107345. [CrossRef]

34. Breiman, L.; Friedman, J.H.; Olshen, R.A.; Stone, C.T. *Classification and Regression Trees*, 1st ed.; Routledge: Boca Raton, FL, USA, 1984; 368p. [CrossRef]
35. Apté, C.; Weiss, S. Data mining with decision trees and decision rules. *Future Gener. Comput. Syst.* **1997**, *13*, 197–210. [CrossRef]
36. Gocheva-Ilieva, S.; Kulina, H.; Ivanov, A. Assessment of Students' Achievements and Competencies in Mathematics Using CART and CART Ensembles and Bagging with Combined Model Improvement by MARS. *Mathematics* **2021**, *9*, 62. [CrossRef]
37. Wang, F.; Wang, Q.; Nie, F.; Li, Z.; Yu, W.; Ren, F. A linear multivariate binary decision tree classifier based on K-means splitting. *Pattern Recognit.* **2020**, *107*, 107521. [CrossRef]
38. Azad, M.; Moshkov, M. Multi-stage optimization of decision and inhibitory trees for decision tables with many-valued decisions. *Eur. J. Oper. Res.* **2017**, *263*, 910–921. [CrossRef]
39. Bronfenbrenner, U.; Evans, G.W. Developmental Science in the 21st Century: Emerging Questions, Theoretical Models, Research Designs and Empirical Findings. *Soc. Dev.* **2000**, *9*, 115–125. [CrossRef]
40. Godfrey, M.M.; Melin, C.N.; Muething, S.E.; Batalden, P.B.; Nelson, E.C. Clinical Microsystems, Part 3. Transformation of Two Hospitals Using Microsystem, Mesosystem, and Macrosystem Strategies. *Jt. Comm. J. Qual. Patient Saf.* **2008**, *34*, 591–603. [CrossRef]
41. Federal State Statistics Service. Available online: http://www.gks.ru (accessed on 23 October 2021).
42. HSE University. Available online: https://www.hse.ru (accessed on 23 October 2021).
43. Larissa, B.; Maran, R.M.; Ioan, B.; Anca, N.; Mircea-Iosif, R.; Horia, T.; Gheorghe, F.; Ema Speranta, M.; Dan, M.I. Adjusted Net Savings of CEE and Baltic Nations in the Context of Sustainable Economic Growth: A Panel Data Analysis. *J. Risk Financ. Manag.* **2020**, *13*, 234. [CrossRef]

Article

Development of a Methodology for Forecasting the Sustainable Development of Industry in Russia Based on the Tools of Factor and Discriminant Analysis

Aleksey I. Shinkevich [1,*], Alsu R. Akhmetshina [2] and Ruslan R. Khalilov [2]

[1] Logistics and Management Department, Kazan National Research Technological University, 420015 Kazan, Russia
[2] Graduate School of Business, Kazan (Volga Region) Federal University, 420008 Kazan, Russia; alsu.akhmetshina@kpfu.ru (A.R.A.); barsegyannv@kstu.ru (R.R.K.)
* Correspondence: ashinkevich@mail.ru; Tel.: +7-9272401653

Citation: Shinkevich, A.I.; Akhmetshina, A.R.; Khalilov, R.R. Development of a Methodology for Forecasting the Sustainable Development of Industry in Russia Based on the Tools of Factor and Discriminant Analysis. *Mathematics* **2022**, *10*, 859. https://doi.org/10.3390/math10060859

Academic Editor: Aleksandr Rakhmangulov

Received: 9 February 2022
Accepted: 5 March 2022
Published: 8 March 2022

Publisher's Note: MDPI stays neutral with regard to jurisdictional claims in published maps and institutional affiliations.

Copyright: © 2022 by the authors. Licensee MDPI, Basel, Switzerland. This article is an open access article distributed under the terms and conditions of the Creative Commons Attribution (CC BY) license (https://creativecommons.org/licenses/by/4.0/).

Abstract: The problem of sustainable development is one of the central issues on the agenda of the global community. However, it is difficult to assess the pace and quality of sustainable development of individual economic systems—in particular, industry—due to the lack of a unified methodological approach. In this regard, the following research goal was formulated—to develop and test a methodology for forecasting sustainable development by using statistical tools. The achievement of the goal was facilitated by the application of formalization methods, factor analysis, discriminant analysis, the method of weighted sum of the criteria, and the method of comparison. The results of the study are new scientific and practical solutions that develop the ability to diagnose economic systems for the transition to environmentally friendly production. Firstly, methodological solutions are proposed to assess the nature of the transition of industry to sustainable development (low, medium, or high rate). The methodology is based on the proposed aggregated indicator of sustainable industrial development based on the results of factor analysis (by the method of principal components). As a result, the patterns of sustainable development of the extractive and manufacturing sectors of the Russian economy are revealed. Secondly, integral indicators of economic, environmental and social factors of sustainable development are calculated, and classification functions for each type of industrial transition to sustainable development (low, medium, or high) are formed through discriminant analysis. Scenarios of industrial development are developed, taking into account the multidirectional trajectories of the socioeconomic development of the country. Thirdly, the DFD model of the process of scenario forecasting of sustainable industrial development is formalized, reflecting the movement of data flows necessary for forecasting sustainable industrial development. It is revealed that the manufacturing industry is expected to maintain a low rate of transition to sustainable development. On the contrary, for the extractive industry, if efforts and resources are concentrated on environmental innovations, average transition rates are predicted. The uniqueness of the proposed approach lies in combining two types of multivariate statistical analysis and taking into account the indicators that characterize the contribution of industrial enterprises to sustainable development.

Keywords: sustainable development; industry; factor analysis; discriminant analysis; forecasting; modeling; DFD (Data Flow Diagram)

1. Introduction

Sustainable development issues occupy a central place at all levels of management. The concept is continuously supplemented by new directions that determine the modernization of strategic management of economic systems at the macro-, meso-, and microlevels the principles of ESG (Environmental, Social, and Corporate Governance), "green" economy, the economy of the closed cycle, and nature-inspired algorithms. Of course, the above concepts are related to and focused on achieving synergies, namely on the protection of the environment [1], the construction of "green" supply chains [2–5], and the provision of environmentally friendly industries against the background of intensive industrial development [6–8].

Thus, this article explores an important issue—the methodology of sustainable industrial development, the study of which is devoted to the works of scientists from different countries [9]. First of all, it is important to understand the essence of sustainable development. In our opinion, society has not yet come to a unified understanding of this concept and awareness of its significance in the conditions of approaching ecological catastrophe. The scientific literature presents an extensive array of conceptual studies in the field of sustainable development [10–22], the role of the closed-cycle economy in this process [23–27], and green production [28–30]. Summarizing these approaches, we note that sustainable development is the result of integrated management of information flows, resource provision, business processes and business model, business strategy, and awareness of competitive advantages. The implementation of the concepts presented above is a rather complex process that requires a rational combination of economic and administrative resources. In this regard, the quintessence of competitive and sustainable development of the enterprise is a strategy based on correct and high-quality methodological techniques.

The development of such methodological solutions is devoted to the research of many scientists. We are impressed by the approach of a team of scientists led by Laurett. The authors identified factors (five drivers and two inhibitors) that determine the sustainable development of agriculture [31]. Szabó et al. explored the issues of sustainable development at the regional level [32]. The authors developed an assessment system for the analysis of regional sustainability, taking into account institutional aspects and natural and human resources. At the same time, the authors have only systematized these categories. The study of private performance measures is highlighted in the works of Kashani and Hajian [33]. The authors define a system of sustainable development as a multidimensional concept that includes economic growth, income distribution, and human well-being. Rotmans believes that a comprehensive evaluation of sustainability involves a long-term comprehensive evaluation of international and national policy programs in accordance with specific goals and criteria [34]. He proposed to find new ways to make the most of current sustainability assessment tools and to develop new approaches to integrated assessment. At the same time, the author does not specify the methodology of the integrated assessment.

Moldavska and Welo [35] proposed a new method for assessing corporate sustainability that views sustainability as a process of directed change. Corporate sustainability assessment is related to the Sustainable Development Goals. However, the authors focused mainly on the architecture of corporate sustainability assessment. The relationship between the company's development indicators and global sustainable development goals was presented. The block approach to managing the sustainable development of the company is impressive, but the need to aggregate blocks into a single integral indicator is ignored.

Therefore, the key problem raised in our study covers two fundamentally important issues—the methodology of sustainable industrial development and the implementation of statistical tools in the development of this methodology. The study of this problem is based on reading foreign publications and the critical theoretical analysis of the approaches of other scientists to its solution.

Sustainable development issues and the way in which they are assessed at different levels of government are given high priority, both globally and nationally. In Russian practice, the methodology covers the monitoring of a number of indicators linked to the UN Sustainable Development Goals. These are the real monetary incomes of the population, as a percentage of the previous period, the index of the physical volume of gross domestic product per capita, the index of the volume of environmental expenditures for the conservation of biodiversity, and the protection of natural territories in % of the previous year and other indicators [36]. This technique covers all spheres of society. However, this approach is accompanied by difficulties of comparing an integrated assessment of the level of sustainable development of different economic systems.

We continue to explore methodological issues. Our research background covers the study of statistical tools and the possibility of their application to assess the sustainable development of socioeconomic systems [37–39]. This study proposes a new approach to assessing the sustainable development of industry based on the combined sequential application of factor and discriminant analysis.

Quality strategic planning is based on the application of mathematical methods of data processing, modeling, and identification of latent dependencies between individual subsystems. These methods include factor analysis, decision trees, discriminant analysis, etc. These methods are implemented through big-data and data-mining technologies. Sustainable development involves the collection and processing of a large amount of data characterizing the economic, environmental, and social development of economic systems. This makes it possible to comprehensively assess the patterns of development of a country, region, and industry. A qualitative methodology for assessing and predicting processes and phenomena should be based on statistical methods and techniques, in particular, regression, factor, and discriminant analysis. Their illumination is reflected in the works of Oda et al. [40], Martínez-Regalado et al. [41], Yadav et al. [42], Tavassoli and Farzipoor Saen [43], and other works.

The competitiveness of the Russian economy is determined by the level of industrial development. In this regard, it is important to forecast the development of Russian industry. The application of discriminant analysis in the context of improving production processes was reflected in the work of Zhang and Luo, where the authors developed an approach to the diagnostics of malfunctions of industrial applications [44]; in a study by Sueyoshi et al. they aimed at developing a unified method for assessing the efficiency of the electric power industry [45]; in the scientific article by Rodrigues Luciano and Rodrigues Lucas, who applied discriminant analysis as part of the classification of energy industry enterprises based on an assessment of financial and economic performance [46]; and in the works of Horváthová et al. [47] and Kočišová and Mišanková [48] where the main subject of the study was the financial condition of enterprises. In the context of sustainable development, discriminant analysis was applied in the work of Vazquez-Brust and Plaza-Úbeda, where the authors identify the characteristics of organizations that pollute the environment excessively [49].

As a result of a critical study of scientific papers (Table 1) published in Scopus journals, we have revealed that a generally recognized rational methodology for assessing sustainable development has not yet been developed. Of course, the international scientific groundwork is not limited to the illuminated works. However, it can be stated that there are few studies based on the use of statistical methods. In our opinion, there are very few publications addressing the use of discriminant analysis in order to improve the methodology of sustainable industrial development and forecasting trends in greening.

In this regard, it is of interest to apply a combined mathematical approach to scenario forecasting of sustainable industrial development. As a consequence, the following goals and objectives of the study are formulated. The purpose of the study is to develop and test a methodology for predicting sustainable development using factor and discriminant analysis. Research objectives:

- Using the method of the main components to develop a methodology for assessing the nature of the transition of industry to sustainable development;
- To identify patterns of sustainable development of the extractive and manufacturing sectors of the Russian economy;
- On the basis of discriminant analysis to develop classification functions of the transition of industry to sustainable development;
- To identify scenarios for the development of Russian industry;
- To form a DFD model of the process of scenario forecasting of sustainable industrial development.

Table 1. Methodological approaches to the diagnosis of sustainable development (compiled by the authors).

Authors	The Specifics of the Approach	Limitations of the Approach
Oda et al. (2020) [40]	A mathematical approach to assessing the consistency of variables based on a generalized information criterion in canonical discriminant analysis	Emphasis on mathematical modeling
Martínez-Regalado et al. (2021) [41]	Application of biplot methods as effective machine learning methods in the framework of sustainable development diagnostics	Only the social factor of sustainable development is affected
Yadav et al. (2021) [42]	The use of logistic regression and discriminant analysis in the search for significant variables in the identification of risk factors that determine hypertension	The study is limited to the medical direction, therefore, the authors cover only the social factor
Tavassoli and Farzipoor Saen (2019) [43]	The methodology of assessing the sustainability of suppliers (in the context of economic, environmental, and social components); the classification of suppliers based on stochastic discriminant analysis is presented	Takes into account the specific criteria of suppliers (advertising costs, number of days of delay, cost of delivery, etc.)
Zhang and Luo (2021) [44]	A new dynamic discriminant analysis of the main subspace for monitoring and troubleshooting of industrial applications was developed	Technical nature of the research results
Sueyoshi et al. (2020) [45]	A methodology for evaluating the efficiency of the electric power industry based on combining the capabilities of discriminant analysis and Data Envelope Analysis is presented	Attention is focused on the environmental component
Rodrigues Luciano and Rodrigues Lucas (2018) [46]	Energy companies are classified into 4 groups based on cluster and discriminant analysis	The methodology is based on the analysis of financial indicators
Horváthová et al. (2021) [47]	The comparative analysis of neural networks and discriminant analysis for bankruptcy forecasting is carried out	The study covers the financial component of the activities of the companies under study
Kočišová et al. (2014) [48]	The discriminant analysis for forecasting the financial condition of companies was refined	
Vazquez-Brust and Plaza-Úbeda (2021) [49]	Discriminant analysis was applied to diagnose companies that excessively pollute the environment	Attention is focused on the environmental aspects of development

2. Materials and Methods

As a key modeling method, we used linear discriminant analysis. Its essence is to identify variables that differ significantly on average in the selected groups; see Formulas (A1)–(A4) (Appendix A) [50]:

The canonical discriminant function will have the form (Formula (1)):

$$d_{kn} = a_0 + a_1 x_{1kn} + a_2 x_{2kn}, \qquad (1)$$

where d_{kn} is the value of the discriminant function for object k in group n, and a_i stands for the coefficients of the discriminant function.

The study was based on statistical information on the development of the mining ($i = 1$) and manufacturing ($i = 2$) sectors of the economy for the period 2010–2019, published in the public domain on the website of the Federal Statistical Service [36]. The following 10 variables served as partial indicators.

Economic (Figure 1):

$I_{ecn,1i}$—the volume of shipped products by enterprises of the i-th sector of the economy, trillion rubles;

$I_{ecn,2i}$—gross value added by enterprises of the i-th sector of the economy, trillion rubles.

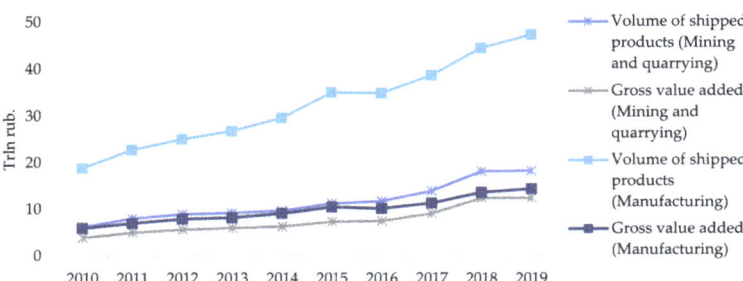

Figure 1. Dynamics of economic indicators of industrial development in Russia.

Ecological:

$I_{ecl,1i}$—the share of enterprises that have introduced innovations to reduce energy costs for production, %;

$I_{ecl,2i}$—the share of enterprises that have introduced innovations to reduce carbon dioxide emissions into the atmosphere, %;

$I_{ecl,3i}$—the share of enterprises that have introduced innovations to reduce environmental pollution, %;

$I_{ecl,4i}$—the share of enterprises that have introduced innovations in the secondary processing of waste, %;

$I_{ecl,5i}$—the volume of recycled and neutralized waste by enterprises of the i-th sector of the economy, billion tons;

$I_{ecl,6i}$—the volume of trapped and neutralized air pollutants emitted by enterprises of the i-th sector of the economy, million tons.

Social:

$I_{s,1i}$—the size of the average monthly salary of employees of enterprises of the i-th sector of the economy, thousand rubles.;

$I_{s,2i}$—average annual number of employees at enterprises of the i-th sector of the economy, million people.

The choice in favor of the listed 10 indicators is due to the following:

- In accordance with the forecast of the long-term socioeconomic development of the Russian Federation for the period up to 2036, the index of industrial production is expected to increase by 67.5% by 2036 (relative to 2018), which determines the importance of the volume of production and sale of industrial products;
- The same document indicates a guideline for increasing the share of products with high added value;
- Greening of production is central to the sustainable development of the national economy; the success of greening is possible as a result of the introduction of innovations, which determines the importance of studying the dynamics of environmental innovation in industry;
- In the conditions of industrial development and dangerous working conditions, the motivation factor is important, which is manifested, in particular, in the number of wages and the level of employment at industry enterprises.

(1) Based on the results of factor analysis, it is proposed to form an aggregated indicator of sustainable development of industry (Formula (2)):

$$I = \sum_{j=1}^{n}(d_j \times F_j), \qquad (2)$$

where j represents the principal components aggregated over the original data, d_j is the proportion of variance of j-th component, and F_j is the value of the main component (factor), calculated by Formula (3):

$$F_j = \sum_{k=1}^{10}(a_k \times I_k), \qquad (3)$$

where a_k represents the factor loadings for the variable k (10 variables indicated above are included in the analysis); and I_k is the value of the indicator (variable k), a private indicator.

(2) At the next stage, the growth rate is determined and the nature of the industry's transition to sustainable development is identified. The growth rate below 8% is proposed to be assessed as low; within 8–13%—as an average; and above 13%—as a high. The scale was determined by an expert method and can be used as a universal one. The scaling results allow us to take the nature of the dynamics (low, average, and high) as a categorical variable when conducting a discriminant analysis.

(3) Next, the weighted sum of criteria method is applied. To do this, private indicators are aggregated into a single generalizing factor, summing up the particular indicators, taking into account the assigned weight (w). The weight is assigned by the authors based on expert opinions and subjective assessment. As a result, it is proposed to calculate 3 indicators, namely $I_{ecn,i}$, $I_{ecl,i}$, and $I_{s,i}$, by Formulas (4)–(6):

$$I_{ecn,\,i} = I_{ecn,1i} \times w_{ecn,1i} + I_{ecn,2i} \times w_{ecn,2i}, \qquad (4)$$

$$\begin{aligned}I_{ecl,\,i} =\; & I_{ecl,1i} \times w_{ecl,1i} + I_{ecl,2i} \times w_{ecl,2i} + I_{ecl,3i} \times w_{ecl,3i} + I_{ecl,4i} \times w_{ecl,4i} \\ & + I_{ecl,5i} \times w_{ecl,5i} + I_{ecl,6i} \times w_{ecl,6i},\end{aligned} \qquad (5)$$

$$I_{s,\,i} = I_{s,1i} \times w_{s,1i} + I_{s,2i} \times w_{s,2i}. \qquad (6)$$

The sum of the weights for each of the three sustainable development factors is 1, as calculated by Formulas (7)–(9):

$$w_{ecn,1i} + w_{ecn,2i} = 1, \qquad (7)$$

$$w_{ecl,1i} + w_{ecl,2i} + w_{ecl,3i} + w_{ecl,4i} + w_{ecl,5i} + w_{ecl,6i} = 1, \qquad (8)$$

$$w_{s,1i} + w_{s,2i} = 1. \qquad (9)$$

(4) Based on the calculated values of sustainable development factors (economic, ecological, and social), a discriminant analysis is carried out, and classification functions (10) are formed for each class of sustainable development (low, average, and high; dependence of I_{categ} from incoming predictors $I_{ecn,i}$, $I_{ecl,i}$, and $I_{s,i}$):

$$I_{categ} = a_0 + a_1 \times I_{ecn,i} + a_2 \times I_{ecl,i} + a_3 \times I_{s,i}. \qquad (10)$$

The tool for statistical analysis was the Statistica program and its Discriminant Analysis module.

The criteria for evaluating the model are as follows:

- Wilks' Lambda, which, at a value close to 0, reflects the high quality of the model and good discrimination (the rate varies between 0 and 1);
- Criterion F, which must exceed the table value of the F-distribution; the criterion indicates that the null hypothesis (that the observations belong to the same class) is rejected and the discriminant analysis is qualitative;
- The significance level of the F-test p should be less than 0.05.

(5) Based on the results of formalized dependencies, scenarios for the sustainable development of industry are developed and the nature of the intensity of the transition to a new format of production systems is predicted.

3. Results

3.1. Patterns of Sustainable Development of the Mining and Manufacturing Industry in Russia

At the first stage of the author's methodological approach, a factor analysis was carried out. As a result, 10 input variables were aggregated into two or three factors, depending on the industry (Table 2).

Table 2. Principal components and factor loadings for two sectors of the economy (Varimax raw).

Mining and Quarrying			Manufacturing			
Variables	F_1	F_2	Variables	F_1	F_2	F_3
$I_{ecn,1}$	0.95	0.28	$I_{ecn,1}$	0.94	0.28	0.10
$I_{ecn,2}$	0.94	0.29	$I_{ecn,2}$	0.93	0.29	0.06
$I_{ecl,1}$	−0.44	−0.79	$I_{ecl,1}$	−0.68	−0.14	−0.54
$I_{ecl,2}$	−0.44	−0.87	$I_{ecl,2}$	0.30	0.90	0.08
$I_{ecl,3}$	0.51	−0.58	$I_{ecl,3}$	0.23	0.84	0.40
$I_{ecl,4}$	0.80	0.04	$I_{ecl,4}$	0.26	0.92	0.08
$I_{ecl,5}$	0.93	0.25	$I_{ecl,5}$	0.47	−0.14	0.31
$I_{ecl,6}$	−0.91	−0.26	$I_{ecl,6}$	−0.16	−0.10	−0.89
$I_{s,1}$	0.97	0.17	$I_{s,1}$	0.94	0.28	0.15
$I_{s,2}$	0.90	0.32	$I_{s,2}$	−0.23	−0.82	0.26
Explained variation	6.52	2.14	Explained variation	3.62	3.33	1.46
Proportion of total variance	0.65	0.21	Proportion of total variance	0.36	0.33	0.15

The factors of sustainable development of the mining industry were mainly included in the first component. Excluded from further analysis is an indicator that characterizes environmental innovations that reduce ecological pollution ($I_{ecl,3}$).

The evaluation of the sustainable development of the manufacturing industry is based on three main components. In this case, two variables (also ecological) are excluded from the matrix—$I_{ecl,1}$ and $I_{ecl,6}$, which is determined by a low factor load (below 0.7).

The formation of an aggregated indicator of industrial sustainable development is based on the dispersion of each selected component (Table 3).

Table 3. Eigenvalues.

Principal Components	Eigenvalue	% Total—Variance	Cumulative—Eigenvalue	Cumulative—%
		Mining and quarrying		
F_1	7.25	72.48	7.25	72.48
F_2	1.40	14.04	8.65	86.52
		Manufacturing		
F_1	5.51	55.13	5.51	55.13
F_2	1.89	18.85	7.40	73.98
F_3	1.01	10.13	8.41	84.11

The resulting factor loadings formed the basis for calculating the indicator of sustainable industrial development (Formula (2)) for the mining and manufacturing industries (Figure 2). There is a significant increase in the indicator in both cases (by 2.5 times). However, the mining industry demonstrates a higher efficiency of measures that contribute to environmental protection in the conditions of active economic development and an increase in production and production volumes. Thus, at the end of 2019, the level of the indicator for the mining industry was 86.44, and for the manufacturing industry, it was only 50.79.

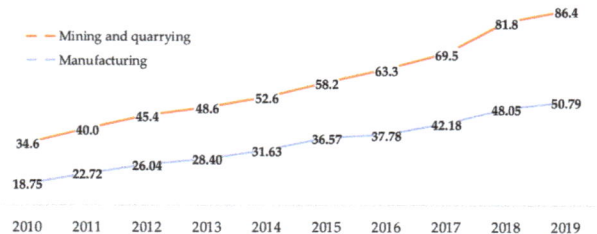

Figure 2. Change of aggregate indicator of sustainable development of industry in Russia.

The identification of patterns in the development of Russian industry is realized by estimating the growth rate of the aggregate indicator (Table 4).

Table 4. Dynamics of the aggregate indicator of sustainable industrial development.

	Mining and Quarrying				Manufacturing		
Year	I	Rate of Increase		Year	I	Rate of Increase	
2010	34.60	-	-	2010	18.75	-	-
2011	40.01	15.66%	high	2011	22.72	21.16%	high
2012	45.41	13.48%	high	2012	26.04	14.61%	high
2013	48.58	6.98%	low	2013	28.40	9.08%	moderate
2014	52.59	8.25%	moderate	2014	31.63	11.36%	moderate
2015	58.17	10.62%	moderate	2015	36.57	15.61%	high
2016	63.28	8.79%	moderate	2016	37.78	3.32%	low
2017	69.47	9.77%	moderate	2017	42.18	11.65%	moderate
2018	81.80	17.75%	high	2018	48.05	13.90%	high
2019	86.44	5.67%	low	2019	50.79	5.70%	low
Average		10.77%				11.82%	

Despite the relatively low values of the aggregate indicator of sustainable development, the manufacturing industry demonstrates higher dynamics: the average growth rate (over 10 years) for the extractive industry was 10.8%, and for the manufacturing, it is 11.8%. The advantage of the manufacturing sector is due to the high volume of production of industrial products, and, accordingly, a relatively high growth rate of this indicator.

Furthermore, the authors assigned weight coefficients to each of the ten variables. The sum of weight coefficients, within the framework of each factor of sustainable industrial development, is 1 and meets Conditions (7)–(9) (Table 5). We applied a differentiated approach to assigning weights to the factors of sustainable development of the extractive and manufacturing sectors, which was dictated by the need to consider the contribution of each of the sectors to the development of the national economy and environmental pollution. Thus, earlier we noted that, within the framework of the economic factor of manufacturing industry, there is a predominance of production and sales volumes over the extractive sector of the economy, but insignificant differences in the value of gross value added (Figure 1).

Table 5. Weighting coefficients (mining and quarrying/manufacturing).

Symbol	Economic Factor	Ecological Factor	Social Factor
$w_{ecn,1}$	0.5/0.9		
$w_{ecn,2}$	0.5/0.1		
$w_{ecl,1}$		0.1/0.3	
$w_{ecl,2}$		0.2/0.1	
$w_{ecl,3}$		0.2/0.2	
$w_{ecl,4}$		0.1/0.1	
$w_{ecl,5}$		0.2/0.1	
$w_{ecl,6}$		0.2/0.2	
$w_{s,1}$			0.6/0.9
$w_{s,2}$			0.4/0.1
Sum total	1	1	1

Using the weighted sum of the criteria method, the importance of sustainability factors can be calculated in an alternative way. In addition, four alternative trajectories were proposed for consideration in order to develop sustainable industrial scenarios (Table 6):

- Development Pathway 1 (DP 1)—negative trends in sustainable development due to a reduction in production and sales, innovative activity in the field of environmental safety, and number of employees;
- Development Pathway 2 (DP 2)—moderate growth rates of indicators relative to the level of 2019;
- Development Pathway 3 (DP 3)—significant improvements, characterized in particular by a substantial increase in innovation activity and improved environmental safety in production;
- Development Pathway 4 (DP 4)—an innovative development trajectory (active efforts of industrial enterprises in the field of economic activity and in the field of environmental protection and social protection of employees of these enterprises).

Based on the weighting factors presented in Table 4 and the expected changes in Russian industrial performance according to Formulas (4) to (6), key factors for sustainable development are also calculated.

Based on the data in Tables 4 and 6, a discriminant analysis was carried out. Its purpose was to predict the pace of sustainable development of the mining and manufacturing sectors of the economy and determine the type of intensity of greening of industrial production. The main elements of the discriminant analysis procedure in the Statistica program are presented below:

- Grouping variable—rate of increase (low, moderate, and high);
- Independent variables—factors of sustainable development (I_{ecn}, I_{ecl}, and I_s);
- Observations—10 (2010–2019 years);
- Method for selecting significant variables—standard.

The calculations were made privately for each sector of the economy. As a result of calculations based on the estimated data of the mining industry, the following results were obtained:

- Wilks' Lambda = 0.0594848—lies near 0, which indicates a qualitative discrimination;
- Approximately $F(6,10) = 5.166873 > F_{table}$ (table value F_{table} (0.05; 6; 10) = 3.21);
- Significance level $p < 0.0115$.

Thus, this classification is correct.

Table 6. Indicators of alternative directions of industrial development in Russia.

DP	$I_{ecn,1}$	$I_{ecn,2}$	$I_{ecl,1}$	$I_{ecl,2}$	$I_{ecl,3}$	$I_{ecl,4}$	$I_{ecl,5}$	$I_{ecl,6}$	$I_{s,1}$	$I_{s,2}$
				Mining and quarrying						
2019	18.32	12.39	0.21	0.25	0.92	0.79	3.56	1.72	89.34	1.15
DP 1	17.00	12.00	0.20	0.20	0.90	0.75	3.40	1.70	85.00	1.10
DP 2	18.40	12.40	0.25	0.30	0.95	0.85	3.50	1.80	92.00	1.15
DP 3	18.50	12.50	0.30	0.40	0.99	0.90	3.60	2.00	95.00	1.16
DP 4	20.00	13.00	0.70	0.70	0.70	0.70	4.00	4.00	100.00	1.17
	Economic, I_{ecn}			Ecological, I_{ecl}					Social, I_s	
2019	15.36			1.39					54.07	
DP 1	14.50			1.34					51.44	
DP 2	15.40			1.42					55.66	
DP 3	15.50			1.52					57.46	
DP 4	16.50			2.02					60.47	
				Manufacturing						
2019	47.44	14.41	0.58	0.46	0.78	0.55	0.18	31.99	43.86	9.96
DP 1	47.00	14.00	0.50	0.40	0.70	0.50	0.15	32.00	45.00	10.00
DP 2	48.00	15.00	0.60	0.50	0.80	0.60	0.20	34.00	46.00	10.20
DP 3	49.00	15.50	0.62	0.52	0.82	0.62	0.22	36.00	46.00	10.20
DP 4	50.00	16.00	0.80	0.80	0.95	0.80	0.30	50.00	55.00	10.30
	Economic, I_{ecn}			Ecological, I_{ecl}					Social, I_s	
2019	44.13			6.85					40.47	
DP 1	30.5			6.75					31	
DP 2	31.5			7.22					31.68	
DP 3	32.25			7.636					31.68	
DP 4	33			10.57					37.12	

Similarly, discrimination was assessed and recognized as qualitative for indicators of the manufacturing industry:

- Wilks' Lambda = 0.0989876—lies near 0, which indicates a qualitative discrimination;
- Approximately $F(6,10) = 3.630678$;
- Significance level $p < 0.0354$.

Moreover, in both cases, the correctness factor of the training samples was 100%. The classification functions for each type of industrial transition to sustainable development are further formalized. For the mining sector of the economy, we have Formulas (11)–(13), and for the manufacturing sector, we have Formulas (14)–(15):

$$\text{high (mining)} = -1555 + 94.69 \times I_{ecn} + 2264.8 \times I_{ecl} - 33.12 \times I_s, \quad (11)$$

$$\text{moderate (mining)} = -1391.41 + 87.96 \times I_{ecn} + 2136.12 \times I_{ecl} - 30.72 \times I_s, \quad (12)$$

$$\text{low (mining)} = -1194.41 + 82.21 \times I_{ecn} + 1981.48 \times I_{ecl} - 28.72 \times I_s, \quad (13)$$

$$\text{high (manuf.)} = -345.06 - 30.06 \times I_{ecn} + 267.97 \times I_{ecl} + 39.89 \times I_s, \quad (14)$$

$$\text{moderate (manuf.)} = -449 - 36.79 \times I_{ecn} + 299.22 \times I_{ecl} + 48.49 \times I_s, \quad (15)$$

$$\text{low (manuf.)} = -467.03 - 36.42 \times I_{ecn} + 306.22 \times I_{ecl} + 48.25 \times I_s. \quad (16)$$

Based on the formalization of classification functions and considering the calculated values of factors of sustainable development (Table 6), the nature of the transition of Russian industry to sustainable development is determined (Table 7).

Table 7. Alternative trajectories of industrial development in Russia (the best values (the largest) are highlighted in bold).

	Mining and Quarrying			Manufacturing			
Qualities	High	Low	Moderate	Qualities	High	Low	Moderate
A Posterior Probability	$p = 0.5$	$p = 0.3$	$p = 0.2$	A Posterior Probability	$p = 0.5$	$p = 0.2$	$p = 0.3$
Economic, I_{ecn}	94.69	82.21	87.96	Economic, I_{ecn}	−30.060	−36.418	−36.788
Ecological, I_{ecl}	2264.80	1981.48	2136.12	Ecological, I_{ecl}	267.971	306.225	299.224
Social, I_s	−33.12	−28.72	−30.72	Social, I_s	39.894	48.246	48.487
Constant	−1555.00	−1194.41	−1391.41	Constant	−345.061	−467.031	−448.995
DP 1	1137.85	**1165.64**	1155.52	DP 1	1783.62	**2125.19**	1951.82
DP 2	1275.81	**1286.86**	1286.62	DP 2	1906.64	**2225.26**	2088.63
DP 3	1447.48	1437.46	**1449.34**	DP 3	1995.57	**3358.87**	2185.52
DP 4	**2579.61**	2428.10	2517.35	DP 4	2976.27	−467.03	**3299.62**

The most likely development alternatives are highlighted in bold in the table, indicating the following:

- For mining industry, high growth rate of the aggregate sustainable development indicator is most likely in the fourth alternative scenario (Development Pathway 4), low growth rate is in the first and second cases (Development Pathways 1 and 2), and moderate rate of transition is in the third case (Development Pathway 3);
- For the manufacturing industry, a low probability of achieving a high growth rate of the aggregate indicator of sustainable development was revealed; achieving breakthrough development requires intensive mobilization of resources to modernize production systems.

3.2. Modeling of a Scenario Prediction Process for Sustainable Industrial Development

The systematization of the proposed methodological solutions is formalized in the form of a decomposition model of the process of scenario forecasting of the sustainable development of industry. The DFD notation was used as a modeling tool, which makes it possible to visually reflect the data flows that are sequentially generated and circulated in an economic system focused on the transition to sustainable development (Figure 3). The description of the model is implemented on a process basis in the All-Fusion Process Modeler (Bpwin) program. Files and databases are presented as a data store—an integral element of the DFD diagram.

The initiative comes from the top managers of an industrial enterprise (at the microeconomic level), from representatives of government, in particular, the Ministry of Industrial Development (at the regional or federal level) in the form of an order to monitor sustainable development and stimulate the greening of production.

The process covers eight sub-processes which are interconnected by data streams. The fundamental models are big data and data mining, which allow us to aggregate a large array of data on the development of the industry.

The proposed model reflects the combined (covering factorial and discriminant analysis) methodical approach of the authors to forecasting industrial development trends. The model differs from previously proposed approaches in the following:

- By combining two types of multivariate statistical analysis,

- By an expanded set of variables taken into account in the aggregate indicator of sustainable development of industrial greening.

The proposed methodological solution makes it possible to implement a flexible approach to planning the activities of industrial enterprises and develop alternative development strategies according to the proposed scenarios.

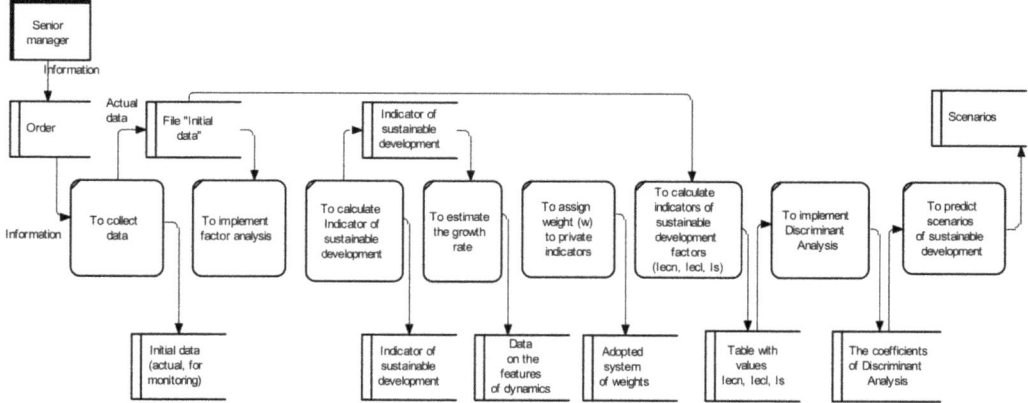

Figure 3. Model of the scenario prediction process of sustainable industrial development in DFD notation.

4. Discussion

In comparing the results of the assessment of the projected rate of transition to sustainable development, a high correlation of r was found (Table 8). In the case of the mining industry, the close link between the projected rate of transition to sustainable development is 87%, and in the case of manufacturing, it is 10%. Thus, it is advisable to recognize the author's methodology as successfully verified.

Table 8. Comparison of the results of factor and discriminant analysis.

DP	Mining and Quarrying		Manufacturing	
	Projected Pace of Transition to Sustainable Development			
	Factor Analysis	Discriminant Analysis	Factor Analysis	Discriminant Analysis
DP 1	low	low	low	low
DP 2	low	low	low	low
DP 3	low	average	low	low
DP 4	average	high	average	average
r	87%		100%	

Comparing the author's approach with previously published studies, it should be emphasized that the methodology proposed in this article is more capacious. We do not limit ourselves to assessing the impact of the functioning of industry on the environment, but take into account measures to reduce negative externalities (in the format of environmental innovations and the activity of enterprises in this area). In contrast to a number of approaches highlighted above [45–49] (analysis of financial and economic activity or environmental aspects), we include four aspects of industrial development (economic, innovative, social, and environmental) in the methodology at once. At the global level, the methodology for calculating the Sustainable Society Index is generally recognized. These are indicators Sufficient Food, Sufficient to Drink, Safe Sanitation, Education, Healthy Life, Gender Equality, Income Distribution, Population Growth, Good Governance, Biodiversity, Renewable Water Resources, Consumption, Energy Use, Energy Savings, Greenhouse Gases, Renewable Energy, Organic Farming, Genuine Savings, GDP, Employment, and Public Debt [51]. However, these indicators are aggregated only to the level of three factors of sustainable development (Human Well-Being, Environmental Well-Being, and Economic Well-Being) and cover society as a whole.

The methodology of sustainable development is also widely presented in the scientific works of Russian scientists. However, territories [52–54], environmental aspects [55], rationalization of water resources use [56,57], etc., prevail as the subject of research.

Of course, the detailed targeted elaboration of methodological solutions reflected in the designated publications is also of particular importance in the development of the methodology of sustainable development. However, the methodological approach we propose allows us to assess the following: firstly, not the statics of sustainable development, but the dynamics; secondly, sustainable development of the industry, which is strategically important in the development of Russia.

The factor and discriminant analysis we used confirmed the viability of the author's approach. The advantage of the first one is that it takes into account the latent patterns of industrial development in the economic, ecological and social planes and the possibility of formalizing the identified dependencies in the form of a function. In contrast to the cluster analysis, which focuses on the classification of observations, the factor analysis classifies variables and enlarges, thereby supplementing the explicit relationship between indicators, taking into account the hidden dependence. An alternative can also be multiple regression, which also formalizes the dependence of the response on predictors, but does not allow aggregating indicators.

Discriminant analysis complements factor analysis, includes elements of regression analysis, contributes to the formalization of the mathematical relationship between variables. In contrast to regression analysis, it includes a categorical variable described by a mathematical function. Thus, the discrimination problem provides the possibility of constructing discriminant functions and their separating power.

Summarizing the results of the study, the following conclusions can be drawn.

Firstly, a methodological solution was proposed for assessing the dynamics of sustainable development of the mining and manufacturing industries in Russia, based on the integrated use of factor and discriminant analysis. The difference of the methodology lies in taking into account the indicators characterizing the activity of enterprises in the context of three subsystems of sustainable development. The solution allows us to identify patterns occurring against the backdrop of greening industry change. The implementation of the methodology is aimed at assessing the contribution of enterprises to achieving harmony between the economic, ecological, and social interests of modern society.

Secondly, on the basis of the proposed methodology, four alternative scenarios of industrial development have been developed, taking into account crisis conditions related to the COVID-19 pandemic. If before 2019 there were periods with active phases of the transition of the Russian industry to a sustainable development model, then, in the short-term, high rates are unlikely. It is confirmed by the results of verification of the author's combined methodology.

Thirdly, the model of the process of scenario forecasting of sustainable industrial development in DFD notation is formalized. It reflects the logic of developing scenarios for future changes in the real sector of the national economy and allows for the implementation of a flexible approach to planning the activities of industrial enterprises.

A set of developments can be reflected in the context of developing a strategy for the socioeconomic development of the country and meso- and macroeconomic systems, encouraging them to participate in achieving sustainable development goals.

Our study has some limitations related to industry specifics, the choice of time series, and taking into account the crisis of 2020. It is planned to develop the methodological basis for managing the sustainable development of economic systems in the format of computer programs, as well as to expand the range of static analysis tools in the search for the most accurate methods and models.

Author Contributions: Conceptualization, A.I.S.; methodology, A.R.A.; formal analysis, R.R.K.; investigation, A.I.S. and A.R.A.; data curation, R.R.K.; writing—original draft preparation, A.I.S. and A.R.A.; writing—review and editing, A.I.S. All authors have read and agreed to the published version of the manuscript.

Funding: The reported study was funded by RSF, project number 22-28-00581.

Institutional Review Board Statement: Not applicable.

Informed Consent Statement: Not applicable.

Data Availability Statement: Not applicable.

Conflicts of Interest: The authors declare no conflict of interest.

Appendix A. Formulas for Calculations

$$\overline{x_1} = \frac{1}{n_1} \sum_{i}^{n_1} x_{1i}, \tag{A1}$$

$$\overline{x_2} = \frac{1}{n_2} \sum_{i}^{n_2} x_{2i}, \tag{A2}$$

$$\overline{x} = \frac{1}{n_1 + n_2}(n_1 x_1 + n_2 x_2), \tag{A3}$$

$$S = \frac{1}{n_1 + n_2 - 2}\left[\sum_{i}(x_{1i} - \overline{x_1})(x_{1i} - \overline{x_1})^{\hat{A}} + \sum_{i}(x_{2i} - \overline{x_2})(x_{2i} - \overline{x_2})^{\hat{A}}\right], \tag{A4}$$

where n_1 and n_2 are conditional groups of observations, $\overline{x_1}$ and $\overline{x_2}$ are average values of conditional variables 1 and 2 for all groups, and S is the variation in groups (should be maximum).

References

1. Keniger, L.E.; Gaston, K.J.; Irvine, K.N.; Fuller, R.A. What are the Benefits of Interacting with Nature? *Int. J. Environ. Res. Public Health* **2013**, *10*, 913–935. [CrossRef] [PubMed]
2. Ali, S.S.; Kaur, R.; Khan, S. Evaluating sustainability initiatives in warehouse for measuring sustainability performance: An emerging economy perspective. *Ann. Oper. Res.* **2022**, *21*, 04454. [CrossRef]
3. Sharma, V.K.; Chandna, P.; Bhardwaj, A. Green supply chain management related performance indicators in agro industry: A review. *J. Clean. Prod.* **2017**, *141*, 1194–1208. [CrossRef]
4. Choi, D.; Hwang, T. The impact of green supply chain management practices on firm performance: The role of collaborative capability. *Oper. Manag. Res.* **2015**, *8*, 69–83. [CrossRef]
5. Centobelli, P.; Cerchione, R.; Esposito, E. Developing the WH 2 framework for environmental sustainability in logistics service providers: A taxonomy of green initiatives. *J. Clean. Prod.* **2017**, *165*, 1063–1077. [CrossRef]
6. Chen, Y.; Lin, B. Towards the environmentally friendly manufacturing industry–the role of infrastructure. *J. Clean. Prod.* **2021**, *326*, 129387. [CrossRef]
7. Sahu, O. Appropriateness of rose (Rosa hybrida) for bioethanol conversion with enzymatic hydrolysis: Sustainable development on green fuel production. *Energy* **2021**, *232*, 120922. [CrossRef]
8. Zhao, X.; Zhang, Y.; Liang, J.; Li, Y.; Jia, R.; Wang, L. The sustainable development of the economic-energy-environment (3E) system under the carbon trading (CT) mechanism: A Chinese case. *Sustainability* **2018**, *10*, 98. [CrossRef]
9. Gandini, A.; Quesada, L.; Prieto, I.; Garmendia, L. Climate change risk assessment: A holistic multi-stakeholder methodology for the sustainable development of cities. *Sustain. Cities Soc.* **2021**, *65*, 102641. [CrossRef]
10. Neto, G.C.d.O.; Leite, R.R.; Lucato, W.C.; Vanalle, R.M.; Amorim, M.; Matias, J.C.O.; Kumar, V. Overcoming Barriers to the Implementation of Cleaner Production in Small Enterprises in the Mechanics Industry: Exploring Economic Gains and Contributions for Sustainable Development Goals. *Sustainability* **2022**, *14*, 2944. [CrossRef]
11. Zodape, H.; Patil, P.; Ranveer, A. Sustainable industrial development. *Int. J. Res. Appl. Sci. Eng. Technol.* **2015**, *3*, 111–116.
12. Yong, L. Towards Inclusive and Sustainable Industrial Development. *Development* **2017**, *58*, 446–451. [CrossRef]

13. Patterson, J.; Widerberg, O.; Schulz, K.; Sethi, M.; Barau, A. Exploring the governance and politics of transformations towards sustainability. *Environ. Innov. Soc. Transit.* **2017**, *24*, 1–16. [CrossRef]
14. Noailly, J.; Shestalova, V. Knowledge spillovers from renewable energy technologies: Lessons from patent citations. *Environ. Innov. Soc. Transit.* **2017**, *22*, 1–14. [CrossRef]
15. Frenken, K. Sustainability perspectives on the sharing economy. *Environ. Innov. Soc. Transit.* **2017**, *23*, 1–2. [CrossRef]
16. Luo, M.; Hwang, B.-G.; Deng, X.; Zhang, N.; Chang, T. Major Barriers and Best Solutions to the Adoption of Ethics and Compliance Program in Chinese International Construction Companies: A Sustainable Development Perspective. *Buildings* **2022**, *12*, 285. [CrossRef]
17. Dyrdonova, A.N.; Lin'kova, T.S. Principles of petrochemical cluster' sustainability assessment based on its members' energy efficiency performance. *E3S Web Conf.* **2019**, *124*, 04013. [CrossRef]
18. Shinkevich, A.I.; Lubnina, A.A.; Chikisheva, N.M.; Simonova, L.M.; Alenina, E.E.; Khrustalev, B.B.; Sadykova, R.S.; Kharisova, R.R. Innovative forms of production organization in the context of high-tech Meso-economic systems sustainable development. *Int. Rev. Manag. Mark.* **2016**, *6*, 219–224.
19. Shinkevich, M.V.; Shinkevich, A.I.; Chudnovskiy, A.D.; Lushchik, I.V.; Kaigorodova, G.N.; Ishmuradova, I.I.; Bashkirtseva, S.A.; Marfina, L.V.; Zhuravleva, T.A. Formalization of sustainable innovative development process in the model of innovations diffusion. *Int. J. Econ. Financ. Issues* **2016**, *6*, 179–184.
20. Linnerud, K.; Holden, E.; Simonsen, M. Closing the sustainable development gap: A global study of goal interactions. *Sustain. Dev.* **2021**, *29*, 738–753. [CrossRef]
21. Švárováá, M.; Vrchota, J. Influence of Competitive Advantage on Formulation Business Strategy. *Procedia Econ. Financ.* **2014**, *12*, 687–694. [CrossRef]
22. Sharifi, A.; Murayama, A. A critical review of seven selected neighborhood sustainability assessment tools. *Environ. Impact Assess. Rev.* **2013**, *38*, 73–87. [CrossRef]
23. Kravchenko, M.; Pigosso, D.C.A.; McAloone, T.C. Towards the ex-ante sustainability screening of circular economy initiatives in manufacturing companies: Consolidation of leading sustainability-related performance indicators. *J. Clean. Prod.* **2019**, *241*, 118318. [CrossRef]
24. Lewandowski, M. Designing the Business Models for Circular Economy—Towards the Conceptual Framework. *Sustainability* **2016**, *8*, 43. [CrossRef]
25. Shen, L.; Wang, X.; Liu, Q.; Wang, Y.; Lv, L.; Tang, R. Carbon Trading Mechanism, Low-Carbon E-Commerce Supply Chain and Sustainable Development. *Mathematics* **2021**, *9*, 1717. [CrossRef]
26. Lahane, S.; Kant, R. Investigating the sustainable development goals derived due to adoption of circular economy practices. *Waste Manag.* **2022**, *143*, 1–14. [CrossRef]
27. Londoño, N.A.C.; Cabezas, H. Perspectives on circular economy in the context of chemical engineering and sustainable development. *Curr. Opin. Chem. Eng.* **2021**, *34*, 100738. [CrossRef]
28. Grafakos, S.; Gianoli, A.; Tsatsou, A. Towards the Development of an Integrated Sustainability and Resilience Benefits Assessment Framework of Urban Green Growth Interventions. *Sustainability* **2016**, *8*, 461. [CrossRef]
29. Baptista, S.L.; Carvalho, L.C.; Romaní, A.; Domingues, L. Development of a sustainable bioprocess based on green technologies for xylitol production from corn cob. *Ind. Crops Prod.* **2020**, *156*, 112867. [CrossRef]
30. Khattak, S.I.; Ahmad, M.; Haq, Z.U.; Shaofu, G.; Hang, J. On the goals of sustainable production and the conditions of environmental sustainability: Does cyclical innovation in green and sustainable technologies determine carbon dioxide emissions in G-7 economies. *Sustain. Prod. Consum.* **2022**, *29*, 406–420. [CrossRef]
31. Laurett, R.; Paço, A.; Mainardes, E.W. Measuring sustainable development, its antecedents, barriers and consequences in agriculture: An exploratory factor analysis. *Environ. Dev.* **2021**, *37*, 100583. [CrossRef]
32. Szabó, M.; Csete, M.S.; Pálvölgyi, T. Resilient regions from sustainable development perspective. *Eur. J. Sust. Dev.* **2018**, *7*, 395–411. [CrossRef]
33. Kashani, S.J.; Hajian, M. Indicators of sustainability. In *Sustainable Resource Management*; Elsevier: Amsterdam, The Netherlands, 2021; pp. 317–334.
34. Rotmans, J. Tools for integrated sustainability assessment: A two-track approach. *Integr. Assess. J. Bridg. Sci. Policy* **2006**, *6*, 35–57.
35. Moldavska, A.; Welo, T. A holistic approach to corporate sustainability assessment: Incorporating sustainable development goals into sustainable manufacturing performance evaluation. *J. Manuf. Syst.* **2019**, *50*, 53–68. [CrossRef]
36. Federal State Statistics Service. Available online: http://www.gks.ru (accessed on 27 January 2022).
37. Shinkevich, A.I.; Ershova, I.G.; Galimulina, F.F.; Yarlychenko, A.A. Innovative Mesosystems Algorithm for Sustainable Development Priority Areas Identification in Industry Based on Decision Trees Construction. *Mathematics* **2021**, *9*, 3055. [CrossRef]
38. Samarina, V.P.; Skufina, T.P.; Savon, D.Y.; Shinkevich, A.I. Management of externalities in the context of sustainable development of the russian arctic zone. *Sustainability* **2021**, *13*, 7749. [CrossRef]
39. Shinkevich, M.V.; Shinkevich, A.I.; Ponkratova, L.A.; Klimova, N.V.; Yusupova, G.F.; Lushchik, I.V.; Zhuravleva, T.A. Models and Technologies to Manage the Institutionalization of Sustainable Innovative Development of Meso-Systems. *Mediterr. J. Soc. Sci.* **2015**, *6*, 32–39. [CrossRef]
40. Oda, R.; Suzuki, Y.; Yanagihara, H.; Fujikoshi, Y. A consistent variable selection method in high-dimensional canonical discriminant analysis. *J. Multivar. Anal.* **2020**, *175*, 104561. [CrossRef]

41. Martínez-Regalado, J.A.; Murillo-Avalos, C.L.; Vicente-Galindo, P.; Jiménez-Hernández, M.; Vicente-Villardón, J.L. Using HJ-Biplot and External Logistic Biplot as Machine Learning Methods for Corporate Social Responsibility Practices for Sustainable Development. *Mathematics* **2021**, *9*, 2572. [CrossRef]
42. Yadav, J.; Allarakha, S.; Shekhar, C.; Jena, G.P. Alcohol and tobacco influencing prevalence of hypertension among 15–54 years old Indian men: An application of discriminant analysis using National Family Health Survey (NFHS), 2015–2016. *Clin. Epidemiol. Glob. Health* **2021**, *12*, 100894. [CrossRef]
43. Tavassoli, M.; Farzipoor Saen, R. Predicting group membership of sustainable suppliers via data envelopment analysis and discriminant analysis. *Sustain. Prod. Consum.* **2019**, *18*, 41–52. [CrossRef]
44. Zhang, M.-Q.; Luo, X.-L. Novel dynamic enhanced robust principal subspace discriminant analysis for high-dimensional process fault diagnosis with industrial applications. *ISA Trans.* **2021**, *114*, 1–14. [CrossRef] [PubMed]
45. Sueyoshi, T.; Qu, J.; Li, A.; Xie, C. Understanding the efficiency evolution for the Chinese provincial power industry: A new approach for combining data envelopment analysis-discriminant analysis with an efficiency shift across periods. *J. Clean. Prod.* **2020**, *277*, 122371. [CrossRef]
46. Rodrigues, L.; Rodrigues, L. Economic-financial performance of the Brazilian sugarcane energy industry: An empirical evaluation using financial ratio, cluster and discriminant analysis. *Biomass Bioenergy* **2018**, *108*, 289–296. [CrossRef]
47. Horváthová, J.; Mokrišová, M.; Petruška, I. Selected Methods of Predicting Financial Health of Companies: Neural Networks Versus Discriminant Analysis. *Information* **2021**, *12*, 505. [CrossRef]
48. Kočišová, K.; Mišanková, M. Discriminant analysis as a tool for forecasting company's financial health. *Procedia Soc. Behav. Sci.* **2014**, *110*, 1148–1157. [CrossRef]
49. Vazquez-Brust, D.A.; Plaza-Úbeda, J.A. What Characteristics Do the Firms Have That Go Beyond Compliance with Regulation in Environmental Protection? A Multiple Discriminant Analysis. *Sustainability* **2021**, *13*, 1873. [CrossRef]
50. Mohammadi-Moghaddam, T.; Firoozzare, A. Investigating the effect of sensory properties of black plum peel marmalade on consumers acceptance by Discriminant Analysis. *Food Chem. X* **2021**, *11*, 100126. [CrossRef]
51. SSI. Sustainable Society Index. Available online: https://ssi.wi.th-koeln.de/history.html (accessed on 26 February 2022).
52. Novoselov, A.; Potravny, I.; Novoselova, I.; Gassiy, V. Social Investing Modeling for Sustainable Development of the Russian Arctic. *Sustainability* **2022**, *14*, 933. [CrossRef]
53. Panteleeva, M.; Borozdina, S. Sustainable Urban Development Strategic Initiatives. *Sustainability* **2022**, *14*, 37. [CrossRef]
54. Degai, T.S.; Khortseva, N.; Monakhova, M.; Petrov, A.N. Municipal Programs and Sustainable Development in Russian Northern Cities: Case Studies of Murmansk and Magadan. *Sustainability* **2021**, *13*, 12140. [CrossRef]
55. Ratner, S.; Gomonov, K.; Revinova, S.; Lazanyuk, I. Ecolabeling as a Policy Instrument for More Sustainable Development: The Evidence of Supply and Demand Interactions from Russia. *Sustainability* **2021**, *13*, 9581. [CrossRef]
56. Proskuryakova, L.N.; Saritas, O.; Sivaev, S. Global water trends and future scenarios for sustainable development: The case of Russia. *J. Clean. Prod.* **2018**, *170*, 867–879. [CrossRef]
57. Galimulina, F.; Zaraychenko, I.; Farrakhova, A.; Misbakhova, C. Rationalization of water supply management in industry within the framework of the concept of sustainable development. *IOP Conf. Ser. Mater. Sci. Eng.* **2020**, *890*, 012177. [CrossRef]

Article

Mathematical Modeling of Changes in the Dispersed Composition of Solid Phase Particles in Technological Apparatuses of Periodic and Continuous Action

Oleg M. Flisyuk *, Nicolay A. Martsulevich, Valery P. Meshalkin and Alexandr V. Garabadzhiu

Department of Processes and Apparatus, Saint Petersburg State Institute of Technology, Technical University, Moskovsky Avenue 26, 109013 Saint Petersburg, Russia; tohm1950@mail.ru (N.A.M.); vpmeshalkin@gmail.com (V.P.M.); gar-54@mail.ru (A.V.G.)
* Correspondence: flissiyk@mail.ru

Abstract: This article presents a methodological approach to modeling the processes of changing the dispersed composition of solid phase particles, such as granulation, crystallization, pyrolysis, and others. Granulation is considered as a complex process consisting of simpler (elementary) processes such as continuous particle growth, agglomeration, crushing and abrasion. All these elementary processes, which are also complex in themselves, usually participate in the formation of the dispersed composition of particles and proceed simultaneously with the predominance of one process or another, depending on the method of its organization and the physicochemical properties of substances. A quantitative description of the evolution of the dispersed composition of the solid phase in technological processes in which the particle size does not remain constant is proposed. Considering the stochastic nature of elementary mass transfer events in individual particles, the methods of the theory of probability are applied. The analysis of the change in the dispersed composition is based on the balanced equation of the particle mass distribution function. The equation accounts for all possible physical mechanisms that effect changes in particle size during chemical and technological processes. Examples of solutions to this equation for specific processes of practical importance are provided. The obtained analytical solutions are of independent interest and are in good agreement with the experimental data, which indicates the adequacy of the proposed approach. These solutions can also be used to analyze similar processes. The effectiveness has been confirmed during the analysis and calculation of the processes of granulation of various solutions and disposal of oil-containing waste to obtain a granular mineral additive.

Keywords: distribution function; integral transformation core; granulation; growth rate; abrasion; fluidized bed; dispersed composition; agglomeration; particle crushing

1. Introduction

Many chemical-technological processes involving the solid phase entail a change in the size of the dispersed particles. These include the processes of crystallization, dissolution, drying, combustion, pyrolysis, gasification, abrasion, and a number of others [1–7]. A change in the dispersed composition of the solid phase during the process can affect it via several mechanisms such as the kinetics of the process, a decrease or increase in the specific interfacial surface area, or a change in the nature of the movement of phases in the working volume. Oftentimes, this influence is so great that it cannot be ignored when estimating and designing industrial processes. For example, during the processes of combustion, pyrolysis and gasification, highly significant changes occur in the size of particles. Solid phase particles can change numerous times and this must be considered to ensure hydrodynamic stability, especially if the processes are carried out in apparatuses with a fluidized bed. In some cases (granulation, grinding), the change in the dispersed composition of solid particles is the essence of the process, which should lead to the

solution of a specific technological problem. Such processes are widely used for recycling waste in order to obtain useful products. For example, granulation allows for the use of a fine-dispersed fraction (dust) as a raw material and by this process, a finished product in the mineral fertilizers industry can be obtained. Similarly, during wastewater treatment, granular organic fertilizers are obtained by means of convective drying in a fluidized bed of activated sludge These types of combined processes of drying and granulation look very promising and proceed with lower energy consumption [1], as they occur simultaneously in one apparatus. Otherwise, the solution would have to be dried first, and only then would the obtained powder be sent for granulation in another apparatus—a granulator. During a combined process, the granulated product is obtained immediately at the outlet of the apparatus.

The change in the granulometric composition of solid particles can be associated with a variety of physical phenomena such as crushing, agglomeration, abrasion, shrinkage, dissolution, etc. Under conditions of intensive hydrodynamic regimes, these phenomena are stochastic and cannot be quantitatively described at the level of a single particle. Therefore, in order to describe the evolution of the dispersed composition of particles it seems natural to use the theory of probability. Previously [1,2,8–14], this approach convincingly proved its effectiveness in modeling processes across various industries. As for the application of mathematical models based on the numerical integration of CFD data for research, these methods have undeniably great capabilities and a degree of universality. However, analytical solutions, whenever they can be obtained, simplify tracing of the dependence of the process on various parameters and can help to quantitatively to describe the real process in some extreme cases. The use of mathematical models based on neural networks (AAN) is a fairly effective analysis tool in most cases. However, when studying chemical and technological processes, their use is unjustified as it is not based on the physical content of the phenomena that constitute the essence of the process.

In addition, a number of papers suggest using the Monte Carlo method to analyze agglomeration processes [15–18]. The literature also presents mathematical models of changes in the dispersed composition based on balance equations which, from a physical point of view, describe such processes more adequately, but are formulated for concrete technological processes and account for their specificity [19–26]. However, the proposed mathematical models are specific rather than universal in nature and are only applicable to certain cases of process organization. Therefore, the main aim of this work is to develop a unified methodological approach to the theoretical analysis of the processes of evolution of the dispersed composition, which would assist in designing accurate mathematical representations of a particular process and to describe it quantitatively with regard to the specificities of the accompanying phenomena.

2. Theoretical Analysis and Methods

For a quantitative description of the change in the dispersed composition of particles caused by several phenomena of different physical nature, the principle of superposition can be used. In this case, the velocity of change in the distribution function of the number of particles by mass is equal to the sum of the velocities of individual processes:

$$\frac{\partial F}{\partial t} = \sum_{i=1}^{k} \left(\frac{\partial F}{\partial t}\right)_i$$

This approach to the mathematical modeling of processes described by linear, quasi-linear differential and integro-differential equations can describe a complex composite process using kinetic equations for individual processes.

Generally, the change in the dispersed composition of the solid phase in a continuous or periodic apparatus is described by equation [1,2]:

$$\frac{\partial f}{\partial t} + div\left(\vec{w} - D_p \vec{\nabla}\right)f + \frac{\partial}{\partial m}\left(u - \frac{\partial}{\partial m}D_m\right)f = I^+ - I^- \tag{1}$$

where $f(\vec{r}, m, t)$ is the particle distribution function by mass m (size). By definition of the distribution function, the expression $f(\vec{r}, m, t)dm$ is the number of particles with a mass in the range $(m, m + dm)$ per unit of the working volume of the apparatus in the vicinity of a point with a radius vector $\vec{r}$ at time t. In Equation (1), $\vec{w}$ is the average velocity of the solid phase, D_p is the mixing coefficient of the solid phase (it is assumed that it is the same for all directions), and $u(\vec{r}, m, t)$ is the total average rate of continuous particle growth, which can occur both due to the adhesion of small particles to large ones and the deposition of the solid phase from solutions on their surface. The D_m coefficient (diffusion coefficient in the mass space) accounts for variations in the growth rate of individual particles. The terms I^+ and I^- on the right side of the equation are responsible for the change in particle size due to coagulation and crushing, respectively. If $k(t, \vec{r}, m, s)$ is used to denote the density of probability of agglomeration of two particles with masses m and s per unit time, and $g(t, \vec{r}, m, m - s, s)$ is used to denote the density of probability of crushing a particle with mass m into two fragments with masses $m - s$ and s, then the values I^+ and I^- take the following forms:

$$I^+ = \frac{1}{2}\int_0^m k(t, \vec{r}, m-s, s) f(\vec{r}, m-s, t) f(\vec{r}, s, t) ds + \int_m^\infty g(t, \vec{r}, s; s-m, m) f(\vec{r}, s, t) ds, \qquad (2)$$

$$I^- = \left[\frac{1}{2}\int_0^m g(t, \vec{r}, m; m-s, s) ds + \int_0^\infty k(t, \vec{r}, m, s) f(\vec{r}, s, t) ds\right] f(\vec{r}, s, t). \qquad (3)$$

Equations (1)–(3) are quite general in nature and can be used to quantitatively describe the evolution of the dispersed composition of the solid phase for many chemical and technological processes with regard to the specific conditions for their implementation. This will be illustrated over several examples.

We applied the proposed approach to the analysis of the granulation process in a flow apparatus of ideal mixing in the solid phase. We assumed that the formation of new centers of granule formation occurs due to the crushing of particles. For crushing occurring in an external circuit, for example, in roller crushers, an analysis is presented in [22]. If crushing is caused by the collision of particles, or thermal stresses inside the particles while agglomeration and abrasion are practically absent, then such conditions are close to the conditions for conducting a continuous process of dehydration of solutions and suspensions in a fluidized bed [27]. At the same time, Equation (1) will be significantly simplified for the stationary mode [1]:

$$\frac{d}{dm}u\phi + \left[\frac{1}{T} + \frac{1}{2}\int_0^m g(m, m-s, s)ds\right]\phi(m) = \int_m^\infty g(s; s-m, m)\phi(s)ds. \qquad (4)$$

Here, $\varphi(m)$ is the density of particle distribution by mass: $\phi = \frac{f(m)}{N}$, $\int_0^\infty \phi(m)dm = 1$; N is the number of particles in the apparatus; T is the average time of residence of the particles in the working volume. It is natural to assume that the probability of crushing a particle is proportional to its mass, since with increasing particle size the inhomogeneities inside the particle also increase. The density of probability of crushing is then a constant: $g(t, \vec{r}, m, m - s, s) = g_0 = $ const. In this case, Equation (4) can be formulated as follows:

$$\frac{d}{dm}u\phi + \frac{1}{T}\phi(m) + \frac{1}{2}mg_0\phi(m) = g_0\int_m^\infty \phi(s)ds. \qquad (5)$$

Experimental studies [28] have established that when granulating solutions in a fluidized bed, the velocity $u(m)$ of particle growth can be approximated by the ratio:

$$u = \frac{dm}{dt} = Am^n \qquad (6)$$

in which the indicator n, depending on the organization of the movement of the solid phase in the apparatus, takes values from 0 to 1. More specifically, $n = 2/3$ in the fluidized bed and $n = 1$ in the gushing bed. Considering the Dependence (6), Equation (5) can be solved numerically. However, an analytical solution can also be extended to both extreme cases: $n = 0$ and $n = 1$. The explicit form of such solutions leads to the conclusion about the limiting behavior of particle distribution functions in actual processes. For $n = 0$ the solution to Equation (5) satisfying the condition $\varphi(0) = 0$ is the function:

$$\phi(m) = g_0 T \left(\xi + \frac{\xi^2}{2} \right) \exp\left[-\left(\xi + \frac{\xi^2}{2} \right) \right], \qquad (7)$$

where $\xi = \frac{m}{\overline{m}} = \frac{m}{uT}$ is the dimensionless parameter and $\overline{m}$ is the average mass of the particles. The Ratio (7) allows to determine all parameters of the distribution of solid phase particles at the outlet of the apparatus.

At $n = 1$, when the particle growth rate is proportional to its size ($u = Am$), the solution to Equation (5) has the form:

$$\phi(m) = \frac{g_0}{2A} \exp\left[-\frac{g_0}{2A} m \right]. \qquad (8)$$

Another example of the effectiveness of Equation (1) in the quantitative description of real practically important processes that are accompanied by a change in the dispersed composition of the solid phase is in the analysis of particle agglomeration in the processing of powdered materials. Many works are currently devoted to the study of agglomeration [29–44]. When agglomerating particles are placed in a flow apparatus of ideal mixing, Equation (1) is simplified and can be formulated as follows:

$$\frac{\partial f}{\partial t} + \frac{1}{T} f + f \int_0^\infty k(m,s) f(s,t) ds = \frac{1}{T} f_0(m,t) + \frac{1}{2} \int_0^m k(m-s,s) f(m-s,t) f(s,t) ds \qquad (9)$$

where $f_0(m, t)$ is the density of the distribution function of the incoming particle flow. If the density of probability of coagulation of two particles is considered as a constant $k(m, s) = k_0 = const$ then the Solution (9) for the steady-state regime can be presented as follows:

$$f(m) = \frac{N_0}{\sqrt{1 + 2Tk_0 N_0}} \sum_{i=1}^{\infty} \left(\frac{2Tk_0 N_0}{1 + 2Tk_0 N_0} \right)^{i-1} \frac{2\Gamma\left(i + \frac{1}{2}\right)}{\sqrt{\pi}(2i-1)\Gamma(i+1)}. \qquad (10)$$

Here, N_0 is the number of particles entering the apparatus per unit of time and $G(x)$ is the gamma function. Expression (10) is used to calculate the number of particles in the apparatus depending on their average time of residence in the working volume, their average mass, as well as estimate the degree of polydispersity of the coagulating particle system. The latter characteristic is determined by the relative dispersion, which in the case under consideration is equal to:

$$\left(\frac{\sigma}{\overline{m}} \right)^2 = \frac{2N_0}{N} - 3 + \frac{N}{N_0} \left[\left(\frac{\sigma_0}{\overline{m}_0} \right)^2 + 1 \right],$$

where the index "0" refers to the flow of particles entering the apparatus. It follows from this expression that with the increase in the probability of the coagulation of particles (i.e., with the decrease in the number of particles N), the degree of polydispersity of the coagulating system increases.

The examples given illustrate the possibility of analytical solutions to Equation (1) in cases where the change in the dispersed composition of solid phase particles is caused mainly by either crushing or coagulation. However, many processes become complicated when coagulation and crushing of solid phase particles occur simultaneously. Such a situation may occur, for instance, when a granulation process is conducted in a flow apparatus of ideal displacement. In this case, Equation (1) takes the form [45]:

$$\frac{\partial f(m,l,t)}{\partial t} + w\frac{\partial f(m,l,t)}{\partial z} + f(m,l,t)\int_0^\infty k(m,s)f(s,l,t)ds + \tfrac{1}{2}f(m,l,t)\int_0^m g(m-s,s)ds \\ = \tfrac{1}{2}\int_0^m k(m-s,s)f(m-s,l,t)f(s,l,t)ds + \int_m^\infty g(s-m,m)f(s,l,t)ds. \quad (11)$$

Here, z is the longitudinal coordinate. Equation (11) should be supplemented with expressions for probabilities $k(m, s)$ and $g(m - s, s)$. The expression for the probability of coagulation of two particles with masses m and s per unit time should account for the fact that the formation of large particles is unlikely, while the collision of two very small particles with a sufficient amount of binder will almost certainly lead to their adhesion.

With regard to this assumption, the kernel of the integral transformation for coagulation can be approximated by the expression:

$$k(m,s) = e^{-B(m+s)} \quad (12)$$

The coefficient B in this expression depends on the conditions of the process including the amount of the binder.

The probability of crushing a particle clearly increases with an increase in its mass, since this entails an increase in the number of inhomogeneities inside it, the number of microcracks, local stresses, and so forth. For this reason, the kernel of the integral transformation for splitting $g(m - s, s)$ can be represented by the following expression:

$$\begin{aligned} g(m-s,s) &= s(m-s)(1-e^{-Cm}), \; s < m \\ g(m-s,s) &= 0, \qquad\qquad\qquad\qquad s > m \end{aligned} \quad (13)$$

The coefficient C depends on the intensity of the mechanical influences on the granules. At the same time, it is assumed that the fragmentation of a particle into two fragments of similar masses is more likely than its fragmentation into fragments of vastly different masses. Accordingly, abrasion is entirely excluded by the proposed models.

For calculating a specific process, the coefficients B and C can be found experimentally based on the results of specially conducted experiments [45].

For known constant values B and C Relations (12) and (13) close Equation (11). The solution to the equation with respect to $f(m, z, t)$ can determine the dynamics of changes in the mass (size) of particles along the course of movement of the processed material under conditions of the competing actions of the following two processes: coagulation and crushing. At the same time, for a continuous steady-state granulation process, the explicit form of the dependence $f(m, z)$ can help to locate the cross-section of the apparatus where crushing begins to prevail over coagulation. For a periodic process under conditions of ideal mixing, it is not difficult to determine the moment in time when the dynamic equilibrium between the processes of coagulation and crushing is established by the explicit form of the dependence $f(m, t)$. At the same time, the derivative $\frac{\partial f(m,t)}{\partial t}$ turns to zero and Equation (11) can be represented as:

$$f(m) = \frac{\tfrac{1}{2}\int_0^m k(m-s,s)f(m-s)f(s)ds + \int_m^\infty g(s-m,m)f(s)ds}{\int_0^\infty k(m,s)f(s)ds + \tfrac{1}{2}\int_0^m g(m-s,s)ds} \quad (14)$$

which uses the method of successive approximations to find the equilibrium function $f(m)$. The solution of this equation allows to determine the final granulometric composition of particles in the periodic granulation process as well as its dependence on the process parameters. As a first approximation of the solution of this equation, it is natural to consider the function:

$$f_1(m) = N\_A^2 m e^{-Am} \quad (15)$$

(N_p is the number of particles in the working volume of the apparatus under dynamic equilibrium conditions) which automatically satisfies the conditions for normalization:

$$\int_0^\infty f_1(m)dm = N_p$$

Substitution of the Relations (12), (13) and (15) to the right side of Equation (14) and the subsequent integration of the second approximation of the equilibrium function $f(m)$ gives:

$$f_2(m) = f_1(m)\varphi(m)$$

where the factor $\varphi(m)$ connecting the first and second approximations has the form:

$$\varphi(m) = \frac{\frac{1}{12}A^2m^2e^{-Bm} + \left[\frac{m}{A^2} - \frac{me^{-Cm}}{(A+C)^2} + \frac{2}{A^3} - \frac{2e^{-Cm}}{(A+C)^3}\right]}{\frac{A^2e^{-Bm}}{(A+B)^2} + \frac{1}{12}m^3(1-e^{-Cm})}$$

The obvious requirement for the behavior of $f_2(m)$ and $f_1(m)$ at $m \to 0$ to coincide leads to the following equation that must be satisfied by the constant A in Expression (17):

$$\left(\frac{A}{1A+C}\right)^3 + \frac{A^3}{2}\left(\frac{A}{A+B}\right)^2 = 1. \tag{16}$$

Consequently, the root of this equation, found after determining the empirical constants B and C, together with Relation (15) results in an explicit form of the first approximation for the equilibrium function $f(m)$. Simple calculations show that the function $\varphi(m) \to 0$ at $m \to \infty$ is close to unity at small values of the variable m. Therefore, the Dependence (15) can be used to analyze the distribution of granules by mass (size) at the stage of the process when the intensity of particle crushing is comparable to the rate of granulation. Specifically, the average mass of granules is equal to:

$$\overline{m}_p = \frac{1}{N_p}\int_0^\infty f_1(m)dm = \frac{1}{N_p}\int_0^\infty A^2m^2e^{-Am}dm = \frac{2}{A}. \tag{17}$$

The modelling of the continuous growth of large particles only at the expense of a small fraction is of great practical interest. In this case, the right side of Equation (1) equals zero, which takes the following form:

$$\frac{\partial f}{\partial t} + div\left(\vec{w} - D_p\vec{\nabla}\right)f + \frac{\partial}{\partial m}\left(u - \frac{\partial}{\partial m}D_m\right)f = 0 \tag{18}$$

For apparatuses with an ideal mixing of the solid phase, the equation will include the average residence time T of particles in the working area:

$$\frac{\partial f}{\partial t} + \frac{1}{T}f + \frac{\partial}{\partial m}uf = \frac{1}{T}f_0(m,t) + \frac{\partial^2}{\partial m^2}D_mF.$$

Under steady-state conditions, the last equation has the exact solution:

$$f(m) = \frac{1}{Tu(m)}\int_{m_0}^m f_0(\zeta)\exp\left(-\int_\zeta^m \frac{d\eta}{Tu(\eta)}\right)d\zeta \tag{19}$$

which is correct in the case when the diffusion in the mass space can be neglected. It can be shown [46] that this is exactly the case when condition $Tu >> m_0$—where m_0 is the mass of a fine fraction particle—is satisfied. The Ratio (19) for the case of a monodispersed composition of large particles and a constant growth rate will take the form:

$$f(m) = \frac{N_0}{Tu} e^{-\frac{m-m_0}{Tu}} \qquad (20)$$

In the processes of granulation and particle enlargement, it is often more convenient to determine the particle distribution function not by mass, but by radius. Equation (19) is invariant with respect to the replacement of m by r, which is the radius of the particle. Consequently, Solution (20) will also be invariant, except in this case, the particle growth rate will be linear rather than mass-related. Moving from the mass of the particle to its radius we get:

$$f(r) = \frac{N_0}{\bar{v}} 4\pi r^2 e^{-\frac{(r^3 - r_0^3)}{Tu} * \frac{4\pi}{3}} \qquad (21)$$

Here, $\bar{v} = Tu$, $f(r)$ is the differential function of the particle distribution over r—the radius of the particle.

3. Results and Discussion

The obtained solutions required experimental verification for a wide class of chemical and technological processes under various conditions of implementation. For this purpose, experimental studies were conducted using technological devices of several types. The results of an experimental study of a cycle-free granulation process with an internal source of granulation in a gushing bed apparatus are given in [1]. In the experiments, a disodium phosphate solution was used, which was fed into the lower part of the apparatus, directly into the fountain core using a pneumatic nozzle. The drying of the solution falling onto the granules occurred very quickly, which ensured the continuous growth of granules in the apparatus. As the nuclei of granulation, small particles of granules were used, which were formed in the apparatus as a result of volumetric and thermal crushing of the granules themselves. This occurred under the influence of local temperature fields formed in the layer that is the core of the fountain and the peripheral zone of the layer.

According to the results of experiments on the study of crushing, the dependences of the density of probability of crushing per unit time g_0 on the magnitude of temperature differences were obtained. The latter, as was found, provides the main factor in the thermal crushing of granules. As is shown, (Figure 1) for a cycle-free process with an internal source of granulation, the experimental values of the differential distribution function of the obtained granules fit well between the distribution curves obtained by calculation according to analytical Dependences (7) and (8).

These analytical dependences obtained for the limiting values of the parameter n determine the boundaries for actual particle distribution functions, provided that the kernel of the integrodifferential equation is a constant. However, if the actual functions reach beyond the boundaries considered, then a different and a more complex type of kernel is needed, which would lead to a significant increase in mathematical difficulties when obtaining solutions.

The adequacy of the proposed model representations was also confirmed for the process of granulating a finely dispersed product in a horizontal cylindrical granulator with a fast-rotating rotor with fingers for intensive mixing of the material [45]. In the experiments, an oil-containing waste disposal product mixed with alkaline earth metal oxide was used to obtain a granular mineral additive in asphalt concrete mixtures. Bitumen BDU 60/90 was used as a binder. The average particle diameter in the initial product was 120 microns with a density of 1.26 g/cm^3. The experiments were carried out at different speeds of rotation. At the same time, the amount of bitumen in all experiments was 12% (wt.) of the total amount of material. The comparison was carried out according to the calculated and experimental values of the average mass of granules at the stage of the process when the effects of crushing and coagulation were comparable, under different operating modes of the granulator. The results of the comparison showed that the Ratios (16) and (17) accurately predict the $\overline{m}_p$ value—see Figure 2.

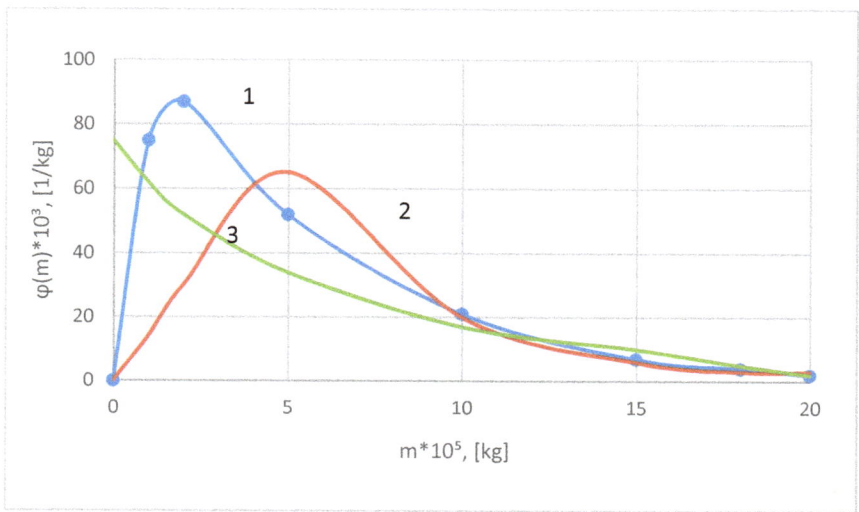

Figure 1. Differential particle mass distribution function. 1—experimental; 2—calculated at $u = const$; 3—calculated at $u = Am$.

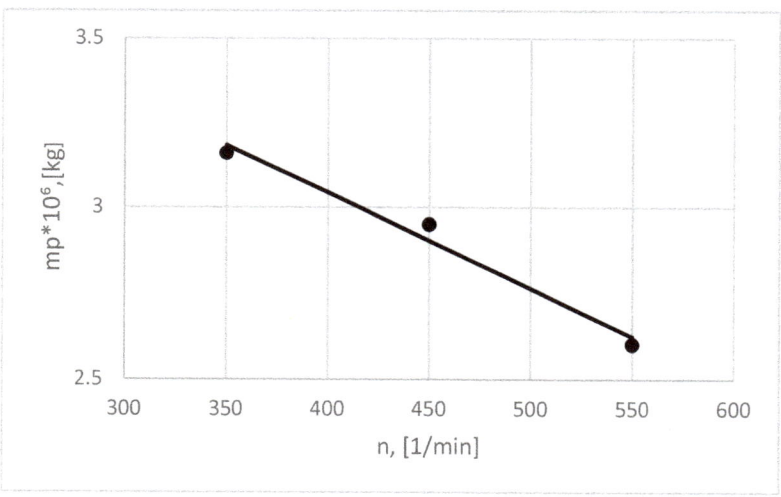

Figure 2. The dependence of the average particle mass $\overline{m}_p$ on the rotation frequency of the rotor n in a high-speed granulator. The line represents calculated values, the points—experimental values.

Consequently, Equation (1) is an acceptable basis, including in the analysis of processes in which the coagulation and crushing of solid particles occur simultaneously. Additionally, the Approximations (12) and (13) can be used for probabilistic estimation of coagulation and particle crushing during the entire time of the process. The dependence $f(m) = N\_(t)A^2 m e^{-Am}$ is flexible enough to correspond with sufficient accuracy to the actual dynamics of changes to the granulometric composition in the periodic mode of operation of the apparatus, or in a continuous process—provided that the design of the apparatus ensures a mode of movement of the material close to ideal displacement.

Another series of experimental studies aimed to verify the validity of the proposed mathematical representations when describing particle enlargement in a gushing bed apparatus [46]. In the experiments, granules of synthetic detergents with a particle diameter of about 1 mm were used and sprayed with small particles of the same material with a diameter of less than 0.2 mm. Water was supplied as a binding fluid. The experiments were carried out in a continuous mode, the volume of the layer in the apparatus was maintained as constant. The liquid-phase water was fed to the surface of the layer by a mechanical nozzle, and the fine fraction for spraying onto the granules was fed through a gas distribution grid, with a flow of heated air as a liquefying agent. To determine the type of the initial distribution function of the initial granules, they were considered a monofraction. In this case, the initial distribution function can be considered as a delta function, $\varphi_0(r) = \delta(r - r_0)$. Here, $\varphi_0 = f(r)/N_0$ is the normalized distribution function for the number of initial particles. Considering this, Equation (21) has the following form:

$$\varphi(r) = \frac{1}{Tu} e^{-\frac{m-r_0}{Tu}} * \theta(r - r_0) \qquad (22)$$

where $\theta(r - r_0)$ is the Heaviside function at $r - r_0 \geq 0$, $\theta(x) = 1$, and at $r - r_0 < 0$, $\theta(x) = 0$. The estimation of the increment of enlarged particles according to Formula (22) and its comparison with the experimental values obtained for the experimental conditions showed a satisfactory convergence of the results. As shown in Figure 3, the deviation between them is about 8%, which indicates the adequacy of both the theoretical and experimental results.

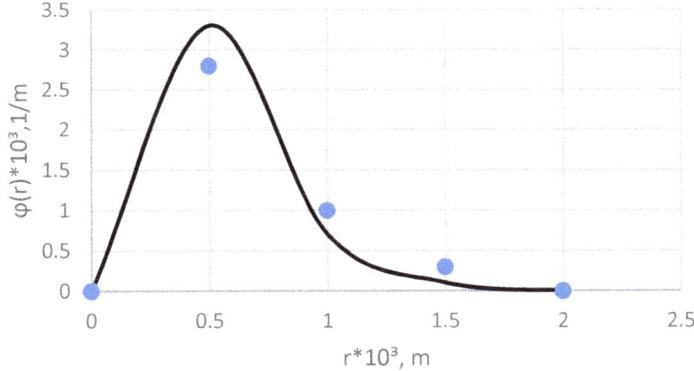

Figure 3. Dependence of the differential particle size distribution function. The line represents calculated values, the points—experimental values.

It is shown in [47] that the proposed approach can also be used to describe the abrasion of particles in suspended bed apparatuses, which is very important for many processes involving the solid phase.

4. Conclusions

A methodological approach to modeling the processes of changing the dispersed composition of solid phase particles such as granulation, crystallization, pyrolysis and others, is presented. Granulation should be considered as a complex process consisting of simpler (elementary) processes such as continuous particle growth, agglomeration, crushing and abrasion. All these elementary processes, which are also complex in themselves, usually participate in the formation of the dispersed composition of particles and proceed simultaneously with the predominance of one process or another, depending on the method of its organization and the physicochemical properties of substances.

Extensive experimental studies carried out by the authors indicate that the general balance Equation (1) for the particle mass distribution function can serve as a universal basis for a quantitative description of the evolution of the dispersed composition of the solid phase in technological apparatuses of periodic and continuous action. The paper presents analytical solutions of this equation for some special cases that are of independent interest.

In addition, it is important to note that a direct numerical or analytical solution of the integro-differential Equation (1) is impossible without experimental data on the kinetics of particle size changes and the probability of their coagulation and crushing. Obtaining such data in each specific case is an independent non-trivial task that requires certain experimental skills. However, if such a problem is solved, then the possibilities of the proposed approach are able to exhaustively assess the characteristics of the granulometric composition of the solid phase at any stage of the process. So, by using the Ratios (7) and (8), it is not difficult to calculate the parameters of the distribution of solid phase particles at the outlet of the flow apparatus of ideal mixing in a continuous mode of the granulation process. Ratios (10), (17) and (21) provide an opportunity to evaluate similar characteristics for other types of processes. At the same time, the calculated ratios implicitly depend on the design features of the devices and their working conditions (for example, after average residence time), which helps to purposefully select the modes of movement of working media in order to achieve the desired dispersed composition at the exit of the apparatus. In practical terms, such a task is of considerable interest.

It is interesting to note that the approach proposed by the authors can also be applied in areas aside from chemical technology. For instance, in [48,49] a similar mathematical apparatus is used in constructing models of economic growth of market participants. In addition, balance equations of the (1) equation type include a distribution function not by size, but by the volume of capital.

Author Contributions: Conceptualization: O.M.F. and N.A.M.; methodology: V.P.M.; validation: O.M.F. and A.V.G.; formal analysis: N.A.M.; research: V.P.M.; writing—original draft preparation: O.M.F.; writing—review and editing: A.V.G.; supervision: V.P.M. All authors have read and agreed to the published version of the manuscript.

Funding: This research received no external funding.

Acknowledgments: The research was funded by the Russian Science Foundation under grant agreement No. 21-79-30029.

Conflicts of Interest: The authors declare that they have no conflict of interest requiring disclosure in the present work.

References

1. Frolov, V.F.; Flisyuk, O.M. *Granulirovanie vo Vzveshennom Sloe (Fluidized-Bed Granulation)*; Khimizdat: St. Petersburg, Russia, 2007.
2. Meshalkin, V.P.; Flisyuk, O.M.; Martzulevich, N.A.; Garabadzhiu, A.V. Theoretical and experimental analysis of change in the dispersed composition of solid phase particles in process apparatus. *Rep. Russ. Acad. Sci.* **2021**, *501*, 32–36. [CrossRef]
3. Ohyama, M.; Amari, S.; Takiyama, H. Operation Design of Reaction Crystallization Using Homogeneity Flisyuk Evaluation for the Quality Improvement of Agglomerated Crystalline Particles. *Crystals* **2021**, *11*, 844. [CrossRef]
4. Mazza, G.; Falcoz, Q.; Gauthier, D.; Flamant, G. A particulate model of solid waste incineration in a fluidized bed combining combustion and heavy metal vaporization. *Combust. Flame* **2009**, *156*, 2084–2092. [CrossRef]
5. Soria, J.M.; Gauthier, D.; Falcoz, Q.; Flamant, G.; Mazza, G.; Hazard, D.J. Local CFD kinetic model of cadmium aporization during fluid bed incineration of municipal solid waste. *J. Hazard. Mater.* **2013**, *248–249*, 276–284. [CrossRef]
6. Osman, A.; Goehring, L.; Patti, A.; Stitt, H.; Shokri, N. Fundamental Investigation of the Drying of Solid Suspensions. *Ind. Eng. Chem. Res.* **2017**, *56*, 10506–10513. [CrossRef]
7. Kotzur, B.A.; Berry, R.J.; Zigan, S.; García-Triñanes, P.; Bradley, M. Particle attrition mechanisms, their characterisation, and application to horizontal lean phase pneumatic Flisyuk conveying systems: A review. *Powder Technol.* **2018**, *334*, 76–105. [CrossRef]
8. Flisyuk, O.M.; Frolov, V.F.; Shininov, T.N. Mathematical Simulation of Granulation Process in a Speed Granulator. *Theor. Found. Chem. Eng.* **2017**, *51*, 432–436. [CrossRef]
9. Flisyuk, O.M.; Martsulevich, N.A.; Krukovskii, O.N. Fluidized-Bed Granulation of Ammonium Sulfate from Solution Formed as By-Product in Production of Manganese Oxides. *Russ. J. Appl. Chem.* **2016**, *89*, 800–804. [CrossRef]
10. Nazli, S.; Burcu, T.; Nazlıcan, Y. Effects of particle size distribution on some physical, chemical and functional properties of unripe banana flour. *Food Chem.* **2016**, *213*, 180–186. [CrossRef]

11. Abbas, A.; Farizhandi, K.; Zhao, H.; Lau, R. Modeling the change in particle size distribution in a gas-solid fluidized bed due to article attrition using a hybrid artificial neural network-genetic algorithm approach. *Chem. Eng. Sci.* **2016**, *155*, 210–220. [CrossRef]
12. Ueda, S.; Miura, K.; Kawata, R.; Furutani, H.; Uematsu, M.; Omori, Y.; Tanimoto, H. Number-size distribution of aerosol particles and new particle formation events in tropical and subtropical Pacific Oceans. *Atmos. Environ.* **2016**, *142*, 324–339. [CrossRef]
13. Holaň, J.; Ridvan, L.; Billot, P.; Štěpánek, F. Design of co-crystallization processes with regard to particle size distribution. *Chem. Eng. Sci.* **2015**, *128*, 36–43. [CrossRef]
14. Koekemoer, A.; Luckos, A. Effect of material type and particle size distribution on pressure drop in packed of large particles: Extending the Ergun equation. *Fuel* **2015**, *158*, 232–238. [CrossRef]
15. Zhao, H.; Maisels, A.; Matsoukas, T.; Zheng, C. Analysis of four Monte Carlo methods for the solution of population balances in dispersed systems. *Powder Technol.* **2007**, *173*, 38–50. [CrossRef]
16. Hussain, M.; Kumar, J.; Peglow, M.; Tsotsas, E. Modeling spray fluidized bed aggregation kinetics on the basis of Monte-Carlo simulation results. *Chem. Eng. Sci.* **2013**, *101*, 35–45. [CrossRef]
17. Hussain, M.; Peglow, M.; Tsotsas, E.; Kumar, J. Modeling of aggregation kernel using Monte Carlo simulations of spray fluidized bed agglomeration. *AIChE J.* **2014**, *60*, 855–868. [CrossRef]
18. Rieck, C.; Schmidt, M.; Bück, A.; Tsotsas, E. Monte Carlo modeling of binder-Less spray agglomeration in fluidized beds. *AIChE J.* **2018**, *64*, 3582–3594. [CrossRef]
19. Vesjolaja, L.; Glemmestad, B.; Lie, B. Population balance modelling for fertilizer granulation process. In Proceedings of the 59th Conference on Simulation and Modelling (SIMS 59), Oslo Metropolitan University, Oslo, Norway, 26–28 September 2018; pp. 95–102. [CrossRef]
20. Wildeboer, W.J.; Litster, J.D.; Cameron, I.T. Modelling nucleation in wet granulation. *Chem. Eng. Sci.* **2005**, *60*, 3751–3761. [CrossRef]
21. Ramkrishna, D. *Population Balances: Theory and Applications to Particulate Systems in Engineering*; Academic Press: San Diego, CA, USA, 2000. [CrossRef]
22. Vreman, A.; van Lare, C.; Hounslow, M. A basic population balance model for fluid bed spray granulation. *Chem. Eng. Sci.* **2009**, *64*, 4389–4398. [CrossRef]
23. Immanuel, C.D.; Doyle, F.J. Solution technique for a multi-dimensional population balance model describing granulation processes. *Powder Technol.* **2005**, *156*, 213–225. [CrossRef]
24. Poon, J.M.H.; Immanuel, C.D.; Francis, J.; Doyle, I.; Litster, J.D. A three-dimensional population balance model of granulation with a mechanistic representation of the nucleation and aggregation phenomena. *Chem. Eng. Sci.* **2008**, *63*, 1315–1329. [CrossRef]
25. Kumar, J.; Peglow, M.; Warnecke, G.; Heinrich, S.; Mörl, L. Improved accuracy and convergence of discretized population balance for aggregation: The cell average technique. *Chem. Eng. Sci.* **2006**, *61*, 3327–3342. [CrossRef]
26. Dürr, R.; Bück, A. Approximate Moment Methods for Population Balance Equations in Particulate and Bioengineering Processes. *Processes* **2020**, *8*, 414. [CrossRef]
27. Cotabarren, I.; Schulz, P.G.; Bucalá, V.; Piña, J. Modeling of an industrial double-roll crusher of a urea granulation circuit. *Powder Technol.* **2008**, *183*, 224–230. [CrossRef]
28. Todes, O.M.; Kaganovich, Y.Y.; Nalimov, S.P.; Golziker, A.D. *Obezvozhivanie Rastvorov v Kipyashchem Sloe (Fluidized-Bed Dehydration of Solutions)*; Metallurgiya: Moscow, Russia, 1973.
29. Dadkhah, M.; Tsotsas, E. Influence of process variables on internal particle structure in spray fluidized bed agglomeration. *Powder Technol.* **2014**, *258*, 165–173. [CrossRef]
30. Terrazas-Velarde, K.; Peglow, M.; Tsotsas, E. Kinetics of fluidized bed spray agglomeration for compact and porous particles. *Chem. Eng. Sci.* **2011**, *66*, 1866–1878. [CrossRef]
31. Chakraborty, J.; Kumar, J.; Singh, M.; Mahoney, A.; Ramkrishna, D. Inverse Problems in Population Balances. Determination of Aggregation Kernel by Weighted Residuals. *Ind. Eng. Chem. Res.* **2015**, *54*, 10530–10538. [CrossRef]
32. Eisenschmidt, H.; Soumaya, M.; Bajcinca, N.; Le Borne, S.; Sundmacher, K. Estimation of aggregation kernels based on Laurent polynomial approximation. *Comput. Chem. Eng.* **2017**, *103*, 210–217. [CrossRef]
33. Bück, A.; Tsotsas, E. Agglomeration. In *Encyclopedia of Food and Health*; Caballero, B., Finglas, P.M., Toldrá, F., Eds.; Academic Press: Oxford, UK, 2016; pp. 73–81. [CrossRef]
34. Auger, J.M.; Martin, S.; Gruy, F. Inverse Population Balance Problems: Heuristics for Aggregation/Breakage of Solid Clusters in Liquid Metals. *Ind. Eng. Chem. Res.* **2020**, *59*, 10373–10388. [CrossRef]
35. Singh, M.; Nayak, R.K.; Walker, G. Convergence analysis of volume preserving scheme for mass based coalescence equation. *Appl. Numer. Math.* **2022**, *173*, 365–379. [CrossRef]
36. Singh, M. New finite volume approach for multidimensional Smoluchowski equation on nonuniform grids. *Stud. Appl. Math.* **2021**, *147*, 955–977. [CrossRef]
37. Ahrens, R.; Le Borne, S. Reconstruction of low-rank aggregation kernels in univariate population balance equations. *Adv. Comput. Math.* **2021**, *47*, 39. [CrossRef]
38. Žižek, K.; Gojun, M.; Grčić, I. Simulating the wet granulation of TiO_2 photocatalyst in fluidized bed: Population balance modelling and prediction of coalescence rate. *Powder Technol.* **2021**, *379*, 1–11. [CrossRef]

39. Singh, M.; Singh, R.; Singh, S.; Walker, G.; Matsoukas, T. Discrete finite volume approach for multidimensional agglomeration population balance equation on unstructured grid. *Powder Technol.* **2020**, *376*, 229–240. [CrossRef]
40. Singh, M.; Singh, R.; Singh, S.; Singh, G.; Walker, G. Finite volume approximation of multidimensional aggregation population balance equation on triangular grid. *Math. Comput. Simul.* **2020**, *172*, 191–212. [CrossRef]
41. Singh, M.; Matsoukas, T.; Walker, G. Mathematical analysis of finite volume preserving scheme for nonlinear Smoluchowski equation. *Phys. D Nonlinear Phenom.* **2020**, *402*, 132221. [CrossRef]
42. Singh, M.; Ismail, H.Y.; Singh, R.; Albadarin, A.B.; Walker, G. Finite volume approximation of nonlinear agglomeration population balance equation on triangular grid. *J. Aerosol Sci.* **2019**, *137*, 105430. [CrossRef]
43. Singh, M.; Kaur, G. Convergence analysis of finite volume scheme for nonlinear aggregation population balance equation. *Math. Methods Appl. Sci.* **2019**, *42*, 3236–3254. [CrossRef]
44. Singh, M.; Vuik, K.; Kaur, G.; Bart, H.J. Effect of different discretizations on the numerical solution of 2D aggregation population balance equation. *Powder Technol.* **2019**, *342*, 972–984. [CrossRef]
45. Flisyuk, O.M.; Martsulevich, N.A.; Shininov, T.N. Granulation of Powdered Materials in a High-Speed Granulator. *Russ. J. Appl. Chem.* **2016**, *89*, 585–590. [CrossRef]
46. Flisyuk, O.M.; Frolov, V.F. Modeling of the evolution of the particle size distribution in batch and continuous fluidized bed apparatus. *Theor. Found. Chem. Eng.* **2007**, *41*, 315–318. [CrossRef]
47. Flisyuk, O.M.; Martsulevich, N.A. Attrition of particles in fluidized bed apparatuses. *Russ. J. Appl. Chem.* **2020**, *93*, 1538–1543. [CrossRef]
48. Turnovsky, S.J. Applications of continuous-time stochastic methods to models of endogenous economic growth. *Annu. Rev. Control* **1996**, *20*, 155–166. [CrossRef]
49. Boucekkine, R.; Fabbri, G.; Federico, S.; Gozzi, F. Growth and agglomeration in the heterogeneous space: A generalized ak approach. *J. Econ. Geogr.* **2019**, *19*, 1287–1318. [CrossRef]

Article

Family of Distributions Derived from Whittaker Function

Maha A. Omair, Yusra A. Tashkandy, Sameh Askar * and Abdulhamid A. Alzaid

Department of Statistics and Operations Research, College of Sciences, King Saud University, Riyadh 145111, Saudi Arabia; maomair@ksu.edu.sa (M.A.O.); ytashkandi@ksu.edu.sa (Y.A.T.); alzaid@ksu.edu.sa (A.A.A.)
* Correspondence: saskar@ksu.edu.sa

Abstract: In this paper, we introduce a general family of distributions based on Whittaker function. The properties of obtained distributions, moments, ordering, percentiles, and unimodality are studied. The distributions' parameters are estimated using methods of moments and maximum likelihood. Furthermore, a generalization of Whittaker distribution that contains a wider class of distributions is developed. Validation of the obtained results is applied to real life data containing four data sets.

Keywords: Whittaker function; confluent hypergeometric series; Whittaker distribution; generalized Whittaker distribution

Citation: Omair, M.A.; Tashkandy, Y.A.; Askar, S.; Alzaid, A.A. Family of Distributions Derived from Whittaker Function. *Mathematics* **2022**, *10*, 1058. https://doi.org/10.3390/math10071058

Academic Editor: Aleksey I. Shinkevich

Received: 28 January 2022
Accepted: 21 March 2022
Published: 25 March 2022

Publisher's Note: MDPI stays neutral with regard to jurisdictional claims in published maps and institutional affiliations.

Copyright: © 2022 by the authors. Licensee MDPI, Basel, Switzerland. This article is an open access article distributed under the terms and conditions of the Creative Commons Attribution (CC BY) license (https://creativecommons.org/licenses/by/4.0/).

1. Introduction

There is no single definition of "special functions", as the term has been used for a variety of functions. They are important to many mathematicians, such as mathematical analysis, functional analysis, applied mathematics, and distribution theory. Such functions can be written as a summation or an integration. Examples include the relatively exponential, gamma, Bessel, hypergeometric, and Whittaker functions. For more instances of special functions, see [1–3]. Most of these functions are non-negative and finite over a certain range, and thus can be used to define probability distributions. Typical examples are the Poisson, gamma, and Bessel distributions.

There was an early interest in special functions in the theory of distribution. This included studies by [4,5], who introduced Bessel function distributions of types I and II. The exact distribution of the product of two independent generalized gamma variables with the same shape parameters using the modified Bessel function of the second kind was given by [6]. A power series distribution generated by the first type of modified Bessel function has been studied [7]. The generalized beta of the first and second kinds of distribution was considered by [8]. The Kummer-beta distribution in the problem of common value action, which features confluent hypergeometric functions, was defined [9]. The type I distribution of the inverted hypergeometric function that includes a Gaussian hypergeometric function is obtained [10]. A generalized Laplacian distribution using the modified Bessel function of second kind has been introduced [11]. The product distribution of two independent random variables featuring the Kummer-beta distribution was obtained by [12] using a confluent hypergeometric series of a two-variable function. The distribution of the product of two independent random variables, beta type II (beta prime) and beta type III, featuring the hypergeometric function of two variables is derived [13]. The distribution of the difference between independent gamma random variables with different shapes and scale parameters, called the bilateral gamma, is introduced [14]. This distribution has used the Whittaker function. The density of the product of type I variables of the Kummer–beta and the inverted hypergeometric functions containing a confluent hypergeometric series of a two-variable function was developed by [15]. They also derived the distribution of the product of the beta type III and type I variables of the inverted hypergeometric function that uses the hypergeometric function of two variables. Several properties of the extended Gauss hypergeometric and extended confluent hypergeometric functions have been studied [16]. The distribution of the products of independent central normal variables involving Meijer G-functions has been developed [17]. A new distribution was obtained as a solution of the generalized Pearson differential equation by [18], and a generalization of this distribution was also defined using the Whittaker functions. This Distribution includes as special cases distributions obtained as the product of well-known distributions. A distribution based on the generalized Pearson differential equation using a modified Bessel function of the second kind was introduced by [19] and named as generalized inverse Gaussian distribution (GGIG). The GGIG distribution is also defined in terms of the Whittaker function.

The current paper belongs to the above studies. We use the Whittaker function to introduce a new life distribution called the Whittaker distribution. This distribution is a generalization of many important continuous distributions. The gamma, exponential, chi-square, generalized Lindley, Lindley, beta prime, and Lomax are special cases of the Whittaker distribution. In some applications, the Whittaker distribution has outperformed the generalized gamma and log-normal distributions. We also define the generalized Whittaker distribution as $Y = X^{1/c}$, where X is the Whittaker distribution and $c \neq 0$. The generalized gamma, half-normal, Weibull, half-t, half-Cauchy, Nakagami, Rayleigh, Dagum, Lévy, type-2 Gumbel, inverse gamma, inverse chi-square, inverse exponential, inverse Weibull, and inverse-Rayleigh distributions are special cases of the proposed generalized Whittaker distribution.

The current paper is organized as follows: In Section 2, we proposed the Whittaker distribution and examined some of its properties. Several important special distributions are presented in Section 3. The parameters are estimated by methods of moments and maximum likelihood in Section 4. To illustrate the usefulness of the proposed Whittaker distribution, four data sets are analyzed in Section 5. Finally, some concluding remarks are given in Section 6.

2. Whittaker Distribution

The Whittaker function is defined as in [2] (Ch. Confluent Hypergeometric Functions, page 1024),

$$W_{\alpha,\beta}(z) = \frac{z^\alpha e^{-\frac{z}{2}}}{\Gamma\left(\beta - \alpha + \frac{1}{2}\right)} \int_0^\infty e^{-t} t^{\beta - \alpha - \frac{1}{2}} \left(1 + \frac{t}{z}\right)^{\alpha + \beta - \frac{1}{2}} dt, \quad \beta - \alpha > -\frac{1}{2} \tag{1}$$

This function can be used to introduce a probability distribution on $(0, \infty)$ as follows:

Theorem 1. *The function:*

$$f(x) = Ce^{-\lambda x} x^{\alpha - 1} \left(\frac{\gamma}{\lambda} + x\right)^{\beta - 1}; \quad x > 0, \tag{2}$$

where $C = \frac{e^{-\frac{\gamma}{2}}}{\Gamma(\alpha)} \left(\frac{\lambda}{\sqrt{\gamma}}\right)^{\alpha + \beta - 1} \frac{\sqrt{\gamma}}{W_{\frac{\beta - \alpha}{2}, \frac{\alpha + \beta - 1}{2}}(\gamma)}, \alpha > 0, \lambda > 0, \gamma > 0,$ *and* $-\infty < \beta < \infty$ *is a probability density function.*

Proof of Theorem 1. As $b > a - \frac{1}{2}$ and $z > 0$, the Whittaker function $W_{a,b}(z)$ is non-negative and finite, hence $f(x) \geq 0$ $\alpha > 0, \lambda > 0, \gamma > 0,$ and $-\infty < \beta < \infty$.

To show that $\int_0^\infty f(x) dx = 1$, we will use the following relation [3] (Ch. Laplace Transforms-Arbitrary Powers p. 139 Equation (22)),

$$\int_0^\infty (t+a)^{2u-1}(t-b)^{2v-1} e^{-pt} dt = \frac{(a+b)^{u+v-1}}{p^{u+v}} e^{\left[\frac{(a-b)p}{2}\right]} \Gamma(2v) W_{u-v,u+v-\frac{1}{2}}(ap+bp), \tag{3}$$

for $t > b$, Re $v > 0$, $|\arg(a+b)| \langle \pi,$ Re $p \rangle 0$.

Therefore, by setting $b = 0$, $u = \frac{\beta}{2}$, $v = \frac{\alpha}{2}$, $p = \lambda$, and $a = \frac{\gamma}{\lambda}$. The proof is complete. □

Definition 1. *Let X be a non-negative random variable with probability density function (pdf) (2). Then, we say that X has a Whittaker distribution and is denoted by $WD(\alpha, \beta, \gamma, \lambda)$.*

Figure 1 gives sample plots of the Whittaker probability density function for different values of the relevant parameters. We first note that λ is a scale parameter as exhibited in Figure 1. In Figure 1b–k, we fix $\lambda = 1$.

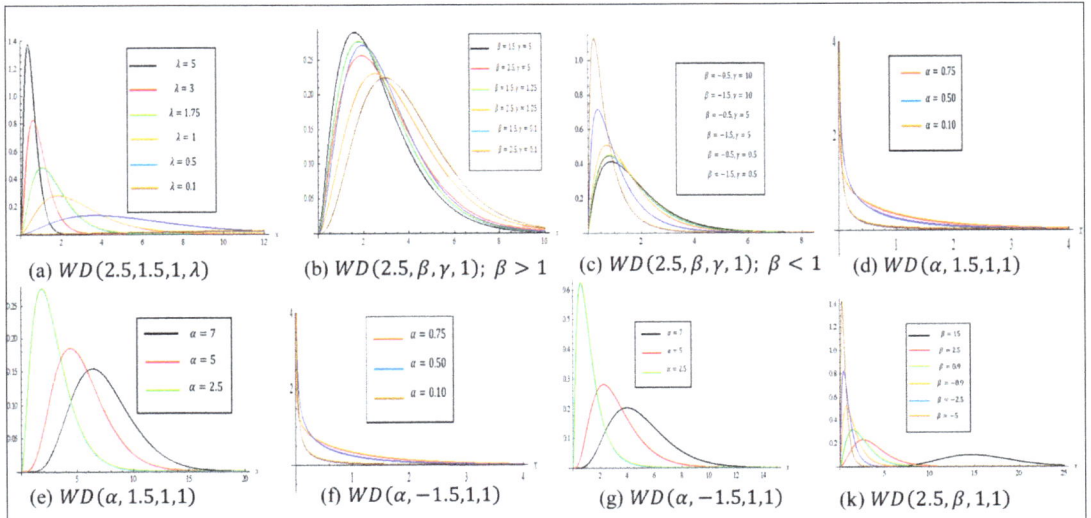

Figure 1. Plots of density function $WD(\alpha, \beta, \gamma, \lambda)$ for some parameters values.

From the plot in Figure 1b, when $\alpha + \beta > 2$, we note that the change in the value of γ has a negligible effect on the shape of the Whittaker probability density function. In Figure 1c, when $\alpha + \beta \leq 2$, note that the change in the value of γ is taken as a scale parameter, and has a greater effect when $\gamma < 1$. For $\beta > 1$ ($\beta < 1$), the distribution peaks further as γ increases (decreases). In Figure 1d–k, we fix $\gamma = 1$. For $\alpha < 1$, the Whittaker pdf attains ∞ and decreases sharply to zero as shown in Figure 1d,f. In Figure 1e,g, as the value of α decreases, the distribution peaks more.

From the plot in Figure 1k, we note that when the value of β increases, the mode increases. Finally, we note that the Whittaker distribution is unimodal.

Theorem 2. *The cumulative distribution function of the $WD(\alpha, \beta, \gamma, \lambda)$ is given by,*

$$F(x) = \frac{e^{-\frac{\gamma}{2}}}{\Gamma(\alpha+1)} \frac{\lambda^\alpha}{\gamma^{\frac{\alpha-\beta}{2}}} x^\alpha \frac{\Phi_1\left(\alpha, 1-\beta, \alpha+1, -\lambda x, -\frac{\lambda x}{\gamma}\right)}{W_{\frac{\beta-\alpha}{2}, \frac{\alpha+\beta-1}{2}}(\gamma)}; \quad x > 0, \tag{4}$$

where $\alpha > 0$, $\lambda > 0$, $\gamma > 0$, $-\infty < \beta < \infty$, and $\Phi_1(\alpha, \beta, \gamma, x, y)$ is the confluent hypergeometric series of two variables defined in [2] (Ch. Exponentials and arbitrary powers, page 349),

$$\Phi_1(\alpha, \beta, \gamma, x, y) = \frac{1}{B(\alpha, \gamma-\alpha)} \int_0^1 t^{\alpha-1}(1-t)^{\gamma-\alpha-1}(1-yt)^{-\beta} e^{xt} dt, \text{ for } \gamma > \alpha > 0 \; arg(1-\beta) < \pi. \tag{5}$$

Proof of Theorem 2. $F(x) = A \int_0^x u^{\alpha-1} \left(\frac{\gamma}{\lambda} + u\right)^{\beta-1} e^{-\lambda u} du; y > 0$, where $A = \frac{1}{\Gamma(\alpha)} \frac{\lambda^{\alpha+\beta-1}}{\gamma^{\frac{\alpha+\beta}{2}-1}} e^{-\frac{\gamma}{2}}$ $\left(W_{\frac{\beta-\alpha}{2}, \frac{\alpha+\beta-1}{2}}(\gamma)\right)^{-1}$.

Using (5) one acquires,

$$\int_0^x u^{\alpha-1}\left(\frac{\gamma}{\lambda}+u\right)^{\beta-1}e^{-\lambda u}du = x^\alpha\left(\frac{\gamma}{\lambda}\right)^{\beta-1}\int_0^1 u^{\alpha-1}\left(1+\frac{\lambda x}{\gamma}u\right)^{-(1-\beta)}e^{-\lambda x u}du = \frac{x^\alpha}{\alpha}\left(\frac{\gamma}{\lambda}\right)^{\beta-1}\Phi_1\left(\alpha,1-\beta,\alpha+1,-\lambda x,-\frac{\lambda x}{\gamma}\right);$$

$\lambda > 0$, $\alpha > 0$. □

Using the properties of the cumulative distribution function, the following lemma provides new properties of the confluent hypergeometric series of two variables:

Lemma 1. *Let $\alpha > 0$, the confluent hypergeometric series of two variables $\Phi_1(\alpha, \beta, \gamma, x, y)$ satisfies the following conditions:*

1- $\lim_{x\to 0}\left[x^\alpha \Phi_1\left(\alpha,1-\beta,\alpha+1,-\frac{\lambda x}{\gamma},-\lambda x\right)\right] = 0$

2- $\lim_{x\to \infty}\left[x^\alpha \Phi_1\left(\alpha,1-\beta,\alpha+1,-\frac{\lambda x}{\gamma},-\lambda x\right)\right] = 1$

3- $x^\alpha \dfrac{\Phi_1\left(\alpha,1-\beta,\alpha+1,-\lambda x,-\frac{\lambda}{\gamma}x\right)}{W_{\frac{\beta-\alpha}{2},\frac{\alpha+\beta-1}{2}}(\gamma)}$ *is a non-decreasing and right continuous function.*

The proof is straightforward using the properties of the cumulative distribution function (cdf).

3. Statistical Properties

This section presents the statistical properties and main characteristics of $WD(\alpha,\beta,\gamma,\lambda)$. We summarize these properties in the following theorem:

Theorem 3.

I. *The Laplace transformation is* $L(t) = \left(\frac{\lambda}{\lambda+t}\right)^{\frac{\alpha+\beta}{2}} e^{\frac{\gamma t}{2\lambda}} \dfrac{W_{\frac{\beta-\alpha}{2},\frac{\alpha+\beta-1}{2}}\left(\gamma\left(1+\frac{t}{\lambda}\right)\right)}{W_{\frac{\beta-\alpha}{2},\frac{\alpha+\beta-1}{2}}(\gamma)}.$

II. *The rth moment about the origin is* $\mu'_r = E(X^r) = \dfrac{\Gamma(\alpha+r)}{\Gamma(\alpha)}\left(\frac{\gamma}{\lambda^2}\right)^{\frac{r}{2}} \dfrac{W_{\frac{\beta-\alpha-r}{2},\frac{\alpha+\beta+r-1}{2}}(\gamma)}{W_{\frac{\beta-\alpha}{2},\frac{\alpha+\beta-1}{2}}(\gamma)}$; $r = 1,2,\ldots$

III. *The mean is* $\mu = \alpha\dfrac{\sqrt{\gamma}}{\lambda}\dfrac{W_{\frac{\beta-\alpha-1}{2},\frac{\alpha+\beta}{2}}(\gamma)}{W_{\frac{\beta-\alpha}{2},\frac{\alpha+\beta-1}{2}}(\gamma)}.$

IV. *The variance is* $\sigma^2 = \alpha(\alpha+1)\dfrac{\gamma}{\lambda^2}\dfrac{W_{\frac{\beta-\alpha}{2}-1,\frac{\alpha+\beta+1}{2}}(\gamma)}{W_{\frac{\beta-\alpha}{2},\frac{\alpha+\beta-1}{2}}(\gamma)} - \alpha^2\dfrac{\gamma}{\lambda^2}\left[\dfrac{W_{\frac{\beta-\alpha-1}{2},\frac{\alpha+\beta}{2}}(\gamma)}{W_{\frac{\beta-\alpha}{2},\frac{\alpha+\beta-1}{2}}(\gamma)}\right]^2.$

V. *The mode x_{mo} of $WD(\alpha, \beta, \gamma, \lambda)$ for $\alpha \geq 1$ is* $x_{mo} = \dfrac{\alpha+\beta-\gamma-2+\sqrt{(\alpha+\beta-\gamma-2)^2+4\gamma(\alpha-1)}}{2\lambda}.$

VI. *The measures of skewness (γ_1), kurtosis (γ_2), and the coefficient of variation C_v of $WD(\alpha,\beta,\gamma,\lambda)$ distribution are, respectively,*

$$\gamma_1 = \dfrac{\left[\frac{\Gamma(\alpha+3)}{\Gamma(\alpha)}\dfrac{W_{\frac{\beta-\alpha-3}{2},\frac{\alpha+\beta}{2}+1}(\gamma)}{W_{\frac{\beta-\alpha}{2},\frac{\alpha+\beta-1}{2}}(\gamma)} - 3\alpha^2(\alpha+1)\dfrac{W_{\frac{\beta-\alpha-1}{2},\frac{\alpha+\beta}{2}-1}(\gamma)W_{\frac{\beta-\alpha}{2},\frac{\alpha+\beta+1}{2}}(\gamma)}{W_{\frac{\beta-\alpha}{2},\frac{\alpha+\beta-1}{2}}(\gamma)^2} + 2\alpha^3\left[\dfrac{W_{\frac{\beta-\alpha-1}{2},\frac{\alpha+\beta}{2}}(\gamma)}{W_{\frac{\beta-\alpha}{2},\frac{\alpha+\beta-1}{2}}(\gamma)}\right]^3\right]}{\left[\alpha(\alpha+1)\dfrac{W_{\frac{\beta-\alpha}{2}-1,\frac{\alpha+\beta+1}{2}}(\gamma)}{W_{\frac{\beta-\alpha}{2},\frac{\alpha+\beta-1}{2}}(\gamma)} - \alpha^2\left[\dfrac{W_{\frac{\beta-\alpha-1}{2},\frac{\alpha+\beta}{2}}(\gamma)}{W_{\frac{\beta-\alpha}{2},\frac{\alpha+\beta-1}{2}}(\gamma)}\right]^2\right]^{3/2}}, \gamma_2 =$$

$$\left[\dfrac{\Gamma(\alpha+4)}{\alpha\Gamma(\alpha+1)}W_{\frac{\beta-\alpha}{2}-2,\frac{\alpha+\beta+3}{2}}(\gamma)W_{\frac{\beta-\alpha}{2},\frac{\alpha+\beta-1}{2}}(\gamma) - 4\dfrac{\Gamma(\alpha+3)}{\Gamma(\alpha+1)}W_{\frac{\beta-\alpha-1}{2},\frac{\alpha+\beta}{2}}(\gamma)W_{\frac{\beta-\alpha-3}{2},\frac{\alpha+\beta}{2}+1}(\gamma) + \right.$$

$$\left. 6\alpha(\alpha+1)\dfrac{W_{\frac{\beta-\alpha-1}{2},\frac{\alpha+\beta}{2}}(\gamma)^2 W_{\frac{\beta-\alpha}{2}-1,\frac{\alpha+\beta+1}{2}}(\gamma)}{W_{\frac{\beta-\alpha}{2},\frac{\alpha+\beta-1}{2}}(\gamma)} - 3\alpha^2\dfrac{W_{\frac{\beta-\alpha-1}{2},\frac{\alpha+\beta}{2}}(\gamma)^4}{W_{\frac{\beta-\alpha}{2},\frac{\alpha+\beta-1}{2}}(\gamma)^2}\right]/$$

$$\left[\frac{(\alpha+1)}{\alpha}W_{\frac{\beta-\alpha}{2}-1,\frac{\alpha+\beta+1}{2}}(\gamma) - \frac{W_{\frac{\beta-\alpha-1}{2},\frac{\alpha+\beta}{2}}(\gamma)^2}{W_{\frac{\beta-\alpha}{2},\frac{\alpha+\beta-1}{2}}(\gamma)}\right]^2,$$

$$\text{and } C_v = \sqrt{\frac{\alpha+1}{\alpha} \frac{W_{\frac{\beta-\alpha}{2}-1,\frac{\alpha+\beta+1}{2}}(\gamma) W_{\frac{\beta-\alpha}{2},\frac{\alpha+\beta-1}{2}}(\gamma)}{W_{\frac{\beta-\alpha-1}{2},\frac{\alpha+\beta}{2}}(\gamma)^2}} - 1.$$

VII. The survival function is $\overline{F}(t) = 1 - F(t) = 1 - \frac{e^{-\frac{\gamma}{2}}}{\Gamma(\alpha+1)} \frac{\lambda^\alpha}{\gamma^{\frac{\alpha-\beta}{2}}} t^\alpha \frac{\Phi_1\left(\alpha, 1-\beta, \alpha+1, -\lambda t, -\frac{\lambda}{\gamma}t\right)}{W_{\frac{\beta-\alpha}{2},\frac{\alpha+\beta-1}{2}}(\gamma)}$.

VIII. The hazard function is $h(t) = \dfrac{\alpha\gamma\left(\frac{\lambda^2}{\gamma}\right)^{\frac{\alpha+\beta}{2}} e^{-\lambda x - \frac{\gamma}{2}} x^{\alpha-1}\left(\frac{\gamma}{\lambda}+x\right)^{\beta-1}}{\Gamma(\alpha+1)W_{\frac{\beta-\alpha}{2},\frac{\alpha+\beta-1}{2}}(\gamma) - \gamma^{\frac{\beta-\alpha}{2}}\lambda^\alpha e^{-\frac{\gamma}{2}} x^\alpha \Phi_1\left(\alpha, 1-\beta, \alpha+1, -\lambda x, -\frac{\lambda x}{\gamma}\right)}$.

Proof of Theorem 3.

I. The Laplace transformation: $L(t) = \frac{\lambda^{\alpha+\beta-1}}{\gamma^{\frac{\alpha+\beta}{2}-1}} \frac{e^{-\frac{\gamma}{2}}}{\Gamma(\alpha)W_{\frac{\beta-\alpha}{2},\frac{\alpha+\beta-1}{2}}(\gamma)} \int_0^\infty x^{\alpha-1}\left(\frac{\gamma}{\lambda}+x\right)^{\beta-1}$

$e^{-(\lambda+t)x}dx = \frac{\gamma^{-\frac{\alpha+\beta}{2}+1}\lambda^{\alpha+\beta-1}e^{-\frac{\gamma}{2}}}{\Gamma(\alpha)W_{\frac{\beta-\alpha}{2},\frac{\alpha+\beta-1}{2}}(\gamma)}\left(\frac{\gamma}{\lambda}\right)^{\frac{\alpha+\beta}{2}-1} \frac{\Gamma(\alpha)}{(\lambda+t)^{\frac{\alpha+\beta}{2}}} \exp\left[\frac{\gamma(\lambda+t)}{2\lambda}\right] W_{\frac{\beta-\alpha}{2},\frac{\alpha+\beta-1}{2}}\left(\gamma\left(\frac{\lambda+t}{\lambda}\right)\right)$

$= \left(\frac{\lambda}{\lambda+t}\right)^{\frac{\alpha+\beta}{2}} e^{\frac{\gamma t}{2\lambda}} \frac{W_{\frac{\beta-\alpha}{2},\frac{\alpha+\beta-1}{2}}\left(\gamma\left(\frac{\lambda+t}{\lambda}\right)\right)}{W_{\frac{\beta-\alpha}{2},\frac{\alpha+\beta-1}{2}}(\gamma)}$, by using (3).

II. The rth moment function is, $\mu'_r = E(X^r) = \frac{\lambda^{\alpha+\beta-1}}{\gamma^{\frac{\alpha+\beta}{2}-1}} \frac{e^{-\frac{\gamma}{2}}}{\Gamma(\alpha)W_{\frac{\beta-\alpha}{2},\frac{\alpha+\beta-1}{2}}(\gamma)} \int_0^\infty x^{\alpha+r-1}$

$\left(\frac{\gamma}{\lambda}+x\right)^{\beta-1} e^{-\lambda x} dx = \frac{\Gamma(\alpha+r)}{\Gamma(\alpha)} \frac{\gamma^{\frac{r}{2}}}{\lambda^r} \frac{W_{\frac{\beta-\alpha-r}{2},\frac{\alpha+\beta+r-1}{2}}(\gamma)}{W_{\frac{\beta-\alpha}{2},\frac{\alpha+\beta-1}{2}}(\gamma)}$, By using (3).

III. We have from II that, $\mu'_1 = \mu = \alpha \frac{\sqrt{\gamma}}{\lambda} \frac{W_{\frac{\beta-\alpha-1}{2},\frac{\alpha+\beta}{2}}(\gamma)}{W_{\frac{\beta-\alpha}{2},\frac{\alpha+\beta-1}{2}}(\gamma)}$, and $\mu'_2 = \alpha(\alpha+1)\frac{\gamma}{\lambda^2}$

$\frac{W_{\frac{\beta-\alpha}{2}-1,\frac{\alpha+\beta-1}{2}}(\gamma)}{W_{\frac{\beta-\alpha}{2},\frac{\alpha+\beta-1}{2}}(\gamma)}$.

IV. The variance is given by $\sigma^2 = \mu'_2 - \mu^2$.

V. The mode x_{m0} can be obtained by differentiating the pdf of $WD(\alpha, \beta, \gamma, \lambda)$ with respect to x as follows, $f'(x) = A\left[(\alpha-1)x^{\alpha-2}(\gamma+\lambda x)^{\beta-1}e^{-\lambda x} + \lambda(\beta-1)x^{\alpha-1}\right.$
$\left.(\gamma+\lambda x)^{\beta-2}e^{-\lambda x} - \lambda x^{\alpha-1}(\gamma+\lambda x)^{\beta-1}e^{-\lambda x}\right] = \left[\frac{(\alpha-1)}{x} + \frac{\lambda(\beta-1)}{(\gamma+\lambda x)} - \lambda\right]f(x)$.

However, the mode x_{m0} is obtained as the solution of $f'(x_{m0}) = 0$. Therefore, we have $\left[\frac{(\alpha-1)}{x_{m0}} + \frac{\lambda(\beta-1)}{(\gamma+\lambda x_{m0})} - \lambda\right]f(x_{m0}) = 0$, that leads to $f(x_{m0}) = 0$, or $\left[\frac{(\alpha-1)}{x_{m0}} + \frac{\lambda(\beta-1)}{(\gamma+\lambda x_{m0})} - \lambda\right] = 0$.

By solving $\left[\frac{(\alpha-1)}{x_{m0}} + \frac{\lambda(\beta-1)}{(\gamma+\lambda x_{m0})} - \lambda\right] = 0$, one acquires, $x_{mo} = \frac{(\alpha+\beta-\gamma-2)\pm\sqrt{(\alpha+\beta-\gamma-2)^2+4\gamma(\alpha-1)}}{2\lambda}$.

Since the distribution is defined on the set $(0, \infty)$, we acquire x_{m0} as in the form, $x_{mo} = \frac{(\alpha+\beta-\gamma-2)+\sqrt{(\alpha+\beta-\gamma-2)^2+4\gamma(\alpha-1)}}{2\lambda}$. □

Note: The skewness (γ_1), kurtosis (γ_2), and the coefficient of variation C_v of $WD(\alpha, \beta, \gamma, \lambda)$ do not depend on λ.

Some recurrence relations of the Whittaker function are provided in [1]. From the above theorem, we can deduce other recurrence relations for the Whittaker function as follows.

Corollary 1. *For $z > 0$ and $b > a - \frac{1}{2}$, we have,*

1- $W_{a-\frac{1}{2},b+\frac{1}{2}}(z) = \frac{2(a+b-z)+1}{[2(b-a)+1]\sqrt{z}} W_{a,b}(z) + \frac{2}{[2(b-a)+1]\sqrt{z}} W_{a+1,b}(z)$.

2- $W_{a+2,b}(z) = \left(b-a+\frac{1}{2}\right)\left(b-a+\frac{3}{2}\right)z\, W_{a-1,b}(z) - \left(a+b+\frac{1}{2} + \left(a+b+\frac{1}{2}-z\right)^2\right)$
$W_{a,b}(z) - 2\left(a+b-z+\frac{3}{2}\right)W_{a+1,b}(z).$

3- $\frac{2(b-a)+3}{2(b-a)+1}W_{a-1,b+1}(z)W_{a,b}(z) > \left[W_{a-\frac{1}{2},b+\frac{1}{2}}(z)\right]^2.$

Proof of Corollary 1. From Theorem 3, one can acquire the mean and the second order moment using the Laplace transformation as follows, $\mu'_1 = \mu = -\frac{\partial}{\partial t}L(t)\big|_{t=0} = \frac{\beta}{\lambda} - \frac{\gamma}{\lambda} + \frac{1}{\lambda}\frac{W_{\frac{\beta-\alpha}{2}+1,\frac{\alpha+\beta-1}{2}}(\gamma)}{W_{\frac{\beta-\alpha}{2},\frac{\alpha+\beta-1}{2}}(\gamma)},$ and $\mu'_2 = E(X^2) = \frac{\partial^2}{\partial t^2}L(t)\big|_{t=0} = \frac{\beta}{\lambda^2} + \frac{1}{\lambda^2}(\beta-\gamma)^2 + \frac{2}{\lambda^2}(\beta-\gamma+1)\frac{W_{\frac{\beta-\alpha}{2}+1,\frac{\alpha+\beta-1}{2}}(\gamma)}{W_{\frac{\beta-\alpha}{2},\frac{\alpha+\beta-1}{2}}(\gamma)} + \frac{1}{\lambda^2}\frac{W_{\frac{\beta-\alpha}{2}+2,\frac{\alpha+\beta-1}{2}}(\gamma)}{W_{\frac{\beta-\alpha}{2},\frac{\alpha+\beta-1}{2}}(\gamma)}.$

The mean and the second order moment can also be derived from the rth moment formula in Theorem 3, $\mu'_1 = \mu = \alpha\frac{\sqrt{\gamma}}{\lambda}\frac{W_{\frac{\beta-\alpha-1}{2},\frac{\alpha+\beta}{2}}(\gamma)}{W_{\frac{\beta-\alpha}{2},\frac{\alpha+\beta-1}{2}}(\gamma)},$ and $\mu'_2 = E(X^2) = \frac{\Gamma(\alpha+2)}{\Gamma(\alpha)}\frac{\gamma}{\lambda^2}\frac{W_{\frac{\beta-\alpha}{2}-1,\frac{\alpha+\beta+1}{2}}(\gamma)}{W_{\frac{\beta-\alpha}{2},\frac{\alpha+\beta-1}{2}}(\gamma)}.$

Hence, by equating the two formulas of μ, we acquire $W_{\frac{\beta-\alpha-1}{2},\frac{\alpha+\beta}{2}}(\gamma) = \frac{\beta-\gamma}{\alpha\sqrt{\gamma}}W_{\frac{\beta-\alpha}{2},\frac{\alpha+\beta-1}{2}}(\gamma) + \frac{1}{\alpha\sqrt{\gamma}}W_{\frac{\beta-\alpha}{2}+1,\frac{\alpha+\beta-1}{2}}(\gamma).$

By replacing $\alpha, \beta,$ and γ with $b-a+\frac{1}{2}$, $a+b+\frac{1}{2}$, and z, respectively, we acquire,
$W_{a-\frac{1}{2},b+\frac{1}{2}}(z) = \frac{2(a+b-z)+1}{[2(b-a)+1]\sqrt{z}}W_{a,b}(z) + \frac{2}{[2(b-a)+1]\sqrt{z}}W_{a+1,b}(z).$

Similarly, by equating the two formulas of $E(X^2)$, we acquire, $\left(\beta + (\beta-\gamma)^2\right)W_{\frac{\beta-\alpha}{2},\frac{\alpha+\beta-1}{2}}(\gamma) = \alpha(\alpha+1)\gamma W_{\frac{\beta-\alpha}{2}-1,\frac{\alpha+\beta-1}{2}}(\gamma) - 2(\beta-\gamma+1)W_{\frac{\beta-\alpha}{2}+1,\frac{\alpha+\beta-1}{2}}(\gamma) - W_{\frac{\beta-\alpha}{2}+2,\frac{\alpha+\beta-1}{2}}(\gamma).$

By replacing $\alpha, \beta,$ and γ with $b-a+\frac{1}{2}$, $a+b+\frac{1}{2}$, and z, respectively, we acquire,
$W_{a+2,b}(z) = \left(b-a+\frac{1}{2}\right)\left(b-a+\frac{3}{2}\right)z\, W_{a-1,b}(z) - \left(a+b+\frac{1}{2} + \left(a+b+\frac{1}{2}-z\right)^2\right)W_{a,b}(z) - 2\left(a+b-z+\frac{3}{2}\right)W_{a+1,b}(z).$

Since $\sigma^2 = \alpha(\alpha+1)\frac{\gamma}{\lambda^2}\frac{W_{\frac{\beta-\alpha}{2}-1,\frac{\alpha+\beta+1}{2}}(\gamma)}{W_{\frac{\beta-\alpha}{2},\frac{\alpha+\beta-1}{2}}(\gamma)} - \alpha^2\frac{\gamma}{\lambda^2}\left[\frac{W_{\frac{\beta-\alpha}{2}-1,\frac{\alpha+\beta}{2}}(\gamma)}{W_{\frac{\beta-\alpha}{2},\frac{\alpha+\beta-1}{2}}(\gamma)}\right]^2 > 0.$

By replacing $\alpha, \beta,$ and γ with $b-a+\frac{1}{2}$, $a+b+\frac{1}{2}$, and z, respectively, we acquire,
$\frac{2(b-a)+3}{2(b-a)+1}W_{a-1,b+1}(z)W_{a,b}(z) > \left[W_{a-\frac{1}{2},b+\frac{1}{2}}(z)\right]^2.$
The proof is complete. □

Corollary 2. For $a > 0$ and $z > 0$, the Whittaker function satisfies the following conditions,

I. $W_{\frac{1}{2}-a,a}(z) = z^{\frac{1}{2}-a}e^{-\frac{z}{2}}.$

II. $W_{1-a,\,a+\frac{1}{2}}(z) = z^{1-a}e^{-\frac{z}{2}}(2az^{-1}+1); \; a,\, z > 0.$

Proof of Corollary 2.

I. $W_{\frac{1}{2}-a,\,a}(z) = \frac{z^{\frac{a}{2}+\frac{1}{2}}e^{-\frac{z}{2}}}{\Gamma(2a)}\int_0^\infty e^{-zt}t^{2a-1}dt = z^{\frac{1}{2}-a}e^{-\frac{z}{2}}.$

II. $W_{1-a,\,a+\frac{1}{2}}(z) = \frac{z^{a+1}e^{-\frac{z}{2}}}{\Gamma(2a)}\int_0^\infty e^{-zt}t^{2a-1}(1+t)dt = \frac{z^{a+1}e^{-\frac{z}{2}}}{\Gamma(2a)}\left(z^{-2a}\Gamma(2a) + z^{-(2a+1)}\Gamma(2a+1)\right) = z^{1-a}e^{-\frac{z}{2}}(2az^{-1}+1).$ □

Corollary 3. For $\alpha + \beta < 1$ and $\alpha > 0$, the confluent hypergeometric function of the second kind satisfies the relation,

$$U(\alpha, \alpha+\beta, 0) = \frac{\Gamma(1-\alpha-\beta)}{\Gamma(1-\beta)}. \quad (6)$$

Proof of Corollary 3. The confluent hypergeometric function of the second kind is defined in [1] (Ch. Confluent Hypergeometric functions/Integral Representations page 505),

$$U(a,b,z) = \frac{1}{\Gamma(a)} \int_0^\infty e^{-zt} t^{a-1}(1+t)^{b-a-1} dt.$$

At $z=0$, we acquire $U(\alpha, \alpha+\beta, 0) = \frac{1}{\Gamma(\alpha)} \int_0^\infty t^{\alpha-1}(1+t)^{\beta-1} dt = \frac{\Gamma(1-\alpha-\beta)}{\Gamma(1-\beta)}$. □

Theorem 4. *Let $X \sim WD(\alpha,\beta,\gamma,\lambda)$. Then,*
(a) *For $\alpha > 1$ and $\alpha+\beta > 2$, $f(x)$ is log-concave.*
(b) *For $\alpha < 1$ and $\alpha+\beta < 2$, $f(x)$ is log-convex.*

Proof of Theorem 4. It is simple to see that, $\frac{\partial}{\partial x} \log f(x) = \frac{(\alpha+\beta-2)}{(\frac{\gamma}{\lambda}+x)} + \frac{(\alpha-1)\frac{\gamma}{\lambda}}{x(\frac{\gamma}{\lambda}+x)} - \lambda$.

It is a decreasing (increasing) function for $\alpha+\beta > 2 \ (<2)$, and $\alpha > 1 \ (<1)$. Thus, $f(x)$ is log-concave (convex). □

Theorem 4 does not cover all ranges of α and β as shown in Figure 2. In the following example, we illustrate that there is no obvious conclusion outside the above ranges.

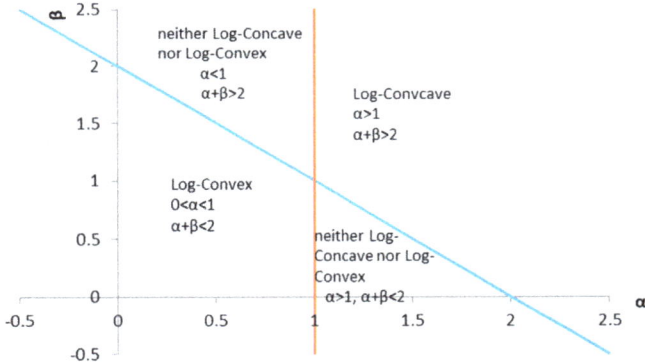

Figure 2. The relation between α and β, and the concavity of $WD(\alpha,\beta,\gamma,\lambda)$.

Example: The second derivative of the log of density is,

$$g(x) = \frac{\partial^2}{\partial x^2} \log f(x) = -\frac{(\alpha-1)}{x^2} - \frac{(\beta-1)}{\left(\frac{\gamma}{\lambda}+x\right)^2}.$$

Figure 3 shows the function $g(x)$ for the two cases where $(\alpha,\beta) = (0.5,4)$ and $(\alpha,\beta) = (1.5,-4)$. When $(\alpha,\beta) = (0.5,4)$, $g(x)$ is positive for $x < 0.69$, and for $x \geq 0.69$, $g(x)$ is negative. Therefore $f(x)$ is neither log-convex nor log-concave. Further, when $(\alpha,\beta) = (1.5,-4)$, $g(x)$ is negative for $x < 0.46$, and for $x \geq 0.46$ is positive. Therefore, $f(x)$ is neither log-convex nor log-concave.

The distributions with log-concave density are unimodal and have increasing failure rate property.

Theorem 5.
I. *The Whittaker distribution has a monotonic likelihood ratio in x with respect to α when the other parameters are constant.*
II. *The Whittaker distribution has a monotonic likelihood ratio in x with respect to β when the other parameters are constant.*

III. The Whittaker distribution has a monotonic likelihood ratio in x with respect to γ when the other parameters are constant and $\beta < 1$.

Proof of Theorem 5.

I Let $\alpha_2 > \alpha_1$. Then, $\frac{\partial}{\partial x}\left(\frac{f_{\alpha_2}(x)}{f_{\alpha_1}(x)}\right) = C(\alpha_2 - \alpha_1)x^{\alpha_2 - \alpha_1 - 1} > 0$, where $C = \left[\frac{\Gamma(\alpha_1)}{\Gamma(\alpha_2)}\right]^n \frac{\lambda^{n(\alpha_2 - \alpha_1)}}{\gamma^{n\frac{\alpha_2 - \alpha_1}{2}}}$

$\left[\frac{W_{\frac{\beta-\alpha_1}{2},\frac{\alpha_1+\beta-1}{2}}(\gamma)}{W_{\frac{\beta-\alpha_2}{2},\frac{\alpha_2+\beta-1}{2}}(\gamma)}\right]^n$.

II. The proof is similar to that of I.

1. For $\gamma_1 < \gamma_2$, we acquire $\frac{\partial}{\partial x}\left(\frac{f_{\gamma_2}(x)}{f_{\gamma_1}(x)}\right) = (\beta - 1)(\gamma_1 - \gamma_2)\frac{(\gamma_2 + \lambda x)^{\beta - 2}}{(\gamma_1 + \lambda x)^{\beta}}$, where $C = \lambda e^{-\frac{\gamma_2 - \gamma_1}{2}}\left(\frac{\gamma_1}{\gamma_2}\right)^{\frac{\alpha+\beta}{2}} \frac{W_{\frac{\beta-\alpha}{2},\frac{\alpha+\beta-1}{2}}(\gamma_1)}{W_{\frac{\beta-\alpha}{2},\frac{\alpha+\beta-1}{2}}(\gamma_2)}$

If $\beta < 1$, then $\frac{\partial}{\partial x}\left(\frac{f_{\gamma_2}(x)}{f_{\gamma_1}(x)}\right) > 0$. □

Note: The Whittaker distribution is not a member of the monotonic likelihood ratio family with respect to λ when other parameters are constant.

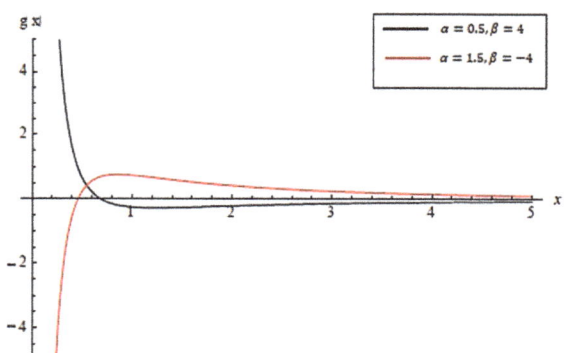

Figure 3. $g(x)$ for $WD(0.5, 4, 1, 1)$, and $WD(1.5, -4, 1, 1)$.

Percentiles

Now, we compute the percentiles of Whittaker distribution. For any $0 < q < 1$, the $100q$-th percentile is a number x_q such that the area under $f(x)$ to the left of x_q is q. That is, x_q is any root of the equation,

$$F(x_q) = \int_0^{x_q} f(x)dx = q$$

Using numerical simulation, the percentage points x_q associated with the cdf of X are computed for some selected values of the parameters using Mathematica software (The code is provided in Appendix A).

Definition 2. *Let $X \sim WD(\alpha, \beta, \gamma, \lambda)$ and $Y = X^{1/c}$, then, Y is defined as the generalized Whittaker distribution given by,*

$$f(y) = \frac{e^{-\frac{\gamma}{2}}}{\Gamma(\alpha)}\frac{|c|\lambda^\alpha}{\gamma^{\frac{\alpha+\beta}{2}-1}}e^{-\lambda y^c}\frac{y^{\alpha c - 1}(\gamma + \lambda y^c)^{\beta - 1}}{W_{\frac{\beta-\alpha}{2},\frac{\alpha+\beta-1}{2}}(\gamma)}; \quad y > 0, \quad (7)$$

where $\alpha > 0$, $\lambda > 0$, $\gamma > 0$, $-\infty < \beta < \infty$, and $\forall c \neq 0$. For simplicity, we use the notation $GWD(\alpha, \beta, \gamma, \lambda, c)$.

4. Special Cases

Many well-known distributions can be viewed as special cases of the WD and GWD. Figure 4 summarizes all these findings. Whereas the distribution defined in [18,19] are neither a generalization nor a special cases of the WD.

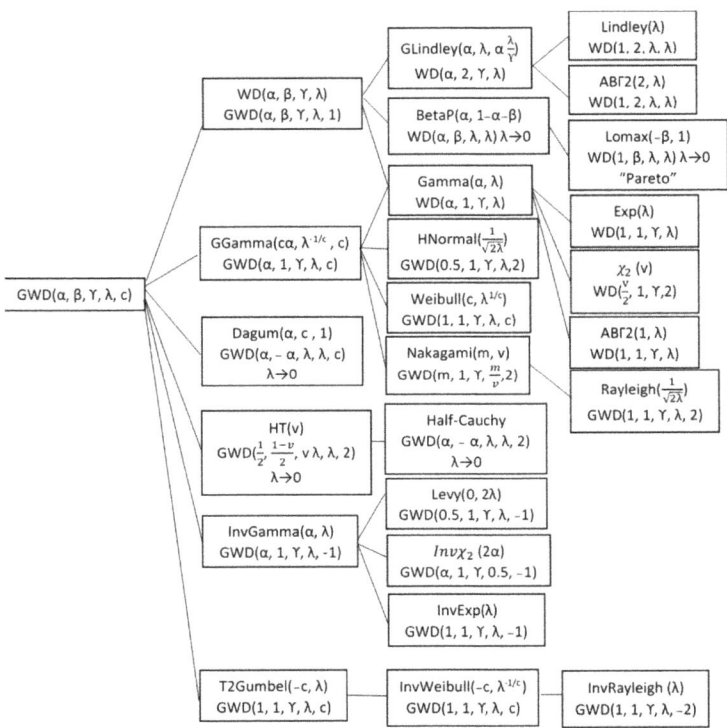

Figure 4. The special cases of $GWD(\alpha, \beta, \gamma, \lambda, c)$ and $WD(\alpha, \beta, \gamma, \lambda)$.

4.1. Generalized Lindley Distribution

If $\beta = 2$, then the Whittaker distribution is reduced to the generalized Lindley distribution proposed by [20], as follows:

At $\beta = 2$, the mgf $M_X(t) = \left(\frac{\lambda}{\lambda-t}\right)^{\frac{\alpha}{2}+1} e^{\frac{-\gamma t}{2\lambda}} \frac{W_{\frac{2-\alpha}{2}, \frac{\alpha+1}{2}}\left(\gamma\left(\frac{\lambda-t}{\lambda}\right)\right)}{W_{\frac{2-\alpha}{2}, \frac{\alpha+1}{2}}(\gamma)}$.

By using Corollary 2(II) at $a = \frac{\alpha}{2}$, we acquire $W_{\frac{2-\alpha}{2}, \frac{\alpha+1}{2}}(z) = z^{-\frac{\alpha}{2}+1} e^{-\frac{z}{2}} \left(\alpha z^{-1} + 1\right)$.

Then,

$$M_X(t) = \left(\frac{\lambda}{\lambda-t}\right)^{\frac{\alpha}{2}+1} e^{\frac{-\gamma t}{2\lambda}} \frac{\left(\gamma\left(\frac{\lambda-t}{\lambda}\right)\right)^{-\frac{\alpha}{2}+1} e^{-\frac{\gamma}{2}\left(\frac{\lambda-t}{\lambda}\right)} \left(\alpha\left(\gamma\left(\frac{\lambda-t}{\lambda}\right)\right)^{-1} + 1\right)}{\gamma^{-\frac{\alpha}{2}+1} e^{-\frac{\gamma}{2}} (\alpha\gamma^{-1} + 1)}, M_X(t) = \left(\frac{\lambda}{\lambda-t}\right)^{\alpha+1} \frac{\alpha\lambda + \gamma(\lambda-t)}{\alpha\lambda + \gamma\lambda}.$$

Thus, if $\alpha = 1$, $\beta = 2$, and $\lambda = \gamma$, the Whittaker distribution is reduced to the Lindley distribution [21].

4.2. Beta Prime Distribution

If $\beta < min(0, (1-\alpha))$, $\gamma = \lambda$, and $\lambda \to 0$, the Whittaker distribution is reduced to the beta prime distribution [22].

For $\gamma = \lambda$, the pdf of $WD(\alpha, \beta, \lambda, \lambda)$ is reduced to $f(x) = \frac{1}{\Gamma(\alpha)} \lambda^{\frac{\alpha+\beta}{2}} e^{-\lambda(x+\frac{1}{2})} \frac{x^{\alpha-1}(1+x)^{\beta-1}}{W_{\frac{\beta-\alpha}{2}, \frac{\alpha+\beta-1}{2}}(\lambda)}$.

By using [1] (Ch. Confluent Hypergeometric functions, page 505),

$$W_{\lambda,\mu}(z) = exp(-z/2) z^{\mu+\frac{1}{2}} U\left(\mu - \lambda + \frac{1}{2}, 1 + 2\mu; z\right). \tag{8}$$

we acquire $W_{\frac{\beta-\alpha}{2}, \frac{\alpha+\beta-1}{2}}(\lambda) = e^{-\frac{\lambda}{2}} \lambda^{\frac{\alpha+\beta}{2}} U(\alpha, \alpha + \beta; \lambda)$.

Then, $f(x) = \frac{1}{\Gamma(\alpha)} e^{-\lambda x} \frac{x^{\alpha-1}(1+x)^{\beta-1}}{U(\alpha, \alpha+\beta; \lambda)}$. By taking the limit as λ tends to zero, one acquires $\lim_{\lambda \to 0} \left(\frac{1}{\Gamma(\alpha)} e^{-\lambda x} \frac{x^{\alpha-1}(1+x)^{\beta-1}}{U(\alpha, \alpha+\beta; \lambda)} \right) = \frac{1}{\Gamma(\alpha)} \frac{1}{U(\alpha, \alpha+\beta, 0)} x^{\alpha-1}(1+x)^{\beta-1}$.

Using Corollary 3, we acquire the pdf $f(x) = \frac{\Gamma(1-\beta)}{\Gamma(\alpha)\Gamma(1-\alpha-\beta)} x^{\alpha-1}(1+x)^{\beta-1}; y > 0$.

Thus, if $\alpha = 1$, $\beta < 0$, $\gamma = \lambda$, and $\lambda \to 0$, the Whittaker distribution is reduced to Lomax [23] and the Pareto distribution [24].

4.3. Generalized Gamma Distribution

If $X \sim GWD(\alpha, 1, \gamma, \lambda, c)$, then X follows a generalized gamma distribution [25]. Hence the corresponding pdf is,

$$f(x) = \frac{e^{-\frac{\gamma}{2}}}{\Gamma(\alpha)} \frac{c\lambda^{\alpha}}{\gamma^{\frac{\alpha-1}{2}}} e^{-\lambda x^c} \frac{x^{\alpha c - 1}}{W_{\frac{1-\alpha}{2}, \frac{\alpha}{2}}(\gamma)}.$$

From Corollary 2 (I), we acquire $W_{\frac{1-\alpha}{2}, \frac{\alpha}{2}}(\gamma) = \gamma^{\frac{1-\alpha}{2}} e^{-\frac{\gamma}{2}}$.

Therefore, $f(x) = \frac{c}{\Gamma(\alpha)} \lambda^{\alpha} x^{\alpha c - 1} e^{-\lambda x^c}$.

Notes:

(a) If $\beta = 1$, $c = 2$, and $\lambda = \frac{\alpha}{\nu}$, the generalized Whittaker distribution is reduced to the Nakagami distribution [26].
(b) If $\alpha = 1$, $\beta = 1$, and $c = 2$, the generalized Whittaker distribution is reduced to Rayleigh distribution [27].
(c) If $\alpha = 0.5$, $\beta = 1$, and $c = 2$, the generalized Whittaker distribution is reduced to the half-normal distribution.
(d) If $\alpha = 1$, and $\beta = 1$, the generalized Whittaker distribution is reduced to the Weibull distribution.
(e) If $\beta = 1$, and $c = 1$, the generalized Whittaker distribution is reduced to the gamma distribution.
(f) If $\alpha = 1$ and $\beta = 1$, the Whittaker distribution is reduced to an exponential distribution.
(g) If $\beta = 1$, $2\alpha = n$, and $\lambda = 2$, the Whittaker distribution is reduced to a chi-square distribution with n degrees of freedom.

4.4. Dagum Distribution

If $X \sim GWD(\alpha, -\alpha, \lambda, \lambda, c)$, X follows the Dagum distribution [28] with $f(y) = \frac{c}{\Gamma(\alpha)} e^{-\lambda y^c} \frac{y^{\alpha c - 1}(1+y^c)^{-(\alpha+1)}}{U(\alpha, 0; \lambda)}$.

Recalling Corollary 3, we acquire the pdf as $f(y) = c\alpha y^{\alpha c - 1}(1+y^c)^{-(\alpha+1)}$.

4.5. Half-t Distribution

If X follows a generalized Whittaker distribution with $\frac{\gamma}{\lambda} = v$, $\alpha = \frac{1}{2}$, $\beta = \frac{1-v}{2}$, $c = 2$, and at $\lambda \to 0$, the generalized Whittaker distribution is reduced to the half-t distribution.

The pdf of $GWD\left(\frac{1}{2}, \frac{1-v}{2}, \lambda v, \lambda, 2\right)$ is given by $f(x) = \frac{e^{-\frac{\lambda v}{2}}}{\Gamma(\frac{1}{2})} \frac{2\lambda^{\frac{2-v}{4}}}{v^{\frac{-v-2}{4}}} e^{-\lambda x^2} \frac{(v+x^2)^{\frac{-1-v}{2}}}{W_{\frac{-v}{4}, \frac{-v}{4}}(\lambda v)}$.

From (8), we acquire $W_{\frac{-v}{4}, \frac{-v}{4}}(\lambda v) = e^{-\frac{\lambda v}{2}} (\lambda v)^{\frac{2-v}{4}} U\left(\frac{1}{2}, 1 - \frac{v}{2}; \lambda v\right)$. Then,

$$f(x) = \frac{1}{\Gamma\left(\frac{1}{2}\right)} \frac{2}{v^{\frac{-v}{2}}} e^{-\lambda x^2} \frac{(v+x^2)^{\frac{-1-v}{2}}}{U\left(\frac{1}{2}, 1-\frac{v}{2}; \lambda v\right)} \lim_{\lambda \to 0} \left(\frac{1}{\Gamma\left(\frac{1}{2}\right)} \frac{2}{v^{\frac{-v}{2}}} e^{-\lambda x^2} \frac{(v+x^2)^{\frac{-1-v}{2}}}{U\left(\frac{1}{2}, 1-\frac{v}{2}; \lambda v\right)} \right) = \frac{v^{\frac{v}{2}}}{\Gamma\left(\frac{1}{2}\right)} \frac{2}{U\left(\frac{1}{2}, 1-\frac{v}{2}, 0\right)} (v+x^2)^{\frac{-1-v}{2}}$$

From Corollary 3, at $\alpha = \frac{1}{2}$, $\beta = \frac{1-v}{2}$, we acquire $U\left(\frac{1}{2}, 1-\frac{v}{2}, 0\right) = \frac{\Gamma\left(\frac{v}{2}\right)}{\Gamma\left(\frac{v+1}{2}\right)}$.

Therefore,

$$f(y) = 2v^{-\frac{v+1}{2}} v^{\frac{v}{2}} \frac{\Gamma\left(\frac{v+1}{2}\right)}{\Gamma\left(\frac{1}{2}\right)\Gamma\left(\frac{v}{2}\right)} \left(1 + \frac{y^2}{v}\right)^{-\frac{v+1}{2}} = 2\frac{\Gamma\left(\frac{v+1}{2}\right)}{\sqrt{v\pi}\Gamma\left(\frac{v}{2}\right)} \left(1 + \frac{y^2}{v}\right)^{-\frac{v+1}{2}}.$$

Thus, if $\alpha = \frac{1}{2}$, $\beta = 0$, $c = 2$, $\gamma = \lambda$, and $\lambda \to 0$, the generalized Whittaker distribution is reduced to a half-Cauchy distribution.

4.6. Inverse Gamma Distribution

If $X \sim GWD(\alpha, 1, \gamma, \lambda, -1)$, X follows the inverse gamma distribution [23], as,

$$f(x) = \frac{e^{-\frac{\gamma}{2}}}{\Gamma(\alpha)} \frac{\lambda^\alpha}{\gamma^{\frac{\alpha-1}{2}}} e^{-\frac{\lambda}{x}} \frac{x^{-\alpha-1}}{W_{\frac{1-\alpha}{2}, \frac{\alpha}{2}}(\gamma)}$$

From Corollary 2 (I), we acquire $W_{\frac{1-\alpha}{2}, \frac{\alpha}{2}}(\gamma) = \gamma^{\frac{\alpha-1}{2}} e^{-\frac{\gamma}{2}}$.

Therefore,

$$f(x) = \frac{\lambda^\alpha}{\Gamma(\alpha)} x^{-\alpha-1} e^{-\frac{\lambda}{x}}.$$

Notes:

(a) If $\alpha = \frac{1}{2}$, $\beta = 1$, and $c = -1$, the generalized Whittaker distribution is reduced to Lévy distribution [29].
(b) If $\alpha = 1$, $\beta = 1$, and $c = -1$, the generalized Whittaker distribution is reduced to the inverse exponential distribution.
(c) If $2\alpha = v$, $\beta = 1$, $\lambda = \frac{1}{2}$, and $c = -1$, the generalized Whittaker distribution is reduced to the inverse chi-square distribution.

4.7. Type-2 Gumbel Distribution

If $X \sim GWD(1, 1, \gamma, \lambda, c)$, then X follows a Type-2 Gumbel distribution [30], as,

$$f(x) = e^{-\frac{\gamma}{2}} |c|\lambda e^{-\lambda x^c} \frac{x^{c-1}}{W_{0,\frac{1}{2}}(\gamma)}.$$

From Corollary 2 (I), we acquire $W_{0,\frac{1}{2}}(\gamma) = e^{-\frac{\gamma}{2}}$.

Therefore, $f(x) = |c|\lambda x^{c-1} e^{-\lambda x^c}$.

Note: If $\alpha = 1$, $\beta = 1$, and $c = -2$, then the generalized Whittaker distribution is reduced to inverse Rayleigh distribution [31].

5. Estimation

In this section, we focus on the estimation of the parameters α, β, λ, and γ of the Whittaker distribution. We introduce the estimation of parameters via the moments' and the maximum likelihood methods, denoted by MME and MLE, respectively.

Let $X_1, X_2, \ldots X_n$ be i.i.d. $WD(\alpha, \beta, \gamma, \lambda)$, the we have the following estimates.

5.1. Method of Moments

$$\hat{\lambda}_{MM} = \hat{\alpha}_{MM} \frac{\sqrt{\hat{\gamma}_{MM}}}{\overline{X}} \frac{W_{\frac{\hat{\beta}_{MM}-\hat{\alpha}_{MM}-1}{2}, \frac{\hat{\alpha}_{MM}+\hat{\beta}_{MM}}{2}}(\hat{\gamma}_{MM})}{W_{\frac{\hat{\beta}_{MM}-\hat{\alpha}_{MM}}{2}, \frac{\hat{\alpha}_{MM}+\hat{\beta}_{MM}-1}{2}}(\hat{\gamma}_{MM})}, \quad (9)$$

where $\hat{\alpha}_{MM}, \hat{\beta}_{MM}$, and $\hat{\gamma}_{MM}$ can be calculated by solving the following system of non-linear equations:

$$S^2 = \overline{X}^2 \left(1 + \frac{1}{\hat{\alpha}_{MM}}\right) \frac{W_{\frac{\hat{\beta}_{MM}-\hat{\alpha}_{MM}}{2}, \frac{\hat{\alpha}_{MM}+\hat{\beta}_{MM}-1}{2}}(\hat{\gamma}_{MM}) W_{\frac{\hat{\beta}_{MM}-\hat{\alpha}_{MM}}{2}-1, \frac{\hat{\alpha}_{MM}+\hat{\beta}_{MM}+1}{2}}(\hat{\gamma}_{MM})}{\left[W_{\frac{\hat{\beta}_{MM}-\hat{\alpha}_{MM}-1}{2}, \frac{\hat{\alpha}_{MM}+\hat{\beta}_{MM}}{2}}(\hat{\gamma}_{MM})\right]^2} - \overline{X}^2 \quad (10)$$

$$\frac{\sum_{i=1}^n X_i^3}{n\overline{X}^3} = \frac{\Gamma(\hat{\alpha}_{MM}+3)}{\hat{\alpha}_{MM}^2 \Gamma(\hat{\alpha}_{MM}+1)} \frac{\left[W_{\frac{\hat{\beta}_{MM}-\hat{\alpha}_{MM}}{2}, \frac{\hat{\alpha}_{MM}+\hat{\beta}_{MM}-1}{2}}(\hat{\gamma}_{MM})\right]^2 W_{\frac{\hat{\beta}_{MM}-\hat{\alpha}_{MM}}{2}-3, \frac{\hat{\alpha}_{MM}+\hat{\beta}_{MM}}{2}+1}(\hat{\gamma}_{MM})}{\left[W_{\frac{\hat{\beta}_{MM}-\hat{\alpha}_{MM}-1}{2}, \frac{\hat{\alpha}_{MM}+\hat{\beta}_{MM}}{2}}(\hat{\gamma}_{MM})\right]^3} \quad (11)$$

In addition,

$$\frac{\sum_{i=1}^n X_i^4}{n\overline{X}^4} = \frac{\Gamma(\hat{\alpha}_{MM}+4)}{\hat{\alpha}_{MM}^3 \Gamma(\hat{\alpha}_{MM}+1)} \frac{\left[W_{\frac{\hat{\beta}_{MM}-\hat{\alpha}_{MM}}{2}, \frac{\hat{\alpha}_{MM}+\hat{\beta}_{MM}-1}{2}}(\hat{\gamma}_{MM})\right]^3 W_{\frac{\hat{\beta}_{MM}-\hat{\alpha}_{MM}}{2}-2, \frac{\hat{\alpha}_{MM}+\hat{\beta}_{MM}}{2}+3}(\hat{\gamma}_{MM})}{\left[W_{\frac{\hat{\beta}_{MM}-\hat{\alpha}_{MM}-1}{2}, \frac{\hat{\alpha}_{MM}+\hat{\beta}_{MM}}{2}}(\hat{\gamma}_{MM})\right]^4}, \quad (12)$$

where $\overline{X}$ is the sample mean, and S^2 is the sample variance.

5.2. Maximum Likelihood Estimates

The log-likelihood function is given by,

$\ln L = n\alpha \ln \lambda - n\left(\frac{\alpha+\beta}{2} - 1\right) \ln \gamma - n \ln \Gamma(\alpha) - n \ln W_{\frac{\beta-\alpha}{2}, \frac{\alpha+\beta-1}{2}}(\gamma) - \lambda \sum_{i=1}^n x_i - n\frac{\gamma}{2} + (\alpha - 1)\sum_{i=1}^n \ln x_i + (\beta - 1)\sum_{i=1}^n \ln(\gamma + \lambda x_i).$

The MLE of α, β, γ, and λ can be obtained by solving numerically the equations $\frac{\partial \ln L}{\partial \alpha} = 0, \frac{\partial \ln L}{\partial \beta} = 0, \frac{\partial \ln L}{\partial \gamma} = 0$, and $\frac{\partial \ln L}{\partial \lambda} = 0$, respectively:

$$\frac{\partial \ln L}{\partial \lambda} = \frac{n\alpha}{\lambda} - \sum_{i=1}^n x_i + (\beta - 1)\sum_{i=1}^n \frac{x_i}{\gamma + \lambda x_i}, \quad (13)$$

$$\frac{\partial \ln L}{\partial \gamma} = -\frac{n\left(\frac{\alpha+\beta}{2} - 1\right)}{\gamma} - \frac{n}{2} + (\beta - 1)\sum_{i=1}^n \frac{1}{\gamma + \lambda x_i} - \frac{n}{2}\left(1 - \frac{\beta - \alpha}{\gamma}\right) + \frac{n}{\gamma} \frac{W_{\frac{\beta-\alpha}{2}+1, \frac{\alpha+\beta-1}{2}}(\gamma)}{W_{\frac{\beta-\alpha}{2}, \frac{\alpha+\beta-1}{2}}(\gamma)}, \quad (14)$$

$$\frac{\partial \ln L}{\partial \alpha} = n \ln \lambda - n \ln \gamma + \sum_{i=1}^n \ln x_i - \frac{n\left[\frac{\gamma^{\frac{\alpha+\beta}{2}} e^{-\frac{\gamma}{2}}}{\Gamma(\alpha)} \int_0^\infty e^{-\gamma t} t^{\alpha-1}(1+t)^{\beta-1} \log(t) dt\right]}{W_{\frac{\beta-\alpha}{2}, \frac{\alpha+\beta-1}{2}}(\gamma)}. \quad (15)$$

where,

$$\frac{\partial}{\partial \alpha} W_{\frac{\beta-\alpha}{2}, \frac{\alpha+\beta-1}{2}}(\gamma) = \frac{\log(\gamma)}{2} W_{\frac{\beta-\alpha}{2}, \frac{\alpha+\beta-1}{2}}(\gamma) - \psi(\alpha) W_{\frac{\beta-\alpha}{2}, \frac{\alpha+\beta-1}{2}}(\gamma) + \frac{\gamma^{\frac{\alpha+\beta}{2}} e^{-\frac{\gamma}{2}}}{\Gamma(\alpha)} \int_0^\infty e^{-\gamma t} t^{\alpha-1}(1+t)^{\beta-1} \log(t) dt,$$

In addition,

$$\frac{\partial \ln L}{\partial \beta} = -n\ln\gamma + \sum_{i=1}^{n}\ln(\gamma+\lambda x_i) - \frac{n\left[\frac{\gamma^{\frac{\alpha+\beta}{2}}e^{\frac{-\gamma}{2}}}{\Gamma(\alpha)}\int_0^\infty e^{-\gamma t}t^{\alpha-1}(1+t)^{\beta-1}\log(1+t)dt\right]}{W_{\frac{\beta-\alpha}{2},\frac{\alpha+\beta-1}{2}}(\gamma)}, \quad (16)$$

where,

$$\frac{\partial}{\partial \beta}W_{\frac{\beta-\alpha}{2},\frac{\alpha+\beta-1}{2}}(\gamma) = \frac{\log(\gamma)}{2}W_{\frac{\beta-\alpha}{2},\frac{\alpha+\beta-1}{2}}(\gamma) + \frac{\gamma^{\frac{\alpha+\beta}{2}}e^{\frac{-\gamma}{2}}}{\Gamma(\alpha)}\int_0^\infty e^{-\gamma t}t^{\alpha-1}(1+t)^{\beta-1}\log(1+t)dt.$$

and $\psi(.)$ is the di-gamma function.

6. Validations

In this section, we consider the application of GWD and WD to four different data sets to study the behavior of the parameters $c, \alpha, \beta, \lambda$, and γ. Mathematica software is adopted to find the parameter estimates (The computer codes are provided in Appendix B). The four data sets are described below.

Data set 1: The data set consisted of third-party motor insurance data for Sweden (1977), described and analyzed in [32].

Data set 2: The data set represented an uncensored data set corresponding to remission times (in months) of a random sample of 128 patients of bladder cancer reported in [33].

Data set 3: It represented the survival times (in days) of 72 guinea pigs infected with virulent tubercle bacilli, observed and reported in [34].

Data set 4: It represented waiting times (in minutes) before service of 100 bank customers as discussed [35].

Table 1 lists the model evaluation statistics for fitting the GWD and the WD together with some other distributions. The best model is shown in bold.

Table 2 presents the values of the Vuong test for WD against normal, Johnson S_L, and log-normal distributions for all data sets.

The variance covariance matrix $I(\theta)^{-1}$ of the MLEs under the Whittaker distribution for data set 1 are computed as,

$$\begin{pmatrix} 93.8653 & -227.9330 & 0.0029 & -5.3054 \\ -227.9330 & 555.0520 & 0.0154 & 13.0219 \\ 0.0029 & 0.0154 & 0.0163 & 0.0004 \\ -5.3054 & 13.0219 & 0.0004 & 0.3127 \end{pmatrix}$$

Thus, the 95% confidence intervals for α, β, γ, and λ were (0, 21.1722), (42.6242, 134.978), (39.733, 40.2333), and (3.6761, 5.8683), respectively. Since α is always nonegative, the lower bound of the confidence interval of α was set to zero.

For GWD (WD), the value of Pearson's chi-square test was $\chi^2 = 1.758$ (2.1865) with p-value 0.1849 (0.3351), which implies that GWD (WD) fits the data well. Regarding the maximum values of the log-likelihood, and the minimum values of the AIC and BIC for GWD, and WD, the results of both models are nearly identical. From the result of fitting $GWD(\alpha, \beta, \gamma, \lambda, c)$, the estimated value is $c = 1.03$. Therefore, we perform an LRT for the hypothesis $H_0: c = 1$ against $H_0: c \neq 1$. The value of the test statistic is $\chi^2 = 0.18$ with a p-value of 0.671, providing $c = 1$. This implies that we can reduce the model GWD to the model WD with fewer parameters. Figure 5 illustrates the estimated density of WD for data set 1.

The WD distribution is better than the log-normal distribution in terms of log-likelihood, AIC, and BIC. The value of the Vuong test for WD versus log-normal is $V = 2.873$ (p-value = 0.0041), which implies that the WD yielded a significantly better fit than the log-normal distribution. While the WD distribution outperforms the normal distribution in terms of log-likelihood and AIC, this was not the case in terms of BIC. The value of the Vuong test for the WD distribution versus the normal distribution is $V = 0.8716$ (p-value = 0.3834), indicating no significant difference between the models.

Table 1. Estimation results for all data sets.

	Data Set 1		Data Set 2		Data Set 3		Data Set 4	
Model	MLE Parameters	Log(L)	MLE Parameters	Log(L)	MLE Parameters	Log(L)	MLE Parameters	Log(L)
GWD	$\alpha = 3.6368$ $\beta = 91.5863$ $\lambda = 4.3822$ $\gamma = 46.4312$ $c = 1.0304$	−3768.62	$\alpha = 0.9679$ $\beta = -3.5285$ $\lambda = 0.0051$ $\gamma = 0.1665$ $c = 1.0921$	−400.762	$\alpha = 3.2583$ $\beta = 1.0196$ $\lambda = 1.8831$ $\gamma = 134.651$ $c = 0.9701$	−94.2268	$\alpha = 32.4000$ $\beta = -29.696$ $\lambda = 0.2028$ $\gamma = 0.0054$ $c = 0.9707$	−316.930
WD	$\alpha = 2.1829$ $\beta = 88.8009$ $\lambda = 4.7722$ $\gamma = 39.9831$	−3768.71	$\alpha = 1.0959$ $\beta = -4.8971$ $\lambda = 0.0033$ $\gamma = 0.1030$	−400.815	$\alpha = 3.0834$ $\beta = 1.0000$ $\lambda = 1.7438$ $\gamma = 2.9426$	−94.2291	$\alpha = 31.5464$ $\beta = -28.9529$ $\lambda = 0.1775$ $\gamma = 0.0050$	−316.931
Log-normal	$\mu = 2.3506$ $\sigma = 0.1899$	−3788.58	$\mu = 1.5109$ $\sigma = 1.2819$	−406.802	$\mu = 0.3991$ $\sigma = 0.629$	−97.5222	$\mu = 2.0211$ $\sigma = 0.7801$	−319.174
Normal	$\mu = 10.6786$ $\sigma = 1.9757$	−3773.45	$\mu = 8.5688$ $\sigma = 10.5191$	−482.883	$\mu = 1.7682$ $\sigma = 1.0273$	−104.106	$\mu = 9.877$ $\sigma = 7.2007$	−339.312
Johnson S_L			$\delta = 1.1633$ $\gamma = -2.2532$ $\tau = -1.3757$	−406.447	$\delta = 1.5878$ $\gamma = -1.9284$ $\lambda = 0.7481$ $\tau = 0.3849$	−92.9256	$\delta = 1.2306$ $\gamma = 2.6058$ $\lambda = 78.0372$ $\tau = -0.5843$	−317.086
Generalized Gamma	$\alpha = 31.9737$ $\lambda = 0.1925$ $c = 0.8918$	−3774.44	$\alpha = 1.6997$ $\lambda = 0.2410$ $c = 0.4266$	−401.66	$\alpha = 3.1607$ $\lambda = 0.5208$ $c = 0.9701$	−94.2268	$\alpha = 3.7429$ $\lambda = 0.1178$ $c = 0.4788$	−317.225
Weibull	$\lambda = 11.5022$ $k = 5.8106$	−3818.69	$\lambda = 8.2303$ $k = 0.9227$	−402.191	$\lambda = 1.996$ $k = 1.8254$	−95.790	$\lambda = 10.9553$ $k = 1.4585$	−318.731
Gamma	$\alpha = 28.5388$ $\lambda = 2.6725$	−3773.27	$\alpha = 0.9155$ $\lambda = 0.1068$	−402.624	$\alpha = 3.0834$ $\lambda = 1.7438$	−94.2291	$\alpha = 2.0088$ $\lambda = 0.2034$	−317.3
Exponential			$\lambda = 0.1167$	−402.96				
Generalized Lindley	$\alpha = 28.0971$ $\lambda = 2.6938$ $\gamma = 5.4342$	−3773.13	$\alpha = 0.3594$ $\lambda = 0.1455$ $\gamma = 1.1499$	−407.868	$\lambda = 1.8248$ $\alpha = 2.3367$ $\gamma = 14.7453$	−94.0893	$\lambda = 0.2300$ $\alpha = 1.4949$ $\gamma = 0.8024$	−317.836
Lindley			$\lambda = 0.2129$	−417.924				

Table 2. Vuong test of WD vs. some models for all data sets.

	Data Set 1		Data Set 2		Data Set 3		Data Set 4	
WD vs	Test statistic	p-value	Test statistic	p-value	Test statistic	p-value	Test statistic	p-value
Log-normal	2.8733	0.0041	1.4188	0.1559	0.3568	0.7212	0.1284	0.8979
Normal	0.8716	0.3834	4.4671	<0.001	2.0183	0.0436	3.5893	0.0003
Johnson			(Johnson S_L) 2.3096	0.0209	(Johnson S_U) −1.0613	0.2885	(Johnson S_B) 0.3735	0.7088

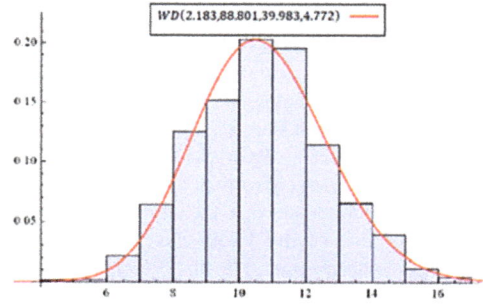

Figure 5. Estimated density of $WD(\alpha, \beta, \gamma, \lambda)$ for data set 1.

The generalized gamma distribution and Weibull distributions are special cases of the generalized Whittaker distribution. Therefore, there is no need to fit these distributions. The gamma and generalized Lindley distributions are special cases of the Whittaker distribution at $\beta = 1$ and $\beta = 2$, respectively. It is clear that $\hat{\beta} = 88.8$ in the WD is neither one nor two. For the gamma distribution, the value of LRT is $\chi^2 = 9.12$ (p-value = 0.0104). Then, $\beta \neq 1$. The same conclusion is obtained under the generalized Lindley, $\beta \neq 2$, where the value of the test statistic is $\chi^2 = 8.84$ (p-value = 0.003).

The variance covariance matrix $I(\theta)^{-1}$ of the MLEs under the Whittaker distribution for data set 2 was computed as,

$$\begin{pmatrix} 0.0238 & 0.1390 & -2.65 \times 10^{-6} & 0.0002 \\ 0.1390 & 5.9668 & -0.00004 & 0.0051 \\ -2.65 \times 10^{-6} & -0.00004 & 8.32 \times 10^{-6} & 2.16 \times 10^{-7} \\ 0.0002 & 0.0051 & 2.16 \times 10^{-7} & 4.86 \times 10^{-6} \end{pmatrix}$$

Thus, the 95% confidence intervals of $\alpha, \beta, \gamma,$ and λ are (0.7937, 1.3981), (−9.684, −0.1094), (0.09735, 0.1087), and (0, 0.0076), respectively. The lower bound of the confidence interval of λ is negative. Since λ is always non-negative, zero is considered the lower bound.

The results of Pearson's chi-square test for GWD (WD) yield $\chi^2 = 12.0676$ (12.3476) with a p-value 0.0984 (0.1944), which implies that GWD (WD) fits the data well. The result of GWD shows that the estimated value of c is 1.09, and the other parameters are nearly the same as those of WD. Therefore, we perform the LRT for hypotheses $H_0 : c = 1$ and $H_0 : c \neq 1$. The value of the test statistic is $\chi^2 = 0.106$ (p-value = 0.7447). This implies that we can reduce GWD to WD, which has fewer parameters. Figure 6 illustrates the estimated density of WD for data set 2.

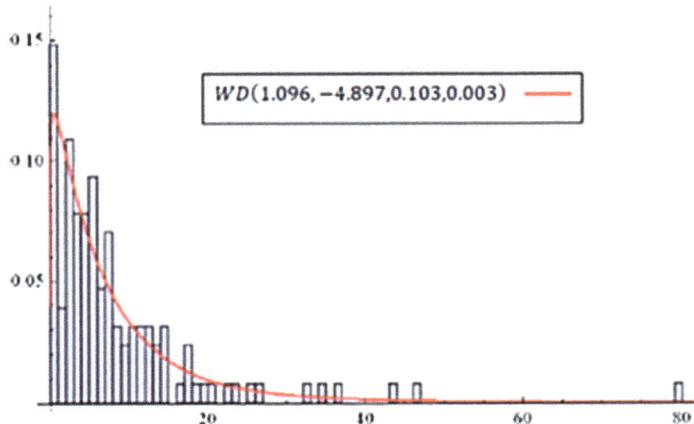

Figure 6. Estimated density of $WD(\alpha, \beta, \gamma, \lambda)$ for data set 2.

According to the Vuong test, we can conclude that WD fits the data better than the normal distribution and Johnson's S_L with (V = 4.47 with p-value < 0.001) and (V = 2.31 with p-value = 0.021), respectively. There is no significant difference between the WD distribution and the log-normal distribution with a p-value of 0.156.

The generalized gamma and Weibull distributions are special cases of GWD, and thus are eliminated from the comparison. Using the LRT to check where the data had been drawn from an exponential distribution, the value of the test statistic becomes $\chi^2 = 4.29$ (p-value = 0.2318). This implies that the exponential distribution fits the data.

The variance covariance matrix $I(\theta)^{-1}$ of the MLEs under the Whittaker distribution for data set 3 is computed as follows.

$$\begin{pmatrix} 3.0194 & -14.3655 & 0.0022 & -2.1450 \\ -14.3655 & 74.2163 & -0.0114 & 11.7791 \\ 0.0022 & -0.0114 & 0.0095 & -0.0018 \\ -2.1450 & 11.7791 & -0.0018 & 1.9596 \end{pmatrix}$$

Thus, the 95% confidence intervals of $\alpha, \beta, \gamma,$ and λ were $(0, 6.4892), (-15.8852, 17.8852), (2.7513, 3.1339)$, and $(0, 4.4875)$, respectively. The lower bounds of the confidence intervals of α and λ are negative; and as both α and λ are always non-negative, zero is used as lower bound.

We fit the models WD and GWD to data on survival times. The results of Pearson's chi-square test for GWD (WD) yield a value $\chi^2 = 3.766$ (3.8114) with p-value 0.1521 (0.2826), which implies that GWD (WD) fits the data well. The results (in Table 1) of GWD show that the estimated value of c is 0.97, and the other parameters are nearly identical to those of WD. Using the LRT, the value of the test statistic is $\chi^2 = 0.005$ (p-value = 0.946). This implies that we can reduce the model GWD to WD, which has fewer parameters. Figure 7 illustrates the estimated density of WD for data set 3.

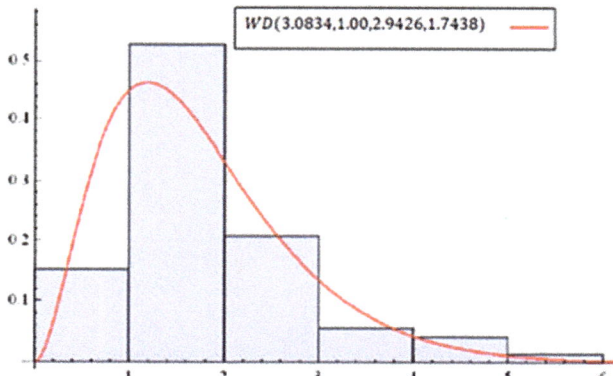

Figure 7. Estimated density of $WD(\alpha, \beta, \gamma, \lambda)$ for data set 3.

Using the Vuong test (in Table 2), there is no significant difference between the fitted model using the WD distribution and all remaining tested distributions.

The generalized gamma and Weibull distributions are a special case of GWD, and thus are eliminated from the comparison. From the results of fitting WD, we note that the estimated value of β is one, and the other fitting measures of α and λ are identical to those of $Gamma(\alpha, \lambda)$. Therefore, we perform the LRT ($H_0 : \beta = 1$) with a p-value of one, with providing $\beta = 1$. The generalized Lindley is a special case of the WD when β is two. Without testing, we know that the gamma distribution yields a better fit than the generalized Lindley for this data set.

The variance covariance matrix $I(\theta)^{-1}$ of the MLEs under the Whittaker distribution for data set 4 is computed as follows.

$$\begin{pmatrix} 1442.85 & -1461.15 & -0.0001 & -0.9952 \\ -1461.15 & 1479.8 & 0.0001 & 1.0190 \\ -0.0001 & 0.0001 & 1.78 \times 10^{-8} & -1.67 \times 10^{-9} \\ -0.9952 & 1.0190 & -1.67 \times 10^{-9} & 0.0019 \end{pmatrix}$$

Thus, the 95% confidence intervals for $\alpha, \beta, \gamma,$ and λ are $(0, 106.00)$, $(-104.35, 46.4446)$, $(0.0047, 0.0053)$, and $(0.0922, 0.2627)$, respectively. The lower bound of the confidence interval of α is negative. As α is non-negative, zero is used as lower bound.

We fit the models WD and GWD to data of waiting times. The results of Pearson's chi-square test for GWD (WD) yield a value of $\chi^2 = 10.9955$ (11.0327) with a p-value 0.202 (0.2735), which implies that GWD (WD) fits the data well. The result (in Table 1) for GWD shows that the estimated value of c is 0.97. Using the LRT for $c = 1$, the value of the test statistic is $\chi^2 = 0.002$ (p-value = 0.964). This implies that we can reduce the model GWD to WD, which has fewer parameters. Figure 8 illustrates the estimated density of WD for data set 4.

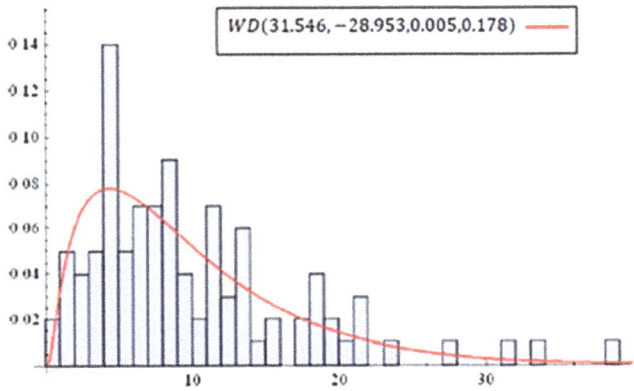

Figure 8. Estimated density of $WD(\alpha, \beta, \gamma, \lambda)$ for data set 4.

According to the Vuong test, we can conclude that WD yields a better fit than the normal with (V = 4.47 with p-value < 0.001), and there is no significant difference between the fitted model using the WD distribution, and the log-normal and Johnson's S_B distributions. The generalized gamma and Weibull distributions are special cases of GWD, and thus are eliminated from the comparison. Using the LRT, the value of the test statistic of $H_0 : \beta = 2$ was $\chi^2 = 1.81$ (p-value = 0.179). This implies that the generalized Lindley distribution fits the data. Finally, the value of the test statistic of the LRT for $H_0 : \beta = 1$ is $\chi^2 = 0.738$ (p-value = 0.691). This implies that the gamma distribution fits the data as well.

7. Conclusions

Based on Whittaker function a modified life distribution that is called Whittaker distribution has been introduced. The Whittaker distribution is a generalization of many well-known continuous distributions such as gamma, exponential, chi-square, generalized Lindley, Lindley, beta prime, and Lomax distributions. Furthermore, we have defined the generalized Whittaker distribution that also has the generalized gamma, half-normal, Weibull, half-t, half-Cauchy, Nakagami, Rayleigh, Dagum, Lévy, type-2 Gumbel, inverse gamma, inverse chi-square, inverse exponential, inverse Weibull, and inverse-Rayleigh distributions as special cases. We Validated the proposed distributions on four real data sets. The results of Pearson's chi-square test confirmed that the Generalized Whittaker distribution and the Whittaker distribution fit the data well for all the four data sets. In some applications, the vuong test showed that the Whittaker distribution has significantly better fit than the normal, log-normal and Jhonson distributions.

Author Contributions: Conceptualization, A.A.A.; methodology, A.A.A., M.A.O. and Y.A.T.; software, Y.A.T. and M.A.O.; validation, M.A.O. and A.A.A.; formal analysis, Y.A.T. and M.A.O.; investigation, S.A. and A.A.A.; resources, Y.A.T.; data curation, Y.A.T. and M.A.O.; writing—original draft preparation, M.A.O. and Y.A.T.; writing—review and editing, A.A.A. and S.A.; visualization, A.A.A.;

supervision, A.A.A.; project administration, S.A.; funding acquisition, Y.A.T. All authors have read and agreed to the published version of the manuscript.

Funding: This research project was supported by the Researchers Supporting Project Number (RSP2022R488), King Saud University, Riyadh, Saudi Arabia.

Institutional Review Board Statement: Not applicable.

Informed Consent Statement: Not applicable.

Data Availability Statement: Data set 1: The third-party motor insurance data for Sweden for the year 1977 described and analyzed by Hallin and Ingenbleek (1983) in The Swedish automobile portfolio in 1977 [DATA TYPE: the logarithm of the total number which had at least one claim]. The data can be found in www.math.uni.wroc.pl/~dabr/R/motorins.html (1 March 2022). Data set 2: The data set represents an uncensored data set corresponding to remission times (in months) of a random sample of 128 bladder cancer patients reported in Lee and Wang (2003) in Statistical Methods for Survival Data Analysis [DATA TYPE: the remission times (in months)]. The data can be found in http://www.naturalspublishing.com/files/published/j9wsil53h390x8.pdf (1 March 2022). Data set 3: The data are given in Bjerkedal (1960) in Acquisition of resistance in guinea pies infected with different doses of virulent tubercle bacilli [DATA TYPE: the survival times (in days)]. The data can be found in https://rivista-statistica.unibo.it/article/viewFile/6282/6061 (1 March 2022). Data set 4: The data represent the waiting times (in minutes) before service of 100 bank customers as discussed by Ghitany et al. (2008). The data can be found in http://biomedicine.imedpub.com/on-generalized-lindley-distribution-and-its-applications-to-model-lifetime-data-from-biomedical-science-and-engineering.pdf (1 March 2022).

Conflicts of Interest: The authors declare no conflict of interest. The funders had no role in the design of the study; in the collection, analyses, or interpretation of data; in the writing of the manuscript, or in the decision to publish the results.

Appendix A

The code for calculating the 25th percentiles of the Whittaker distribution:
(Code file)

```
Clear[a1,a2,b1,b2,x,f,g,cf]
a1 = 10.5; a2 = 1.25; b = 3.5; v = 2.5;
f[x_]:= Exp[−v/2]/Gamma[a1] b^a1/v^((a1 + a2)/2 − 1)*(x^(a1 − 1) (v + b*x)^(a2 − 1))/WhittakerW[(a2 − a1)/2,(a1 + a2 − 1)/2,v] Exp[−x*b]
cf[u_]: = Exp[−v/2]/Gamma[a1] b^a1/v^((a1 + a2)/2 − 1)*1/WhittakerW[(a2 − a1)/2,(a1 + a2−1)/2,v] NIntegrate[x^(a1 − 1) (v + b*x)^(a2 − 1) Exp[−x*b],{x,0,u}]
w1 = FindRoot[Exp[−v/2]/Gamma[a1] b^a1/v^((a1 + a2)/2−1)*1/WhittakerW[(a2−a1)/2,(a1 + a2−1)/2,v] NIntegrate[x^(a1 − 1) (v + b*x)^(a2 − 1) Exp[−x*b],{x,0,u}]−0.25,{u,0.12}]
q1 = u//.w1
cf[q1]
{u− > 2.38469}
2.38469
0.25
```

Appendix B

The computer codes for the maximum likelihood estimation, the Voung test and for the variance covariance matrix $I(\theta)^{-1}$ of the MLEs under the Whittaker distribution for data set 2:
(Code file)

y = {0.08,0.52,0.22,0.82,0.62,0.39,0.96,0.19,0.66,0.4,0.26,0.31,0.73,3.48,6.97,25.74,2.54,5.32, 14.83,1.05,4.26,17.14,4.34,19.13,6.54,3.36,6.94,13.29,2.46,5.17,10.06,0.9,4.23,7.63,1.35,7.93,3.25, 12.03,8.65,13.11,2.26,5.09,9.74,32.15,4.18,7.62,46.12,5.62,18.1,6.25,2.02,22.69,0.2,5.06,9.47,26.31, 3.88,7.59,16.62,2.83,11.64,4.4,12.02,6.76,2.09,4.98,13.8,0.51,3.82,10.34,36.66,2.75,11.25,3.02,11.98, 4.51,2.07,4.87,9.02,0.5,3.7,7.32,34.26,2.69,5.41,79.05,5.71,1.76,8.53,6.93,8.66,0.4,3.64,7.28,14.77,

2.69,5.41,17.12,2.87,11.79,4.5,20.28,12.63,23.63,3.57,7.26,14.76,2.64,5.34,10.75,1.26,7.87,1.46,8.37,
3.36,5.49,2.23,7.09,14.24,0.81,5.32,10.66,43.01,4.33,17.36,5.85,2.02,12.07};
 n = 128;
 w1 = FindRoot[{c*Sum[Log[y[[i]]], {i, 1, n}] − (n*((1/2)*Derivative[0, 1, 0][WhittakerW]][(a2 − a1)/2, (1/2)*(a1 + a2 − 1), v] −
(1/2)*Derivative[1, 0, 0][WhittakerW][(a2 − a1)/2, (1/2)*(a1 + a2 − 1), v]))/Whittaker
W[(a2 − a1)/2, (1/2)*(a1 + a2 − 1), v] − n*PolyGamma[0, a1] + n*Log[b] − (1/2)*n*Log[v],
Sum[Log[b*y[[i]]^c + v], {i, 1, n}] − (n*((1/2)*Derivative[0, 1, 0][WhittakerW][(a2 − a1)/2,
(1/2)*(a1 + a2 − 1), v] +
(1/2)*Derivative[1, 0, 0][WhittakerW][(a2 − a1)/2, (1/2)*(a1 + a2 − 1), v]))/Whittaker
W[(a2 − a1)/2, (1/2)*(a1 + a2 − 1), v] − (1/2)*n*Log[v],
(a2 − 1)*Sum[1/(b*y[[i]]^c + v), {i, 1, n}] − (n*((1/2 − (a2 − a1)/(2*v))*WhittakerW[(a2
− a1)/2, (1/2)*(a1 + a2 − 1), v] − WhittakerW[(a2 − a1)/2 + 1, (1/2)*(a1 + a2 − 1),
v]/v))/WhittakerW[(a2 − a1)/2, (1/2)*(a1 + a2 − 1), v] − (n*((a1 + a2)/2 − 1))/v − n/2,
(a2 − 1)*Sum[y[[i]]^c/(b*y[[i]]^c + v), {i, 1, n}] − Sum[y[[i]]^c, {i, 1, n}] + (a1*n)/b && a1 > 0
&& v > 0 && b > 0}, {{a1, 1.08}, {a2, −4.57}, {b, 0.005}, {v, 0.15}}]
 {a1−> 1.09587,a2−> −4.89705,b−> 0.00331532,v−> 0.103035}
 Clear[a1, a2, v, b, c]
 w = FindRoot[{n*Log[b] − (1/2)*n*Log[v] − n*PolyGamma[0, a1] + c*Sum[Log[y[[i]]]],
{i, 1, n}] − (n*((1/2)*Derivative[0, 1, 0][WhittakerW][(1/2)*(−a1 + a2), (1/2)*(−1 + a1
+ a2), v] − (1/2)*Derivative[1, 0, 0][WhittakerW][(1/2)*(−a1 + a2), (1/2)*(−1 + a1 +
a2), v]))/ WhittakerW[(1/2)*(−a1 + a2), (1/2)*(−1 + a1 + a2), v], (−(1/2))*n*Log[v] +
Sum[Log[v + b*y[[i]]^c], {i, 1, n}] − (n*((1/2)*Derivative[0, 1, 0][WhittakerW][(1/2)*(−a1
+ a2), (1/2)*(−1 + a1 + a2), v] + (1/2)*Derivative[1, 0, 0][WhittakerW][(1/2)*(−a1 + a2),
(1/2)*(−1 + a1 + a2), v]))/ WhittakerW[(1/2)*(−a1 + a2), (1/2)*(−1 + a1 + a2), v], −(n/2)
− ((−1 + (a1 + a2)/2)*n)/v + (−1 + a2)*Sum[1/(v + b*y[[i]]^c), {i, 1, n}] − (n*((1/2 − (-a1
+ a2)/(2*v))*WhittakerW[(1/2)*(−a1 + a2), (1/2)*(−1 + a1 + a2), v] − WhittakerW[1 +
(1/2)*(−a1 + a2), (1/2)*(−1 + a1 + a2), v]/v))/ WhittakerW[(1/2)*(−a1 + a2), (1/2)*(−1
+ a1 + a2), v], (a1*n)/b − Sum[y[[i]]^c, {i, 1, n}] + (−1 + a2)*Sum[y[[i]]^c/(v + b*y[[i]]^c),
{i, 1, n}], n/c + a1*Sum[Log[y[[i]]], {i, 1, n}] − b*Sum[Log[y[[i]]]*y[[i]]^c, {i, 1, n}] + (−1 +
a2)*Sum[(b*Log[y[[i]]]*y[[i]]^c)/(v + b*y[[i]]^c), {i, 1, n}] && a1 > 0 && v > 0 && b > 0}, {{a1,
0.98}, {a2, −3.47}, {b, 0.005}, {v, 0.15}, {c, 1.5}}]
 {a1−> 0.967908,a2−> −3.52849,b−> 0.00510853,v−> 0.166534,c−> 1.09214}
 "Vuong test"
 k = 4;
 a1 = 1.09587;
 a2 = −4.897054;
 b = 0.0033153184;
 v = 0.103034;
 f[x_]:= (Exp[−v/2]/Gamma[a1])*(b^a1/v^((a1 + a2)/2 − 1))*((x^(a1 − 1)*(v + b*x)^(a2
− 1))/WhittakerW[(a2 − a1)/2, (a1 + a2 − 1)/2, v])*Exp[(−x)*b]
 "Log-normal"
 Clear[u, se]
 wln = FindRoot[{−(n/se) − Sum[−((−u + Log[y[[i]]])^2/se^3), {i, 1, n}], −Sum[−((−u
+ Log[y[[i]]])/se^2), {i, 1, n}]}, {{u, 2.3}, {se, 0.2}}]
 se = se //. wln;
 u = u //. wln;
 fln[x_]:= (1/(x*se*Sqrt[2*Pi]))*Exp[−((Log[x] − u)^2/(2*se^2))];
 lln = (−n)*Log[Sqrt[2*Pi]] − Sum[Log[y[[i]]], {i, 1, n}] − n*Log[se] − Sum[(Log[y[[i]]]
− u)^2/(2*se^2), {i, 1, n}]
 lrln = Sum[Log[f[y[[i]]]/fln[y[[i]]]], {i, 1, n}] − (k − 2);
 wnln = (1/n)*Sum[Log[f[y[[i]]]/fln[y[[i]]]]^2, {i, 1, n}] − ((1/n)*Sum[Log[f[y[[i]]]/fln[y[[i]]]],
{i, 1, n}])^2;
 vln = lrln/Sqrt[n*wnln]

```
2*(1 − CDF[NormalDistribution[], Abs[vln]])
"Normal"
Clear[sn, un, w1, vnor, lrnor, wnnor, fn, lnor]
w1 = FindRoot[{−(n/sn) + Sum[(−un + y[[i]])^2, {i, 1, n}]/sn^3, −(Sum[−2*(−un +
y[[i]]), {i, 1, n}]/(2*sn^2))}, {{un, 1}, {sn, 1}}]
un = un //. w1;
sn = sn //. w1;
fn[x_]:= (1/Sqrt[2*Pi*sn^2])*Exp[−((x − un)^2/(2*sn^2))]
lnor = (−(n/2))*Log[2*Pi] − n*Log[sn] − Sum[(y[[i]] − un)^2, {i, 1, n}]/(2*sn^2)
lrnor = Sum[Log[f[y[[i]]]/fn[y[[i]]]], {i, 1, n}] − (k − 2);
wnnor = (1/n)*Sum[Log[f[y[[i]]]/fn[y[[i]]]]^2, {i, 1, n}] − ((1/n)*Sum[Log[f[y[[i]]]/
fn[y[[i]]]], {i, 1, n}])^2;
vnor = lrnor/Sqrt[n*wnnor]
2*(1 − CDF[NormalDistribution[], Abs[vnor]])
"Johnson"
Clear[bj, tj, cj]
vjo = −2.25315;
cj = 1.1633;
tj = −1.37569;
fj[x_]:= (cj/Sqrt[2*Pi])*(1/(x − tj))*Exp[(−2^(−1))*(vjo + cj*Log[x − tj])^2]
lnj = n*Log[cj/Sqrt[2*Pi]] − Sum[Log[y[[i]] − tj], {i, 1, n}] − (1/2)*Sum[(vjo + cj*Lo
g[y[[i]] − tj])^2, {i, 1, n}]
lrj = Sum[Log[f[y[[i]]]/fj[y[[i]]]], {i, 1, n}] − (k − 3);
wnj = (1/n)*Sum[Log[f[y[[i]]]/fj[y[[i]]]]^2, {i, 1, n}] − ((1/n)*Sum[Log[f[y[[i]]]/f
j[y[[i]]]], {i, 1, n}])^2;
vj1 = lrj/Sqrt[n*wnj]
2*(1 − CDF[NormalDistribution[], Abs[vj1]])
Vuong test0e
Log-normal
{u− > 1.51087,se− > 1.28189}
−406.802
1.41883
0.155948
Normal
{un− > 8.56875,sn− > 10.5191}
−482.833
4.46717
7.92596 × 10^−6
Johnson
−406.447
2.30962
0.0209092
"CI"
a11 = n*((v^((a1 + a2)/2)*Exp[−v/2])/Gamma[a1])*(NIntegrate[Exp[(−v)*t]*t^(a1 −
1)*(1 + t)^(a2 − 1)*Log[t]^2, {t, 0, Infinity}]/WhittakerW[(a2 − a1)/2, (a1 + a2 − 1)/2, v]) −
n*(((v^((a1 + a2)/2)*Exp[-v/2])/Gamma[a1])*(NIntegrate[Exp[(−v)*t]*t^(a1 − 1)*(1 + t)^(a2
− 1)*Log[t], {t, 0, Infinity}]/WhittakerW[(a2 − a1)/2, (a1 + a2 − 1)/2, v]))^2;
    a12 = n*((v^((a1 + a2)/2)*Exp[−v/2])/Gamma[a1])*(NIntegrate[Exp[(−v)*t]*t^(a1 −
1)*(1 + t)^(a2 − 1)*Log[t]*Log[1 + t], {t, 0, Infinity}]/WhittakerW[(a2 − a1)/2, (a1 + a2 −
1)/2, v]) − n*((v^((a1 + a2)/2)/Gamma[a1])*(Exp[−v/2]/WhittakerW[(a2 − a1)/2, (a1 +
a2 − 1)/2, v]))^2*NIntegrate[Exp[(−v)*t]*t^(a1 − 1)*(1 + t)^(a2 − 1)*Log[t], {t, 0, Infinity}]*
NIntegrate[Exp[(−v)*t]*t^(a1 − 1)*(1 + t)^(a2 − 1)*Log[1 + t], {t, 0, Infinity}];
    a13 = −(−(n/v) − n*(a2 − v)*((v^((a1 + a2)/2 − 1)*Exp[−v/2])/Gamma[a1])*(NInteg
rate[Exp[(−v)*t]*t^(a1 − 1)*(1 + t)^(a2 − 1)*Log[t], {t, 0, Infinity}]/
```

WhittakerW[(a2 − a1)/2, (a1 + a2 − 1)/2, v]) + n*((v^((a1 + a2)/2)*Exp[-v/2])/Gamma[a1])*(NIntegrate[Exp[(−v)*t]*t^a1*(1 + t)^(a2 − 1)*Log[t], {t, 0, Infinity}]/ WhittakerW[(a2 − a1)/2, (a1 + a2 − 1)/2, v]) − n*((v^((a1 + a2)/2 − 1)*Exp[-v/2])/Gamma[a1])*WhittakerW[(a2 − a1)/2 + 1, (a1 + a2 − 1)/2, v]*
(NIntegrate[Exp[(−v)*t]*t^(a1 − 1)*(1 + t)^(a2 − 1)*Log[t], {t, 0, Infinity}]/WhittakerW[(a2 − a1)/2, (a1 + a2 − 1)/2, v]^2));
a14 = −(n/b);
a22 = n*((v^((a1 + a2)/2)*Exp[-v/2])/Gamma[a1])*(NIntegrate[Exp[(−v)*t]*t^(a1 − 1)*(1 + t)^(a2 − 1)*Log[1 + t]^2, {t, 0, Infinity}]/WhittakerW[(a2 − a1)/2, (a1 + a2 − 1)/2, v]) − n*(((v^((a1 + a2)/2)*Exp[−v/2])/Gamma[a1])*(NIntegrate[Exp[(−v)*t]*t^(a1 − 1)*(1 + t)^(a2 − 1)*Log[1 + t], {t, 0, Infinity}]/WhittakerW[(a2 − a1)/2, (a1 + a2 − 1)/2, v]))^2;
a23 = −(−(n/v) + Sum[1/(v + b*y[[i]]), {i, 1, n}] + n*((v^((a1 + a2)/2)*Exp[-v/2])/Gamma[a1])*(NIntegrate[Exp[(-v)*t]*t^a1*(1 + t)^(a2 − 1)*Log[1 + t], {t, 0, Infinity}]/WhittakerW[(a2 − a1)/2, (a1 + a2 − 1)/2, v]) + n*(1 − a2/v)*((v^((a1 + a2)/2)*Exp[-v/2])/Gamma[a1])*(NIntegrate[Exp[(-v)*t]*t^(a1 − 1)*(1 + t)^(a2 − 1)*Log[1 + t], {t, 0, Infinity}]/WhittakerW[(a2 − a1)/2, (a1 + a2 − 1)/2, v]) − (n/v)*((v^((a1 + a2)/2)*Exp[-v/2])/Gamma[a1])*WhittakerW[(a2 − a1)/2 + 1, (a1 + a2 − 1)/2, v]* (NIntegrate[Exp[(-v)*t]*t^(a1 − 1)*(1 + t)^(a2 − 1)*Log[1 + t], {t, 0, Infinity}]/WhittakerW[(a2 − a1)/2, (a1 + a2 − 1)/2, v]^2));
a24 = −(n/b − Sum[v/((v + b*y[[i]])*b), {i, 1, n}]);
a33 = −((n/v^2)*(a1 − 1) + (n/v^2)*(v/2 − (a2 − a1)/2 − 2)*(WhittakerW[(a2 − a1)/2 + 1, (a1 + a2 − 1)/2, v]/WhittakerW[(a2 − a1)/2, (a1 + a2 − 1)/2, v]) −
(n/v^2)*(WhittakerW[(a2 − a1)/2 + 2, (a1 + a2 − 1)/2, v]/WhittakerW[(a2 − a1)/2, (a1 + a2 − 1)/2, v]) − (a2 − 1)*Sum[1/(v + b*y[[i]])^2, {i, 1, n}]);
a34 = (a2 − 1)*Sum[y[[i]]/(v + b*y[[i]])^2, {i, 1, n}];
a44 = −(−((n*(a1 + a2 − 1))/b^2) + (−1 + a2)*Sum[(y[[i]]*v)/(b*(v + b*y[[i]]))^2), {i, 1, n}] + (−1 + a2)*Sum[v/(b^2*(v + b*y[[i]]))), {i, 1, n}]);
beta = {{a11, a12, a13, a14}, {a12, a22, a23, a24}, {a13, a23, a33, a34}, {a14, a24, a34, a44}};
inbeta = Inverse[beta];
MatrixForm[inbeta]
CI
(_{{0.0237651, 0.139018, −2.65017 × 10^−6, 0.00020543},
{0.139018, 5.96683, −0.0000375354, 0.00511258},
{−2.65017 × 10^−6, −0.0000375354, 8.32295 × 10^−6, 2.16077 × 10^−7},
{0.00020543, 0.00511258, 2.16077 × 10^−7, 4.85993 × 10^−6}}_)
"a1"
Sqrt[inbeta[[1,1]]]
"p-value"
2*(1 − CDF[NormalDistribution[], a1/Sqrt[inbeta[[1,1]]]])
a1 + 1.96*Sqrt[inbeta[[1,1]]]
a1 − 1.96*Sqrt[inbeta[[1,1]]]
"a2"
Sqrt[inbeta[[2,2]]]
"p-value"
2*(1 − CDF[NormalDistribution[], Abs[a2/Sqrt[inbeta[[2,2]]]]])
a2 + 1.96*Sqrt[inbeta[[2,2]]]
a2 − 1.96*Sqrt[inbeta[[2,2]]]
"v"
Sqrt[inbeta[[3,3]]]
"p-value"
2*(1 − CDF[NormalDistribution[], v/Sqrt[inbeta[[3,3]]]])
v + 1.96*Sqrt[inbeta[[3,3]]]
v − 1.96*Sqrt[inbeta[[3,3]]]
"b"
Sqrt[inbeta[[4,4]]]

"p-value"
2*(1 − CDF[NormalDistribution[], b/Sqrt[inbeta[[4,4]]]])
b + 1.96*Sqrt[inbeta[[4,4]]]
b − 1.96*Sqrt[inbeta[[4,4]]]
a1
0.154159
p-value
1.16995×10^{-12}
1.39805
0.793748
a2
2.44271
p-value
0.0449863
−0.10939
−9.68481
v
0.00288495
p-value
0.
0.108655
0.0973455
b
0.00220453
p-value
0.134414
0.00762087
−0.00102087

References

1. Abramowitz, M.; Stegun, I.A. *Handbook of Mathematical Functions with Formulas, Graphs, and Mathematical Tables*; 9th Printing; Dover: New York, NY, USA, 1972.
2. Gradshteyn, I.S.; Ryzhik, I.M. *Table of Integrals, Series, and Products*, 7th ed.; Elsevier: Burlington, MA, USA, 2007.
3. Bateman, H. *Tables of Integral Transforms [Volumes I & II]*; McGraw-Hill Book Company: New York, NY, USA, 1954; Volume 1.
4. McKay, A.T. A Bessel function distribution. *Biometrika* **1932**, *1*, 39–44. [CrossRef]
5. Laha, R.G. On some properties of the Bessel function distributions. *Bull. Calcutta. Math. Soc.* **1954**, *46*, 59–72.
6. Malik, H.J. Exact distribution of the product of independent generalized gamma variables with the same shape parameter. *Ann. Math. Stat.* **1968**, *39*, 1751–1752. [CrossRef]
7. Pitman, J.; Yor, M.A. decomposition of Bessel bridges. *Z. Wahrscheinlichkeit.* **1982**, *59*, 425–457. [CrossRef]
8. McDonald, J.B. Some generalized functions for the size distribution of income. In *Modeling Income Distributions and Lorenz Curves*; Springer: New York, NY, USA, 2008; pp. 37–55.
9. Gordy, M.B. Computationally convenient distributional assumptions for common-value auctions. *Comput. Econ.* **1998**, *12*, 61–78. [CrossRef]
10. Gupta, A.K.; Nagar, D.K. *Matrix Variate Distributions*; Chapman & Hall/CRC: Washington, DC, USA, 2000.
11. McNeil, A.J. The Laplace Distribution and generalizations: A revisit with applications to communications, economics, engineering, and finance. *J. Am. Stat. Assoc.* **2002**, *97*, 1210–1211. [CrossRef]
12. Nagar, D.Y.; Zarrazola, E. Distributions of the product and the quotient of independent Kummer-beta variables. *Sci. Math. Jpn.* **2005**, *61*, 109–118.
13. Sánchez, L.E.; Nagar, D.K. Distributions of the product and the quotient of independent beta type 3 variables. *Far. East. J. Theor. Stat.* **2005**, *17*, 239.
14. Küchler, U.; Tappe, S. Bilateral gamma distributions and processes in financial mathematics. *Stoch. Process. Appl.* **2008**, *118*, 261–283. [CrossRef]
15. Zarrazola, E.; Nagar, D.K. Product of independent random variables involving inverted hypergeometric function type I variables. *Ing. Cienc.* **2009**, *5*, 93–106.
16. Nagar, D.K.; Morán-Vásquez, R.A.; Gupta, A.K. Properties and applications of extended hypergeometric functions. *Ing. Cienc.* **2014**, *10*, 11–31. [CrossRef]

17. Gaunt, R.E. Products of normal, beta and gamma random variables: Stein operators and distributional theory. *Braz. J. Probab. Stat.* **2018**, *32*, 437–466. [CrossRef]
18. Shakil, M.; Singh, J.N.; Kibria, B.G. On a family of product distributions based on the Whittaker functions and generalized Pearson differential equation. *Pak. J. Statist.* **2010**, *26*, 111–125.
19. Shakil, M.; Kibria, B.G.; Singh, J.N. A new family of distributions based on the generalized Pearson differential equation with some applications. *Austrian J. Stat.* **2010**, *39*, 259–278. [CrossRef]
20. Zakerzadeh, H.; Dolati, A. Generalized Lindley distribution. *J. Math. Ext.* **2009**, *3*, 13–25.
21. Lindley, D.V. Fiducial distributions and Bayes' theorem. *J. R Stat. Soc. Ser. B Stat. Methodol.* **1958**, *1*, 102–107. [CrossRef]
22. Johnson, N.L.; Kotz, S.; Balakrishnan, N. *Continuous Univariate Distributions*, 2nd ed.; Wiley: Hoboken, NJ, USA, 1995; Volume 2, ISBN 0-471-58494-0.
23. Lomax, K.S. Business failures: Another example of the analysis of failure data. *J. Am. Stat. Assoc.* **1954**, *49*, 847–852. [CrossRef]
24. Arnold, B.C. *Pareto Distributions*; International Co-operative Publishing House: Fairlan, MD, USA, 1983.
25. Stacy, E.W. A generalization of the gamma distribution. *Ann. Math. Stat.* **1962**, *33*, 1187–1192. [CrossRef]
26. Nakagami, M. The m-Distribution—A General Formula of Intensity Distribution of Rapid Fading. *Stat. Methods Radio Wave Propag.* **1960**, *1*, 3–36.
27. Beckmann, P. Rayleigh distribution and its generalizations. *Radio Sci. J. Res. NBS/USNC-URSIs* **1962**, *68d*, 927–932. [CrossRef]
28. Dagum, C. A model of income distribution and the conditions of existence of moments of finite order. *Bull. Int. Stat. Inst.* **1975**, *46*, 199–205.
29. Lévy, P. Calcul des probabilités. *Rev. Metaphys. Morale* **1926**, *33*, 3–6.
30. Gumbel, E.J. *Statistics of Extremes*; Columbia University Press: New York, NY, USA, 1958.
31. Treyer, V.N. Doklady Acad. Nauk, Belorus, U.S.S.R., 1964.
32. Hallin, M.; Ingenbleek, J.F. The swedish automobile portfolio in 1977: A statistical study. *Scand. Actuar. J.* **1983**, *1*, 49–64. [CrossRef]
33. Lee, E.T.; Wang, J.W. *Statistical Methods for Survival Data Analysis*, 3rd ed.; Wiley: Hoboken, NJ, USA, 2003.
34. Bjerkedal, T. Acquisition of Resistance in Guinea Pies infected with Different Doses of Virulent Tubercle Bacilli. *Am. J. Hyg.* **1960**, *72*, 130–148. [PubMed]
35. Ghitany, M.E.; Al-Mutairi, D.K.; Nadarajah, S. Zero-truncated Poisson–Lindley distribution and its application. *Math. Comput. Simul.* **2008**, *79*, 279–287. [CrossRef]

Article

Choosing Industrial Zones Multi-Criteria Problem Solution for Chemical Industries Development Using the Additive Global Criterion Method

Aleksey I. Shinkevich [1,*], Nadezhda Yu. Psareva [2] and Tatyana V. Malysheva [1]

[1] Department of Logistics and Management, Kazan National Research Technological University, 420015 Kazan, Russia; tv_malysheva@mail.ru
[2] Department of Organization and Management Theory, State University of Management, 109542 Moscow, Russia; n.v.barsegyan@yandex.ru
* Correspondence: ashinkevich@mail.ru; Tel.: +7-9272401653

Citation: Shinkevich, A.I.; Psareva, N.Y.; Malysheva, T.V. Choosing Industrial Zones Multi-Criteria Problem Solution for Chemical Industries Development Using the Additive Global Criterion Method. *Mathematics* **2022**, *10*, 1434. https://doi.org/10.3390/math10091434

Academic Editor: Víctor Yepes

Received: 20 March 2022
Accepted: 22 April 2022
Published: 24 April 2022

Publisher's Note: MDPI stays neutral with regard to jurisdictional claims in published maps and institutional affiliations.

Copyright: © 2022 by the authors. Licensee MDPI, Basel, Switzerland. This article is an open access article distributed under the terms and conditions of the Creative Commons Attribution (CC BY) license (https:// creativecommons.org/licenses/by/ 4.0/).

Abstract: The safe development of chemical industries requires adequate control of the environmental sustainability of the areas where enterprises are located. The purpose of the article is to develop and test a methodology for solving the multicriteria problem of choosing industrial zones for the development of chemical industries using the method of an additive global criterion. The novelty of the methodology lies in the multi-criteria and complexity of the tool and the presence of a statistical base, which allows it to be used for various socio-economic purposes at all levels of government. As the main research tools, the methods of multi-criteria selection of objects, one-dimensional data scaling, additive convolution of criteria, and methods of multivariate statistical analysis for verifying the results obtained and making a decision were used. The article describes the mathematical apparatus of the technique for solving the multicriteria problem of selecting objects by the method of an additive global criterion. The solution algorithm provides for a three-level integration of particular indicators using the methods of mathematical processing of an array of different-dimensional values. The procedure for selecting the vectors of the criterion space makes it possible to select industrial zones and obtain a global criterion using the additive convolution method. In order to test the methodology, the problem of choosing industrial zones for the potential development of chemical industries in the Russian region was solved. For the development of chemical production, industrial zones have been selected that are included in the above-average environmental sustainability group: Bavlinskaya, Nurlatskaya, Bugulminskaya, and Leninogorskaya. Tendencies of decrease in ecological stability of the zones, which have relatively safe industries on their territory but are adjacent to the zones of location of environmentally unfavorable industries, are revealed. The materials of the article can be used in the development of intelligent systems for monitoring and controlling the development of chemical industries, which allow monitoring the level of environmental safety of industrial zones, identifying sources of negative environmental impact with pursuing decision-making on the organization and planning of production systems in the territorial space.

Keywords: multi-criteria selection problem; additive global criterion; multivariate statistical analysis; criteria convolution; criteria vectors; industrial zones; chemical production

MSC: 62C25; 90B50

1. Introduction

Chemical enterprises, as open production systems, carry out an intensive exchange of production resources with the environment. Currently, when designing new chemical and technological facilities, insufficient attention is paid to assessment of ecology negative factors of an industrial zone impact. The territorial development of chemical technological systems should be carried out with continuous monitoring of environmental sustainability and balance of enterprises operation zones.

According to new Russian legislation, first category enterprises of negative impact on environment must obtain an integrated environmental permit to conduct their activities, including mathematical calculation and justification confirming production site environmental safety. In this regard, this study is relevant and has high scientific theoretical and practical significance.

Numerous works of foreign and domestic scientists are devoted to industrial zones development in conditions of negative impact of chemical industries on the environment.

The main research directions in the field of territories concept and principles sustainable development are determined by works of the following scientists. Zhou Y., Kong Y., Sha J. and others examined industrial structure modernization in the evolution of eco-efficiency in a spatial aspect [1]; Fernando L., Suarez M., Eugenia M. proposed a multidisciplinary model to ensure territories sustainability [2]; Chertow M., Gordon M., Hirsch P. assessed industrial symbiosis and infrastructure potentials [3]; and John B., Luederitz C., Lang D. et al. [4], Cui X. [5] proposed a concept and system model for the development of ecologically safe industrial zones.

The study of sustainable development possibilities in the western regions of China based on the DEA method is reflected in the articles of Niu D.H. and Gu Kh.Ch. [6]; the conceptual categorical policy toolkit for stimulating region sustainable development is considered by V.G. Polishchuk [7]; the preconditions and prospects for state regulation of state and region sustainable development of the state and regions were studied by A. Merzlyak and U. Vikhort [8]; and methodological tools for choosing a sustainable development strategy the region is reflected in the writings of Szabo, M; Chete M.S., Palvolgi T., Ye B.N. [9,10]. Russia regions example demonstrates socio-ecological-economic system and methodological aspects sustainable development model for assessment of factors affecting sustainable development in the publications of M.A. Dugarovich, D.E. Buyantuev, S.M. Reznichenko, O.V. Takhumova, and Filatova V.V. [11,12].

The problems of chemical industries environmental safety are widely considered in scientific works of researchers, chemists, ecologists, and process engineers. The fundamental concept of "green" chemistry belongs to the researchers Anastas P.T. and Warner J.C. [13], who proposed twelve principles of "green engineering" as the basis for sustainable development [14]. Co-authored with Zimmerman J.B., the principles of waste recycling are considered in the work "When is waste not waste?" [15]. The scientific team consisting of Vest S., Aguedo M., Anastas P.T. focused on the targeted modification of raw materials using green chemistry to produce high value-added products [16]. Under the direction of Falinsky M.M. for the purposes of sustainable development, they proposed methods of water purification based on nanotechnologies [17]. Golden J.C. and co-authors from the position of social security considered the trends of ecological trade [18].

A significant contribution to the modern development of low-waste chemical-technological systems at the world level was made by the Russian academician V.P. Meshalkin. Under his scientific guidance, a lot of works were created in theory analysis field and synthesis of energy-efficient environmentally friendly chemical industries [19,20] and methods of automation of systems for optimal control of chemical-technological processes [21,22]. Problems of efficiency, competitiveness and environmental safety of industrial production in Russia and Tatarstan are considered in the works of Malysheva T., Shinkevich A., Ostanin L., Dyrdonova A. and others [23–25].

Methods for solving multi-criteria decision-making problems are widely used by specialists in various economy areas. Approaches to solving such problems are described in the works of domestic and foreign scientists: Bezruk V., Svid Y., and Korsun Y. who investigated methods of multi-criteria optimization in planning and management of telecommunication networks [26]; Roy B. and Slouinski R. who proposed solution to multi-criteria problems with limited bandwidth and mutual exclusion [27]; Shi Ts. and Hao F. who developed a strategy for ranking the tasks of making multi-criteria decisions in social networks [28];

Bobs D., Pascual F. who applied multi-criteria decision analysis in medical substitution therapy programs [29]; and Nunez A. and Dondo J. who considered the possibility of resource planning for reconfigurable systems based on the multi-criteria method [30]. Approaches to solving problems of multi-criteria optimization in the construction industry, energy, transport complex, social sphere, regional economy are presented in the works [31–34].

Methods of multivariate statistical analysis are also presented in the literature in relation to various research problems including factorial, discriminant, cluster analysis, multivariate scaling, and other approaches. Wang Yu and Xu Ch. used statistical analysis to evaluate work with contracts in Chinese universities [35]; Yang Ch. applied multivariate statistical analysis in monitoring equipment condition [36]; Du V., Han Y. and Chen S. developed approaches to analysis with the preservation of confidentiality [37]; Gavrilko Yu.V. et al. demonstrated temporal multivariate critical attributes analysis of production process quality with data factorization [38]; and Qian X., Min Ch. and Huang X. applied multivariate statistical analysis to assess enterprises efficiency, a comprehensive assessment of regions [39,40].

Nevertheless, despite extensive theoretical and methodological data set and practical solutions presence, there is a lack of research that may solve diagnostics and a differentiated approach problem to the organization of production systems from the standpoint of industrial zones sustainable development. This leads to the fact that when designing chemical plants with complex technological processes without taking into account territories environmental sustainability, project environmental justification may be incorrectly presented, and this is important to consider when preparing documentation for obtaining an integrated environmental permit.

The developed toolkit has a high practical value, since it is necessary for chemical industries to obtain a comprehensive environmental permit for the operation of enterprises. According to the current Russian legislation, industrial facilities of the first category of negative impact on the ecosystem are required to assess the environmental sustainability of the areas of their location or planned expansion. Unlike previously existing methods, the proposed approach to solving the problem of selecting territories is a universal tool based on a ready-made database of state statistics. The novelty of the approach also lies in the multi-criteria and complex nature of the tool, which allows it to be used for various socio-economic purposes at all levels of management (enterprise, industry, region).

The purpose of the study is to develop and test a methodology for solving the multi-criteria problem of choosing industrial zones for the development of chemical industries by the additive global criterion method. The study includes three key sections:

- Development of a three-level multi-criteria system for chemical production development zones environmental sustainability assessment;
- Indicators of one to three levels of integration calculation for industrial zones, links analysis between environmental sustainability criteria K_1–K_4;
- Calculation of additive global criterion for environmental sustainability with the choice of industrial zones for the potential development of chemical production.

2. Methodology

To solve the problem of choosing industrial zones for chemical industries development, the authors have developed a methodology that provides solving the multi-criteria problem of objects selection by the method of the additive global criterion. Unlike the classical methods of multi-criteria decision analysis (MCDM), the proposed approach evaluates not only conflicting criteria, but also dependent causal criteria. Depending on the purpose of the study, each of the criteria can be used both in the general space and separately, taking into account weight coefficients. This choice is due to the specifics of the area of application of the methodology, namely the assessment of the environmental friendliness of industrial zones. Structuring complex problems and considering consistent criteria leads to more informed decisions.

As a rule, some solutions work well for one method, and some for others. In this regard, the proposed approach is an integration of elements of MCDM methods:
- Analytical hierarchy process (structuring the problem of selecting industrial zones into a hierarchy with criteria and alternatives);
- Scalarization of the vector criterion (scalar global criterion of environmental sustainability);
- Clustering of the numerical space (classification of industrial zones in relation to the value of the global criterion);
- Randomization of aggregated indices (convolution of single indices in a criterion).

Let us present a detailed description of the methodology for solving the multicriteria problem of choosing industrial zones for the development of chemical industries using the method of an additive global criterion. The multi-criteria selection method, unlike other approaches, is the most preferable for decision-making in conditions of multitasking, a multidimensional set of source data, the presence of two or more criteria for object management. It is with these characteristics that we can describe the task of assessing the environmental sustainability of chemical production development zones.

The transformation of selection problem into a one-criterion problem is carried out in several stages: by combining private local indicators (set $\{P_1, P_2, P_3, P_4 \ldots P_{48}\}$) into summary indices ($I_{11}, I_{12}, I_{13}; I_{21} I_{22}, I_{23}; I_{31}, I_{32}, I_{33}; I_{41}, I_{42}$) with subsequent convolution into criteria (K_1, K_2, K_3, K_4) and the general global criterion for environmental sustainability (ES_{KA}).

Note that each integral index I is assigned a number or place of this index in the set of indices. For example, "I_{12}", where "1" means that the index will form criterion No. 1 (K_1) in the future, and "2" means that this is the second index in the group of indices that form the criterion K_1.

The following well-known mathematical and logical methods were used in the methodology for industrial zones selection for chemical industries development:
- One-dimensional scaling (point assessment) method—for integrating a large number of different-sized parameters of environmental sustainability (indices In in the criterion Kn);
- Additive convolution of criteria method—for transforming a multi-criteria problem into a one-criterion one, including the definition of criteria vectors (K_1, K_2, K_3, K_4) and a procedure for filtering out the worst objects, as well as the use of weight coefficients (aK_1, aK_2, aK_3, aK_4) when folding the criteria (K_1, K_2, K_3, K_4) into an additive global criterion (ES_{KA});
- Correlation analysis of data method—to identify the direction and closeness of the re lationship between dependent criteria (K_2, K_3) and an independent criterion (K_2), that are in consistent ecological chain;
- Data clustering method (hierarchical objects classification by the method of single connection according to the criteria K_1–K_4)—to verify the results of industrial zones selection for the development of chemical production according to the classification scale of environmental sustainability global criterion ES_{KA};
- Expert assessment method—for assessment of environmental sustainability criteria significance and determining the weight coefficients based on vectors of preferences and focal objects method.

A total of 48 particular indicators were used for the sequential formation of the global additive ESKA criterion. Table 1 provides a detailed description of private indicators by criteria.

Table 1. Base of partial indicators for the formation of criteria for environmental sustainability of industrial zones.

Criteria	Particular Indicators
K_1 "Load on industrial zone ecosystem"	P_1—is the amount of pollutants departing from all stationary sources of discharge per person; P_2—the amount of pollutants departing from all stationary sources of isolation without purification, in % of the total amount of pollutants; P_3—formation of industrial waste per unit area; P_4—formation of industrial waste by hazard classes (1st class—extremely dangerous and 2nd class—highly dangerous) per unit area; P_5—availability of operating waste sorting complexes per unit area; P_6—the area of authorized landfills in relation to the territory of the industrial zone; P_7—the proportion of respondents who noted the problem of the presence of enterprises polluting the environment; P_8—the percentage of respondents who noted the problem of oil pollution; P_9—the percentage of respondents who noted the problem of outdated treatment systems; P_{10}—the number of vehicles per unit area of the industrial zone; P_{11}—mineral fertilizers applied per unit area; P_{12}—the specific weight of arable land in the structure of farmland; P_{13}—density of cattle per unit of farmland; P_{14}—livestock waste relative to the area of the industrial zone; P_{15}—is the percentage of respondents who noted the problem of fertilizers and pesticides flowing from the fields.
K_2 "Industrial zone ecosystem state"	P_{16}—caught harmful substances per person; P_{17}—disposed of harmful substances per person; P_{18}—emissions of pollutants into the atmosphere from stationary sources per person; P_{19}—emissions of air pollutants from vehicles per person; P_{20}—the share of respondents who noted the problem of exhaust gases from auto transport; P_{21}—is the proportion of respondents who indicated "wastewater entering rivers and lakes" as an environmental factor affecting health; P_{22}—the percentage of respondents satisfied with the quality of drinking water; P_{23}—discharge of pollutants with wastewater relative to the area of the industrial zone; P_{24}—the proportion of insufficiently treated wastewater; P_{25}—the proportion of wastewater without treatment; P_{26}—exceeding the maximum permissible concentration of pollutants in waters; P_{27}—soil quality; P_{28}—exceeding the maximum permissible concentration of exogenous chemicals in the soil; P_{29}—the average weighted content of heavy metal salts % in the total amount of the maximum permissible concentration; P_{30}—is the total indicator of chemical contamination of the soil.
K_3 "Industrial zone life quality"	P_{31}—is the average life expectancy of the population in the industrial zone; P_{32}—natural increase (decrease) in relation to the population of the industrial zone; P_{33}—the level of morbidity of the population in the industrial zone per population; P_{34}—neoplasms per population; P_{35}—diseases of the blood, hematopoietic organs and individual disorders involving the immune mechanism, per population; P_{36}—diseases of the endocrine system, eating disorders and metabolic disorders per population; P_{37}—respiratory diseases per population; P_{38}—the percentage of respondents who noted the absence of chronic diseases in children; P_{39}—the percentage of respondents who noted their health status as "Good", "Very good"; P_{40}—the proportion of respondents who noted being on "sick leave" 3 or more times a year; P_{41}—the proportion of respondents who noted the absence of chronic diseases in the adult population; P_{42}—the share of disabled people in the industrial zone; P_{43}—availability of sanatoriums per unit of population.
K_4 "Restoration potential of industrial zone ecosystem"	P_{44}—forecast operational resources of fresh groundwater relative to the area of the industrial zone; P_{45}—creation of protective forest plantations to the total area of the industrial zone; P_{46}—the share of forest plantations in the total area of the industrial zone; P_{47}—current environmental protection costs relative to the area of the industrial zone; P_{48}—the cost of capital repairs of fixed assets for environmental protection relative to the area of the industrial zone.

Solving the problem of choosing industrial zones for chemical production development involves seven sequential steps. The algorithm for solving a multi-criteria problem by the additive global criterion method is visualized in Figure 1.

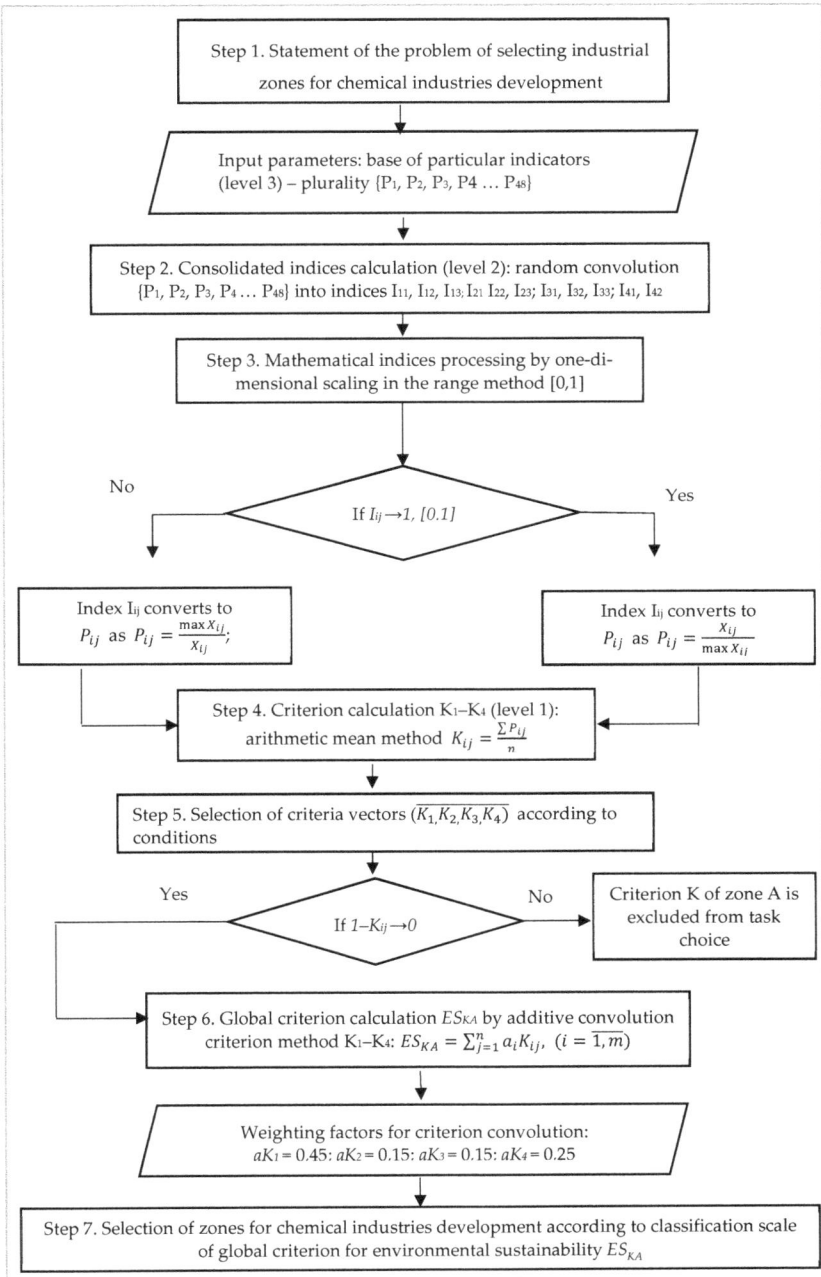

Figure 1. Algorithm for solving the multi-criteria problem of choosing industrial zones for chemical industries development using the additive global criterion method.

The technique for solving the problem is as follows:

Step 1. The task of selecting industrial zones for the development of chemical industries is being formulated. The input parameters or indicators of the third level of integration are determined—the base of private indicators representing a set $\{P_1, P_2, P_3, P_4 \ldots P_{48}\}$ in industrial zones (A_1–A_{11}).

Step 2. Composite indices (level 2 indicators) are calculated by arbitrary convolution of private indicators $\{P_1, P_2, P_3, P_4 \ldots P_{48}\}$ to composite indices $I_{11}, I_{12}, I_{13}; I_{21}, I_{22}, I_{23}; I_{31}, I_{32}, I_{33}; I_{41}, I_{42}$.

Step 3. Environmental sustainability different-sized indices array by one-dimensional scaling method is converted into one-dimensional indicators within the range [0,1]. At the same time, primary multi-directionality of indicators is leveled: the essence of the indices improves as their value approaches 1.

Step 4. On the basis of one-dimensional indices of environmental sustainability, there is a calculation of K_1–K_4 criteria (indicators of the 1st level) by the arithmetic mean method.

Step 5. To make a decision on the choice of the most optimal according to criterion of industrial zones environmental sustainability choice, the vectors of criteria $(\overline{K_1, K_2, K_3, K_4})$ are its best values close to 1. Procedure for filtering out the worst objects in relation to vector values is undertaken.

Step 6. The global ES_{KA} criterion is calculated by additive convolution method of K_1–K_4 criteria. Since, for making a decision, criteria K_1–K_4 are not equal, they are assigned weight coefficients ai by carrying out the expert evaluation procedure.

Step 7. The selection of industrial zones for chemical industries development is made according to the global criterion for environmental sustainability classification scale ES_{KA}. Objects are classified into four levels of environmental sustainability (high level, above average level, below average level and low level), making it possible to decide on the choice of potential industrial zones for the development of chemical production.

Mathematical data processing is performed using Microsoft Office Excel software and the Statistica software package.

3. Results

3.1. Development of a Three-Level Multi-Criteria System for Chemical Production Development Zones Environmental Sustainability Assessment

The condition for industrial zones selection for chemical industries development is the ecological sustainability of the regions. Particular indicators and criteria were selected typical for regions with industrial complexes on their territory and most informatively reflecting the impact effect of unfavorable environmental factors.

According to the developed methodology 48 particular indicators (multiplicity $\{P_1, P_2, P_3, P_4 \ldots P_{48}\}$) form four criteria for industrial zones environmental sustainability of (K_1, K_2, K_3, K_4):

K_1—load on industrial zone ecosystem;
K_2—industrial zone ecosystem state;
K_3—life quality of industrial zone;
K_4—restoration potential of industrial zone ecosystem.

Accordingly, criteria K_1–K_4 are a certain function of the corresponding particular indicators:

$$\begin{aligned} K_1 &= f(P_1, P_2, P_3 \ldots P_{15}), \\ K_2 &= f(P_{16}, P_{17}, P_{18} \ldots P_{30}), \\ K_3 &= f(P_{31}, P_{32}, P_{33} \ldots P_{43}), \\ K_4 &= f(P_{44}, P_{45}, P_{46}, P_{47}, P_{48}). \end{aligned} \quad (1)$$

Private indicators information base is based on forms of state statistical observation, reports from relevant government departments, and on sociological surveys results. In view of the large data array on private local indicators, their list is not provided in the article.

view of the large data array on private local indicators, their list is not provided in the article.

The criteria for the environmental sustainability of industrial zones represent a dependent ecological chain, where the criteria K_1—independent, K_2—dependent, K_3—dependent, K_4—independent:

$$\begin{cases} K_3 = f(K_1, K_2, K_4); \\ K_4; \end{cases} \qquad (2)$$

or

$$\begin{cases} K_2 = f(K_1, K_4); \\ K_3 = f(K_1, K_2, K_4); \\ K_4; \end{cases}$$

or

$$\begin{cases} K_1 = f(P_1, P_2, P_3 \ldots P_{15}); \\ K_2 = f(P_1, P_2, P_3 \ldots P_{15}; P_{44}, P_{45}, P_{46}, P_{47}, P_{48}); \\ K_3 = f(P_1, P_2, P_3 \ldots P_{15}; P_{44}, P_{45}, P_{46}, P_{47}, P_{48}); \\ K_4 = f(P_{44}, P_{45}, P_{46}, P_{47}, P_{48}). \end{cases} \qquad (3)$$

It is also taken into account that environmental sustainability level of an industrial zone is closely related to the fourth criterion—industrial zones potential to preserve and restore ecosystem (K_4) at the expense of available natural resources and investment opportunities.

The calculation of K_1–K_4 criteria is carried out on the basis of a three-tier approach by sequentially folding the previous level indicators (Figure 2).

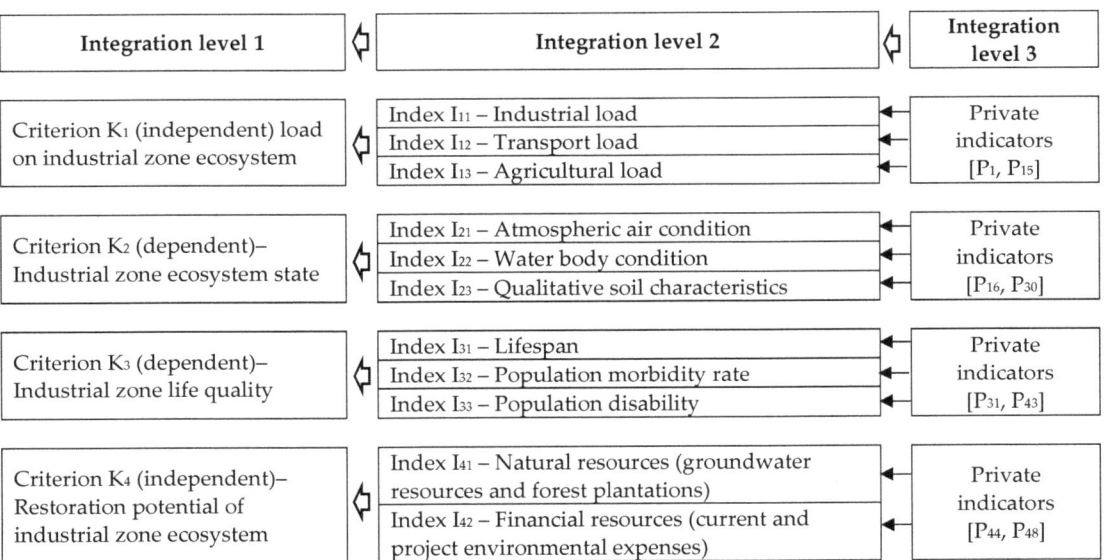

Figure 2. Multi-criteria three-level system for environmental sustainability of chemical production development zones assessment.

The task provides for the following levels of integration:

- Integration level 3—formation of primary private indicators (multiplicity {$P_1, P_2, P_3, P_4 \ldots P_{48}$});
- Integration level 2—calculation of second order indicators, where indices I_{11} (industrial load) are formed for K_1
- Second order indicators calculation, where for K_1 I_{11} (industrial load), I_{12} (transport load), I_{13} (agricultural load) are formed; for K_2—indexes I_{21} (atmospheric air condition), I_{22} (water body condition), I_{23} (qualitative soil characteristic); for K_3—indexes I_{31} (life span), I_{32} (population morbidity rate), I_{33} (population disability); for K_4—indexes I_{41} (natural resources (groundwater resources and forest plantations)), I_{42} (financial resources (current and project environmental expenses));

- Integration level 3—first order indicators calculation—directly, criteria for the environmental sustainability of industrial zones K_1, K_2, K_3, K_4.

Thus, multi-criteria task of selecting industrial zones methodology for chemical industries development is complemented by the formation stage of second-order indicators, that at the next step form criteria or indicators of the first order. K_1 "Industrial zone ecosystem load" includes the negative impact of industrial production as stationary sources, the transport subsystem as mobile pollutants and agricultural load due to land cultivation with chemicals and pollution of water bodies on the external environment. K_2 "Industrial zone ecosystem state" includes ecological characteristics of the environment-forming elements, namely the state of atmospheric air, water bodies, soil characteristics, including taking into account heavy metals content of salts. K_3 "Industrial zone life quality" includes life expectancy level, population morbidity and disability. This criterion is the final one in the ecological chain $K_1 \rightarrow K_2 \rightarrow K_3$. In this case, K_2 is a dependent criterion from K_1, K_3 is a dependent criterion from K_2. Criterion K_1 in this chain is independent. Criterion K_4 includes the industrial zone natural potential, taking into account the predicted operational resources of groundwater and forest plantations, and the financial potential expressed by the expenses level for environmental purposes, including for current needs and expenses for capital repairs of fixed assets for environmental protection.

The objects of assessment according to K_1–K_4 criteria are Republic of Tatarstan industrial zones with a predominance of petrochemical industries in the industrial structure (11 territorial units A_1–A_{11}): Aznakaevsky (A_1), Almetyevsky (A_2), Bavlinsky (A_3), Bugulminsky (A_4), Yelabuzhsky (A_5), Zainskiy (A_6), Leninogorskiy (A_7), Mendeleevskiy (A_8), Nizhnekamskiy (A_9), Nurlatskiy (A_{10}) municipal districts, and Kazan (A_{11}). Mostly, these are representatives of the Kama (processing enterprises of the chemical and petrochemical industry) and the Almetyevsk industrial agglomeration (suppliers of raw materials for chemical production, e.g., oil and natural gas production enterprises). The city of Kazan is characterized by large production facilities for chemical products and production of rubber and plastic products presence.

3.2. Indicators of 1–3 Levels of Integration Calculation for Industrial Zones, Links Analysis between Environmental Sustainability Criteria K_1–K_4

The second level indicators formation and directly the criteria K_1–K_4 themselves (level 1 integration) for the objects of assessment (A_1–A_{11}) is carried out by the method of one-dimensional scaling. This approach is used to integrate indicators system due to environmental sustainability parameters large number, as well as their diversity. The methodology is intended for the purposes of ranking industrial zones according to the criteria of environmental sustainability K_1–K_4.

The algorithm for calculating second level indicators (indices I_{kn}) and the first level of integration (criteria K_1–K_4) is as follows:

(1) The logical orientation of indicators is determined: some indicators are maximized (that is, with an indicator value increase, its essence improves), others are minimized (that is, with an indicator value decrease, its essence improves).

(2) At each stage of integration, due to different dimensions and different directions, the indicators are normalized on a scale from 0 to 1.

(3) If the indicator x_{ij} is maximized, then it is normalized according to the following formula:

$$P_{ij} = \frac{X_{ij}}{\max X_{ij}}, \ (i = \overline{1,m},\ j = \overline{1,n}), \qquad (4)$$

где x—previous level of integration indicator;
P—next level of integration indicator;
i—object number (industrial zone);
m—objects quantity (11 industrial zones);
j—indicator or criterion number;
n—given integration level indicators quantity.

(4) If indicator is minimized, it is normalized according to the following formula:

$$P_{ij} = \frac{\max X_{ij}}{X_{ij}}, \ (i = \overline{1,m}, \ j = \overline{1,n}). \tag{5}$$

Table 2 shows the matrix of the highest first integration level with standardized objects A_1–A_{11} and calculated environmental criteria K_1–K_4. All elements of the matrix are in the range [0,1], while the best or optimal criterion value is 1.

Table 2. Matrix of criteria for environmental sustainability assessment of industrial zones (level of integration 1) with the allocation of criteria vectors.

Industrial zones (A_1–A_{11})	Environmental Sustainability Criterion (K_1–K_4)			
	Ecosystem Load (K_1)	Ecosystem State (K_2)	Life Quality (K_3)	Ecosystem Restoration Potential (K_4)
Aznakaevskaya (A_1)	0.39	0.37	0.42	0.49
Almetyevskaya (A_2)	0.35	0.29	0.68	0.35
Bavlinskaya (A_3)	0.65	0.59	0.65	0.73
Bugulminskaya (A_4)	0.63	0.54	0.65	0.61
Yelabugskaya (A_5)	0.52	0.37	0.44	0.37
Zainskaya (A_6)	0.55	0.34	0.45	0.34
Leninogorskaya (A_7)	0.52	0.61	0.58	0.71
Mendeleevskaya (A_8)	0.41	0.38	0.32	0.31
Nignekamskaya (A_9)	0.32	0.27	0.49	0.27
Nurlatskaya (A_{10})	0.61	0.65	0.61	0.62
Kazan (A_{11})	0.51	0.64	0.41	0.42
Optimal values	max	max	max	max
Criterion vectors	0.65; 0.63	0.65; 0.64	0.68; 0.65	0.73; 0.71

The gray cells in the table contain criteria vectors.

The pair correlation coefficient according to K_1–K_2 criteria shows a fairly strong direct dependence of the industrial zone ecosystem state on the industrial load on it (the tightness of the relationship $Kkor = 0.74$). At the same time, the criteria dependence is not absolutely linear, which is confirmed graphically on the concentration diagram "Industrial zone ecosystem load—Industrial zone ecosystem state" (Figure 3).

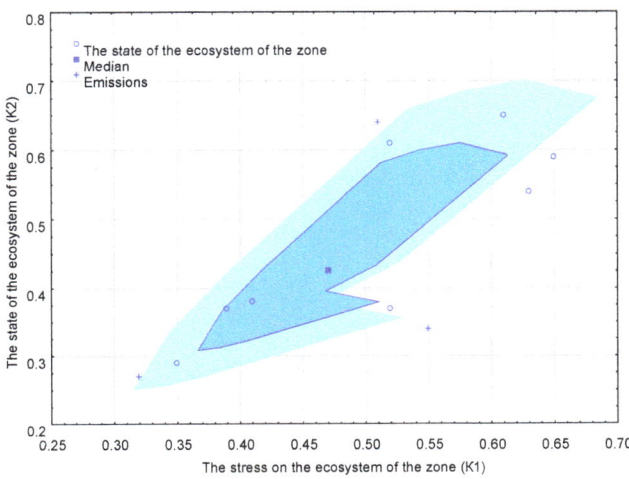

Figure 3. Criterion concentration chart K_1–K_2 "Industrial zone ecosystem load—Industrial zone ecosystem state".

The diagram shows individual points—emissions from the concentration zone, characteristic of industrial zones that do not have a high environmental load due to the specifics and scale of petrochemical industries, but adjacent to disadvantaged areas. For example, the Yelabuga industrial zone (A_5), located in close proximity to a large

The diagram shows individual points—emissions from the concentration zone, characteristic of industrial zones that do not have a high environmental load due to the specifics and scale of petrochemical industries, but adjacent to disadvantaged areas. For example, the Yelabuga industrial zone (A_5), located in close proximity to a large petrochemical center—the city of Nizhnekamsk: with a relatively favorable level of industrial load of 0.52, the state of the ecosystem is 0.37.

Weak relationship is observed between the criteria K_1–K_3 "Industrial zone ecosystem load—Industrial zone life quality" (tightness of connection *Kkor* = 0.37) (Figure 4). We believe that the formation of a criterion for industrial zone life quality is influenced by a number of other factors related, inter alia, by health care system characteristics. One of the emission points on the concentration diagram is the Almetyevsk industrial zone, where, against the background of an unfavorable load (0.35) and the state of the environment (0.29), a fairly high level of life quality (0.68) is observed, probably due to the presence of medical institutions of the largest oil company.

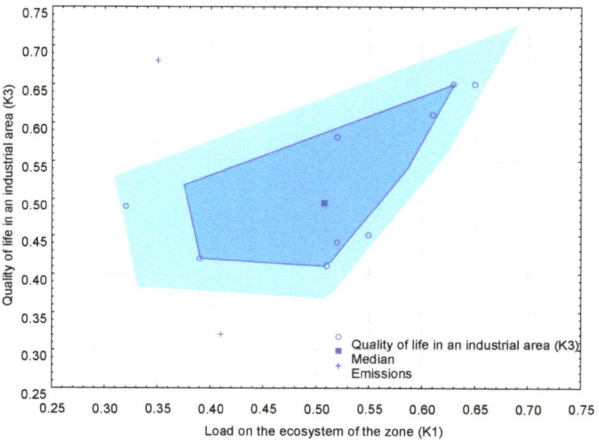

Figure 4. Criterion concentration chart K_1–K_3 «Industrial zone ecosystem load—Industrial zone life quality».

3.3. Calculation of Additive Global Criterion for Environmental Sustainability with the Choice of Industrial Zones for the Potential Development of Chemical Production

To make a decision on the choice of the most optimal industrial zones for potential development of chemical industries, let us single out the vectors of environmental sustainability criteria—the best values close to 1. These are most likely the Bavlinskaya (A_3) and Bugulminskaya (A_4) industrial zones, where in the first case three vector criterion (K_1, K_3, K_4), in the second—two vector criteria (K_1, K_3).

In case of multi-criteria problems, before proceeding to a single-criterion problem, a procedure is performed to filter out the worst objects with respect to vector values. Nevertheless, the purpose of our solution is not only to select the optimal industrial zones for petrochemical industries potential development, according to the criterion of environmental sustainability, but also to assess the impact of enterprises on ecosystem state and life quality in the territories. In addition, certain optimal zones (Bavlinskaya, Bugulminskaya) based on the feature of vector criteria require confirmation, since not all of the four criteria have vector significance. Furthermore, the importance of K_1–K_4 criteria is not equivalent for making a decision that will be discussed below.

In this regard, we will convolve criteria K_1–K_4 for all studied objects A_1–A_{11}. Let us accept the condition that for making a decision, the criteria K_1–K_4 are not equal and are assigned to the corresponding weight coefficients a_i by carrying out the expert evaluation procedure:

$$\sum a_i = 1, \text{ that is } 0.45 + 0.15 + 0.15 + 0.25 = 1.$$

$$a_1 = 0.45;$$
$$a_2 = 0.15;$$
$$a_3 = 0.15; \quad (6)$$
$$a_4 = 0.25;$$
where $\sum a_i = 1$, that is $0.45 + 0.15 + 0.15 + 0.25 = 1$.

The expert decision on assigning weight coefficients to the criteria is based on the opinions of six specialists—representatives of the environmental safety services of petrochemical enterprises and employees of state structures in terms of managing and monitoring processes in the industry and ecosystem.

The survey of experts was conducted by the interview method based on the developed regulations for the collection and analysis of expert assessments. The development of expert assessments by specialists was carried out on the basis of the method of preference vectors and focal objects. Further, the examination of the received opinions and assessments of experts was carried out by comparing the obtained average estimates.

As you can see, the key criterion is industrial zone ecosystem load ($aK_1 = 0.45$), which we consider quite justified in view of the fact that K_1 serves as a "starting" link and "launches" the entire further chain of criteria. The second most important K_4, which represents the potential to restore lost environmental sustainability of an industrial zone ($aK_4 = 0.25$). Criteria K_2 and K_3, which are a consequence of the cause of K_1, have equal importance and weight coefficients—1.5 each.

The transformation of multi-criteria problem into a one-criterion problem was carried out by the method of additive convolution of criteria according to the formula:

$$ES_{K,A} = \sum_{j=1}^{n} a_i K_{ij}, \left(i = \overline{1,m}\right), \quad (7)$$

where ES_{KA}—integral criterion of environmental sustainability obtained from a set of criteria K_j on objects (industrial zones) A_i.

For the integral criterion ES_{KA}, scale of environmental sustainability of an industrial zone in the range [0,1] is proposed, corresponding to four sustainability states:

$0.75 < ES_{KA} < 1.0$—high environmental sustainability;
$0.50 < ES_{KA} < 0.75$—environmental sustainability above average;
$0.25 < ES_{KA} < 0.50$—environmental sustainability below average;
$0.0 < ES_{KA} < 0.25$—low environmental sustainability.

Table 3 shows industrial zones classification with chemical-technological facilities on their territory, according to the level of environmental sustainability. The convolution of K_1–K_4 criteria made it possible to obtain an additive global criterion and to group the industrial zones.

Table 3. Additive global criterion value for ES_{KA} environmental sustainability and industrial zones classification.

Industrial Zone Name	Integral Criterion Value ES_{KA}	Value Range ES_{KA}	Industrial Zones Environmental Sustainability Classification
No representatives in this selection		$0.75 < ES_{KA} < 1.0$	high environmental sustainability
Bavlinskaya (A_3)	0.661		
Nurlatskaya (A_{10})	0.619	$0.50 < ES_{KA} < 0.75$	environmental sustainability above average
Bugulminskaya (A_4)	0.615		
Leninogorskaya (A_7)	0.590		
Kazan (A_{11})	0.492		
Zainskaya (A_6)	0.451		
Yelabugskaya (A_5)	0.448		
Aznakayevskaya (A_1)	0.417	$0.25 < ES_{KA} < 0.50$	environmental sustainability below average
Almetyevskaya (A_2)	0.391		
Mendeleevskaya (A_8)	0.367		
Nignekamskaya (A_9)	0.326		
No representatives in this selection		$0.0 < ES_{KA} < 0.25$	low environmental sustainability

According to ES_{KA} not one of the research objects has been assigned to the zone of "ideal" high environmental sustainability. The situation is similar with the group of low environmental sustainability. Thus, all industrial zones are divided into the second and third groups with environmental sustainability above and below average. Furthermore, in the second group, there are mainly regions with oil-producing companies, in the third (i.e., the production of chemical and petrochemical products). Our earlier assumptions about the optimality of Bavlinskaya (A_3) and Bugulminskaya (A_4) industrial zones on the basis of 4 criteria are confirmed by additive criterion present calculations. We believe that industrial zones included in the group of environmental sustainability above average may be considered as optimal for the development of petrochemical industries: Bavlinskaya (A_3), Nurlatskaya (A_{10}), Bugulminskaya (A_4), Leninogorskaya (A_7) industrial zones.

To verify the results of industrial zones selection for the development of chemical industries according to the classification scale of the global criterion for environmental sustainability ES_{KA}, a hierarchical classification of objects is carried out according to the criteria K_1–K_4 by multidimensional clustering method. The method of single connection is used where the distance between observation objects is determined on the basis of the Euclidean metric. The distance (S_{eu}) between the values of K_1–K_4 for industrial zones (A_i) is determined by the formula:

$$S_{eu} = \sqrt{\sum_{i=1}^{4}(K_{Ai} - K_{Ai+1})^2}. \tag{8}$$

The results of cluster analysis confirm industrial zones distribution by the level of environmental sustainability, which is confirmed by the matrix of Euclidean distances (Table 4). Objects with a value of the Euclidean distance $S_{eu} \leq 0.18$ are included in the group of industrial zones of environmental sustainability above average; with the value of the Euclidean distance $S_{eu} \geq 0.18$ are included in the group of industrial zones of ecological stability below the average.

Table 4. Euclidean distances matrix between industrial zones when clustering objects by levels of environmental sustainability according to the criteria K_1–K_4.

	A_3	A_7	A_{10}	A_4	A_1	A_{11}	A_5	A_2	A_6	A_8	A_9
	environmental sustainability above average										
A_3	0.00	0.15	0.14	0.13	0.48	0.42	0.49	0.57	0.51	0.62	0.67
A_7	0.15	0.00	0.14	0.18	0.39	0.34	0.44	0.52	0.48	0.54	0.60
A_{10}	0.14	0.14	0.00	0.12	0.42	0.30	0.42	0.52	0.45	0.54	0.60
A_4	0.13	0.18	0.12	0.00	0.39	0.34	0.38	0.46	0.40	0.52	0.56
	environmental sustainability below average										
A_1	0.48	0.39	0.42	0.39	0.00	0.30	0.18	0.31	0.22	0.21	0.26
A_{11}	0.42	0.34	0.30	0.34	0.30	0.00	0.28	0.48	0.32	0.31	0.45
A_5	0.49	0.44	0.42	0.38	0.18	0.28	0.00	0.31	0.05	0.17	0.25
A_2	0.57	0.52	0.52	0.46	0.31	0.48	0.31	0.00	0.31	0.38	0.21
A_6	0.51	0.48	0.45	0.40	0.22	0.32	0.05	0.31	0.00	0.20	0.25
A_8	0.62	0.54	0.54	0.52	0.21	0.31	0.17	0.38	0.20	0.00	0.23
A_9	0.67	0.60	0.60	0.56	0.26	0.45	0.25	0.21	0.25	0.23	0.00

The presented classification of industrial zones according to the level of environmental sustainability is relevant at this point in time and may be mobile in dynamics. With a high degree of probability, it may be assumed that in the case of putting into operation low-ecological petrochemical plants in industrial zones with environmental sustainability above average, the territories may move to a worse group of environmental sustainability below the average. On the contrary, the modernization of existing production facilities, and the organization of ecological industrial chemical engineering systems with a corresponding decrease in industrial load on the territory may raise the level of sustainability to a higher one.

In this regard, we believe that the proposed and tested methodology for multi-criteria environmental sustainability assessment of industrial zones is relevant and practically significant for programs creation aimed for development of petrochemical complex at the level of state coordinating structures (ministries, departments), at the level of holdings or groups of companies (for example, in Tatarstan JSC Tatneftekhiminvest Holding, GC Taif). In turn, the further methodology development, taking into account the natural resource potential, seems valid. The study of financial resources in two projections—as pre-costs (for measures to improve technological processes in order to minimize the negative impact) and post-costs (costs for the elimination, neutralization and compensation of already committed environmental violations) allows you to justify the direction and feasibility of environmental engineering projects.

4. Conclusions

Achievement of the set goal of choosing industrial zones for chemical industries development made it possible to obtain the following scientific and practical results:

1. To solve the question of choosing industrial zones for chemical industries development, a method that provides for solving a multi-criteria problem of selecting objects by the method of an additive global criterion has been developed. The algorithm for solving the problem provides for seven consecutive steps, including the calculation of indicators of the third level (partial indicators), the second level (summary indices) and the first level (criteria) using methods of mathematical processing of different quantities array. The procedure for identifying criterion vectors space allows you to optimize the sample of industrial zones and to obtain a global criterion for environmental sustainability using the additive convolution method. The final algorithm step is objects classification according to the level of environmental sustainability, which makes it possible to make a decision on the selection of potential industrial zones for the development of chemical production.

2. A multi-criteria system for assessing zones environmental sustainability for the development of chemical industries of three-level integration has been developed. The assessment system combines 48 private local indicators into 11 composite integral indices with their further convolution into 4 criteria: industrial zone ecosystem load (K_1), industrial zone ecosystem state (K_2), industrial zone life quality (K_3), and the potential for ecosystem restoration industrial zone (K_4). The criteria for the environmental sustainability of industrial zones represent a dependent ecological chain. The objects of assessment according to the K_1–K_4 criteria are industrial zones with a predominance of chemical production in the industrial structure (11 territorial units A_1–A_{11}).

3. By three-level integration method of basic indicators using one-dimensional scaling of values and their linear convolution, the key criteria of environmental sustainability K_1–K_4 are obtained for the industrial zones under study. Pairwise correlation showed a fairly strong direct dependence ($Kkor$ = 0.74) of the state of the ecosystem of the industrial zone (K_2) on the industrial load on the territory (K_1) with individual emissions of points-objects from the concentration zone. A weak relationship ($Kkor$ = 0.37) is observed between industrial zone ecosystem load (K_1) and industrial zone life quality (K_3), which is explained by a number of other social factors and the indirect criteria impact. The tendencies of a decrease in the environmental sustainability of industrial zones that have relatively environmentally friendly production facilities on their territory, but are adjacent to the zones where environmentally unfavorable production facilities are located, are revealed.

4. The problem of selecting industrial zones for the potential development of chemical industries is solved on the basis of obtained additive global criterion for environmental sustainability. When transforming a multi-criteria problem into a one-criterion problem, the procedure for determining the criteria vectors, screening out non-dominated objects relative to the vectors, weighing the criteria during convolution based on expert assessment is performed. Industrial zones classification according to the level of environmental

sustainability relative to the value of the additive global criterion is made, which is verified by the method of clustering objects according to the set of criteria K_1–K_4. Industrial zones that are included in the group of environmental sustainability above average Bavlinskaya (A_3), Nurlatskaya (A_{10}), Bugulminskaya (A_4), and Leninogorskaya (A_7) are selected for the development of chemical production.

The practical significance of the results of the study lies in the need to develop methodological tools for enterprises of the first category in order to assess the negative impact on the ecosystem. The new legislation obliges chemical industries to assess the environmental sustainability of their areas. Approbation of the proposed tools clearly shows the practical applicability of the methodology and the multivariance of its use in the real economy.

Author Contributions: Conceptualization, methodology—A.I.S., T.V.M.; formal analysis—N.Y.P.; investigation—A.I.S., T.V.M.; data curation—T.V.M.; writing—original draft preparation—A.I.S.; writing—review and editing—N.Y.P. All authors have read and agreed to the published version of the manuscript.

Funding: The research was carried out at the expense of the grant of the Russian Science Foundation, project number 22-28-00581, https://rscf.ru/en/project/22-28-00581/.

Conflicts of Interest: The authors declare no conflict of interest.

References

1. Zhou, Y.; Kong, J.; Hankun, W. The role of industrial structure upgrades in eco-efficiency evolution: Spatial correlation and spillover effects. *Sci. Total Environ.* **2019**, *687*, 1327–1336. [CrossRef]
2. Fernando, M.; Suarez-Serrano, L.; Eugenia, M. Multidisciplinary loop for urban sustainability. *Rev. De Arquit.* **2019**, *21*, 76–89.
3. Chertow, M.; Gordon, M.; Hirsch, P.; Ramaswami, A. Industrial symbiosis potential and urban infrastructure capacity in Mysuru, India. *Environ. Res. Lett.* **2019**, *14*, 075003. [CrossRef]
4. John, B.; Luederitz, C.; Lang, D.; Wehrden, H. Toward Sustainable Urban Metabolisms. From System Understanding to System Transformation. *Ecol. Econ.* **2019**, *157*, 402–414. [CrossRef]
5. Cui, X. How can cities support sustainability: A bibliometric analysis of urban metabolism? *Ecol. Indic.* **2018**, *93*, 704–717. [CrossRef]
6. Li, L.; Lei, Y.; Pan, D.; Si, C. Research on Sustainable Development of Resource-Based Cities Based on the DEA Approach: A Case Study of Jiaozuo, China. *Math. Probl. Eng.* **2016**, *2016*, 5024837. [CrossRef]
7. Polishchuk, V.G. Conceptual categorial policy toolkit for promoting sustainable development of the region. *Top. Probl. Econ.* **2009**, *101*, 168–174.
8. Merzlyak, A.; Vikhort, U. Background and prospects for state regulation of sustainable development of the state and regions. *Balt. J. Econ. Res.* **2016**, *2*, 83–89.
9. Sabo, M.; Chete, M.C.; Palvolga, T. Sustainable Regions in terms of sustainable development. *Eur. Sustain. Dev. J.* **2018**, *7*, 395–411.
10. Ye, B.N. Methodological tools for selecting a strategy for sustainable development of the region. *Indep. Manag. Prod. J.* **2020**, *11*, 1803–1818.
11. Dugarovich, M.A.; Buyantuevna, D.E.; Alexandrovna, A.D. Model of sustainable development of the socio-ecological-economic system of the municipal formation in Russia. In Proceedings of the International Conference on Social Science and Educational Research (ACSS-SSTR 2015), Singapore, 6–7 November 2015; Volume 14, pp. 138–142.
12. Reznichenko, S.M.; Takhumova, O.V.; Filatov, V.V. Methodological aspects of assessing factors affecting sustainable development Region. *Mod. J. Teach. Foreign Lang.* **2018**, *8*, 70–80.
13. Anastas, P.T.; Warner, J.C. *Green Chemistry: Theory and Practice*; Oxford University Press: New York, NY, USA, 1998; p. 135.
14. Anastas, P.T.; Zimmerman, J.B. Twelve principles of green engineering as a foundation for sustainable development. *Sustain. Dev. Sci. Technol. Defin. Princ.* **2006**, *1*, 11–32.
15. Zimmerman, J.B.; Anastas, P.T. When is waste not waste? *Sustain. Dev. Sci. Technol. Defin. Princ.* **2006**, *1*, 201–221.
16. Vest, S.; Aguedo, M.; Anastas, P.T. Lignin Conversions for High Value Added Applications: Towards Targeted Modifications Using Green Chemistry. *Green Chem.* **2017**, *19*, 4200–4233.
17. Falinsky, M.M.; Turley, R.; Zimmerman, J.B. Proper Water Treatment Using Nanotechnology: Considerations of Sustainability from Design and Research to Development and Implementation. *Environ. Sci.-Nano* **2020**, *7*, 3255–3278. [CrossRef]
18. Golden, J.C.; Subramanian, V.; Zimmerman, J.B. Sustainable Development and Trade Trends. *J. Ind. Ecol.* **2011**, *15*, 821–824. [CrossRef]
19. Meshalkin, V.P.; Gartman, T.N.; Kokhov, T.A.; Korelshtein, L.B. Approximate mathematical model of heat exchange in a complex thermal engineering system of several product pipelines carrying a motionless isothermal product within a single insulating jacket. *Dokl. Chem.* **2018**, *481*, 152–156. [CrossRef]

20. Meshalkin, V.; Shinkar, E.; Okhlobystin, A. Logical-information model of energy-saving production of organic sulfur compounds from low-molecular sulfur waste fuel oil. *Energy* **2020**, *13*, 5286. [CrossRef]
21. Makarova, H.; Meshalkin, V.; Kolybanov, K. System analysis of the efficiency of imitation of processes of chemical immobilization of mercury in waste using multivariate visualization tools. *Theor. Basis Chem. Eng.* **2020**, *54*, 872–878. [CrossRef]
22. Meshalkin, V.P.; Shulaev, N.S.; Aristov, V.M. Physicochemical Basics of Energy and Resource Efficient Combined Technology of Wastewater Treatment of Soda Ash Production. *Rep. Chem.* **2020**, *494*, 145–148.
23. Shinkevich, A.I.; Malysheva, T.V.; Ostanin, L.M.; Muzhzhavleva, T.V.; Kandrashina, E.A. Organization challenges of competitive petrochemical products production. *Espacios* **2018**, *39*, 28–41.
24. Dyrdonova, A.N.; Shinkevich, A.I.; Galimulina, F.F.; Malysheva, T.V.; Zaraychenko, I.A.; Petrov, V.I.; Shinkevich, M.V. Issues of Industrial Production Environmental Safety in Modern Economy. *Ekoloji* **2018**, *106*, 193–201.
25. Malysheva, T.; Shinkevich, A.; Ostanina, S.; Vodolazhskaya, E.; Moiseyev, V. Perspective directions of improving energy efficiency on the meso and micro levels of the economy. *J. Adv. Res. Law Econ.* **2016**, *7*, 75.
26. Bezruk, V.; Svid, I.; Korsun, I. Methods of multicriteria optimization in planning and management of telecommunication networks. In Proceedings of the International Conference on Contemporary Problems of Radio Engineering, Telecommunications and Informatics, Lvov, Ukraine, 28 February–3 March 2006; pp. 381–383.
27. Roy, B.; Slowinski, R. Distribution of multicriteria tasks to heterogeneous processors with limited bandwidth and mutual exclusion. *Comb. Optim. Appl.* **2014**, *2*, 327–364.
28. Shi, Z.; Hao, F. Ranking strategy for the tasks of making multicriteria decisions in social networks. *J. Super Comput. Technol.* **2013**, *66*, 556–571.
29. Bobs, J.; Pascual, F.; Casado, M. A multicriteria analysis of decisions in opioid substitution therapy programs for opioid use disorders. *Adicciones* **2018**, *30*, 167–169.
30. Nunez, A.; Dondo, F.; Murdochka, M. Scheduling and Resource Scheduling Based on a multicriteria method for Partially Dynamically Reconfigurable Systems. *IEEE Trans. Lat. Am.* **2020**, *18*, 414–421. [CrossRef]
31. Zhao, L.; Tan, V.; Huang, L. Collaborative task distribution based on crowd using Multi-Criteria Optimization and Decision Making. *IEEE Syst. J.* **2020**, *14*, 3904–3915. [CrossRef]
32. Mitkus, S.; Trinkuniene, E. Analysis of the construction contract evaluation criteria system model. *Technol. Econ. Dev. Econ.* **2007**, *13*, 244–252. [CrossRef]
33. Jelohani-Niaraki, M. Joint spatial multicriteria assessment: Overview and directions for future research. *Int. J. Geogr. Inform.* **2021**, *35*, 9–42. [CrossRef]
34. Jakovljevic, V.; Zizovic, M.; Pamucar, D.; Stević, Ž.; Albijanic, M. Evaluation of Human Resources in Transportation Companies Using Multi-Criteria Model for Ranking Alternatives by Defining Relations between Ideal and Anti-Ideal Alternative (RADERIA). *Mathematics* **2021**, *9*, 976. [CrossRef]
35. Wang, Y.; Xu, Z. Statistical Analysis of Contract Fraud in Chinese Universities. *Mathematics* **2021**, *9*, 1684. [CrossRef]
36. Yang, C. How to Use the Multivariate Statistical Analysis Method in Equipment Condition Monitoring. In Proceedings of the 4th International Conference on Mechatronics, Materials, Chemistry and Computing (ICMMCCE 2015), Xi'an, China, 12–13 December 2015; Volume 39, pp. 176–181.
37. Du, V.; Han, Y.; Chen, S. Confidentiality-Preserving Multivariate Statistical Analysis: Linear Regression and Classification. In Proceedings of the 4th International SIAM Conference on Data Mining, Lake Buena Vista, FL, USA, 22–24 April 2004; pp. 222–223.
38. Gavrilko, Y.; Kurchenko, O.; Tereshchenko, A. Method for multi-dimensional statistical analysis of temporary multi-dimensional critical atri-butes of the quality of the production process with data factorization. *Radio Electron. Inform. Manag.* **2019**, *1*, 167–177.
39. Qian, X. Multivariate statistical methods the level of our comprehensive analysis of all regions. In Proceedings of the International Colloquium on Computing, Communications, Control and Management (CCCM 2010), Yangzhou, China, 20–22 August 2010; Volume 3, pp. 454–457.
40. Min, C.; Huang, X. Assessment of the economic efficiency of enterprises based on the method of multivariate statistical analysis. In Proceedings of the International Conference on Quality, Reliability, Risk, Maintenance and Safety (QR2MSE), Chengdu, China, 15–18 June 2012; pp. 971–974.

Article

The Allocation of Base Stations with Region Clustering and Single-Objective Nonlinear Optimization

Jian Chen, Jiajun Tian, Shuheng Jiang, Yunsheng Zhou, Hai Li and Jing Xu *

School of Mechanical Engineering, Yangzhou University, Yangzhou 225127, China; jian.chen@yzu.edu.cn (J.C.); jiajun_tian2022@163.com (J.T.); shuheng_jiang@163.com (S.J.); yunsheng_zhou2022@163.com (Y.Z.); hai.li200888@gmail.com (H.L.)
* Correspondence: jingxu@yzu.edu.cn

Abstract: For the problem of 5G network planning, a certain number of locations should be selected to build new base stations in order to solve the weak coverage problems of the existing network. Considering the construction cost and some other factors, it is impossible to cover all the weak coverage areas so it is necessary to consider the business volume and give priority to build new stations in the weak coverage areas with high business volume. Aimed at these problems, the clustering of weak point data was carried out by using k-means clustering algorithm. With the objective function as the minimization of the total construction cost of the new base stations, as well as the constraints as the minimal distance between adjacent base stations and the minimal coverage of the communication traffic, the single-objective nonlinear programming models were established to obtain the layout of macro and micro base stations in order to illustrate the impact of the shape of the station coverage area, the circular and the "shamrock" shaped coverage areas were compared in this paper. For the "shamrock" base station, a secondary clustering was undertaken to judge the main directions of the three sector coverage areas. Then, an improved model taking the coverage overlapping into consideration was proposed to correct the coverage area of different sectors. Finally, the optimal layout was obtained by adjusting the distribution of all base stations globally. The results show that the optimal planning method proposed in this paper has good practicability, which also provides a very good reference for solving similar allocation problems of dynamic resources.

Keywords: 5G network planning; k-means clustering algorithm; "shamrock" shaped coverage area; secondary clustering; single-objective nonlinear optimization model

MSC: 90C90

Citation: Chen, J.; Tian, J.; Jiang, S.; Zhou, Y.; Li, H.; Xu, J. The Allocation of Base Stations with Region Clustering and Single-Objective Nonlinear Optimization. *Mathematics* **2022**, *10*, 2257. https://doi.org/10.3390/math10132257

Academic Editor: Aleksey I. Shinkevich

Received: 4 June 2022
Accepted: 24 June 2022
Published: 27 June 2022

Publisher's Note: MDPI stays neutral with regard to jurisdictional claims in published maps and institutional affiliations.

Copyright: © 2022 by the authors. Licensee MDPI, Basel, Switzerland. This article is an open access article distributed under the terms and conditions of the Creative Commons Attribution (CC BY) license (https://creativecommons.org/licenses/by/4.0/).

1. Introduction

The location–allocation problem is a classic mathematical optimization problem that determines the best location for a facility to be placed based on geographical demands, facility costs, and transportation distances. They are widely utilized in many industries to find the optimal placement of various facilities, including public transportation terminals, power plants, polling locations, warehouses, and cell towers, to maximize efficiency, impact, and profit [1].

With the rapid development of mobile communication technology, its operation scale is getting bigger and bigger; the communication network is getting more and more complex. Especially with the arrival of the 5G era, the effective range that a base station can cover is getting smaller and smaller with the increase of the communication bandwidth. At the same time, with the increasing types of base stations and antennas, communication network planning—especially the site selection of base stations—is more complex.

Generally, base station planning is usually considered as a typical single-objective or multi-objective programming problem. The location and the configuration of base stations have to be chosen so that the majority of the traffic is served, while at the same time the amount of interference and multi-coverage is kept minimal [2]. During this process, the selection of the best location is only a decision variable. The ultimate goal of the selection is usually to achieve the shortest weighted distance, to minimize the cost of network construction, to maximize energy efficiency, or to obtain the optimal site layout scheme, while considering the optimal signal coverage.

For a given area requiring base station planning, a large number of weak signal coverage points scatter in this region. The attributes of each weak coverage point include the location coordinates and the mobile data traffic (the data volume transmitted over mobile networks). In practical network planning, it is almost impossible to cover all weak coverage points due to the prohibitive construction cost and the geographical constrains. Therefore, it is necessary to consider the volume of business and to give priority to the area with high traffic volume. Conventionally, when 90% of the total traffic volume in the area was covered, the construction scheme was considered to have met the deployment requirements [3]. Besides, the shape of the signal coverage domain is very important for planning the base station, but it is in general assumed to be a circle, and there are few discussions on planning the base station combining signal coverage in a "shamrock" shape.

The objective of this work is to build the optimization model of planning base stations in consideration of the actual shape of the coverage area. The main contributions of this paper are the following: (1) the clustering of weak point data was implemented by the k-means clustering; (2) two different single-objective nonlinear programming models were established to obtain the layout scheme of base stations; and (3) discussion and comparison of two cases with a circular coverage area and "shamrock" shaped areas.

The rest of this paper is organized as follows: Section 2 presents the previous work on base station selection. Section 3 introduces the preprocess of the original data. Section 4 shows the establishment of the single-objective nonlinear programming models. Section 5 discusses the obtained results. Section 6 concludes the entire work and gives an outlook for future work.

2. Related Works

In this section, we focus on related works about the optimization location–allocation problem of macro and micro base stations.

A variety of according analytical optimization problems were introduced by Mathar et al. [2] in 2000. Each was formalized as an integer linear program, and the optimum solutions can be given in most cases. When the exact solution cannot be obtained due to the complexity of the problem, simulated annealing was used as an approximate optimization technique. Besides, in 2001, Mathar et al. [4] also used discrete mathematical programming approaches to solve the frequency allocation and cell site selection problem in an integrated setup. The site selection problem of the base station was expressed as integer linear programming and solved by combinatorial optimization methods by which the two objectives can be solved simultaneously in a single programming step.

In 2003, a multi-objective optimization model for the antenna layout problem, which involves interference, traffic demand, area coverage, different parameterized antenna types and cell geometry, was proposed by Zimmermann et al. [5]. An evolutionary algorithm was presented to deal with more than 700 candidate sites in the working area.

Between 2003–2008, different mathematical programming models and algorithms were described by Amaldi et al. [6–8] for locating and configuring base stations in order to maximize the coverage and to minimize the costs. In 2006, Amaldi et al. [9] also outlined some of the most significant optimization problems emerging in planning second and third generation cellular networks. The main corresponding mathematical models were introduced, and some of the computational methods designed to solve these models were also briefly described.

The problem of site placement was formulated as an optimization problem by Khalek et al. [10] in 2010. The objective function, variables, and constraints were defined in this paper. Taking the base station location as a decision variable and the powers allocated to its designated users as a state variable, an algorithm using pattern search techniques was proposed and implemented.

The antenna placement problem involving locating and configuring infrastructure for mobile networks was studied by Fattouh et al. [11,12] between 2008–2011. Aiming at the problems existing in mobile network planning, a density-based spatial clustering algorithm combined with a cluster partition based on Medoids algorithm was improved.

For fourth generation (4G) wireless network base station planning, a multi-objective mathematical model was proposed by Mai et al. [13]. The goal of the model was to minimize construction costs, while maximizing coverage and capacity. In this model, factors such as orthogonal frequency division multiplexing, co-channel interference, reference signal received power, base station density, and cell edge rate were considered in detail.

An integer programming mathematical model with the goal of minimizing network costs was proposed by Selim et al. [14] in 2015 to study the location and the configuration of base stations in cellular mobile networks. The IP model was solved using the commercial software LINGO12.

In 2016, a multi-objective genetic algorithm (NSGA-II) that fulfills three criteria related to coverage, capacity, and total network cost was proposed by Valavanis et al. [15] by which the optimum location of base stations, satisfying certain coverage and capacity limitations in a cellular network size planning, was investigated.

The supplement problem of the capacity of existing in a network of macro base stations was studied by Iellamo et al. [16] in 2017 by dynamically placing a 5G network of small base stations in the form of unmanned aerial vehicles (UAV). Two clustering algorithms were proposed to maximize the capacity boost provided by the UAVs during each considered period and to extend the battery life of the mobile users served. Real Beijing downtown trajectory data was used for the numerical analysis, the simulation results show that the proposed algorithm has a good performance, and it can be used to realize real-time connection configuration.

Goudos et al. [17] focused on the efficient maximizing of the average user rate, average area rate, and energy efficiency. These three goals are in conflict with each other, and they require the use of multi-objective optimization techniques. So, a comprehensive optimization framework based on multi-objective evolutionary algorithms (MOEAs) was proposed in 2018 to solve such multi-objective problems in 5G networks and to achieve the best compromise solution.

A 5G base station deployment method considering cost and signal coverage was proposed by Wang et al. [18] in 2020. The optimization problem of 5G macro and micro base station location was proposed. Aiming at reducing the setup cost and strengthening the signal coverage, while deploying 5G base stations, an implementation procedure was carried out for the cooperative operation and the deployment scheme of optimizing the location of 5G heterogeneous base stations. The effectiveness of the proposed method was verified by a series of numerical examples, and the optimal deployment scheme for the number of macro and micro base stations was determined by cost-benefit analysis.

A multi-objective methodology for optimizing radio base station positioning was presented by Fraiha et al. [19] in 2021. The proposed methodology aims to improve the work of [20], with meeting the largest coverage and serving the largest number of users.

The comprehensive performance of 5G base stations was evaluated by Liang et al. [21] in 2022 from the perspectives of financial performance, operational performance, social influence, and environmental impact so as to clarify problems such as poor user experience and frequently insufficient coverage area existing in the construction of base stations. A mixed multicriteria decision-making model based on the difference quotient gray correlation analysis technique and the Bayesian best worst method was proposed. The results show that the signal coverage area and per capita investment costs are the most important indicators affecting the overall performance of the 5G base station.

For most of the planning methods mentioned above, the signal coverage domain was mainly simply assumed as a circle. However, in actual scenarios, no matter whether a macro or a micro base station, the signal coverage domain mostly has three sectors ("shamrock" shaped) and each sector points to a direction. In the main direction of each sector, the range of signal coverage points is the largest, the coverage of the area around the main direction roughly decreases in a nonlinear relation with the angle.

Based on the propagation characteristics of signals, Liu et al. [22] and Blanch et al. [23] have discussed the sector distribution shape of base stations in detail; the characteristics of base station sector antennas were investigated. The scattering surfaces were designed by Wu et al. [24] to improve the radiation patterns of the base-station antennas, thus improving the efficiency and the coverage quality of the antenna. However, their discussion was limited to a single sector of a single base station, and it did not consider the planning of three sectors of each base station. Furthermore, the overall construction plan of the base station was not discussed.

In addition, there is some research on transmission power distribution in wireless sensor networks. Wireless sensor network design requires a high-quality location and energy saving power allocations to maximize network lifetime and coverage. The traditional deployment and power assignment approaches is to optimize these two goals separately, or combine them together as one objective, or constrain one and optimize the other. Aiming at the problem of multi-objective deployment and power distribution, a decomposition-based multi-objective evolutionary algorithm was proposed by Konstantinidis et al. [25] to decompose the multi-objective optimization problem into multiple single-objective problems. The neighborhood information was simultaneously used to solve sub-problems. A memetic ant colony algorithm combining transmission power assignment with the network-coding-based-multicast routing was proposed by Khalily-Dermany et al. [26] to improve network efficiency.

3. Data Preprocessing

For the area selected in this paper, the range of horizontal and vertical coordinates is defined as integer numbers from 0 to 2499, which results in 2500 × 2500 points [3]. In 5G base station planning, two different base stations are mainly established: macro station (the maximum coverage assumed to be 30 in this paper) and micro base station (maximum coverage assumed to be 10). The coverage of base stations is the area after scaling and converting according to the actual situation. For convenience of subsequent calculations, the unit price of a micro base station is assumed to be 1, and that of a macro base station is assumed to be 10.

3.1. Selection of Weak Coverage Points

The construction of a 5G base station is usually based on the existing 4G base station. It is necessary to judge all weak coverage points in the studied area and to determine whether these points have been covered by the original 4G base station. For a given point, if the distance between the coordinates of the planned base station and the given point is greater than the coverage range of the base station, it is considered that the point is not covered by the base station; otherwise, it is covered. The data of 182,807 weak points (the coordinates and the business volume) as well as the location coordinates of 1474 existing base stations are provided by [3].

For convenience of calculation, the coordinate data of all weak coverage points before and after filtering are numbered. The coordinates of provided weak points are expressed as X_i, i represents the series number of each point assigned in sequence, $i = 1, 2, 3, \ldots, 182,807$. The coordinates of all points that still meet the requirements of weak coverage points after filtering are expressed as Y_j, j represents the series number of remaining points after filtering. Meanwhile, the coordinates of all old base stations are numbered and expressed as J_k, $k = 1, 2, 3, \ldots, 1474$. The distance D_{ij} between the coordinates of old base stations and weak coverage points can be expressed as:

$$D_{ij} = \|X_i - J_k\|, (i = 1, 2, 3 \cdots 1,882,807; k = 1, 2, 3 \cdots 1474) \quad (1)$$

If $D_{ij} < 10$, this indicates that this weak coverage point has been covered by the old stations, which is not necessary to be considered. If $D_{ij} > 10$, the corresponding X_i values will be assigned to Y_j and form a new coordinate data set of weak coverage points.

3.2. Filtering of "Noise" Points

For an ideal solution, it doesn't have to cover 100% of the traffic volume, further filtering of "noise" points was considered in this paper. The "noise points" here refer to the weak coverage points with low traffic volume, which correspond to the areas with few traffic users and poor traffic signals. Since the deployment scheme in this paper only needs to meet more than 90% of the business volume, reasonably giving up some "noise points" with very low business volume can not only simplify the data volume but also better meet the needs of the actual base station construction.

By deleting weak coverage points with service values ranging from 1 to 5 one by one, the ratio of lost service volume and the percentage of the deleted points were calculated. The results are shown in Table 1:

Table 1. Traffic loss results after filtering some weak signal coverage points.

Weak Coverage Points to Be Deleted	1	2	3	4	5
Percentage of the deleted points	31.1%	40.7%	47.0%	51.6%	55.2%
Ratio of lost service volume	0.26%	0.63%	1.03%	1.44%	1.91%

After several calculation attempts, the weak coverage points with service value lower than four were finally filtered as "noise points" in this paper. The comparison of weak coverage points before and after data processing is shown in Figure 1. After the above data preprocessing, the number of weak coverage points were reduced from the initial 182,807 to 83,841.

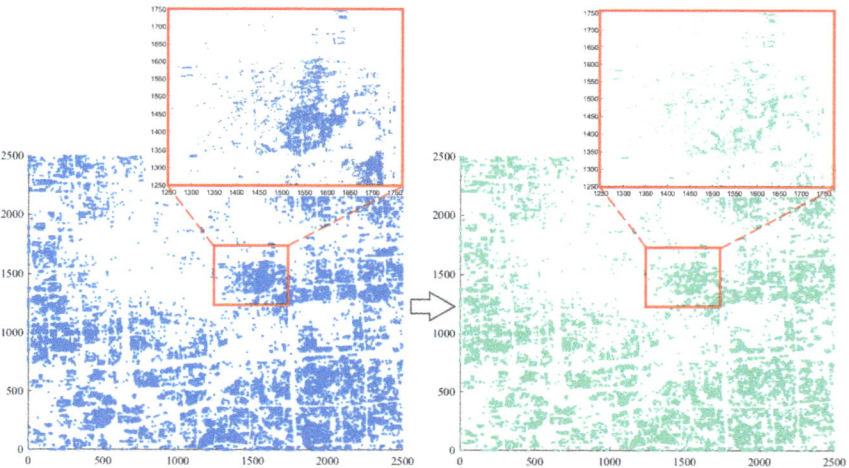

Figure 1. Comparison diagram of weak coverage point distribution before and after deleting "noise" points.

4. Methodology

Factors to be determined in base station construction planning mainly include three aspects: (1) coordinates of the site where the base station needs to be constructed; (2) the type of base station to be built; and (3) orientation of the three sectors of each base station. Considering that the judgment of the base station sector orientation is more complex than determining the base station type and location, two models were established in this paper to conduct a comparative study on this problem: (1) the location and type decision model of a single base station with circular coverage area and (2) the base station orientation decision model based on a "shamrock" shaped coverage area.

4.1. Decision Model of a Single Base Station with Circular Coverage Area

In this paper, the k-means clustering algorithm [27] was adopted to group the discrete weak coverage points and gather the small-scale weak coverage areas. The schematic diagram of 0–1 clustering planning model used in this paper is shown in Figure 2.

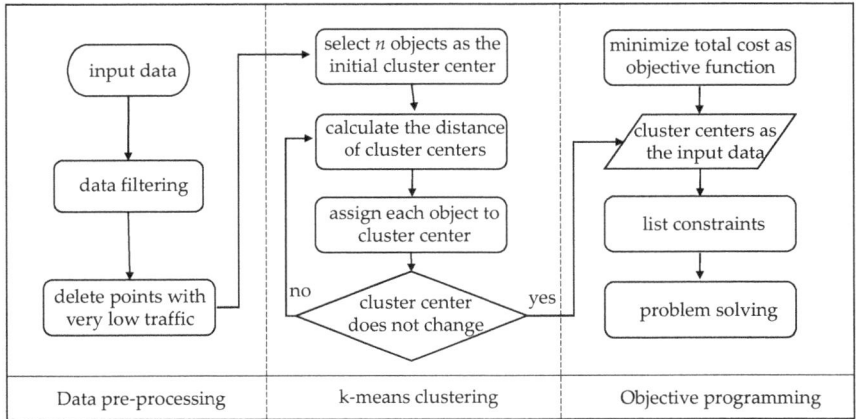

Figure 2. Schematic diagram of 0–1 clustering planning.

4.1.1. Classification of Weak Coverage Data Sets by k-Means Clustering Algorithm

As shown in Figure 2, the main steps of k-means clustering algorithm are: setting the number of groups n that you want to divide all data into; selecting n objects as the initial cluster center; calculating the distance from each object to each cluster center; and assigning each object to its nearest cluster center. At the same time, after each object is allocated, the cluster center will be re-determined, the final process is repeated until the set termination condition is satisfied.

(1) Determining the number of required clustering centers

In this paper, the ratio of the number of weak coverage points to the total number of points in the distribution area was denoted as the distribution density of weak coverage points, expressed by ρ.

$$\rho = M/Z \tag{2}$$

where M represents the total number of weak coverage points and Z is the total number of weak coverage points in the distribution area. In reality, only when the distribution of the base station is not uniform will the weak coverage point appear. Therefore, the distribution area of weak coverage points needs to be divided separately. A more scientific approach is to gather all the circular areas with radius 30 around the weak coverage points into a total area so that the area with a good signal can be excluded. On this basis, all ranges with the coordinates of the old base station as the circle center and 30 as the radius were further excluded. In this way, the influence of the old base station on the weak coverage area can be eliminated. The range obtained by the final filtering is the area where the weak coverage points distribute. According to the above process, the calculation was carried out, the distribution area of weak coverage points obtained is shown in Figure 3.

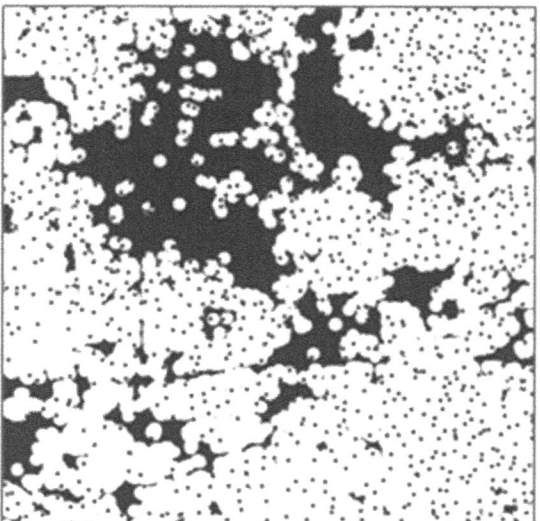

Figure 3. Distribution area of weak coverage points (the white area is weak coverage area).

The white area in Figure 3 represents the distribution area of weak coverage points, which contains 4,351,125 coordinate points. It is more accurate to calculate the distribution density of weak coverage points ρ by applying Equation (2).

After obtaining the distribution density of weak coverage points, it is necessary to estimate how many base stations are needed to cover all the weak coverage points evenly distributed in the region, under conditions of using both a micro base station with a radius of 10 and macro stations with a radius of 30. The calculation formula can be expressed as follows:

$$A = \frac{M}{S \times \rho} \quad (3)$$

where S represents the number of points that the base station can cover. The corresponding calculated average value of a micro base station is 317 and that of a macro base station is 2821. A indicates the number of base stations to be built. By substituting the existing data into the formula, we can get the number of two different types of base stations to be established. Then, we assign weights to the two types of base stations according to the actual situation. The number of clustering centers can be finally determined.

(2) Clustering of weak coverage points

If the number of the k-means cluster is known, clustering can be implemented. MATLAB was used for programming calculation. The clustering distribution results obtained by classification is shown in Figure 4. The clusters of points of different colors shown in the figure are weak coverage points assigned to a cluster.

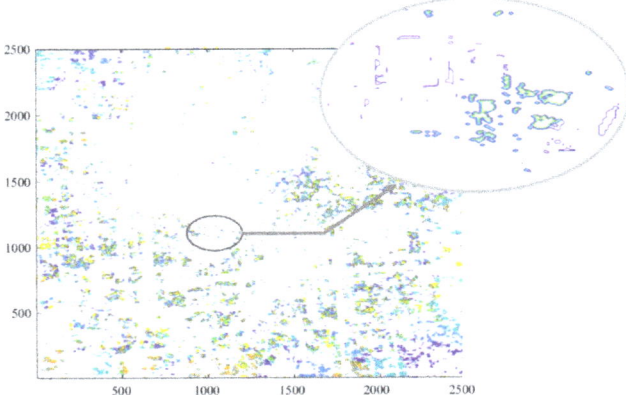

Figure 4. Distribution result of the weak coverage points after clustering.

4.1.2. Total Covered Business Amount of a Circular Coverage Area

After that, the problem was simplified to calculate the total traffic volume covered according to the site coordinates, quantity, and distribution of three known types of base stations (old base station, new micro and macro base stations). For different types of base stations, the method of calculating the coverage traffic is essentially the same. Taking the macro base station as an example.

Suppose that for a given macro station Z_i, its coordinates in Cartesian coordinates are (A_i, B_i), the weak coverage points in the circular coverage range are denoted as $R_j(a_j, b_j)$. According to the Euclidean distance formula, the distance d_{ij} between the weak coverage point and the base station can be expressed as:

$$d_{ij} = \|Z_i - R_j\|_2 \qquad (4)$$

Obviously, when the radius is greater than the distance between the weak coverage point and the base station site, this point cannot be covered, and the coefficient of the weak coverage point was assigned to 0; otherwise, the coefficient was assigned to 1.

$$R_j = \begin{cases} 1, d_{ij} \leq R \\ 0, d_{ij} > R \end{cases} \qquad (5)$$

Therefore, by summing all the business volume y_j covered by the base station numbered j, the total business volume S_j covered by all macro base stations can be obtained.

$$S_j = \sum_{j=1}^{n} R_j \cdot y_j \qquad (6)$$

Similarly, for the micro base station, the only difference is that the coverage radius of the micro base station is 1, while that of the macro station is 10. The total business volume S_k covered by all base stations can also be obtained.

4.1.3. Establishment of Single-Objective Nonlinear Programming Model

In this paper, the single-objective nonlinear programming model was used to determine the site deployment by which the theoretical global optimal solution can be obtained.

(1) Determination of objective function

Obviously, construction planning belongs to the planning model involving cost; the most common objective function for this type of question is to minimize the cost, while satisfying all constraints. Therefore, the objective function set in this paper is:

$$\text{Min } W = \left\{ 10 \sum_{i=0}^{n} a_i + \sum_{i=0}^{n} b_i \right\} \tag{7}$$

where W represents the total cost of building new base stations; a_i represents the situation of constructing macro station in the location with series number as i; b_i refers to the construction of micro-base station at the location with series number as i.

(2) Determination of the constraints

After confirming the coordinates of points that can establish a base station, three situations need to be discussed for each point: don't build a base station, build a micro base station, or build a macro base station. If a_i represents the 0–1 variable of a coordinate point to build a macro station; b_i represents the 0–1 variable of a coordinate point to build a micro base station. The 0~1 constraint can be expressed as follows:

$$\begin{cases} a_i = 0, 1 \\ b_i = 0, 1 \\ a_i + b_i \leq 1 \end{cases} \tag{8}$$

In the meantime, the distance between different planned construction base stations should also be limited to avoid overlapping coverage. A_m is used to represent the location of the new base station with series number m; A_n represents the location of the new base station with series number n; and the distance constrain can be written as follows:

$$\|A_m - A_n\|_2 > 10 \tag{9}$$

Finally, it is necessary to ensure that the signal area covers at least 90% of the total business volume. The constraint of business volume can be expressed as:

$$\sum_{i=0}^{n} \sum_{j=0}^{n} S_j \cdot a_i + \sum_{i=0}^{n} \sum_{k=0}^{n} S_k \cdot b_i + P_o \geq 0.9 \times P_t \tag{10}$$

in which P_t represents the total business volume and P_o represents the sum of all the business volume covered by the old base station.

4.1.4. Final Single-Objective Programming Model Based on Circular Coverage Area

Finally, by taking the total cost of constructing new base stations as the objective function, the 0–1 constraint to limit one base station built in each point, the distance between adjacent base stations is bigger than 10, and the signal area covering at least 90% of the traffic as the constraint conditions. A single-objective nonlinear programming model can be established as follows.

$$\text{Min } W = \left\{ 10 \sum_{i=0}^{n} a_i + \sum_{i=0}^{n} b_i \right\}$$

subject to (8)–(10).

4.2. Base Station Orientation Decision Model Based on "Shamrock" Coverage Area

In fact, the signal coverage of each base station is not circular. Most base stations have three sectors, each pointing in different directions. The sector has the farthest signal coverage distance in the main direction. It can be covered in a certain range around the main direction, but the coverage gradually decreases with the angle according to a certain law. In this paper, it is assumed that the coverage of the area around the main direction of

60° attenuates to approximately 75% of the maximum range. At the same time, considering the utilization of coverage, generally, the included angle between the main direction should be not less than 45° for any two "blades" of the same base station.

In order to determine the main direction orientation of the "shamrock" blade, three angle variables need to be introduced. Therefore, the polar coordinate system obviously has great advantages compared with the Cartesian coordinate system in the model establishment. Considering the huge number of base stations to be established in this paper, a polar coordinate system set was finally established, the poles of each polar coordinate system fall on the coordinates of the site where the base station is to be established. Subsequent discussions were taken at each polar coordinate system of each coordinate system set.

4.2.1. Proposed "Shamrock" Shaped Coverage Area Model

(1) Introduction of the area covered by the "shamrock" model

According to the previous description as well as the established polar coordinate system, a schematic diagram of the "shamrock" shaped coverage area is shown in Figure 5.

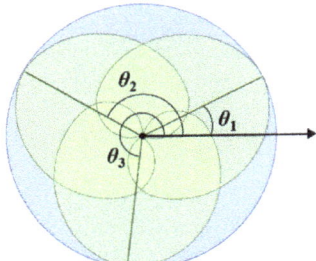

Figure 5. Schematic diagram of the "shamrock" covering model built in polar coordinate system.

The figure above shows a particular state of the "shamrock" coverage area combined with polar coordinates. The light blue circle area represents the traditional circular coverage area. The "shamrock" shaped coverage area is colored in light green. Different lines indicate the direction of the center of each sector. The three angles represent the rotation angle of each sector based on polar coordinates. It can be seen there are great differences in coverage areas between the two different models.

In this case, by determining the rotation angle of each sector at a particular pole, the state of the area covered by that pole can be obtained. Meanwhile, in order to ensure that the included angle between the main directions of each two sectors is not less than 45°, the following constrain should be met:

$$\begin{cases} \theta_2 - \theta_1 > 45° \\ \theta_3 - \theta_2 > 45° \\ \theta_3 - \theta_2 < 315° \end{cases} \quad (11)$$

Meanwhile, the relation between the real coverage area of a base station and the angle change value can be approximated as a heart-shaped line. Assuming the radius is ρ, the coverage area of any sector can be expressed in the following formula according to polar coordinates, where θ_0 represents the angle of a sector with polar axis rotation:

$$\rho = \frac{2\arctan|\theta| + \pi}{\pi}[1 + \cos(\theta_0 - \theta)] \cdot R \quad (12)$$

(2) Simplify data by analyzing coverage areas

The details for a sector of any "shamrock" shaped coverage area are shown in Figure 6:

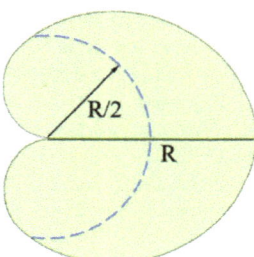

Figure 6. Detail of a sector of the "shamrock" shaped coverage area.

It can be seen from Figure 6 that in any case, a sector of 120° radian with radius $R/2$ can always be guaranteed to be fully covered. At the same time, under the given constraints, the three sectors of each base station will overlap, resulting in the central area also being affected by overlap. However, considering that the purpose of each base station is to cover as much business volume as possible, different sectors are distributed relatively evenly in most cases so that the area with $R/2$ radius as the center of each base station can be completely covered, as the shadow area shown in Figure 7:

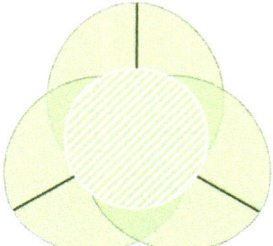

Figure 7. Idealized signal coverage diagram.

In the subsequent calculation, by default, for all base stations, it is regarded that the weak coverage points with a Euclidean distance less than $R/2$ can be fully covered. In this way, the number of weak coverage points needs to be discussed as they can be reduced theoretically, and the spatial complexity of the model can be greatly reduced.

(3) Determination of the main direction based on k-means clustering algorithm

According to the analysis above, the problem has been simplified to cover as many weak coverage points in the ring region as possible. A schematic diagram is shown in Figure 8.

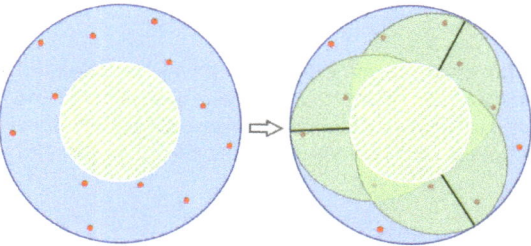

Figure 8. Schematic diagram of a ring signal cover region.

In order to determine the main directions of the three sectors and to cover as many points as possible, the k-means clustering algorithm was used again to separate all points according to the pole angle of the polar coordinate system. The number of cluster centers selected for this division was three.

It is assumed that the coordinates of the clustering center point obtained after calculation are M_m (a_i, b_i). Then, this point was connected to the coordinates of base station N_n (A_i, B_i); the obtained line direction is the main direction. The transformation formula can be obtained from the relation between the Cartesian coordinate and polar coordinate angle. θ_i was used to represent the polar coordinate angle of the "blade" with series number i in a "shamrock" model; the transformation formula can be written as follows:

$$\begin{cases} \theta_i' = \arctan\left(\frac{|b_i - B_i|}{|a_i - A_i|}\right) \\ \theta_i = \begin{cases} \theta_i' & , a_i > A_i, b_i > B_i \\ \pi - \theta_i' & , a_i > A_i, b_i < B_i \\ \pi + \theta_i' & , a_i < A_i, b_i < B_i \\ 2\pi - \theta_i' & , \text{else} \end{cases} \end{cases} \qquad (13)$$

For each base station, the clustering center coordinates of the three ring weak coverage points obtained by the k-means algorithm were substituted into the above formula, the optimal coverage distribution state of each base station after changing the shape of the coverage range could be obtained.

4.2.2. Solution of the Total Amount of Covered Business

According to Formula (13), the deflection angle of the weak coverage point in the polar coordinate system θ_{ij} can be written as:

$$\begin{cases} \theta_i' = \arctan\left(\frac{|b_j - B_i|}{|a_j - A_i|}\right) \\ \theta_{ij} = \begin{cases} \theta_i' & , a_j > A_i, b_j > B_i \\ \pi - \theta_i' & , a_j > A_i, b_j < B_i \\ \pi + \theta_i' & , a_j < A_i, b_j < B_i \\ 2\pi - \theta_i' & , \text{else} \end{cases} \end{cases} \qquad (14)$$

According to Formula (12), the radius length ρ corresponding to a specific angle in any sector can be determined by the formula:

$$\rho = \begin{cases} \left(1 - \frac{3\theta_0}{2\pi}\right) \cdot R + \frac{3R}{2\pi} \cdot \theta_{ij}, & \theta_0 - \frac{\pi}{3} \leq \theta_{ij} < \theta_0 \\ \left(1 + \frac{3\theta_0}{2\pi}\right) \cdot R - \frac{3R}{2\pi} \cdot \theta_{ij}, & \theta_0 \leq \theta_{ij} < \theta_0 + \frac{\pi}{3} \end{cases} \qquad (15)$$

For a macro base station, it is the same as the circular coverage area, according to the Euclidean distance formula, the distance d'_{ij} between the weak coverage point and the base station can be expressed as:

$$d'_{ij} = \|Z'_i - R'_j\|_2 \qquad (16)$$

Obviously, when the radius of the blade is greater than the distance between the weak coverage point and the base station site, the point cannot be covered, and the value of R'_j is assigned to 0. Otherwise, it is assigned to 1.

$$R'_j = \begin{cases} 1, & d_{ij} \leq \rho \\ 0, & d_{ij} > \rho \end{cases} \qquad (17)$$

Therefore, by summing all the business volume y'_j covered by the base station numbered j, the total business volume S'_j covered by all macro base stations can be obtained.

$$S'_j = \sum_{j=1}^{n} R'_j \cdot y'_j \tag{18}$$

Similarly, for the micro base station, the total business volume S'_k covered by all base stations can also be obtained.

4.2.3. Improved Model with Considering the Coverage Domain Overlap

After completing all the steps above, the model in this paper has basically realized the judgment of the sector orientation; but, in an actual situation it is necessary that the angle between the main directions of any two sectors not be less than 45°. In this paper, all sectors of a coverage area were numbered as 1, 2, and 3 in the counterclockwise direction. When considering the angle in the main direction, we need only to consider the angle between 1–2, 2–3, and 3–1. It is assumed in this paper that if the detected angle between the main direction is less than 45°, the former of the two sectors should be fixed and its angle remain unchanging, the angle increased to the critical condition by rotating the latter angle. At the same time, for the second blade, if the changing of the angle leads to the angle between the second and the third sectors being less than 45°, these two blades were gathered into a new group and the above operations were repeated. Obviously, the most extreme case of each "shamrock" requires only two rotations of the blades, as shown in Figure 9:

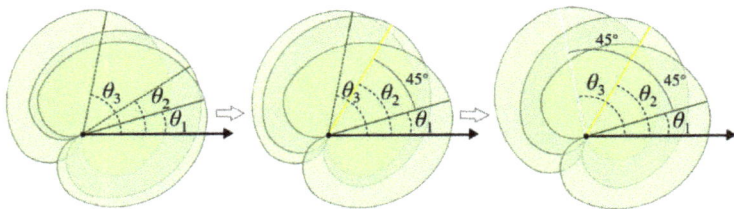

Figure 9. Illustration of extreme case correction.

Based on the above analysis, the formula of a regional overlap modification model can be expressed as:

$$\begin{cases} \theta_2 = \theta_1 + \pi/4, & |\theta_2 - \theta_1| < \pi/4 \\ \theta_3 = \theta_2 + \pi/4, & |\theta_3 - \theta_2| < \pi/4 \\ \theta_1 = \theta_3 + \pi/4, & |\theta_1 - \theta_3| < \pi/4 \end{cases} \tag{19}$$

Using the above method, the coverage area of the base station can be modified. Eventually, all base station coverage can be changed to a realistic "shamrock" state.

4.2.4. Decision by Using Single-Objective Nonlinear Programming Model

The same as the model built for a circular coverage area, a single-objective nonlinear programming model can also be established for "shamrock" shaped areas.

The objective function established was:

$$\text{Min } W' = \left\{ 10 \sum_{i=0}^{n} a'_i + \sum_{i=0}^{n} b'_i \right\} \tag{20}$$

where W' represents the total cost of building new base stations; a'_i represents the situation of constructing a macro station in the location with a series number as i; and b'_i refers to the construction of a micro-base station at the location with a series number as i. All constraints can be determined as:

Judging whether to build base station and the type of base station to be built:

$$\begin{cases} a'_i = 0, 1 \\ b'_i = 0, 1 \\ a'_i + b'_i \leq 1 \end{cases} \tag{21}$$

Constrain used to avoid overlapping coverage:

$$\|A'_m - A'_n\|_2 > 10 \tag{22}$$

Constraints on region overlap modification:

$$\begin{cases} \theta_2 = \theta_1 + \pi/4, \ |\theta_2 - \theta_1| < \pi/4 \\ \theta_3 = \theta_2 + \pi/4, \ |\theta_3 - \theta_2| < \pi/4 \\ \theta_1 = \theta_3 + \pi/4, \ |\theta_1 - \theta_3| < \pi/4 \end{cases}$$

Also, to ensure that the signal area covers at least 90% of the total business volume:

$$\sum_{i=0}^{n}\sum_{j=0}^{n} S'_j \cdot a'_i + \sum_{i=0}^{n}\sum_{k=0}^{n} S'_k \cdot b'_i + P_o \geq 0.9 \times P_t \tag{23}$$

4.2.5. Final Model Based on "Shamrock" Shaped Coverage Area

Finally, for the "shamrock" shaped coverage area, the single-objective nonlinear programming model can be established as follows.

$$\text{Min } W' = \left\{ 10\sum_{i=0}^{n} a'_i + \sum_{i=0}^{n} b'_i \right\}$$

subject to Equations (19), (21)–(23).

For this proposed model, the objective function and the constraints are very clear. The commercial optimization modelling software, LINGO 18, can be used to find the optimal layout scheme and the least cost.

5. Results and Discussion

A flow chart of planning the base station is shown in Figure 10. The whole solving process of this paper can be divided into three main steps: (1) data preprocessing and K-means clustering by using MATLAB software; (2) based on the data processed by MATLAB, LINGO was used for the programming solution to obtain the minimum cost and the location of the base station, two different approaches based on the circular and the "shamrock" shaped coverage areas were presented, respectively; and (3) according to the results of LINGO, MATLAB was used again to draw the position of the base station in the region to be planned.

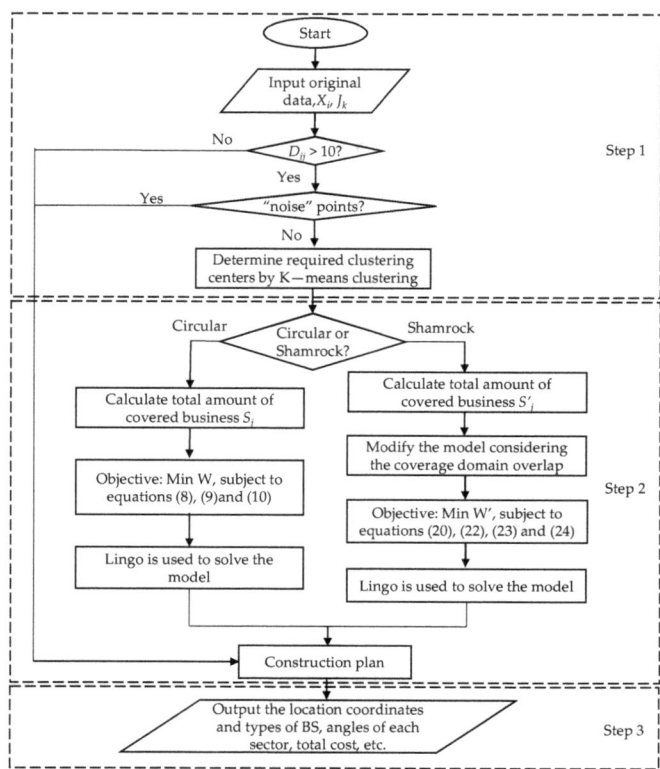

Figure 10. Flow chart of proposed algorithm.

5.1. Solution of Single Base Station with Circular Coverage Area

Based on the single-objective linear programming model established in Section 4.1 (Equations (7)–(10)) as well as the flow chart shown in Figure 10, the optimal layout scheme and the least cost can be calculated. According to the result, 8856 micro base stations are to be built and the number of macro stations is 412, which covers 6,599,691 businesses and accounts for 93.53% of the total business volume, the nominal cost is 10,092.

For a detailed construction plan, it is necessary to determine the coordinates and types of base stations to be constructed. Considering the huge amount of data, only 20 results are listed in this paper, as shown in Table 2.

Table 2. Part results of the location coordinates and types of base stations needed to be established.

Series Number	X Coordinates	Y Coordinates	Type	Series Number	X Coordinates	Y Coordinates	Type
1	1985	1495	Micro BS	11	493	629	Micro BS
2	1662	1191	Micro BS	12	540	438	Micro BS
3	1501	1501	Micro BS	13	1641	1153	Micro BS
4	1532	241	Micro BS	14	1836	1331	Micro BS
5	218	2328	Micro BS	15	158	929	Micro BS
6	1009	1009	Micro BS	16	168	2006	Micro BS
7	1228	963	Macro BS	17	555	282	Micro BS
8	1864	1528	Micro BS	18	1733	656	Micro BS
9	602	1024	Micro BS	19	1637	667	Macro BS
10	914	671	Micro BS	20	1867	1325	Micro BS

5.2. Solution Based on "Shamrock" Shaped Coverage Area Model

Similarly, according to Equations (19)–(23) as well as the flow chart shown in Figure 10, it can be obtained that a total of 9043 micro base stations and 437 macro stations need to be established, which covers 6,499,493 businesses and accounts for 92.11% of the total business volume, the total nominal cost is 10,530. Results of 10 base stations are listed in Table 3.

Table 3. Part results of the location coordinates and types of base stations needed to be established.

Serial Number	X Coordinates	Y Coordinates	Type	θ_1	θ_2	θ_3
1	309	1486	Micro BS	42°	148°	284°
2	77	1299	Micro BS	17°	151°	240°
3	1905	127	Micro BS	103°	228°	324°
4	2464	1539	Micro BS	95°	197°	282°
5	1063	438	Micro BS	51°	166°	268°
6	1838	1838	Micro BS	7°	133°	226°
7	2338	741	Micro BS	22°	152°	248°
8	2212	1062	Macro BS	65°	165°	255°
9	1889	2420	Micro BS	26°	142°	234°
10	1955	128	Micro BS	49°	133°	267°

It can be seen from Table 3 that based on the proposed model, both the coordinates and the angles of all sectors can be obtained.

5.3. Discussion

According to the above method, the optimal plannings of base station construction for both circular and "shamrock" shaped coverage areas were calculated, respectively, the comparison results are shown in Figure 11.

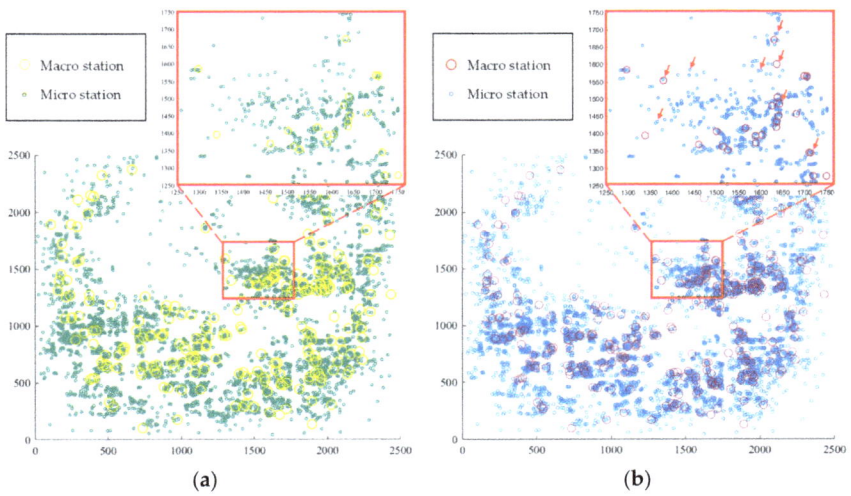

Figure 11. Diagrams showing the locations and the types of base stations need to be constructed. (**a**) shows— the results based on a circular coverage area, the big circles with ochre yellow are the macro stations, and the dark green circles are the positions of the micro stations. (**b**) shows the results based on the "shamrock" shaped coverage area, the big red circles are the macro stations and the blue circles are the positions of the micro stations. The red arrows in the zoom window shows part of the differences compared with the corresponding positions in (**a**).

For the results based on a circular coverage area, the number of macro stations needed to be built is 8856, the number of micro stations is 412, and the nominal cost is 10,092. For the results based on the "shamrock" shaped coverage area, the numbers of macro and micro stations are 9102 and 476, respectively, and the total nominal cost is 10,530.

According to the results of the two methods, it can be found that the number of base station planning using the "shamrock" shaped coverage area algorithm increased slightly, and it results in a slight increase in cost compared with the circular coverage area. However, since the two coverage models have very different coverage areas, the improved "shamrock" model proposed in this paper can effectively reduce the occurrence of repeated coverage, which is also more reasonable.

6. Conclusions

Firstly, the complexity of calculation is configurable by multi-step data filtering. The stepwise design of the model greatly improves the degree of flexibility. The available scenarios of the model can be broadened by adjusting parameters, which also makes the adjustment of the model more convenient.

Secondly, in order to get closer to reality, the "shamrock" shaped of the coverage area model was used in comparison with the circular coverage area model. When determining the sector orientation of the "shamrock" coverage area model, a k-means clustering algorithm was introduced again in a small range. These changes make the planning of base station construction more reasonable with the observation that the final signal coverage is more uniform and the overlapping waste of signal coverage domain is reduced.

Thirdly, single-objective nonlinear programming was used to plan the base station construction. This method permits finding the global optimal solution theoretically, but the disadvantage is the excessive demand on computing power. The model used in this paper can be further extended to a multi-objective function so that more evaluation indicators can be taken into account; the model will be much closer to the real situation.

Finally, some factors related to propagation, such as shadowing or effects related to antenna radiation patterns, were not taken into account in this paper, which can have a detrimental effect on coverage in certain points. These factors are left for future study.

This model is mainly based on clustering of a large dataset sample and optimization based on density distribution for resource allocation problems. Although the capacity of the model is manifested by the special case of the base station construction planning, theoretically, this model can also be used to solve various problems related to dynamic resource allocation regulation with a wide range of application scenarios.

Author Contributions: Conceptualization, J.C.; methodology, J.C.; software, J.T. and S.J.; validation, J.C., J.T. and S.J.; formal analysis, J.C. and S.J.; investigation, J.C. and Y.Z.; resources, J.C.; data curation, J.C. and J.T.; writing—original draft preparation, J.C., J.T. and S.J.; writing—review and editing, J.C., J.X. and H.L.; visualization, J.T.; supervision, J.X. and H.L.; project administration, J.X.; funding acquisition, J.C. and J.X. All authors have read and agreed to the published version of the manuscript.

Funding: This research was funded by the National Natural Science Foundation of China (Grant Number: 52105344), the Natural Science Foundation of Jiangsu Province (Grant Number: BK20190873), the Postgraduate Education Reform Project of Yangzhou University (Grant Number: JGLX2021_002), the Undergraduate Education Reform Project of Yangzhou University (Special Funding for Mathematical Contest in Modeling) (Grant Number: xkjs2022002), as well as the Lvyang Jinfeng Plan for Excellent Doctors of Yangzhou City.

Institutional Review Board Statement: The study was conducted according to the guidelines of the Declaration of Helsinki, and it was approved by the Ethics Committee of the Military Institute of Aviation Medicine (decision number 11/2015).

Informed Consent Statement: Informed consent was obtained from all subjects involved in the study.

Data Availability Statement: The data presented in this study are available on request from the corresponding author.

Conflicts of Interest: The authors declare no conflict of interest.

References

1. Cantlebary, L.; Li, L. Facility Location Problem. Available online: https://optimization.cbe.cornell.edu/index.php?title=Facility_location_problem (accessed on 20 May 2022).
2. Mathar, R.; Niessen, T. Optimum Positioning of Base Stations for Cellular Radio Networks. *Wirel. Netw.* **2000**, *6*, 421–428. [CrossRef]
3. MathorCup-University Mathematical Modeling Competition, Question 2022D. Chinese Society of Optimization, Overall Planning and Economic Mathematics. Available online: http://mathorcup.org/detail/2378 (accessed on 20 May 2022).
4. Mathar, R.; Schmeink, M. Optimal Base Station Positioning and Channel Assignment for 3G Mobile Networks by Integer Programming. *Ann. Oper. Res.* **2001**, *107*, 225–236. [CrossRef]
5. Zimmermann, J.; Höns, R.; Mühlenbein, H. ENCON: An evolutionary algorithm for the antenna placement problem. *Comput. Ind. Eng.* **2003**, *44*, 209–226. [CrossRef]
6. Amaldi, E.; Capone, A.; Malucelli, F.; Signori, F. Radio Planning and Optimization of W-CDMA Systems. In Proceedings of the 2003 International Federation for Information Processing, Venice, Italy, 23–25 September 2003; Volume 2775, pp. 437–447.
7. Amaldi, E.; Capone, A.; Malucelli, F. Planning UMTS Base Station Location: Optimization Models with Power Control and Algorithms. *IEEE Trans. Wirel. Commun.* **2003**, *2*, 939–952. [CrossRef]
8. Amaldi, E.; Capone, A.; Malucelli, F. Radio Planning and Coverage Optimization of 3G Cellular Networks. *Wirel. Netw.* **2008**, *14*, 435–447. [CrossRef]
9. Amaldi, E.; Capone, A.; Malucelli, F.; Mannino, C. Optimization Problems and Models for Planning Cellular Networks. In *Handbook of Optimization in Telecommunications*; Springer: Berlin/Heidelberg, Germany, 2006.
10. Khalek, A.A.; Ai-Kanj, L.; Zaher, D.; Turkiyyah, G. Site Placement and Site Selection Algorithms for UMTS Radio Planning with Quality Constraints. In Proceedings of the 2010 International Conference on Telecommunications, Doha, Qatar, 4–7 April 2010; pp. 375–381.
11. Ibrahim, L.F.; Hamed, M.H. Using clustering technique M-PAM in mobile network planning. In Proceedings of the 12th WSEAS International Conference on Computers, Heraklion, Greece, 23–25 July 2008.
12. Ibrahim, L.F.; Salman, H.A. Using Hyper Clustering Algorithms in Mobile Network Planning. *Am. J. Appl. Sci.* **2011**, *8*, 1004–1013. [CrossRef]
13. Mai, W.; Liu, H.; Chen, L.; Li, J.; Xiao, H. Multi-objective Evolutionary Algorithm for 4G Base Station Planning. In Proceedings of the 2013 International Conference on Computational Intelligence and Security, Emeishan, China, 14–15 December 2013; pp. 85–89.
14. Selim, S.Z.; Almoghathawi, Y.A.; Aldajani, M. Optimal Base Stations Location and Configuration for Cellular Mobile Networks. *Wirel. Netw.* **2015**, *21*, 13–19. [CrossRef]
15. Valavanis, I.; Athanasiadou, G.; Zarbouti, D.; Tsoulos, G.V. Multi-Objective Optimization for Base-Station Location in Mixed-Cell LTE Networks. In Proceedings of the 10th European Conference on Antennas and Propagation (EuCAP), Davos, Switzerland, 10–15 April 2016.
16. Iellamo, S.; Lehtomaki, J.J.; Khan, Z. Placement of 5G Drone Base Stations by Data Field Clustering. In Proceedings of the 2017 IEEE Vehicular Technology Conference (VTC Spring), Sydney, Australia, 4–7 June 2017; pp. 1–5.
17. Goudos, S.; Diamantoulakis, P.; Karagiannidis, G. Multi-objective Optimization in 5G Wireless Networks with Massive MIMO. *IEEE Commun. Lett.* **2018**, *22*, 2346–2349. [CrossRef]
18. Wang, C.H.; Lee, C.J.; Wu, X. A Coverage-Based Location Approach and Performance Evaluation for the Deployment of 5G Base Stations. *IEEE Access* **2020**, *8*, 123320–123333. [CrossRef]
19. Fraiha, R.; Gomes, I.; Gomes, C.; Gomes, H.; Cavalcante, G. Improved Multi-objective Optimization for Cellular Base Stations Positioning. *Journal of Microwaves. Optoelectron. Electromagn. Appl.* **2021**, *20*, 870–882.
20. Gomes, C.; Gomes, I.; Fraiha, R.; Gomes, H.; Cavalcante, G. Optimum Positioning of Base Station for Cellular Service Devices Using Discrete Knowledge Model. *J. Microwaves. Optoelectron. Electromagn. Appl.* **2020**, *19*, 428–443. [CrossRef]
21. Liang, M.; Li, W.; Ji, J.; Zhou, Z.; Zhao, Y.; Zhao, H.; Guo, S. Evaluating the Comprehensive Performance of 5G Base Station: A Hybrid MCDM Model Based on Bayesian Best-Worst Method and DQ-GRA Technique. *Math. Probl. Eng.* **2022**, *2022*, 4038369. [CrossRef]
22. Liu, J.; Ting, S.; Sarkar, T. Base-station Antenna Modeling for Full-wave Electromagnetic Simulation. In Proceedings of the 2014 IEEE International Symposium on Antennas and Propagation & USNC/URSI National Radio Science Meeting, Memphis, TN, USA, 6–11 July 2014; pp. 2106–2107.
23. Blanch, S.; Romeu, J.; Cardama, A. Near Field in the Vicinity of Wireless base-station Antennas: An Exposure Compliance Approach. *IEEE Trans. Antennas Propag.* **2002**, *50*, 685–692. [CrossRef]
24. Wu, C.H.; Yang, C.F.; Wang, T.S.; Liao, K.C.; Chen, Y.M. A Method to Improve the Radiation Patterns of the Base Station Sector Antenna for Mobile Communications by Adding Scattering Structures on the Front Panel of the Antenna. In Proceedings of the 2006 IEEE Antennas and Propagation Society International Symposium, Albuquerque, NM, USA, 9–14 July 2006; pp. 4357–4360.
25. Konstantinidis, A.; Yang, K.; Zhang, Q. An Evolutionary Algorithm to a Multi-Objective Deployment and Power Assignment Problem in Wireless Sensor Networks. In Proceedings of the IEEE GLOBECOM 2008—2008 IEEE Global Telecommunications Conference, New Orleans, LA, USA, 30 November–4 December 2008; pp. 1–6.

26. Khalily-Dermany, M. Transmission power assignment in network-coding-based-multicast-wireless-sensor networks. *Comput. Netw.* **2021**, *196*, 108203. [CrossRef]
27. MacQueen, J. Some Methods for Classification and Analysis of Multivariate Observations. In Proceedings of the 5th Berkeley Symposium on Mathematical Statistics and Probability, Berkeley, CA, USA, 21 June–18 July 1965 and 27 December 1965–7 January 1966; Statistical Laboratory of the University of California: Berkeley, CA, USA, 1967; Volume 1, pp. 281–297.

Article

Forecasting the Efficiency of Innovative Industrial Systems Based on Neural Networks

Aleksey I. Shinkevich [1,*], Irina G. Ershova [2] and Farida F. Galimulina [1]

[1] Logistics and Management Department, Kazan National Research Technological University, 420015 Kazan, Russia
[2] Department of Finance and Credit, Southwest State University, 305040 Kursk, Russia
* Correspondence: ashinkevich@mail.ru; Tel.: +7-9272401653

Abstract: Approaches presented today in the scientific literature suggest that there are no methodological solutions based on the training of artificial neural networks to predict the direction of industrial development, taking into account a set of factors—innovation, environmental friendliness, modernization and production growth. The aim of the study is to develop a predictive model of performance management of innovative industrial systems by building neural networks. The research methods were correlation analysis, training of neural networks (species—regression), extrapolation, and exponential smoothing. As a result of the research, the estimation efficiency technique of an innovative industrial system in a complex considering the criteria of technical modernization, development, innovative activity, and ecologization is developed; the prognostic neural network models allow to optimize the contribution of signs to the formation of target (set) values of indicators of efficiency for macro and micro-industrial systems that will allow to level a growth trajectory of industrial systems; the priority directions of their development are offered. The following conclusions: the efficiency of industrial systems is determined by the volume of sales of goods, innovative products and waste recycling, which allows to save resources; the results of forecasting depend significantly on the DataSet formulated. Although multilayer neural networks independently select important features, it is advisable to conduct a correlation analysis beforehand, which will provide a higher probability of building a high-quality predictive model. The novelty of the research lies in the development and testing of a unique methodology to assess the effectiveness of industrial systems: it is based on a multidimensional system approach (takes into account factors of innovation, environmental friendliness, modernization and production growth); it combines a number of methodological tools (correlation, ranking and weighting); it expands the method of effectiveness assessment in terms of the composition of variables (previously presented approaches are limited to the aspects considered).

Keywords: innovative industrial system; extractive industry; manufacturing industry; efficiency; forecasting; neural networks; radial basis functions (RBF); multilayer perceptron (MLP)

MSC: 90C35

1. Introduction

The growing demands on industry and the conditions of modernity are caused by a number of objective reasons: the problem of the exhaustion of natural resources, intensive environmental pollution, and concern for future generations. Industrial systems that do not meet the requirements of the external (interaction with the environment and excessive emissions of pollutants, external effects in relation to society, etc.) and internal environment (working conditions, the state of fixed assets, etc.), need significant modernization. This affects the efficiency of the functioning of industrial systems, due to the level of rationality of capital investment, operating costs, organization and automation of production, digitalization of industrial systems, and innovation activities. The importance of managing the efficiency of innovative industrial systems in Russia is due to the high indices of industrial production: over a ten-year period (2010–2020) the index in Russia was 124%, Turkey—167%, Poland—143%, Australia—126%, the Republic of Korea—115%, USA—104%, Japan—88%, etc. [1]. However, Russian industry operates under conditions of high depreciation of fixed assets (at the end of 2021 in the extractive industry the index was 60.8%, and in the manufacturing sector—52.5%), which increases production risks and, presumably, affects the performance. Thus, under the conditions of tightening economic conditions, the management of efficiency and its factors becomes especially important, which makes the problems studied in this article urgent.

The aim of the study is to develop a predictive model of performance management of innovative industrial systems by building neural networks. The theoretical significance of the formulated provisions consists of the development of the methodology of performance management. The practical significance of the research lies in the possibility of predicting the performance of enterprises based on data management of the assets of industrial systems, and the identification of the degree of influence of production factors on the results of the functioning of industrial systems.

The object of the study is innovative industrial systems. The key features of such systems are, firstly, notable innovation activity, supported by human capital, scientific potential, availability of resources, investments, and secondly, production of products. Consequently, the considered category is based on a combination of the designated key features with an orientation on technological development. Let us highlight the provisions characterizing the functioning of innovative industrial systems in modern economic conditions.

First, industrial innovations determine the competitiveness of companies on the market and make a significant contribution to improving the quality of products [2–4].

Second, the ongoing structural transformation of industrial systems is accompanied by modernization, the quality of which is determined by innovation [5,6].

Third, the level of change management determines the category of the system, in connection with which modern scientists distinguish such types of innovation systems as national, regional, technological, and sectoral [7–15]. Our research is focused on innovative branch systems, i.e., systems which unite organizations (links of production system), processing raw materials into finished products, and interacting with each other and with infrastructural organizations of a national innovation system.

Fourthly, the interaction of agents in the innovative development of industry takes place under various forms of cooperation, which include clusters [16–18], technological platforms [19,20], consortia [21,22] and other types of cooperation.

Generalizing the above provisions, as well as relying on [23], let us clarify the definition of «innovation industrial system». Under it, we understand a set of interconnected subsystems, processes, elements, and participants, united by commodity-raw, energy, information, financial and service flows, contributing to the production of industrial products and the formation of GDP. By subsystems, we mean a subsystem of R&D, supply, production, distribution, transport, storage subsystems, and related infrastructure. Industrial systems can be considered at the scale of micro, meso- and macro levels. In the first case we should understand a production system and its functioning subsystems, in the second case—an industrial complex (a set of interacting enterprises located in a particular territory and united by industry, in particular, industrial clusters, holdings), in the third case—national industry as an independent branch of the national economy, uniting extractive, manufacturing, and energy production.

The behavior of complex systems, in particular industrial systems, is influenced by many external and internal factors, predictable and random. In this regard, the processes occurring in innovative industrial systems are stochastic in nature. Simulation tools allow us to assess and predict the behavior of such a system, as well as the nature and degree of influence of factors. In the conditions of the necessity of processing large arrays of data (on equipment operation, technological and business processes, stocks, etc.) methods of predictive analytics: Data mining, statistical and econometric methods, and methods of artificial intelligence are recognized as valuable tools. The latter is based on the training of neural networks, which has gained popularity in practice today: the search for minerals, solving logistics problems, the prediction of equipment failures, etc. Against the background of the advantages of neural networks, statistical methods of data processing (correlation and regression, cluster analysis, factor analysis and the principal component method, classification, and regression trees, etc.) have a certain weakness—the prediction of results based only on available data; neural networks can generate a prediction based on data not encountered in the training.

The practical application of neural network tools is popular and covered in the studies of many scientists. Conceptually, the neural network training methodology is widely covered in the scientific literature [24–31]. According to scientists, the quality and adequacy of models, and their predictive properties for extrapolation purposes are conditioned by the data set and their volume. Learning neural networks contribute to the structuring of information about complex dynamic systems, which include industrial systems. In this regard, neural networks are widely used in industry, due to the need for high-quality processing of large amounts of data on resource consumption, energy consumption, and business processes. In the context of oil pipeline monitoring and petroleum product volume prediction, this tool is highlighted in Mayet et al. where pipeline performance characteristics (amplitudes) are defined as inputs of the neural network, with percentages of four petroleum products as outputs [32]. To ensure continuous pharmaceutical production, the neural network model was tested by Wong et al. [33].

One of the purposes of the neural network technique is forecasting. A one-dimensional GDP prediction model was proposed by Longo et al. [34]. The problems of forecasting the regional industrial systems, where the authors proposed a neural network model with two blocks of input data (block 1—regional system and regional GDP level; block 2—panel data network and indicators of regional GDP growth index, mining, manufacturing and service sector growth values), and output parameters—forecasted values of industrial growth are disclosed in the works of Tuo et al. [35]. A predictive neural network model was proposed by Zhao and Niu [36]. The authors investigated the dependence of CO_2 emissions on four factors—population, GDP per capita, standard coal consumption and the share of thermal power generation. Adesanya et al. use neural networks to predict process parameters in the thermoplastic extrusion process in the cable industry, whereby the authors set nine neurons (parameters describing physical material properties) as the input and 11 neurons (temperature parameters) as the output layer [37].

Under the conditions of implementation of resource and energy-saving policies, energy consumption management is of particular importance, and in this regard, neural network models have become very popular in the context of rationalization of energy consumption. The study by Leite Coelho da Silva et al. presents the results of building a one-dimensional model for predicting energy consumption and reveals that a better prediction is obtained by building an MLP mode [38]. Shinkevich et al. propose energy resource optimization methods based on neural network training: the input parameters of the model are optimal, minimal and average energy consumption values, deviation and variance, and the output parameter is the optimal energy consumption in the chemical industry [39]. Ramos et al. propose a model to predict the electricity consumption of industrial facilities by analyzing online data (consolidated every 5 min) and applying an artificial neural network (ANN) [40]. Seawram et al. propose a predictive model of specific heat capacity (one neuron per output) based on the latent dependence of the target variable on the input parameters (nine neurons per input—different parameters of base fluid, nanoparticles and temperature) consistent with sustainable development and direction to reduce carbon dioxide emissions [41]. The team of scientists, Dli et al., built a process state prediction model using recurrent neural networks [42]. Thus, the key effect of modeling industrial systems based on a neural network is to improve the quality of manufactured products and the level of safety of production systems.

The methodology for training neural networks to assess the performance of enterprises (microindustrial systems) is covered in a number of papers [43–45], which demonstrates the high practical value and widespread application of deep learning tools as part of the evaluation and prediction of enterprise performance. However, studies limited to economic and innovation indicators, ignoring the environmental aspects of the functioning of enterprises prevail. Thus, Du combines such a wide range of indicators, including innovation activities, but does not focus on the analysis of a series of dynamics and prospection, but on a set of enterprises with an identical set of indicators, and does not consider environmental issues [43]. A similar approach is outlined in a study by Luo and Ren [45], but it also omits the environmental issue.

At the same time, the literature review of scientific positions allows us to judge the presence of a certain unrealized potential in the methodology of industrial systems efficiency management: there are no methodological solutions based on the training of artificial neural networks, allowing us to evaluate and predict the direction of industrial development, considering a complex of factors—innovation, environmental friendliness, modernization and production growth. An interesting approach to regional industry management based on neural networks was found in [35], but the authors limited the study to the inclusion of GDP and production index indicators. The above determines the relevance and importance of the development of predictive models and directions of development of both macro- and micro-industrial systems with the use of intelligent data processing tools.

2. Materials and Methods

The algorithm of this study is built on the principle of decomposition at the macro- and micro levels of management of industrial systems. In the first case, we are talking about the industrial sector of the Russian economy, represented mainly by extractive and manufacturing industries. The array of data for diagnostics and forecasting of the development of industrial systems (in retrospect) covers the period from 2005 to 2021—the period of structural transformation of industry in Russia [1,46]. In addition, speaking of innovative industrial systems, we refer not only to the output of innovative products but also to the investment of resources in improving the environmental friendliness of production. In the second case—at the micro level—the object of the research was a Russian industrial petrochemical enterprise PJSC «Nizhnekamskneftekhim»; the initial data set represented by the time series for 2009–2021 (quarterly data). The choice in favor of this enterprise is due to its strategic importance since it is one of the largest petrochemical enterprises in Russia and in Europe, one of the largest producers of synthetic polyisoprene in the world and the third largest supplier of butyl rubbers in the world.

1. Consequently, it is strategically important to develop adequate predictive models that can not only consider the history of the development of the industrial system but also be able to predict the results of activity under the influence of certain factors. In this regard, the following stages of research are outlined:
    1. identification of patterns and trends in the development of macro- and micro-industrial systems;
    2. forecasting the efficiency of innovative macro-industrial systems;
    3. predicting the efficiency of the microindustrial system.
2. The methodological basis of this study is a set of the following stages of modeling:
    1. information gathering;
    2. identification of significant relationships between indicators (correlation analysis);
    3. formation of a mathematical model;
    4. model verification;
    5. analysis of simulation results.

As an indicator of efficiency at the macro level, the use of the gross value added, combining the interests of all participants of the industrial system and the economy as a whole state proposed. It is a value equal to the difference between the volume of produced goods and services and their intermediate consumption [1]. The latter covers payroll, net profit, taxes, and depreciation, which is of interest not only to owners, but also to the state, investors, and employees.

We took the gross value added (Y_i) as the dependent variable:

Y_{mining}—is the gross value added created in the mining sector (billion rubles);

$Y_{manufacturing}$—is the gross value added created in the manufacturing sector (billion rubles).

Taking into consideration current trends in economic development, the following indicators are taken as independent variables:

$DFA_{(i)}$—degree of depreciation of fixed assets on the full range of organizations of the i-th sector of industry (%)—criterion of technical modernization;

$VSG_{(i)}$—volume of shipped goods of own production, work and services performed by own forces in the i-th sector of industry (million rubles)—development criterion;

$VIG_{(i)}$—volume of innovative goods, works, and services in the Russian Federation (million rubles)—criterion of innovative activity;

$RW_{(i)}$—use and neutralization of production and consumption waste in the i-th sector of industry (million tons)—greening criterion.

At the micro level, the evaluation efficiency of the classical indicators of profitability, taken as dependent (output) variables carried out, and taken as dependent (output) variables:

R_{ps}—profitability of sold products;

R_s—return on sales.

As input variables (independent) investigated:

CA—current assets (thousand rubles);

FA—fixed assets (thousand rubles);

GP—gross profit (thousand rubles);

PS—profit from sales (thousand rubles).

Based on the identified relationships between the criteria variables and predictors the author's methodology for assessing the effectiveness of innovative industrial systems (IIS) is proposed. Our approach is based on the method of rating assessments and benchmarks and focused on a comprehensive assessment of the development of an innovative industrial system. For this purpose, the index which takes into consideration the correlation of predictors with the gross added value created by a separate sector of the economy—the growth of the innovative industrial system coefficient (K_{iisd}) is developed. It takes into consideration the criteria of technical modernization, development, innovation activity, and ecologization and reflects the complex efficiency of industrial system functioning. The algorithm of the methodology (Figure 1) clearly reflects the stages and the arrays of necessary data formed at each stage.

The suggested methodology is distinguished by taking into account heterogeneous, but significant components of the functioning of industrial enterprises (technical modernization, development, innovation activity, and greening), which allows us to overcome the limitations in assessing the directions of development; correlates with the interests of all stakeholders in the economic system (noted above); is multifaceted, flexible and adaptive (the weighting factors are adjustable and respond to changes in the dynamics of indicators), which affects the correlation coefficients. The formulated methodology develops the previously proposed by us method for assessing the sustainable growth of innovative mesosystems (ISDI) [23] and overcomes the problems of dimensionality of the parameters under study.

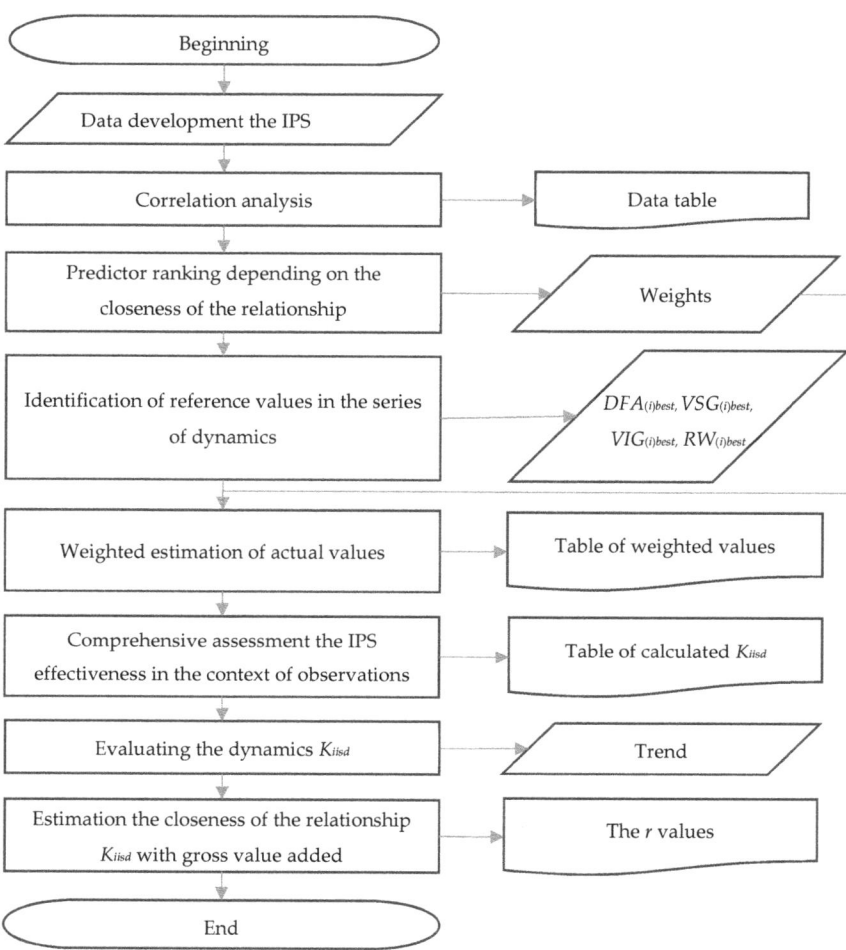

Figure 1. The author's methodology algorithm for assessing the effectiveness of innovative industrial systems.

The suggested methodology is the calculation of the coefficient of development of innovative industrial systems of industrial enterprises (technical modernization, development, innovation activity, and greening), which allows us to overcome the limitations in assessing the directions of development; correlates with the interests of all stakeholders in the economic system (noted above); is multifaceted, flexible and adaptive (the weighting factors are adjustable and respond to changes in the dynamics of indicators), which affects the correlation coefficients. The formulated methodology develops the previously proposed by us method for assessing the sustainable growth of innovative mesosystems (ISDI) [23] and overcomes the problems of dimensionality of the parameters under study.

$$K_{iisd} = \sqrt[4]{\sum_{j=1}^{4} w_j \left(\frac{A_{ij(min)}}{A_{ij(year)}} \right) \sum_{j=1}^{4} w_j \left(\frac{A_{ij(year)}}{A_{ij(max)}} \right)} \quad (1)$$

$$w_j = \frac{a_j}{4} \text{ and } w_j < 1$$

where study one of the four attributes (DFA, VSG, VIG, RW); $A_{ij(min)}$ or $A_{ij(max)}$—is the reference value for the corresponding attribute in the dynamics series; $A_{ij(year)}$—is the actual value of the indicator in a particular year; w_j—is the weight coefficient j attribute; a_j—the rank assigned to the j attribute in accordance with the value of the correlation coefficient ($a_j = 4$ for the attribute with the strongest correlation, $a_j = 1$ for the attribute with the weakest correlation); Y_i—the gross value added created in the i-th industry sector. (1)

At the next stages of the study, modelling and forecasting of the indicators are carried out. The forecasting tool was artificial neural networks (ANN), trained in the Statistica environment. Of the three available modeling strategies (automated neural networks search (ANS), custom neural networks (CNS) and subsampling (random, bootstrap)) the ANS option is used in all modeling cases. The basic problem solved by neural networks is regression. The neural network parameters are weights and shifts of neurons, and the hyperparameters are the number of layers, the number of neurons in each layer, activation functions and the error function. Let us consider these parameters in more detail.

The neural network construction is based on the summation function of a neuron, which consists of the summation of products of input values by their weight coefficients (2):

$$Y = F(WX) = F(x_1\omega_1 + x_2\omega_2 + \ldots + x_n\omega_n) = F\left(\sum_{i=1}^{n} x_i\omega_i\right)$$

or (2)

$$Y = b + x_1\omega_1 + x_2\omega_2 + \ldots + x_n\omega_n = b + \sum_{i=1}^{n} x_i\omega_i$$

where Y—is the output value; $X = (x_1, x_2 \ldots , x_n)$—is a vector of input signals, a feature; $W = (\omega_1, \omega_2 \ldots , \omega_n)$—is a vector of weights reflecting the significance of the corresponding feature (strength of synaptic connection, synapse); b is the activation function bias neuron.

The inputs of the artificial neural network are a mathematical vector of numbers X (3):

$$X = [x_1, x_2, \ldots , x_n]. \quad (3)$$

- An activation function is a function that converts weighted inputs into an adequate output. We distinguish between activation functions for radial basis functions (RBF) and multilayer perceptron (MLP). In the former, we rely on the following functions:
- Gauss function (4):

$$f(x) = \exp\left(\frac{-S^2}{2\sigma^2}\right),$$
$$S^2 = |X - W|^2 = \sum_i (x_i - \omega_i)^2 \quad (4)$$

where σ—is the standard deviation of the width of the radial-baseline function; S is the weighted sum of the neuron;

- the identity function (linear) (5):

$$f(x) = x. \quad (5)$$

The following activation functions in MLP training applied:

- an identical function;
- logistic function (sigmoid) (6):

$$f(x) = \frac{1}{1+e^{-x}},$$
$$f(x) \in (0;1) \quad (6)$$

- function of the hyperbolic tangent (7):

$$f(x) = th(x) = \frac{(e^x - e^{-x})}{(e^x + e^{-x})},$$
$$f(x) \in (-1;1), \quad (7)$$

- exponential function (8):

$$f(x) = e^{-x}. \quad (8)$$

The error function (neural network error) in regression problems is determined by the formula for summing the squares of errors (9):

$$E = \sum_{i=1}^{n}(Y - Y^*)^2, \quad (9)$$

where Y—is the actual value of the output variable and Y^*—Y^* is the predicted value of the output variable.

We evaluated the quality of trained artificial neural networks using the test sample with the average absolute error MAPE (10):

$$MAPE = \frac{1}{n}\sum_{i=1}^{n}\frac{|Y - Y^*|}{Y} = \frac{1}{n}\sum_{i=1}^{n}\frac{Y_{AR}}{Y}, \quad (10)$$

where n—is the number of observations in the test sample (automatically); Y_{AR}—is the absolute residuals on Y in the test sample.

According to the architecture, all neural networks are divided into two types: single-layer and multilayer. A single-layer network is a neural network without hidden layers, the signals of the input layer, including synapses, are fed to the output layer, which provides a relatively high speed of learning; the architecture of such a network is stable and does not vary; pre-processing of predictors is required [47–51]. However, due to the simplicity of tuning and consequently, the low accuracy of the model, we do not use the method of training single-layer neural networks in the study.

We rely on the application of a multilayer neural network (deep), in which the input signals pass through hidden layers with one set of synapses, and only then to the output layer with other weights. While the single-layer network requires careful preparation of the input data, in the multilayer neural networks this problem is overcome by the transformation and selection of features during training. At the same time, the addition of hidden layers causes an increase in the training time of the network, and the ability to process a small amount of data and retraining can contribute to a low quality of prediction [52–55].

Thus, the key type of neural network used in the paper is a multilayer network (1 hidden layer with h neurons), where x—is a set of predictors, inputs, and Y—is a set of categorical variables, outputs (Figure 2).

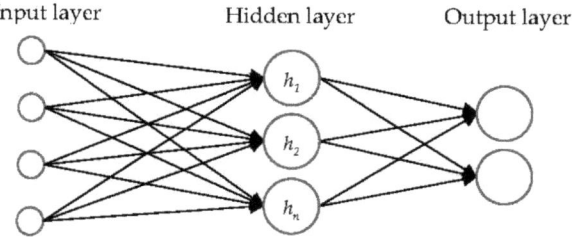

Figure 2. The architecture of the multilayer neural network.

Homogeneous and heterogeneous neural networks are distinguished according to the type of neuronal structures. In the first case, homogeneous networks consist of neurons with one type of activation, while in the second case there is a combination of activation functions [56]. In our study, there are artificial neural networks of both types, but predominantly heterogeneous ones, because in this way the network automatically chooses the best option to calculate the output value.

The methodological basis was the use of such methods of data processing as correlation analysis, training of neural networks (species—regression), extrapolation, and exponential smoothing. An instrumental set of data processing includes such software products as Statistica (module—«Automated neural networks search», «Time series and forecasting») and Deductor Studio (module—Neural network). The calculation of efficiency indicators and the coefficient of development of the innovative industrial system K_{iisd} is implemented in Microsoft Excel.

predominantly heterogeneous ones, because in this way the network automatically chooses the best option to calculate the output value.

The methodological basis was the use of such methods of data processing as correlation analysis, training of neural networks (species—regression), extrapolation, and exponential smoothing. An instrumental set of data processing includes such software products as Statistica (module—«Automated neural networks search», «Time series and forecasting») and Deductor Studio (module—Neural network). The calculation of efficiency indicators and the coefficient of development of the innovative industrial system K_{iisd} is implemented in Microsoft Excel.

3. Results

3.1. Trends in the Development of Stochastic Innovation Industrial Systems in Russia

Industrial systems in Russia are developing steadily to a certain extent, as evidenced by the dynamics of gross value added created in the mining and processing sector. The trend analysis makes it possible to judge the global growth trend in both types of industrial systems (Figure 3) (more data in Appendix A). A more predictable and sustainable dynamic is demonstrated by manufacturing, which, unlike extractive industries, maintained its production momentum in 2020 (the year of the global pandemic, when supply chains around the world were disrupted, negatively affecting technological processes, production costs, and sales volumes). While the index of gross value added in 2020 in the extractive industries decreased by 27% (relative to 2019), the index in the manufacturing industries increased by 1.4%. This trend is due to the specificity of industries, flexibility and ability to restructure and diversify production.

Figure 3. Extrapolation of gross value added by industrial sector of the Russian economy by constructing an exponential trend line for the mining (**a**) and manufacturing (**b**) industries.

According to the author's methodology algorithm (Figure 1), the data collection of the development of the industrial system in Russia allowed to carry out a correlation analysis, which revealed that the dependent variable (Y_i) significantly depends on all four input variables (DFA, VSG, VIG, RW) in both cases—the extractive and manufacturing sectors of the economy in Russia (Table 1, Table 2). The correlation coefficients exceed 0.7, and the closeness of the relationship between all the indicators is high.

Table 1. Correlation matrix and ranking indicators the mining sector of the economy.

	Mean	Y_{mining}	$DFA_{(mining)}$	$VSG_{(mining)}$	$VIG_{(mining)}$	$RW_{(mining)}$	The Rank of the Trait, a	Weight, w
Y_{mining}	6652	1	0.788233	0.997309	0.862541	0.953822		
$x_{1(mining)}$	54	0.788233	1	0.796851	0.666535	0.775370	1	0.25
$x_{2(mining)}$	10,315,429	0.997309	0.796851	1	0.871492	0.948996	4	1
$x_{3(mining)}$	400,421	0.862541	0.666535	0.871492	1	0.785332	2	0.5
$x_{4(mining)}$	2274	0.953822	0.775370	0.948996	0.785332	1	3	0.75

Table 2. Correlation matrix and ranking indicators the manufacturing sector of the economy.

	Mean	$Y_{manufacturing}$	$DFA_{(manuf.)}$	$VSG_{(manuf.)}$	$VIG_{(manuf.)}$	$RW_{(manuf.)}$	The Rank of the Trait, a	Weight, w
$Y_{manuf.}$	9048	1	0.915754	0.996381	0.917357	0.720713		
$x_{1(manuf.)}$	48	0.915754	1	0.920973	0.843458	0.784281	2	0.5
$x_{2(manuf.)}$	29,618,279	0.996381	0.920973	1	0.942095	0.738616	4	1
$x_{3(manuf.)}$	2,035,221	0.917357	0.843458	0.942095	1	0.718756	3	0.75
$x_{4(manuf.)}$	149	0.720713	0.784281	0.738616	0.718756	1	1	0.25

Having all the necessary data, we identified the reference values in the series of dynamics (Table 3).

Table 3. Benchmark values the innovative industrial systems indicators.

	DFA (min)	VSG (max)	VIG (max)	RW (max)
Mining	49.6 (2009)	23,598,403 (2021)	874,337 (2021)	3585 (2018)
Manufacturing	45.6 (2008)	62,978,104 (2021)	3,659,812 (2021)	247 (2021)

Then by Formula (1), we calculated the weighted values of the four indicators for the study period and the final coefficient of growth of the innovative industrial system K_{iisd} for two types of industrial systems (Table 4) and compared them to the dynamics of gross value added (Figure 4).

Table 4. Comprehensive assessment of the development of innovative industrial systems (calculated according to the author's methodology).

Year	Y_{mining} (bln rub.)	K_{iisd} (mining) (Coefficient)	$Y_{manuf.}$ (bln rub.)	K_{iisd} (manufacturing) (Coefficient)
2005	2064	0.63	3388	0.85
2006	2509	0.68	4116	0.92
2007	2866	0.87	5025	0.97
2008	3285	0.90	6164	1.07
2009	2885	0.84	5005	1.00
2010	3843	0.92	5935	1.12
2011	4944	1.25	6896	1.24
2012	5563	1.37	7774	1.46
2013	5911	1.29	8070	1.56
2014	6231	1.46	8959	1.56
2015	7276	1.43	10,289	1.76
2016	7423	1.56	10,017	1.93
2017	9029	1.72	11,308	1.79
2018	12,410	2.09	13,315	1.90
2019	12,622	2.12	14,215	1.99
2020	9185	1.73	14,415	2.17
2021	15,031	2.44	18,926	2.43

nounced in the manufacturing industrial systems sector, as evidenced by the corre coefficient of 0.969 (Figure 4b).

In general, the high quality of the proposed indicator should be noted; it succ and comprehensively describes the characteristics of industrial systems in a particul riod of time and allows a comparative analysis of the development of various obje research.

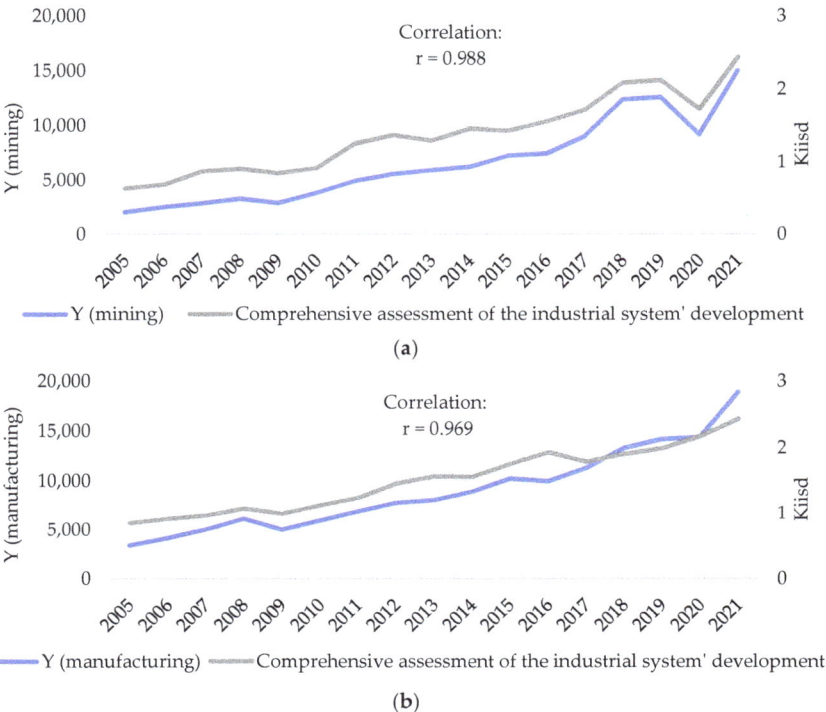

Figure 4. The verification coefficient of development effectiveness the innovation industrial system for the mining (**a**) and manufacturing (**b**) industries (comparison of the actual values of gross value added and calculated by the author's methodology values of the coefficient of development of innovative industrial system).

As in the case of gross value added, the coefficient of integrated development of industrial systems as a whole, increases (in both cases). The quality of the proposed indicator is confirmed by the comparison with the size of the gross value added. The higher quality of the indicator is demonstrated by the mining sector, as evidenced by low deviations and a correlation coefficient of 0.988 (Figure 4a). The deviations are more pronounced in the manufacturing industrial systems sector, as evidenced by the correlation coefficient of 0.969 (Figure 4b).

In general, the high quality of the proposed indicator should be noted; it succinctly and comprehensively describes the characteristics of industrial systems in a particular period of time and allows a comparative analysis of the development of various objects of research.

Thus, the patterns of development of innovative industrial systems should include the steady growth of gross value added, which satisfies the interests of owners, investors, government, and employees; there is direct and high dependence on this performance indicator for the four most important criteria of modern economic system functioning (the criteria of technical modernization, development, innovation activity, greening). The causal relationship (positive) between the depreciation of fixed assets x_1 and the gross added value Y can be explained by the concentration of efforts and resources of production systems not on the renewal of technical infrastructure, but on product and technological innovation, as well as on measures for the recycling of production and consumption waste. Shifting the focus to the purchase of new equipment and the subsequent reduction in the degree of fixed assets will restrain the growth of production and gross value added as a result of the redistribution of income and investment.

3.2. Variative Forecasting of the Efficiency of Innovative Macro-Industrial Systems in Russia

3.2.1. Univariate Prediction

In order to predict the efficiency of industrial systems development the gross value added indicator taken as a basis (modeling for the dependent variable Kiisd showed similar architectures and characteristics of neural networks and corresponding predictions), alternative types of neural networks—Multilayer Perceptron (MLP) and Radial Basis Function (RBF)—evaluated. Univariate prediction assumes a single neuron input and output: the actual value (input value) and the predicted value (output value). The size of the subsamples is set in the following proportions: training—60%, test—20%, validation—20%. By applying the ANS option, five networks with the best quality scores were trained.

1. In the extractive sector, the highest performance is shown by the radial basis function network with five hidden neurons RBF 1-5-1 and a learning performance of 97.55% (Table 5). The error function is defined by the sum of squares formula, the activation function of hidden neurons is Gaussian, and the output neurons are identical (linear). Thus, the obtained one-dimensional neural network is heterogeneous, combining neurons with two different activation functions, and multilayer.

Table 5. Alternative univariate models for predicting Y_{mining} gross value added.

Net. Name	Training Perf.	Test Perf.	Validation Perf.	Training Error	Test Error	Validation Error
RBF 1-5-1	0.975502	0.991997	0.999828	74,038.1	2,517,832	10,540,650
RBF 1-5-1	0.924554	−0.713870	0.999946	290,964.0	13,077,520	29,005,897
RBF 1-5-1	0.958372	0.973763	0.986317	148,272.0	6,215,827	17,400,202
MLP 1-6-1	0.969824	0.931990	0.984887	98,788.5	834,197	4,930,694
RBF 1-5-1	0.750521	−0.862889	0.975379	944,232.3	1,353,0519	29,115,342

The time series graph is plotted in the projection over 25 periods (starting from period 1), which allows us to estimate the near-term performance of the extractive sector of the economy in Russia (in 7 years). According to the best network (RBF 1-5-1), the projected value of gross value added in the industry will remain at 9000 billion rubles (Figure 5a). Forecasting K_{iisd} shows a similar development trend (Figure 5b).

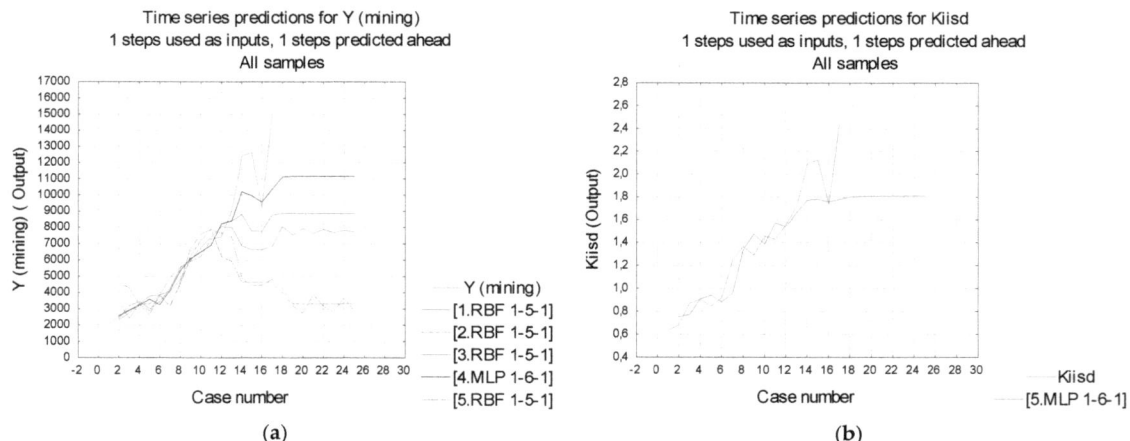

Figure 5. Projection the performance of innovative industrial systems 7 years ahead: (a) forecasting neural networks Y_{mining}; (b) K_{iis} forecasting neural networks.

Since the quality of the model was estimated by the test sample, we estimated the relative error of this model by absolute residuals. We calculated the average absolute error of MAPE and found that the quality of the test sample for Y_{mining} was 31.3%, for K_{iisd}—22%

Since the quality of the model was estimated by the test sample, we estimated the relative error of this model by absolute residuals. We calculated the average absolute error of MAPE and found that the quality of the test sample for Y_{mining} was 31.3%, for K_{iisd}—22% (high error), indicating the low quality of the predicted scenario of changes in gross value added in the mining sector. The difficult-to-predict indicator is due to the previously noted sharp decline in gross value added in the industry.

The application of the exponential smoothing tool ($\alpha = 0,1$; without trend and seasonality) reduces the average absolute error of MAPE to 12%. However, the results of smoothing significantly distort the original data set, which affects the results of forecasting by neural networks. If the actual data provide the forecast of the indicator for future periods at the level of 9000 billion rubles (Figure 5a), then taking into account the exponential smoothing, the forecasted value falls below 6000 billion rubles.

The intermediate conclusion is that the neural network RBF 1-5-1 (MAPE = 31.3%) predicts the value of gross value added in the extractive industry at 9000 billion rubles.

2. In the processing sector, we obtained the best multilayer perceptron type network described by the MLP 1-2-1 architecture—with two hidden neurons, whose activation function is hyperbolic; the activation function of neurons at the output is identical (Table 6). The model is again heterogeneous.

Table 6. Alternative univariate models for forecasting the gross value added of $Y_{manuf.}$.

Net. Name	Training Perf.	Test Perf.	Validation Perf.	Training Error	Test Error	Validation Error
MLP 1-2-1	0.942668	0.965460	0.955398	242,733.9	295,473.1	2,886,074
MLP 1-2-1	0.941358	0.954011	0.961203	251,689.5	348,608.2	2,281,566
MLP 1-8-1	0.942357	0.959377	0.958476	245,806.0	312,927.0	2,445,556
MLP 1-7-1	0.941358	0.954011	0.961203	249,517.3	365,610.0	2,588,421
MLP 1-2-1	0.941099	0.964267	0.956155	287,181.8	277,392.1	2,333,691

According to the projection, the gross value added will fluctuate between 15,000 and 16,000 billion rubles (Figure 6). The average value of the error calculated on absolute residuals in the test sample was 14.6%, which is twice better than in the case of the one-dimensional $Y_{manuf.}$ projection model. The manufacturing industry is expected to grow further, but at a lower growth rate (with a probability of 14.6%).

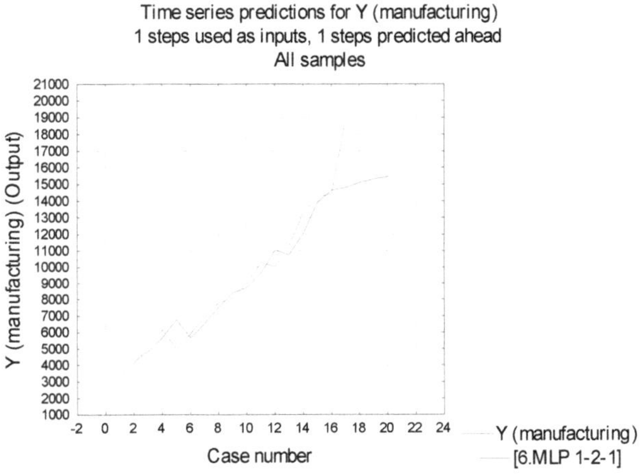

Figure 6. Projection the $Y_{manuf.}$ for 7 years ahead.

The intermediate conclusion is that the multilayer neural network of MLP 1-2-1 architecture (MAPE = 14.6%) predicts the value of $Y_{manuf.}$ in the range of 15,000–16,000 billion rubles.

The intermediate conclusion is that the multilayer neural network of MLP 1-2-1 architecture (MAPE = 14.6%) predicts the value of $Y_{manuf.}$ in the range of 15,000–16,000 billion rubles.

3.2.2. Multivariate Forecasting

As an alternative method of prediction, we trained a neural network taking into account several features—*DFA, VSG, VIG, RW*. The quality of the models has increased significantly.

We modeled the dynamics series, which characterize the efficiency of industrial systems functioning, according to a similar algorithm carried out. However, the architecture of networks has changed in terms of input neurons—their number has increased to 4 (according to a set of features). Both types of neural networks (MLP and RBF) are set for training the largest number of networks, nets for training—50, nets for conservation—5.

1. In the field of mining, it was revealed that MLP models demonstrate a higher quality of prediction of the output variable (Table 7). The balance of the quality of the training and control samples allows the choice to be made in favor of networks with MLP 4-8-1 and MLP 4-9-1 architecture. The choice of the best model was also made according to the MAPE criterion, so network #3 with MLP 4-9-1 architecture was chosen for scenario prediction. The activation function of hidden neurons is a hyperbolic tangent; the activation function of output neurons is identical. A quality check of the test sample confirms the lowest error value for the selected network, but at the same time—high (28%).

Table 7. Alternative multivariate models for predicting Y_{mining} gross value added.

Net. Name	Training Perf.	Test Perf.	Validation Perf.	Training Error	Test Error	Validation Error	MAPE
RBF 4-5-1	0.986852	0.975468	0.999344	24,126.39	3,109,395	12,947,184	42%
MLP 4-8-1	0.991204	0.927100	0.994118	4907.93	1,623,501	7,684,535	32%
MLP 4-9-1	0.992292	0.933468	0.999945	0.00	1,285,083	6,436,301	28%
MLP 4-8-1	0.992292	0.969944	0.998589	0.00	2,112,949	9,731,973	33%
MLP 4-9-1	0.992292	0.943643	0.999955	0.00	1,567,571	7,404,531	29%

The evaluation of the weights in the network connections allows us to judge the high strength of the synaptic connection of the variable $DFA_{(mining)}$, which characterizes the degree of depreciation of fixed assets at the enterprises of the industry, with the hidden neuron #5 (w ($DFA_{(mining)}$; h_5) = 4.20); the hidden neuron #3 has a high positive effect on the output variable, as evidenced by indicates w (h_3; Y_{mining}) = 1.21.

Based on the constructed neural network model, four different scenarios were calculated (Table 8):

- Scenario 1: continuation of the increase in all four variables (by 1%);
- scenario 2: reduction in the degree of depreciation of fixed assets in the industry ($DFA_{(mining)}$) by 1% as a result of the modernization of industrial systems) and an increase in the other three indicators by 1%;
- scenario 3: reduction of $DFA_{(mining)}$ by 1% and growth of the other three indicators by 5%;
- scenario 4: reduction $DFA_{(mining)}$ by 5% (investing in the renovation of fixed assets) and an increase in the other three indicators by 1%.

Table 8. Scenarios of changes in the efficiency of industrial systems in the mining sector of the economy.

Year	Y_{mining}	$DFA_{(mining)}$	$VSG_{(mining)}$	$VIG_{(mining)}$	$RW_{(mining)}$
2021	15,031	60.8	23,598,403	874,336.9	3510.6
Scenarios	Y_{mining} (predicted)	$DFA_{(mining)}$	$VSG_{(mining)}$	$VIG_{(mining)}$	$RW_{(mining)}$
1	11,646.8	61.4	23,834,387	88,3080.3	3545.7
2	11,143.7	60.2	23,834,387	88,3080.3	3545.7
3	11,103.6	60.2	24,778,323.2	91,8053.7	3686.1
4	10,320.2	57.8	23,834,387	88,3080.3	3545.7

According to these scenarios, the efficiency of macro-industrial systems in the field of mining is at the point of bifurcation, the way out of which will be a choice between further increasing economic efficiency to the detriment of the state of fixed assets (which are the core of the production system) and investing in modernization with an economic return only in the future. As noted above, this revealed a high relationship between Y and DFA. Our hypothesis that the redistribution of income and investment in favor of the modernization of fixed assets will restrain the increase in the efficiency of the industrial system is confirmed (the value of Y_{mining} (predicted) will be only 10 320.2 billion rubles). If economic agents concentrate the financial flow on the purchase of new machinery, equipment, and transport, it will provide a decrease in the added value relative to the level of 2021.

2. In the field of manufacturing industries, the lowest value of absolute error MAPE by the network of architecture MLP 4-3-1 is shown (Table 9). The error of 6.9% can be considered satisfactory, and this neural network is applicable in the quality of scenario forecasting of the industrial system. The highest strength of the synaptic connection is also demonstrated by the predictor $DFA_{(manuf.)}$ in connection with the hidden neuron #3 (connection weight is 0.46); in the output—hidden neuron #1 (connection weight is 0.77).

Table 9. Alternative multivariate models for forecasting the gross value added of $Y_{manufacturing}$.

Net. Name	Training Perf.	Test Perf.	Validation Perf.	Training Error	Test Error	Validation Error	MAPE
MLP 4-4-1	0.915479	0.976979	0.985058	457,466.8	384,616	2,737,451	11.6%
RBF 4-5-1	0.944350	0.803836	0.957482	233,871.7	4,591,564	13,365,813	31.4%
RBF 4-5-1	0.956258	0.994056	0.960144	171,935.9	4,136,706	13,562,300	26.9%
RBF 4-5-1	0.963447	0.917787	0.956054	134,166.2	3,415,319	11,026,154	26%
MLP 4-3-1	**0.895015**	**0.941203**	**0.999883**	**549,292.2**	**563,440**	**554,153**	**6.9%**

3. The development of the four scenarios outlined above regarding manufacturing allows us to judge in all cases, a significant increase in the gross value added in the industry compared to 2021 (Table 10).

The development of the four scenarios outlined above regarding manufacturing allows us to judge in all cases, a significant increase in the gross value added in the industry compared to 2021 (Table 10).

Table 10. Scenarios of changes in the efficiency of industrial systems in manufacturing industries.

Year	$Y_{manuf.}$	$DFA_{(manuf.)}$	$VSG_{(manuf.)}$	$VIG_{(manuf.)}$	$RW_{(manuf.)}$
2021	18,926	52.5	62,978,104	36,598,12.3	247
Scenarios	$Y_{manuf.}$ (predicted)	$DFA_{(manuf.)}$	$VSG_{(manuf.)}$	$VIG_{(manuf.)}$	$RW_{(manuf.)}$
1	24113.16	53.02	63,607,885	36,964,10	249.4
2	23101.90	51.98	63,607,885	36,964,10	249.4
3	24959.65	51.98	66,127,009	38,428,03	259.3
4	21224.49	49.88	63,607,885	36,964,10	249.4

A summary of the results of forecasting the efficiency of macro-industrial systems, as well as the priority areas of development that require special attention, is presented in the form of a scheme (Figure 7). The univariate (1 attribute on the input) and multivariate (4 attributes on the input) variant models are reflected.

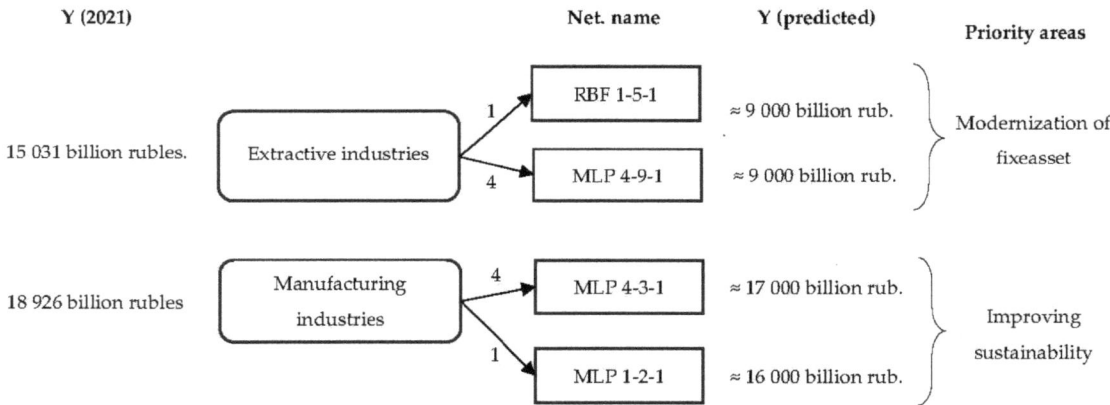

Figure 7. A predictive model for improving the efficiency of macro-industrial systems and priority areas for their development.

Thus, a more predictable trend of changes in the efficiency of industrial systems is observed in the sphere of manufacturing industries. This is due to a more uniform rate of change Y_{fi} (Figure 3). Prediction of the efficiency of extractive innovative industrial systems is complicated by the deterioration of the indicator of gross value added in 2020. This «outlier» in the dynamic series affected the quality of neural networks. Further monitoring of the dynamics of the criteria variables and predictors will allow for adjusting the neural network and improving the quality of the predictive model.

3.3. Predicting the Efficiency of the Microindustrial System

Prediction of the efficiency of microindustrial systems is implemented on the example of a large Russian petrochemical enterprise «Nizhnekamskneftekhim». In this case, the input is four neurons (CA, FA, GP, PS), and the output is—2 (R_{ps} и R_s). The learning quality of the neural network on average has increased; due to the increase in the series of dynamics to 52 periods (quarterly data on the activities of the company for 13 years, Figure 8).

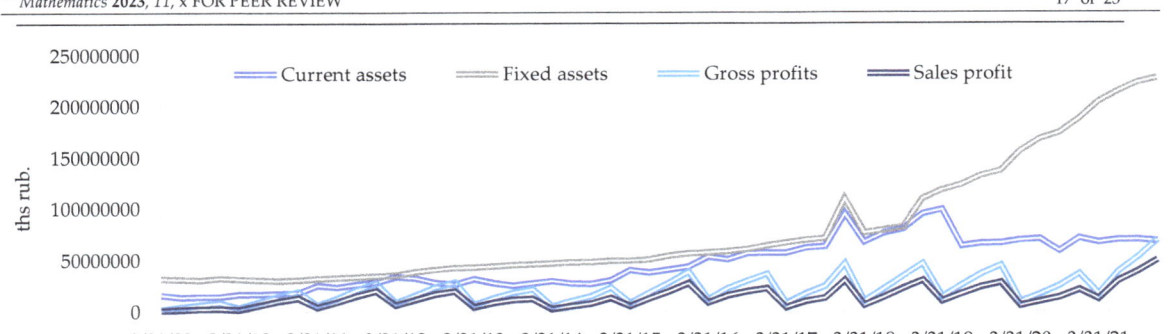

Figure 8. Dynamics of change in input variables over 13 years (quarterly data presented).

The size of the subsamples is set in the following proportions: training—70%, test—15%, validation—15%. ANS option is also applied. 50 networks for training. We obtained five trained MLP networks (Table 11). The best quality of the test sample is observed for network #4 MLP 4-8-2, which is the most adequate and considered by us acceptable for prediction (the average absolute error of MAPE does not exceed 8%).

Table 11. Alternative multivariate models for predicting the profitability of an enterprise.

Net. Name	Training Perf.	Test Perf.	Validation Perf.	Training Error	Test Error	Validation Error	MAPE (R_{ps})	MAPE (R_s)
MLP 4-3-2	0.977628	0.992374	0.986670	0.000158	0.000025	0.000173	9.68%	8.27%
MLP 4-9-2	0.975122	0.995172	0.981610	0.000174	0.000016	0.000325	16.65%	10.60%
MLP 4-9-2	0.983194	0.985588	0.984998	0.000132	0.000056	0.000260	12.15%	10.52%
MLP 4-8-2	0.993344	0.963529	0.991687	0.000046	0.000194	0.000102	7.11%	6.33%
MLP 4-6-2	0.984742	0.928401	0.996516	0.000082	0.000275	0.000057	10.87%	10.48%

The high quality of the trained neural networks is confirmed by the low scatter between the target and output values of the performance indicators, clearly demonstrated by the scatter diagrams (Figure 9).

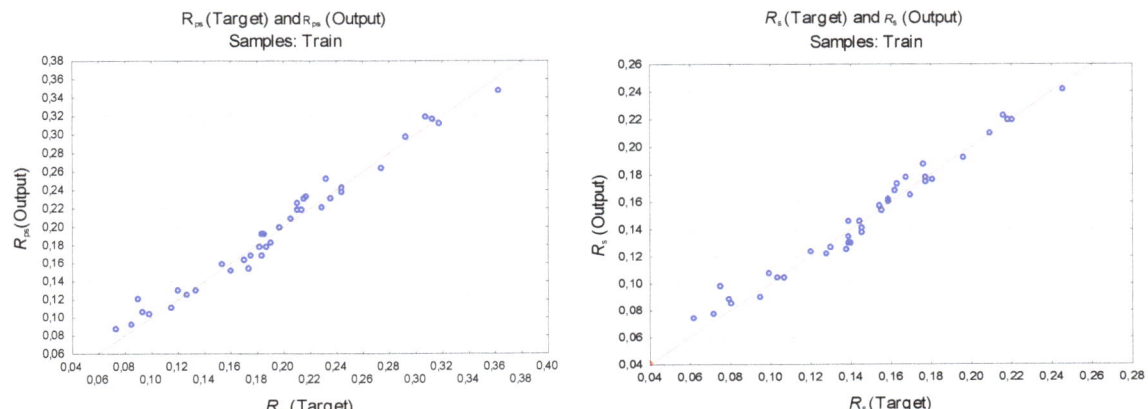

Figure 9. Scatter plot of the training sample (exponential activation function): (**a**) Return on sales R_{ps}; (**b**) Return on sales R_s.

Evaluation of the sensitivity of the neural network to the predictors allows us to conclude that the variables GP and PS are noisy because their sensitivity is many times lower than the predictors CA and FA (Table 12). However, their importance for the formation of performance indicators is unconditional, in connection with which we leave these signs in the DataSet.

Table 12. Evaluation the sensitivity of neural networks to input variables.

Net. Name	CA	FA	GP	PS
1.MLP 4-3-2	110.66	49.02	3.56	2.30
2.MLP 4-9-2	185.18	142.50	3.35	2.38
3.MLP 4-9-2	136.86	57.61	4.31	3.51
4.MLP 4-8-2	120,584.73	813.57	20.61	16.84
5.MLP 4-6-2	159,432.66	1637.65	17.53	4.69
Mean	56,090.02	540.07	9.87	5.95

We considered four scenarios of enterprise development based on the results of neural network modeling (Table 13), according to which different rates of one-time growth of indicators are provided:

- Scenario 1: 1% increase in input variables;
- Scenario 2: 5% increase in input variables;
- Scenario 3: 10% increase in input variables;
- Scenario 4: Reduce the value of input variables by 1%.

Table 13. Scenarios of changes in enterprise efficiency (exponential activation function).

Year	R_{ps} (%)	R_s (%)	CA (ths. rub.)	FA (ths. rub.)	GP (ths. rub.)	PS (ths. rub.)
4 quarter 2021	26.6	19.4	67,879,452	227,152,227	69,003,100	49,405,272
Scenarios	R_{ps} (%)	R_s (%)	CA (ths. rub.)	FA (ths. rub.)	GP (ths. rub.)	PS (ths. rub.)
1	26.8	19.1	68,558,247	229,423,749	69,693,131	49,899,325
2	25.8	18.6	71,273,425	238,509,838	72,453,255	51,875,536
3	24.6	17.9	74,667,397	249,867,450	75,903,410	54,345,799
4	27.2	19.4	67,200,658	224,880,705	68,313,069	48,911,219

Of course, the trajectory of enterprise development is not limited to the considered scenarios. However, the calculations allow us to form a general idea about the patterns of change in the indicators of the effectiveness of the industrial system.

A distinctive feature of the enterprise is the inverse dependence of performance indicators on the size of fixed assets, current assets and profits. As we can see, fixed assets have a high value, which bears a significant contribution to the formation of the criterion variables. However, according to the identified patterns, the variable has little effect on efficiency indicators. The explanation may be idle production facilities or a high degree of depreciation of fixed assets at the enterprise.

Deductor Studio is used as an alternative neural network-training tool. In a similar neural network with eight neurons on a hidden layer, the activation function is sigmoid (Figure 10).

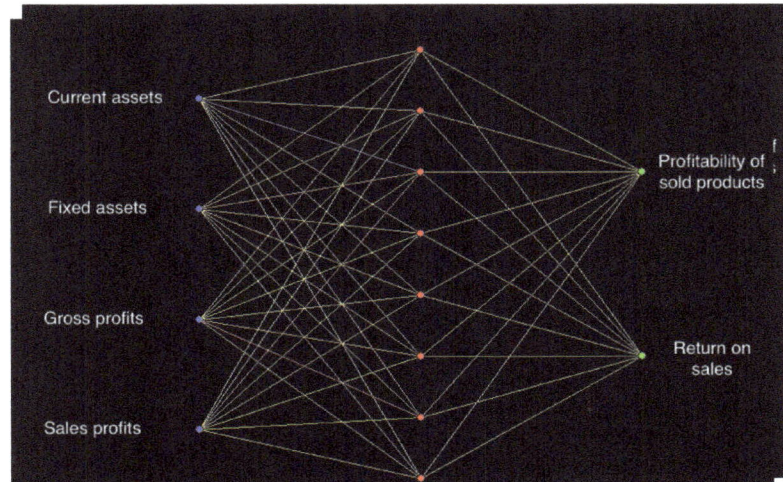

Figure 10. Graph of a neural network with architecture 4-8-2 constructed in Deductor Studio (dependence of the performance indicators of the microindustrial system on the input variables *DFA, VSG, VIG, RW*).

The quality of the models was assessed by the scatter diagram (Figure 11) and the root mean square error, which was 0.86%.

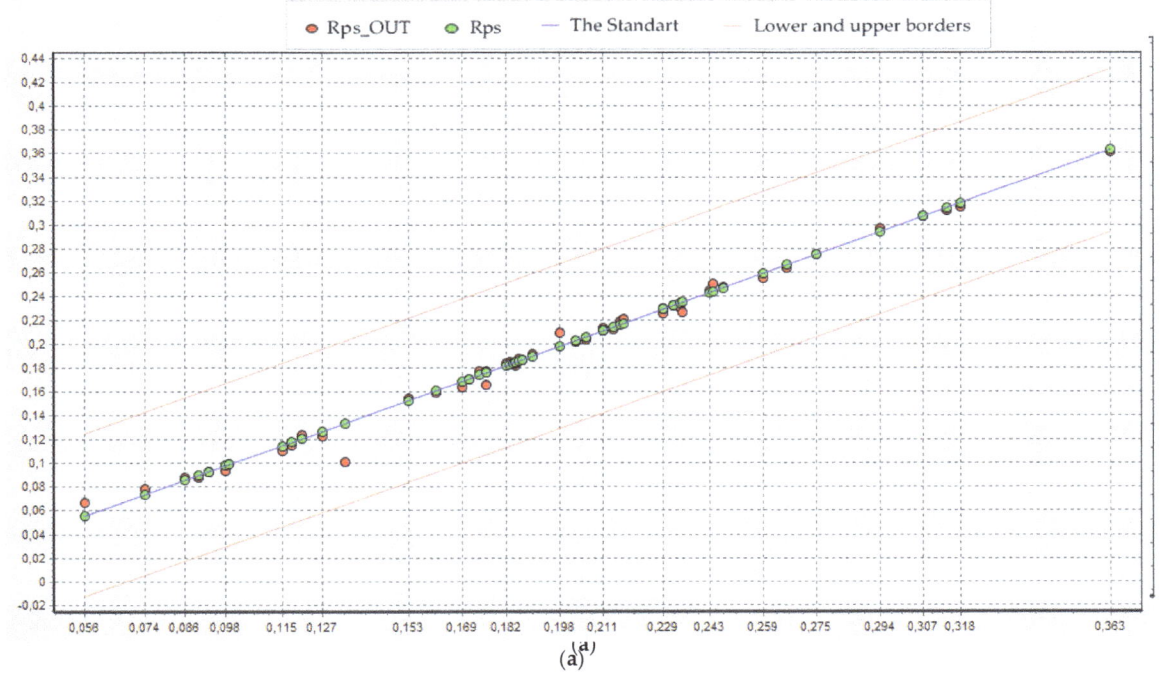

(a)

Figure 11. *Cont.*

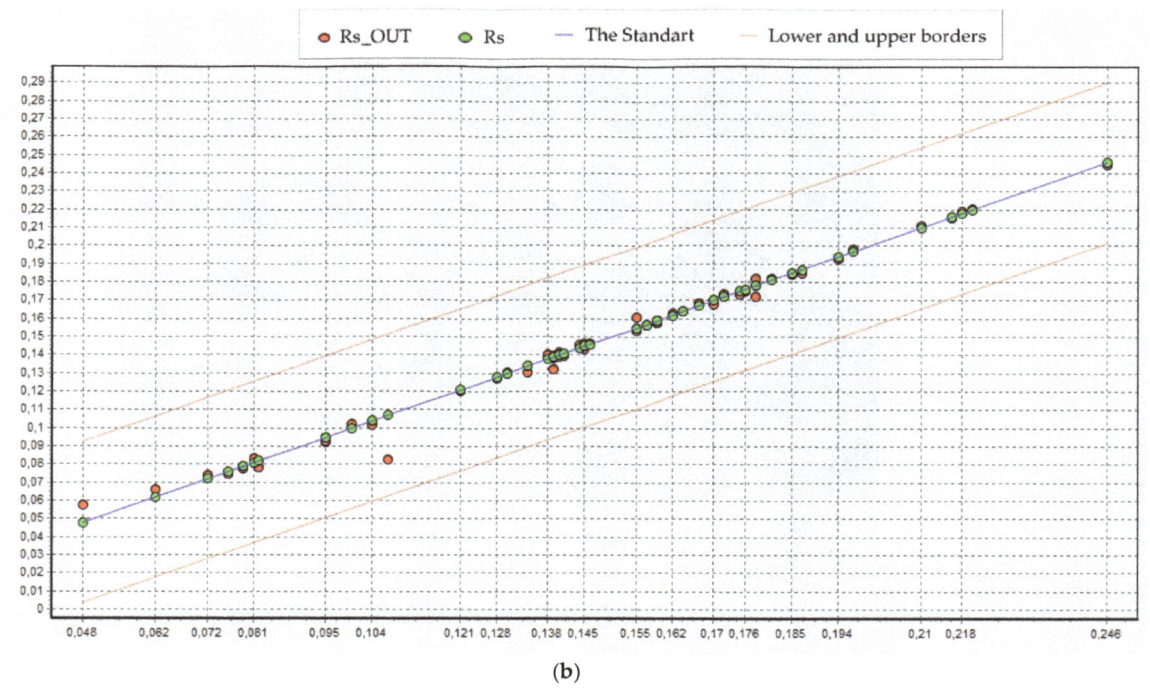

(b)

Figure 14. Scatter plot the training sample (logistic activation function), built in Deductor Studio: (a) Return on sales R_{ps}; (b) Return on sales R_s.

Evaluation of the scenario of forecasting of the enterprise activity consists of the previously identified vectors of changing the performance indicators of the industrial system. The trained neural network made it possible to identify the following values of the output variables:

- scenario 1 (1% increase in input variables): R_{ps} = 23.6% RR = 18.9%;
- scenario 2 (5% increase in input variables): R_{ps} = 23.7% RR = 18.8%;
- scenario 3 (10% increase in input variables): R_{ps} = 23.5% RR = 18.8%;
- scenario 4 (1% reduction in the value of input variables): R_{ps} = 28.5% RR = 20.3%.

Once again, the increase in performance indicators may be noticeable in the case of a decrease in the values of predictors.

Thus, the prediction results are significantly dependent on the DataSet. Despite the fact that multilayer neural networks self-select important features, it is advisable to perform correlation analysis beforehand, which will provide a higher probability of obtaining a high-quality predictive model.

4. Discussion

An analytical review of scientific approaches to performance management allows us to state the widespread use of artificial neural network tools to predict the behavior of complex systems. This work highlights numerous studies aimed at the study and development of neural network modeling methodology, where the object is mathematical tools, industries, enterprises, oil product volumes, GDP, CO_2 emissions, technological parameters, etc. However, in the conditions of Russian industry's transition to sustainable development, circular economy, as well as innovative development, a comprehensive assessment of the efficiency of industrial systems becomes important. Such an attempt in a study by Tuo et al. has been made [35] but is limited to the growth of production and GDP.

GDP. Other studies are limited to either technological processes [41,42], the environmental performance of industrial systems [36], or electricity consumption forecasting [38], etc.

We have come to the conclusion that there is no one-size-fits-all, true methodology for the performance management of industrial systems, which expands the scope for incremental methodology. We continue to emphasize complex solutions, which allow for a comprehensive assessment of a particular system. The tasks set for production enterprises and complexes at the federal level affect the issues of innovative development, modernization, and recycling. This formed the basis of our research and contributed to the identification of patterns of development of industrial systems of different levels and obtaining a number of new scientific results. Thus, we develop the methodology of performance management the industrial systems based on modern data processing tools.

Neural networks of different types and architectures served as a key tool for the processing of a series of dynamics. The advantage of this tool in relation to others (e.g., regression analysis) is that the mechanism of multilayer artificial neural networks automatically selects the best architecture based on the predefined conditions—the given sample structure (training, control, test), choice of neural network type (MLP or RBF), number of neurons on the hidden layer and activation function. This tool allows to train different variants of networks based on the same set of input data and to select the best model in terms of quality.

Thus, this article formulates the following conclusions and results.

1. The methodological solution for calculating the coefficient of development of an innovative industrial system (K_{iisd}), which develops the scientific groundwork in the field of efficiency management, is distinguished by its comprehensiveness and takes into account the most important components for today (the criteria of technical modernization, development, innovation activity, greening is taken into account). The basic principle of calculation of the indicator is universal and based on the results of correlation analysis. The combination of correlation, ranking and the determination of weighting coefficients makes our approach unique. The verification of the methodology confirms the correctness and adequacy of the real dynamics of the effectiveness of industrial systems.

2. The patterns of development of industrial systems in Russia (extractive and manufacturing) are based on the implementation of two methods—trend extrapolation and neural network modeling (univariate and multivariate). The results of comparing the results of the two methods identify different trajectories of development of industrial systems: in the first case—unconditional growth of the efficiency indicator (gross value added), and in the second case—decline. These trends allow us to summarize the difficult predictability of the development of innovative industrial systems, as well as the finding of the Russian industry at the point of bifurcation. The way out of the bifurcation point can be a structural transformation of state support of industrial enterprises of development institutions.

3. Prognostic neural network models, which allow for optimizing the contribution of attributes in the formation of target (set) values of performance indicators have been developed. The models are complemented by the definition of those priority directions of development of macro-industrial systems, which today are not given enough attention (according to the results of economic-mathematical modeling). Our conclusions and proposals will make it possible to align the growth trajectory of production systems.

4. Based on the results of neural network training, scenarios for the development of the micro-industrial system were proposed, allowing the forming of an idea and the potential vector of development of the enterprise—the growth or decline in efficiency. The choice of the direction of development is conditioned by the necessity of rationalization of production capacities and further modernization of technical infrastructure.
5. It is determined that the efficiency of industrial systems is determined by the volume of sales of goods, which is logical and natural. At the same time, innovative products and recycling of waste, which allow for saving resources, also make a significant contribution to the formation of gross value added.

The limitation of the proposed methodological complex is in the data set: a trained neural network will give better results with a larger data set. The wider the data set, the more cases the predictive model will consider.

Summarizing the study, we note that the constructed predictive models are non-linear in nature (the construction of the linear regression equation did not give a qualitative adequate model with significant regression coefficients). Neural networks allow us to overcome the complexity of such dependence, which is comparable to the opinion of other scientists [37,51]: multilayer networks with linear activation functions can be transformed into single-layer ones, which negatively affects network performance and prediction results.

Our findings and recommendations can be useful as a methodological basis for monitoring the effectiveness of industrial systems of different levels (for statistical services and public authorities) and can be included in strategies and programs for the development of industry in the country, and can be applied to the forecasting of activities based on the training of artificial neural networks.

5. Conclusions

This article presents the results of the study of innovative industrial systems, evaluated by their effectiveness at different levels of management (at micro- and macro levels), and using artificial neural networks developed predictive models that allow to identify the priority areas of development of the Russian economy, and align the growth trajectory of industrial systems. The significance of innovations and the ecologization of industrial systems was substantiated by a macroeconomic system. For the micro-economic system, the levers of efficiency have been identified, the management of which serves as the basis for the strategic development of the industrial system.

In future studies, the authors will test the performance of trained neural networks on new data sets for forecasting other industrial systems (macro- and micro-level). An interesting area of research could be the application of the Recurrent neural network (RNN) and Beetle antennae search in diagnosing the efficiency of economic systems.

Author Contributions: Conceptualization—A.I.S., methodology—F.F.G., formal analysis I.G.E., investigation A.I.S., I.G.E., data curation F.F.G., writing—original draft preparation A.I.S., F.F.G., writing—review and editing—A.I.S., I.G.E. All authors have read and agreed to the published version of the manuscript.

Funding: The research was carried out within the framework of the grant of the President of the Russian Federation for state support of leading scientific schools of the Russian Federation, project number NSh–1886.2022.2.

Data Availability Statement: Not applicable.

Conflicts of Interest: The authors declare no conflict of interest.

Appendix A. Symbol Table

Unit Designation	Contents
Macroindustrial systems	
Y_{mining}	the gross value added created in the mining sector
$Y_{manuf.}$	the gross value added created in the manufacturing sector
i	sector of industry (mining sector, manufacturing sector)
$DFA_{(i)}$	degree of depreciation of fixed assets on the full range of organizations of the i-th sector of industry
$VSG_{(i)}$	volume of shipped goods of own production, work and services performed by own forces in the i-th sector of industry
$VIG_{(i)}$	volume of innovative goods, works, services in Russia
$RW_{(i)}$	use and neutralization of production and consumption waste in the i-th sector of industry
K_{iisd} (mining)	the growth of innovation industrial system coefficient (mining sector)
K_{iisd} (manufacturing)	the growth of innovation industrial system coefficient (manufacturing sector)
Microindustrial system	
R_{ps}	profitability of sold products
R_s	return on sales
CA	current assets
FA	fixed assets
GP	gross profit
PS	profit from sales

References

1. Federal State Statistics Service. Available online: http://www.gks.ru (accessed on 2 November 2022).
2. Barsegyan, N.V.; Salimyanova, I.G.; Kushaeva, E.R. Typology of innovation strategies for petrochemical enterprises. *J. Phys. Conf. Ser.* **2020**, *1515*, 042090. [CrossRef]
3. Garina, E.P.; Kuznetsov, V.P.; Romanovskaya, E.V.; Kuznetsova, S.N.; Kornilov, D.A. Formation of the Production System Elements in the Enterprise of the Industry Through the Integration of Production Systems and Product Creation Systems. *Lect. Notes Netw. Syst.* **2020**, *73*, 441–451. [CrossRef]
4. Malysheva, T.V.; Shinkevich, A.I.; Kharisova, G.M.; Nuretdinova, Y.V.; Khasyanov, O.R.; Nuretdinov, I.G.; Zaitseva, N.A.; Kudryavtseva, S.S. The Sustainable Development of Competitive Enterprises through the Implementation of Innovative Development Strategy. *Int. J. Econ. Financ. Issues* **2016**, *6*, 185–191.
5. Kirillova, E.; Kakatunova, T.; Khalin, V. Methodology of Diagnostics and Selection of Industrial Enterprises Development Strategy in the Framework of Innovative Processes Joint Implementation. *Lect. Notes Netw. Syst.* **2022**, *474*, 53–64. [CrossRef]
6. Monetti, F.M.; de Giorgio, A.; Maffei, A. Industrial transformation and assembly technology: Context and research trends. *Procedia CIRP* **2022**, *107*, 1427–1432. [CrossRef]
7. Asheim, B.T.; Isaksen, A. Regional innovation systems: The integration of local 'sticky'and global 'ubiquitous' knowledge. *J. Technol. Tran.* **2002**, *27*, 77–86. [CrossRef]
8. Bergek, A.; Jacobsson, S.; Carlsson, B.; Lindmark, S.; Rickne, A. Analyzing the functional dynamics of technological innovation systems: A scheme of analysis. *Res. Policy* **2008**, *37*, 407–429. [CrossRef]
9. Cooke, P.; Mikel, G.U.; Etxebarria, G. Regional innovation systems: Institutional and organisational dimensions. *Res. Pol.* **1997**, *26*, 475–491. [CrossRef]
10. Li, D.; Liang, Z.; Tell, F.; Xue, L. Sectoral systems of innovation in the era of the fourth industrial revolution: An introduction to the special section. *Ind. Corp. Chang.* **2021**, *30*, 123–135. [CrossRef]
11. Kashani, E.S.; Naeini, A.B.; Gholizadeh, H. Innovation systems and global value chains: A Co-citation analysis of established linkages and possible future trends. *Int. J. Innov. Stud.* **2023**, *7*, 68–86. [CrossRef]
12. Khan, M.S. Absorptive capacities approaches for investigating national innovation systems in low and middle income countries. *Int. J. Innov. Stud.* **2022**, *6*, 183–195. [CrossRef]

13. Palm, A. Innovation systems for technology diffusion: An analytical framework and two case studies. *Technol. Forecast. Soc. Chang.* **2022**, *182*, 121821. [CrossRef]
14. Ortt, J.R.; Kamp, L.M. A technological innovation system framework to formulate niche introduction strategies for companies prior to large-scale diffusion. *Technol. Forecast. Soc. Chang.* **2022**, *180*, 121671. [CrossRef]
15. Shinkevich, A.I.; Kudryavtseva, S.S.; Rajskaya, M.V.; Zimina, I.V.; Dyrdonova, A.N.; Misbakhova, C.A. Integral technique for analyzing of national innovation systems development. *Espacios* **2018**, *39*, 6.
16. Cai, S.; Jiao, J.; Xiang, Q. Research on formation and development of circular industrial clusters and innovative networks. *Energy Procedia* **2011**, *5*, 1519–1524. [CrossRef]
17. Dli, M.; Zaenchkovski, A.; Tukaev, D.; Kakatunova, T. Optimization algorithms of the industrial clusters' innovative development programs. *Int. J. Appl. Eng. Res.* **2017**, *12*, 3455–3460.
18. Yashin, S.N.; Trifonov, Y.V.; Koshelev, E.V.; Garina, E.P.; Andryashina, N.S. Formation of a Linear Functional of Cluster Value for the Innovative Development of a Region. *Adv. Sci. Technol. Innov.* **2022**, 341–346. [CrossRef]
19. Blazquez, D.; Domenech, J.; Garcia-Alvarez-Coque, J.-M. Assessing Technology Platforms for Sustainability with Web Data Mining Techniques. *Sustainability* **2018**, *10*, 4497. [CrossRef]
20. Dezhina, I.G. Technology platforms in Russia: A catalyst for connecting government, science, and business? *Triple Helix* **2014**, *1*, 6. [CrossRef]
21. Lin, F.-J.; Lin, Y.-H. The determinants of successful R&D consortia: Government strategy for the servitization of manufacturing. *Serv. Bus.* **2012**, *6*, 489–502. [CrossRef]
22. Oliver, A.L. Holistic ecosystems for enhancing innovative collaborations in university–industry consortia. *J. Technol. Transf.* **2022**, *47*, 1612–1628. [CrossRef]
23. Shinkevich, A.I.; Ershova, I.G.; Galimulina, F.F.; Yarlychenko, A.A. Innovative Mesosystems Algorithm for Sustainable Development Priority Areas Identification in Industry Based on Decision Trees Construction. *Mathematics* **2021**, *9*, 3055. [CrossRef]
24. Hansen, L.K.; Salamon, P. Neural Network Ensembles. *IEEE Trans. Pattern Anal. Mach. Intell.* **1990**, *12*, 993–1001. [CrossRef]
25. Cheng, B.; Titterington, D.M. Neural networks: A review from a statistical perspective. *Stat. Sci.* **1994**, *9*, 2–30. [CrossRef]
26. Yao, X. Evolving artificial neural networks. *Proc. IEEE* **1999**, *87*, 1423–1447.
27. Dhillon, A.; Verma, G.K. Convolutional neural network: A review of models, methodologies and applications to object detection. *Prog. Artif. Intell.* **2020**, *9*, 85–112. [CrossRef]
28. Zhou, J.; Cui, G.; Hu, S.; Zhang, Z.; Yang, C.; Liu, Z.; Wang, L.; Li, C.; Sun, M. Graph neural networks: A review of methods and applications. *AI Open* **2020**, *1*, 57–81. [CrossRef]
29. Ge, K.; Zhao, J.-Q.; Zhao, Y.-Y. GR-GNN: Gated Recursion-Based Graph Neural Network Algorithm. *Mathematics* **2022**, *10*, 1171. [CrossRef]
30. Guo, M.; Manzoni, A.; Amendt, M.; Conti, P.; Hesthaven, J.S. Multi-fidelity regression using artificial neural networks: Efficient approximation of parameter-dependent output quantities. *Comput. Methods Appl. Mech. Eng.* **2022**, *389*, 114378. [CrossRef]
31. Linka, K.; Schäfer, A.; Meng, X.; Zou, Z.; Karniadakis, G.E.; Kuhl, E. Bayesian Physics Informed Neural Networks for real-world nonlinear dynamical systems. *Comput. Methods Appl. Mech. Eng.* **2022**, 115346. [CrossRef]
32. Mayet, A.M.; Nurgalieva, K.S.; Al-Qahtani, A.A.; Narozhnyy, I.M.; Alhashim, H.H.; Nazemi, E.; Indrupskiy, I.M. Proposing a High-Precision Petroleum Pipeline Monitoring System for Identifying the Type and Amount of Oil Products Using Extraction of Frequency Characteristics and a MLP Neural Network. *Mathematics* **2022**, *10*, 2916. [CrossRef]
33. Wong, W.C.; Chee, E.; Li, J.; Wang, X. Recurrent Neural Network-Based Model Predictive Control for Continuous Pharmaceutical Manufacturing. *Mathematics* **2018**, *6*, 242. [CrossRef]
34. Longo, L.; Riccaboni, M.; Rungi, A. A neural network ensemble approach for GDP forecasting. *J. Econ. Dyn. Control* **2022**, *134*, 104278. [CrossRef]
35. Tuo, S.; Chen, T.; He, H.; Feng, Z.; Zhu, Y.; Liu, F.; Li, C. A Regional Industrial Economic Forecasting Model Based on a Deep Convolutional Neural Network and Big Data. *Sustainability* **2021**, *13*, 12789. [CrossRef]
36. Zhao, W.; Niu, D. Prediction of CO_2 Emission in China's Power Generation Industry with Gauss Optimized Cuckoo Search Algorithm and Wavelet Neural Network Based on STIRPAT model with Ridge Regression. *Sustainability* **2017**, *9*, 2377. [CrossRef]
37. Adesanya, A.; Abdulkareem, A.; Adesina, L.M. Predicting extrusion process parameters in Nigeria cable manufacturing industry using artificial neural network. *Heliyon* **2020**, *6*, e04289. [CrossRef]
38. Leite Coelho da Silva, F.; da Costa, K.; Canas Rodrigues, P.; Salas, R.; López-Gonzales, J.L. Statistical and Artificial Neural Networks Models for Electricity Consumption Forecasting in the Brazilian Industrial Sector. *Energies* **2022**, *15*, 588. [CrossRef]
39. Shinkevich, A.I.; Malysheva, T.V.; Vertakova, Y.V.; Plotnikov, V.A. Optimization of Energy Consumption in Chemical Production Based on Descriptive Analytics and Neural Network Modeling. *Mathematics* **2021**, *9*, 322. [CrossRef]
40. Ramos, D.; Faria, P.; Vale, Z.; Mourinho, J.; Correia, R. Industrial Facility Electricity Consumption Forecast Using Artificial Neural Networks and Incremental Learning. *Energies* **2020**, *13*, 4774. [CrossRef]
41. Seawram, S.; Nimmanterdwong, P.; Sema, T.; Piemjaiswang, R.; Chalermsinsuwan, B. Specific heat capacity prediction of hybrid nanofluid using artificial neural network and its heat transfer application. *Energy Rep.* **2022**, *8*, 8–15. [CrossRef]
42. Dli, M.; Puchkov, A.; Kakatunova, T. Assessment of the technological process condition based on the assembly of deep recurrent neural networks. *Lect. Notes Comput. Sci.* **2020**, *12412*, 393–402. [CrossRef]

43. Du, W. Research on Evaluation of Enterprise Performance Based on BP Neural Network Improved by Levenberg-Marquardt Algorithm. In Proceedings of the 2015 International Conference on Automation, Mechanical Control and Computational Engineering (AMCCE 2015), Changsha, China, 24–25 October 2015; pp. 167–171. [CrossRef]
44. Wenjing, C. BP Neural Network-Based Evaluation Method for Enterprise Comprehensive Performance. *Math. Probl. Eng.* **2022**, *2022*, 7308235. [CrossRef]
45. Luo, Y.; Ren, D. Influence of the enterprise's intelligent performance evaluation model using neural network and genetic algorithm on the performance compensation of the merger and acquisition parties in the commitment period. *PLoS ONE* **2021**, *16*, e0248727. [CrossRef] [PubMed]
46. HSE University. Available online: https://www.hse.ru (accessed on 2 November 2022).
47. Arunapriya, B.; Kavitha Devi, D. Image compression using single layer linear neural networks. *Procedia Comput. Sci.* **2010**, *2*, 345–352. [CrossRef]
48. Dudnikov, E.E.; Rubashov, M.V. Single-layer neural networks with various feedbacks. *Neural Parallel Sci. Comput.* **2001**, *9*, 29–48.
49. Rosenblatt, F. The perceptron: A probabilistic model for information storage and organization in the brain. *Psychol. Rev.* **1958**, *65*, 386–408. [CrossRef]
50. Sazli, M.H. A brief review of feed-forward neural networks. *Commun. Fac. Sci. Univ. Ank. Series A2-A3 Phys. Sci. Eng.* **2006**, *50*, 11–17. [CrossRef]
51. Shokraneh, F.; Geoffroy-Gagnon, S.; Nezami, M.S.; Liboiron-Ladouceur, O. A Single Layer Neural Network Implemented by a 4×4 MZI-Based Optical Processor. *IEEE Photonics J.* **2019**, *11*, 8894848. [CrossRef]
52. Abbas, O.M. Neural Networks in Business Forecasting. *Int. J. Comput. (IJC)* **2015**, *19*, 114–128.
53. Chaudhary, A.; Sharma, M. Multilayer Neural Network Design for the Calculation of Risk Factor Associated with COVID-19. *Augment. Hum. Res.* **2021**, *6*, 6. [CrossRef]
54. Covantes-Osuna, C.; López, J.B.; Paredes, O.; Vélez-Pérez, H.; Romo-Vázquez, R. Multilayer Network Approach in EEG Motor Imagery with an Adaptive Threshold. *Sensors* **2021**, *21*, 8305. [CrossRef] [PubMed]
55. Smetanin, Y.G. Neural networks as systems for recognizing patterns. *J. Math. Sci.* **1998**, *89*, 1406–1457. [CrossRef]
56. Hagg, A.; Mensing, M.; Asteroth, A. Evolving parsimonious networks by mixing activation functions. In Proceedings of the GECCO'17: Genetic and Evolutionary Computation Conference, Berlin, Germany, 15–19 July 2017; pp. 425–432. [CrossRef]

Disclaimer/Publisher's Note: The statements, opinions and data contained in all publications are solely those of the individual author(s) and contributor(s) and not of MDPI and/or the editor(s). MDPI and/or the editor(s) disclaim responsibility for any injury to people or property resulting from any ideas, methods, instructions or products referred to in the content.

Article

Mathematical Model Describing the Hardening and Failure Behaviour of Aluminium Alloys: Application in Metal Shear Cutting Process

Lotfi Ben Said [1,2,*], Alia Khanfir Chabchoub [3] and Mondher Wali [2]

1. Department of Mechanical Engineering, College of Engineering, University of Ha'il, Ha'il City 2440, Saudi Arabia
2. Laboratory of Electrochemistry and Environment (LEE), National Engineering School of Sfax, University of Sfax, Sfax 5080, Tunisia
3. Higher Institute of Technological Studies of Sousse, Sousse 4023, Tunisia
* Correspondence: bensaid_rmq@yahoo.fr or lo.bensaid@uoh.edu.sa

Citation: Ben Said, L.; Chabchoub, A.K.; Wali, M. Mathematical Model Describing the Hardening and Failure Behaviour of Aluminium Alloys: Application in Metal Shear Cutting Process. *Mathematics* 2023, 11, 1980. https://doi.org/10.3390/math11091980

Academic Editor: Aleksey I. Shinkevich

Received: 22 March 2023
Revised: 18 April 2023
Accepted: 21 April 2023
Published: 22 April 2023

Copyright: © 2023 by the authors. Licensee MDPI, Basel, Switzerland. This article is an open access article distributed under the terms and conditions of the Creative Commons Attribution (CC BY) license (https://creativecommons.org/licenses/by/4.0/).

Abstract: Recent research has focused on sheet shear cutting operations. However, little research has been conducted on bar shear cutting. The main objective of the present investigation is to study bar shear cutting with numerical and experimental analysis. Bar shear cutting is an important operation because it precedes bulk metalworking processes for instance machining, extrusion and hot forging. In comparison to sheet shear cutting, bar shear cutting needs thermomechanical modelling. The variational formulation of the model is presented to predict damage mechanics in the bar shear cutting of aluminium alloys. Coupled thermomechanical modelling is required to analyse the mechanical behaviour of bulk workpieces, in which the combined effect of strain and temperature fields is considered in the shear cutting process. For this purpose, modified hardening and damage Johnson–Cook laws are developed. Numerical results for sheet and bar shear cutting operations are presented. The comparison between numerical and experimental results of shearing force/tool displacement during sheet and bar shear cutting operations proves that the use of a thermomechanical model in the case of the bar shear cutting process is crucial to accurately predict the mechanical behaviour of aluminium alloys. The analysis of the temperature field in the metal bar shows that the temperature can reach T = 388 °C on the sheared surface. The current model accurately predicts the shear cutting process and shows a strong correlation with experimental tests. Two values of clearance (c_1 = 0.2 mm) and (c_2 = 1.2 mm) are assumed for modeling the bar shear cutting operation. It is observed that for the low shear clearance, the burr is small, the quality of the sheared surface is better, and the fractured zone is negligible.

Keywords: shear cutting; thermomechanical model; ductile fracture; Johnson–Cook model

MSC: 74R99

1. Introduction

Finite element methods are increasingly being developed and used for predicting the behaviour of workpiece and tool components in manufacturing processes. Metal forming and cutting processes require knowledge of the mechanical behaviour and damage of the workpiece [1]. In fact, the accuracy of a finite element model of any metalworking process is always dependent on the robustness of the identification of the constitutive law of materials [2–4].

In decoupled models, plasticity and damage fields are independent. Various numerical models take into consideration the stress triaxiality term in damage prediction [5,6]. Others models consider the damage variable as a function of the cavity properties in porous materials [7,8]. When predicting the behaviour and ductile damage of metallic materials during cutting and forming processes, Johnson–Cook models are the most widely used laws [9,10]. Their accuracy has been proven in various works [11–14]. The Johnson–Cook plasticity law considers the thermo-plastic behaviour of workpieces in manufacturing processes with high deformation rates and high temperature variations. In addition, the Johnson–Cook damage criterion takes into account the influence of stress triaxialities on damage strain. This model was considered in computational manufacturing processes because it takes into account the high deformation rates and high temperature fields obtained in these processes, such as shear cutting and machining. The material parameters of this model are determined by experimental tests.

Recently, the shear cutting process has been widely used by mechanical industries and investigated by a larger number of numerical studies. This is due to the increasing demand for a reliable and optimal shearing process in aeronautical and automotive developments. In terms of numerical studies, the sheet shear cutting process has interested researchers more than the bar shear cutting process. Sheet and bar metalworking differ in the blank dimensions, evolution of the temperature field during cutting operations, and the anisotropy of the workpiece; each case should be studied distinctly. In this context, research works on sheet shear cutting [15–17] are more developed than those on the bar shear cutting process [18,19]. The impact of cutting parameters such as clearance and cutting speed on the quality of the sheared workpiece, shearing efficiency and tool life has been studied.

Optimization of the workpiece geometry and tool wear during shear cutting operations is a priority in the metalworking industry. Experimental and numerical studies have been performed to analyse the impact of friction, cutting speed, punch force, etc. on workpiece and cutting tools [20–22]. These studies are based on the efficiency of the computed material models, which contain hardening and damage laws. In addition, a burr deformation can frequently be illustrated in shear cutting operations on the cutting edge [23]. The burr should be deburred before the next step of manufacturing operation, such as the blanking and turning steps. Accurate shear cutting parameters have been determined for a burr-free cutting edge. A pre-shear cutting operation was studied from a numerical and experimental point of view [19]. The thermal field was not considered in the 3D numerical model. Behrens et al. [18] develop an experimental study in order to show the influence of microstructural conditions, clearance and shear rate on the shear plane quality of aluminium bars.

In recent years, researchers have studied sheet shear cutting processes with experimental and numerical investigations. However, only a few results have been determined for the bar shear cutting process. Sheet shearing studies are more advanced than bar shearing studies because of the continuous development of automobile and aeronautic fabrication. Accordingly, it is of interest that we conduct a study about the bar shear cutting process, which is an important operation that principally precedes bulk forming processes. In this paper, a mechanical and thermomechanical numerical modelling are developed. Based on experimental and numerical tests, the thermal term should be considered in plasticity and damage models to simulate the bar shear cutting process. For this purpose, a variational formulation of the thermomechanical model of shear cutting operation is developed. The efficiency of the plasticity and damage Johnson–Cook models are proved. The governing laws take into account the effect of the temperature field on the flow stress and the damage strain. Numerical tests of shear cutting operations are presented in order to prove the accuracy of the modified Johnson–Cook models in predicting ductile damage. The numerical results of sheet and bar shearing operations are presented in this paper. The comparison between the numerical and experimental results of the shear force/tool displacement, during the shearing operations of plates and bars, proves that the use of the thermomechanical model in the case of the bar shearing process is essential to flawlessly predict the behaviour of aluminium materials. In fact, the temperature field influences mechanical properties such as hardening, ductility and strain damage. The effect of shear clearance is investigated in order to emphasize the effect of this parameter on burr formation, the quality of the sheared surface and the dimensions of the fractured zone.

2. Materials and Methods

The experiments are carried out using specific shearing tools (Figure 1). The experimental cutting tests are conducted using a universal tensile machine (Figure 1a). Shear cutting tests are carried out with a constant cutting speed and at ambient temperature. Figure 1b,c show the 3D design of the employed shearing tools, which are used to cut aluminium sheets and round bars, respectively.

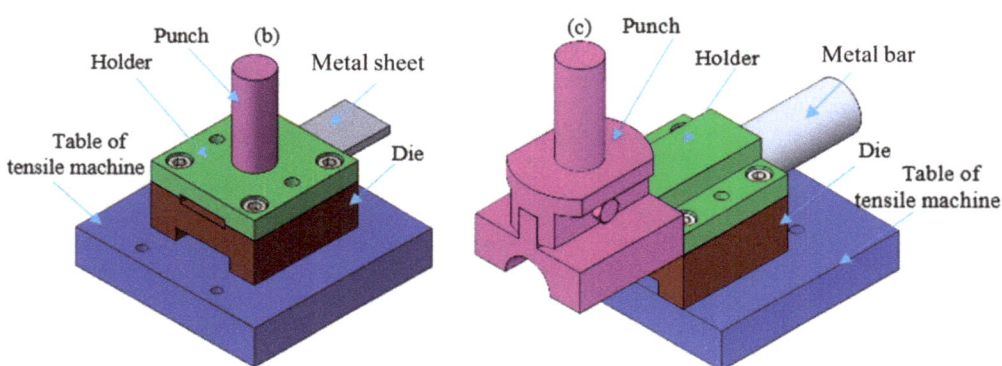

Figure 1. Experimental shear cutting tools: (**a**) tensile machine; (**b**) specific sheet shearing tool; (**c**) specific bar shearing tool.

Two grades of aluminium alloys are considered for the experimental and numerical tests. The first material is the 5083 aluminium sheet. Its thickness is 2 mm, and its elastic properties are illustrated in Table 1. The second material is the Al6061-T6 round bar. This aluminium bar has a diameter of 18 mm. Table 2 illustrates its thermomechanical properties.

Table 1. Elastic properties of 5083 aluminium sheet [24].

Yield Strength (MPa)	Poisson's Ratio	Young's Modulus (MPa)
106.3	0.33	75.6

Table 2. Al6061-T6 aluminium bar properties [25].

Density (g/cm³)	Tensile Strength (MPa)	Yield Strength (MPa)	Young's Modulus (GPa)	Poisson's Ratio	Thermal Conductivity (W/mK)
2.7	310	275	69	0.33	167

3. Constitutive Models of Mechanical Behaviour and Damage

3.1. Governing True Stress–Strain Model

The true stress–strain equation is determined in order to set up a finite element simulation of the shear cutting operation. It is deduced from the engineering stress–strain curve, which is plotted by recording the engineering stress variation with the engineering strain until the bifurcation of the specimen. Both terms are known as nominal stress and nominal strain. The engineering stress–strain curve is obtained by progressively applying load F to a tensile test and measuring the engineering deformation (Equation (1)) from this experimental test. This curve reveals the mechanical properties of the workpiece.

$$\varepsilon = \frac{L - L_0}{L_0} \quad (1)$$

where L is the current length of the gauge section, and L_0 is the original length of the gauge section.

The engineering stress is calculated by dividing the applied load F by the original cross-section S_0. The nominal stress is given by Equation (2).

$$\sigma = \frac{F}{S_0} \quad (2)$$

However, the curve based on the instantaneous cross-section area S is called the true stress–strain curve. The instantaneous applied load divided by the instantaneous cross-sectional area of specimen S gives the true stress, as shown in Equation (3):

$$\sigma_v = \frac{F}{S} \quad (3)$$

For the true strain, Equation (4) gives the definition of this term:

$$d\varepsilon = \frac{dL}{L} \quad (4)$$

Both sides, which are given by Equation (4), are integrated, and the boundary conditions are applied. We obtain the following equation:

$$\varepsilon_v = \int_{L_0}^{L} \frac{dL}{L} \quad (5)$$

True strain is a logarithmic term. It is given by Equation (6):

$$\varepsilon_v = Ln\left(\frac{L}{L_0}\right) = Ln(1 + \varepsilon) \quad (6)$$

3.2. Empirical Formulations and Identification of Hardening Model

Good knowledge of the mechanical properties is needed in order to perform accurate numerical modelling of the manufacturing processes. Diverse empirical formulations have been proposed in order to predict the plastic deformation behaviour of materials in metal forming and cutting processes. One of the most commonly used formulations was proposed by Hollomon [26]. This power-law empirical relationship depends on two parameters: the strain-hardening coefficient and the strain-hardening exponent, respectively. Ludwik's law has an additional stress factor [27]. This model depends on three parameters, which are the yield strength, the coefficient of plastic resistance and the strain-hardening exponent. The Hollomon power law is not capable of describing the plastic behaviour at low strains for face-centred cubic steels with low stacking-fault energy (SFE). In fact, the stacking fault introduces an irregularity into the normal sequence of atoms. This irregularity carries the SFE. A modified Hollomon relationship [28,29] was developed, which is extended to all metals regardless of the SFE. Two additional parameters are added in the modified Holloman law. In the same context, Swift [30] proposed a flow formulation by modifying the Holloman relationship. He takes into account a pre-strain term as a structural parameter.

Furthermore, when a workpiece is subjected to a high temperature as in forming and cutting processes, its strength tends to decrease. The thermal field has an effect on the evaluation of the flow stress model. In fact, in the shear cutting process, the temperature sensitivity should be taken into account when we define the plasticity and the damage laws. We define in these models the temperature sensitivity term $\underline{T}$, which is defined as shown in Equation (7). We denote T_0 and T_m as the reference and melting temperatures, respectively.

$$\underline{T} = \frac{T - T_0}{T_m - T_0} \tag{7}$$

Furthermore, an empirical plasticity law named the Johnson–Cook model (Equation (8)) was developed and is usually used to describe the ductile material's behaviour under strain hardening, strain rate hardening and thermal conditions [31].

$$\sigma_{eq} = \left(A + B\left(\varepsilon_{pl}\right)^n\right)\left(1 + C\,Ln(\underline{\dot{\varepsilon}})\right)\left(1 - (\underline{T})^m\right) \tag{8}$$

The constitutive parameters may be determined experimentally. In the current study, the reference temperature (Equation (7)) and the reference strain rate (Equation (9)) are taken, respectively, as 20° and 1 s^{-1}. In the flow stress model, we have

$$\underline{\dot{\varepsilon}} = \frac{\dot{\varepsilon}}{\dot{\varepsilon}_0} \tag{9}$$

The strain-hardening effect depends on three parameters, which are A, B and n. They are called the yield stress, flow stress and the strain-hardening coefficient, respectively. The strain rate strengthening effect depends on the strain rate coefficient, denoted as C. The last term represents the temperature effect. It contains the temperature dependence coefficient m. In our model of the shear cutting test, the strain rate's strengthening influence is neglected.

However, two laws are considered. In the first one, the temperature effect is not taken into account. The modified Johnson–Cook law is given by Equation (10).

$$\sigma_{eq} = \left(A + B\varepsilon_{pl}^n\right) \tag{10}$$

After rearranging Equation (10) and taking the logarithmic function on both sides of this law, a linear relationship between $Ln(\sigma_{eq} - A)$ and $Ln\left(\varepsilon_{pl}\right)$ was determined, as shown in Equation (11):

$$Ln(\sigma_{eq} - A) = n.Ln\left(\varepsilon_{pl}\right) + Ln(B) \tag{11}$$

This relationship is a linear function. Based on the experimental tensile test, the flow stress model given by Equation (10) is calibrated. Then, the strain-hardening parameters are predicted.

In the second law, the modified Johnson–Cook model is given by Equation (12):

$$\sigma_{eq} = \left(A + B\left(\varepsilon_{pl}\right)^n\right)\left(1 - (\underline{T})^m\right) \tag{12}$$

In order to linearize this relationship, it is necessary to rearrange it, as follows, by considering the logarithmic function of the three terms:

$$Ln\left(1 - \frac{\sigma_{eq}}{A + B\left(\varepsilon_{pl}\right)^n}\right) = m.Ln(\underline{T}) \tag{13}$$

After identification of the strain-hardening parameters (Equation (11)) and fitting of the different data points, the temperature dependence coefficient m can be identified.

3.3. Constitutive Model of Ductile Damage

When the fracture initiation occurs in the workpiece, its strength property reduces during plastic deformation. The relationship between the damaged stress σ_D and the damage parameter D gives the damage evolution, as shown in Equation (14).

$$\sigma_D = (1 - D)\sigma_{eq}; \quad 0 \leq D \leq 1 \tag{14}$$

The damage occurs when D reaches the maximum value $D_{max} = 1$.

Furthermore, numerical models take into account the influence of stress triaxiality η on the strain damage. The triaxiality factor is a dimensionless ratio between hydrostatic and Von Mises equivalent stresses. We denote σ_I, σ_{II} and σ_{III} as the principal tensor stresses. We then have

$$\eta = \frac{\sigma_m}{\sigma_{eq}} = \frac{\frac{\sigma_I + \sigma_{II} + \sigma_{III}}{3}}{\sqrt{\frac{1}{2}\left[(\sigma_I - \sigma_{II})^2 + (\sigma_{II} - \sigma_{III})^2 + (\sigma_{III} - \sigma_I)^2\right]}} \tag{15}$$

The triaxiality factor gives us an idea of the stress states in the sheared piece. Therefore, stress triaxiality is an important factor to consider in the design and analysis of ductile materials, particularly in high-stress and high-strain applications in which the risk of fracture is significant. By understanding the relationship between stress triaxiality and fracture behaviour, engineers can optimize the design of materials and structures to improve their strength, durability, and safety.

One of the damage models used in cutting processes is the Hooputra criterion [32]. It is widely used in the sheet shear cutting process, in which it assumes that the damage strain depends only on the triaxiality factor (Equation (16)).

$$D = \int \frac{\Delta \varepsilon_{pl}}{\varepsilon_f} \tag{16}$$
$$\varepsilon_f = a_1 e^{a_3 \eta} + a_2 e^{-a_3 \eta}$$

where $\Delta \varepsilon$ is the equivalent plastic strain increment, and ε_f is the damage strain. The influence of the thermal term is not considered in this model. The material parameters, which are a_1, a_2 and a_3, should be identified experimentally. The maximal damage variable was fixed to $D_{max} = 1$. The failure happens when the damage variable reaches D_{max}.

Otherwise, as shown in Equation (17), the Johnson–Cook damage model describes the damage strain as a function of the stress triaxiality, strain rate and temperature fields.

$$\varepsilon_f = \left(D_1 + D_2\, e^{D_3 \eta}\right)\left(1 + D_4\, Ln(\dot{\varepsilon})\right)(1 - D_5 \underline{T}) \tag{17}$$

The damage material parameters (D_1 to D_5) are determined from experimental characterization tests. The cumulative damage parameter D is calculated as shown in Equation (18).

$$D = \sum \left(\frac{\Delta \varepsilon_{pl}}{\varepsilon_f}\right) \tag{18}$$

The modified Johnson–Cook law (Equation (19)) describes the fracture strain when the effect of strain rate is neglected. Only four parameters should be identified.

$$\varepsilon_f = \left(D_1 + D_2 \, e^{D_3 \eta}\right)(1 - D_5 \underline{T}) \tag{19}$$

When the effect of temperature is also neglected, the second modified Johnson–Cook law describes the fracture strain:

$$\varepsilon_f = \left(D_1 + D_2 \, e^{D_3 \eta}\right) \tag{20}$$

Both models (Equations (19) and (20)) will be used in numerical computations of shear cutting tests.

4. Variational Formulation of Shear Cutting Operations

Friction forces should be considered in any cutting process, mainly in machining and shear cutting tests. These forces play a critical role in the prediction of cutting parameters. In shear cutting operations, friction is mainly present between the workpiece and the tool. The contact force F_{fr} (Equation (21)) is decomposed into two parts, which are tangential and normal terms.

$$F_{fr} = F_{fr}^n + F_{fr}^t \tag{21}$$

The internal heat flux results only from the plastic strain and the contact friction between the workpiece and the shear cutting tools.

In addition, the fundamental governing equation of the dynamic system in continuum mechanics is given by Equation (22).

$$div(\underline{\sigma}) + f_d = \rho \ddot{U} \tag{22}$$

where $\underline{\sigma}$ is the symmetric stress tensor; it is defined with the behaviour law. f_d is the volume force, ρ is the mass density of workpiece, and $\ddot{U}$ is the acceleration. Based on the principle of virtual work, the total work done by the applied forces during a small virtual displacement δU is zero. This principle is shown in Equation (23):

$$W_{int} + W_{inert} = \sum W_{ext} \tag{23}$$

where W_{int} and W_{inert} are the internal and inertial virtual work, respectively. They are defined, respectively, by the following equations.

$$\begin{aligned} W_{int} &= \int_V \sigma \, \delta \dot{U} \, dV \\ W_{inert} &= \int_V \rho \, \ddot{U} \, \delta U \, dV \end{aligned} \tag{24}$$

In the same context, Equation (25) is the mathematical relationship of the external virtual work.

$$\sum W_{ext} = \int_V f_d \, \delta U \, dV + \int_{S_{fr}} \left(F_{fr}^n + F_{fr}^t\right) \delta U \, dS + \int_{S_\tau} \tau \, \delta U \, dS \tag{25}$$

where τ is the stress vector on the surface S_τ.

The variational form of the mechanical problem is given by the following equation:

$$\begin{array}{c} \int_V \underline{\sigma} : \delta \underline{\varepsilon} \, dV + \int_V \rho \, \ddot{U} \, \delta \dot{U} \, dV \\ = \\ \int_V f_d \, \delta \dot{U} \, dV + \int_{S_{fr}} \left(F_{fr}^n + F_{fr}^t\right) \delta \dot{U} \, dS + \int_{S_\tau} \tau \, \delta U \, dS \end{array} \tag{26}$$

In addition, the thermal equation is given by Equation (27). C_v, T and k are the specific heat of the isotropic materials, the temperature rate and the thermal conductivity, respectively.

$$\rho\, C_v\, \dot{T} = div(k.grad(T)) + Q_{conv} + Q_{mec} \qquad (27)$$

Q_{conv} is the work created by heat convection between the tools and the workpiece. Q_{mec} is generated by the mechanical contribution. It is given by Equation (28).

$$Q_{mec} = \eta_{pl}\, Q_{pl} + \eta_{fr}\, Q_{fr} \qquad (28)$$

where η_p is the fraction of plastic work converted into heat Q_{pl}, η_{fr} is the fraction of friction work converted into heat in the workpiece Q_{fr}. The contact surface between the workpiece and the cutting tool is denoted S_f. The weak variational form of Equation (27) is expressed as follows:

$$\int_V \left(\rho C_p \dot{T} - k\Delta T - \eta_{pl}\, \underline{\sigma} : \underline{\dot{\varepsilon}}\right) \delta T\, dV$$
$$= \qquad (29)$$
$$-\int_{S_{fr}} \left(\eta_{fr} f_{fr} \tau_{fr}\, \dot{U} + h(T - T_{tool})\right) \delta T\, dS$$

The space of functions and their derivatives are L^2-integrable and belong to the H^1 space. We denote δT as an arbitrary temperature variation. T_{tool} is the temperature of the tool, and h is heat transfer coefficient due to thermal convection. Then, thermomechanical problem consists of solving the following system (Equation (30)).

$$\begin{cases} \int_V \left(\underline{\sigma} : \delta\underline{\varepsilon} + \rho\, \ddot{U}\, \delta\dot{U} - f_d\, \delta\dot{U}\right) dV = \int_{S_{fr}} \left(F_{fr}^n + F_{fr}^t\right) \delta\dot{U}\, dS + \int_{S_\tau} \tau\, \delta U\, dS \\ \int_V \left(\rho C_p \dot{T} - k\Delta T - \eta_{pl}\, \underline{\sigma} : \underline{\dot{\varepsilon}}\right) \delta T\, dV = -\int_{S_{fr}} \left(\eta_{fr} f_{fr} \tau_{fr}\, \dot{U} + h(T - T_{tool})\right) \delta T\, dS \end{cases} \qquad (30)$$

Using the finite element method, the continuum mechanical problem described in Equation (30) is discretized, in which the total computation step is decomposed into a Δt time step (Appendix A).

After developing mathematical equations of thermomechanical shear cutting problem, numerical results will be presented in the next sections. The accuracy of the developed numerical models will be evaluated.

5. Numerical Models of Shear Cutting Operation

5.1. Numerical Model of Sheet Shear Cutting

The studied material is the 5083 aluminium alloy. A finite element code ABAQUS/Explicit is used in order to simulate the shear cutting operation of the 5083 aluminium sheet, which is meshed using a four-node bilinear axisymmetric quadrilateral element (CAX4R). In this section, the J2 yield criterion is used to describe the yielding behaviour of the aluminium material. As illustrated in Figure 2, we use a refined mesh in the failure zone. In our numerical model, the punch, the die and the holder are supposed rigid solids.

The diameters of the punch and die are 12 mm and 12.25 mm, respectively. The Coulomb friction model is used with a friction coefficient of 0.3. The parameters corresponding to the isotropic hardening are given in Table 3.

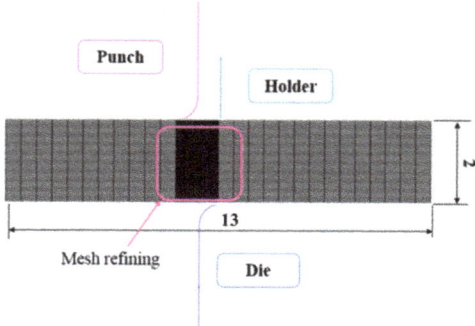

Figure 2. Numerical model of the sheet shear cutting operation.

Table 3. Behaviour parameters of 5083 aluminium sheet [24].

Young's modulus (MPa)	75,636
Poisson's ratio	0.33
Isotropic hardening parameters (MPa)	$\sigma(\varepsilon_{pl}) = 106.36 + 235.77\left(1 - e^{-9\,\varepsilon_{pl}}\right) + 54.36\left(1 - e^{-514\,\varepsilon_{pl}}\right)$

5.2. Numerical Model of Bar Shear Cutting

The bar shear cutting process is modelled in this section. Figure 3 shows the numerical model of this process. The bar is assumed to be composed of isotropic materials. Therefore, The J2 yield criterion, also known as the Von Mises yield criterion, is used for predicting the yield behaviour of the aluminium bar under complex stress states. In order to consider the element deletion method, the sample is fine-meshed in the shear zone. In fact, the element mesh size is 0.1 mm in this zone.

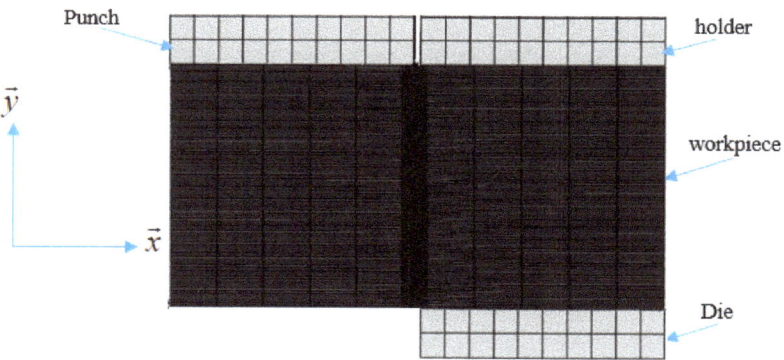

Figure 3. Moving and fixed parts of the shear cutting model.

All tools are considered rigid solids. The aluminium bar is modelled as an elastoplastic solid. The action applied by the punch on the bar causes a high shear deformation in the shear zone. The punch has a shear speed of V_{sh} = 200 mm/min. The holder and the die are clamped in this model. The Coulomb friction model is used with a friction coefficient of 0.3.

Experimental characterization tests are elaborated on the 6061-T6 aluminium bar by [33] in order to predict the Johnson–Cook parameters for the aluminium alloys. They are estimated as drawn in Table 4.

Table 4. Johnson–Cook parameters of Al6061-T6 aluminium bar [33].

A (MPa)	B (MPa)	n	m	D_1	D_2	D_3	D_5
250	79.7	0.5	1.5	−0.77	1.45	−0.47	1.6

The plasticity and damage mechanics are modelled with the modified Johnson–Cook model. For the bar shear cutting process simulations, two models are used. The first one considers only the mechanical behaviour and damage laws of the bar (Equations (10) and (19)). The second considers the thermal effect (Equations (12) and (20)) during the shear cutting process, which can significantly affect the flow stress and damage strain of the material.

For the mechanical model, the sheared workpiece is meshed with an eight-node linear brick element called C3D8 in Abaqus software. It is a fully integrated element. However, if we consider the thermomechanical model, the hexahedral thermally coupled elements with trilinear displacement and temperature (C3D8T) are used. In this model, four degrees of freedom are defined, which are three displacements in spatial directions with the temperature field.

6. Numerical Results and Discussion

6.1. Mechanical Model for Predicting Sheet Shear Cutting Operation

Mechanical models are used for the sheet metal in order to simulate the sheet shear cutting operation. In fact, Figure 4 illustrates the computed result.

Figure 4. Numerical prediction of the sheet shear cutting operation for punch displacement of 1.1 mm.

Figure 5 illustrates a comparison between experimental and numerical curves. Figure 5 depicts the evolution of the shearing force vs. punch displacement during the shearing operation. It is notable that whether for the numerical or experimental results, a sudden drop in the shear force is detected, which is caused by a brutal crack propagation in the sheet metal. There is good correlation between the both curves, which proves the efficiency of the mechanical model in computing the sheet shear cutting operation.

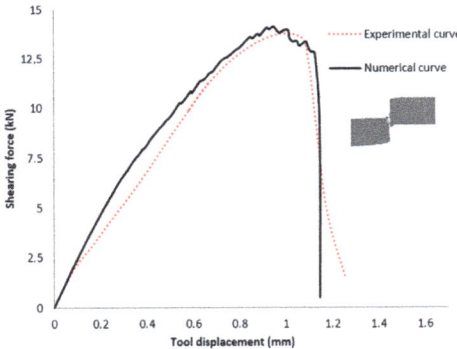

Figure 5. Sheet shear cutting tests: numerical and experimental results.

6.2. Thermomechanical Model for Predicting Bar Shear Cutting Operations

The bar shear cutting process of the Al6061-T6 alloy is simulated with the finite element code ABAQUS/Explicit. We denote with "Model 1" the modified Johnson–Cook plasticity and damage laws (Equations (10) and (19)), and with "Model 2" the modified Johnson–Cook laws (Equations (12) and (20)). Computed shearing force vs. tool displacement curves are illustrated in Figure 6.

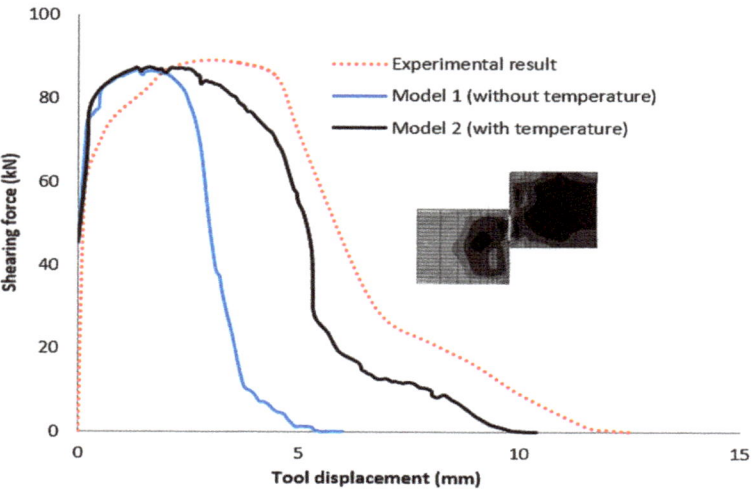

Figure 6. Bar shear cutting tests: numerical and experimental results.

The experimental shearing force was illustrated in the same Figure 6. During the experimental and numerical shear cutting operation, the clearance value is $c = 0.1$ mm.

The force–tool displacement curve contains four parts. The first is the elastic deformation. In this part, the curve evolution is linear. The second is the plastic deformation with hardening. If the curve attains the maximum value of shear cutting force, we obtain the plastic deformation with partial section reduction. Finally, macro crack nucleation and propagation are illustrated in the last zone. In Model 1, the temperature term is not considered in plasticity and damage relationships. This model incorrectly predicts the evolution of shearing force in the function of tool displacement. The numerical plastic deformation parts are smaller than the experimental parts, as shown in Figure 6. However, the maximum shear cutting force is approximately the same for both numerical models and for the experimental test. It has been noted in Figure 6 that using Model 2 gives a result very close to the experimental result. Finally, in the case of the bar shear cutting process, the temperature field should be considered in the constitutive behaviour of the aluminium material. This is because the shear cutting process can generate significant heat due to plastic deformation and friction between the cutting tool and the workpiece. The localized heating can affect the material's flow stress, damage accumulation, and microstructure evolution, leading to changes in the material's mechanical properties and potential failure modes.

A set of numerical tests of Model 2 are carried out in order to predict displacement (Figure 7) and temperature (Figure 8) fields that occur via shear cutting operations.

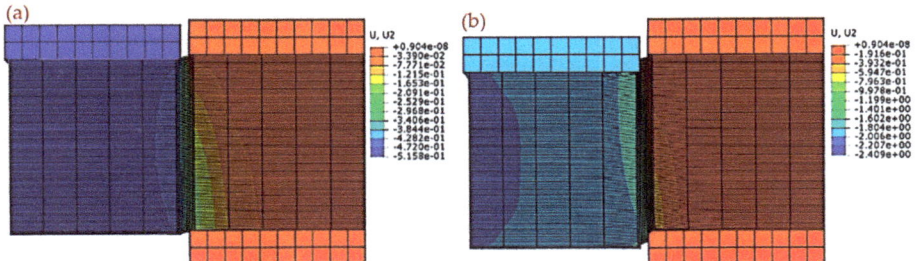

Figure 7. Displacement fields: (**a**) punch displacement U2 = 0.51 mm; (**b**) punch displacement U2 = 2.4 mm.

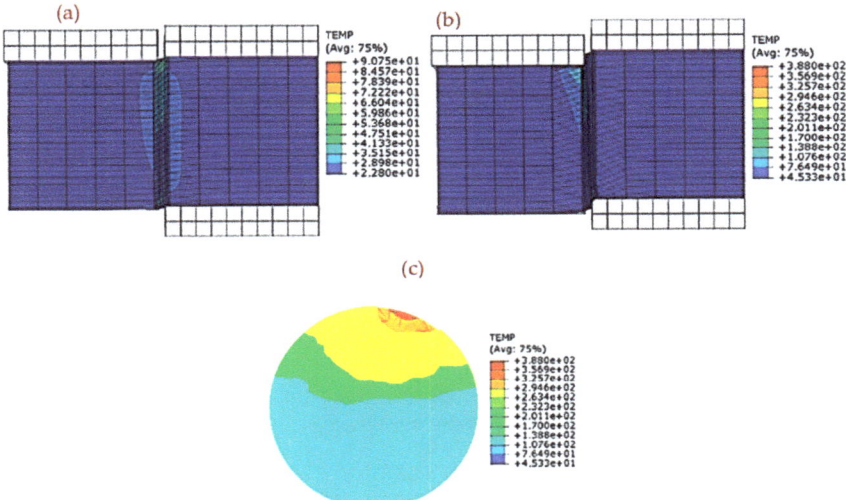

Figure 8. Temperature fields: (**a**) U2 = 0.51 mm; (**b**) U2 = 2.4 mm; (**c**) Temperature distribution on sheared surface (U2 = 2.4 mm).

The computed temperature fields in the bar metal show that the sheared surface reaches T = 90.7 °C with a punch displacement U2 = 0.51 mm (Figure 8a), and T = 388 °C with U2 = 2.4 mm (Figure 8b). The temperature distribution on the sheared surface with U2 = 2.4 mm is illustrated in Figure 8c. We deduce that the temperature increases significantly with the displacement of punch.

Friction work has a significant effect on the temperature fields in the bar workpiece generated during a shear cutting process. In fact, frictional forces are generated during the displacement of punch, which causes energy to be converted into heat. This explains the increase in temperature on the sheared surface. Therefore, this temperature, which is generated by friction, affects the mechanical properties of the bar workpiece.

In the shear cutting process, it is important to consider thermomechanical modelling that takes into account the temperature generated during cutting. This is because the temperature has a significant effect on the mechanical behaviour of the workpiece. This can lead to a more efficient and effective process of shear cutting bar metal. Thermomechanical modelling is used to predict the temperature distribution within the workpiece as well as the resulting deformation and stresses.

Figure 9 illustrates the damage evolution in workpiece. An element deletion method that eliminates the damaged element is applied to this model. This method allows a better simulation of the contact between the workpiece and the tools. An element is deleted from numerical model if the cumulative damage parameter reaches $D_{max} = 1$ at the integration points of the element. The output variables for this element are set to zero. In the next steps, the removed element has no energetic contribution to the shear cutting simulation.

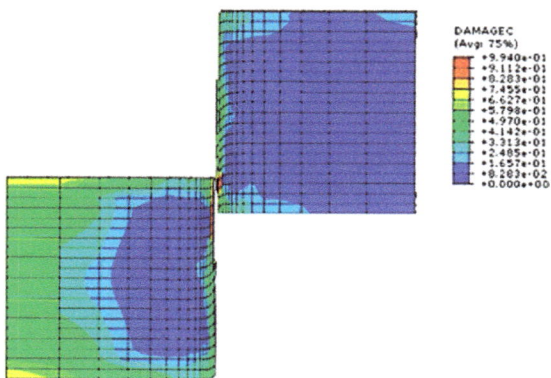

Figure 9. Damage fields.

6.3. Influence of Clearance on the Sheared Surface Quality

After proving the accuracy of Model 2 in predicting the shearing force and the ductile failure of the bar workpiece, a parametric analysis will be conducted in this section in order to determine the influence of clearance c, as a shear cutting parameter, on the sheared bar geometry. Three clearance values are chosen: $c_1 = 0.2$ mm, $c_2 = 0.5$ mm and $c_3 = 1.2$ mm. The most useful measures of sheared workpiece geometry are the burr (b) and the roughness of the sheared surface (a).

The computed burr created in the bar is analyzed. Figure 10 illustrates the final geometry of the workpiece.

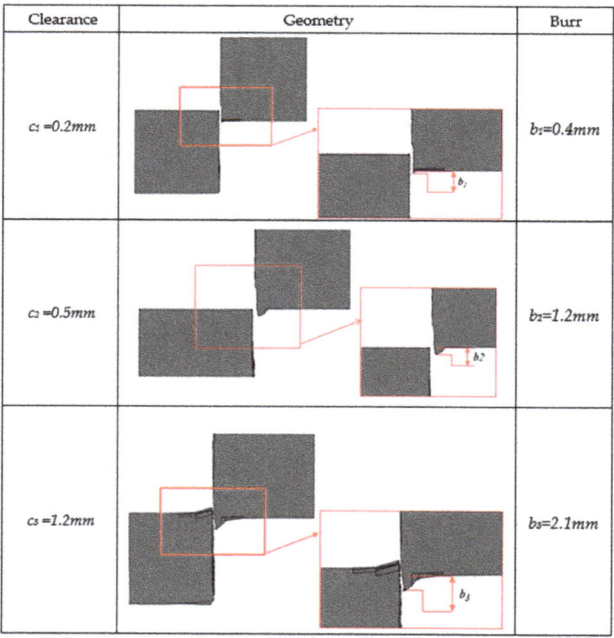

Figure 10. Influence of shear clearance on the burr with $c_1 = 0.2$ mm, $c_2 = 0.5$ mm, and $c_3 = 1.2$ mm.

For the low shear clearance (c_1), the burr ($b_1 = 0.4$ mm) is small and the fractured zone is minimal. However, when the shear clearance increases (c_3), a larger fractured zone is obtained and the burr ($b_3 = 2.1$ mm) increases. We deduce from Figure 10 that the increase in the shear clearance causes a high burr value.

In the same context, the influence of shear clearance on the quality of the sheared surface is studied (Figure 11).

Clearance	Geometry	sheared surface roughness
$c_1 = 0.2$ mm	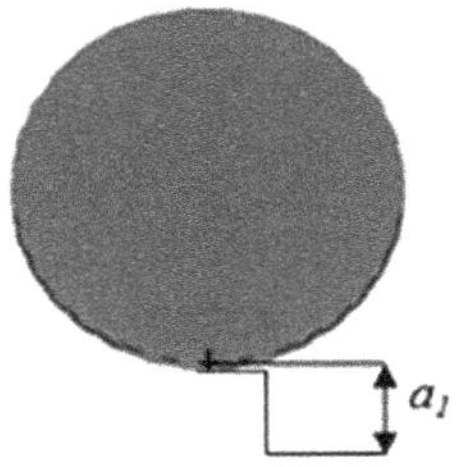	$a_1 = 0.6$ mm
$c_2 = 0.5$ mm	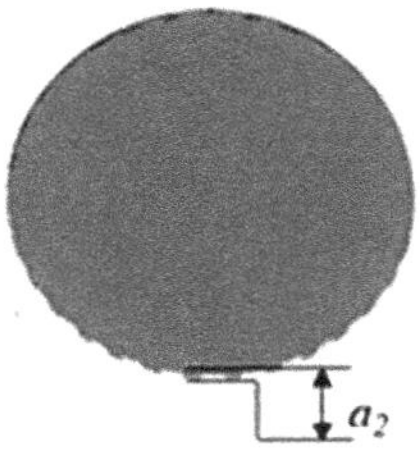	$a_2 = 0.9$ mm
$c_3 = 1.2$ mm	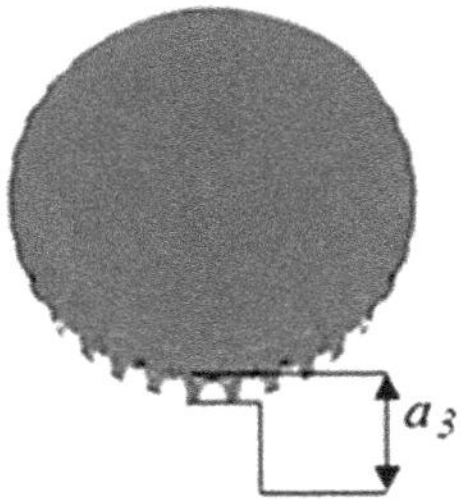	$a_3 = 1.7$ mm

Figure 11. Influence of shear clearance on the sheared surface roughness with $c_1 = 0.2$ mm, $c_2 = 0.5$ mm, and $c_3 = 1.2$ mm.

With a low shear clearance (c_1), the best quality of sheared surface ($a_1 = 0.6$ mm) is obtained. However, with a high shear clearance value (c_3), a worse quality ($a_3 = 1.7$ mm) is found. As shown in Figure 11, the increase in the shear clearance causes the quality to worsen.

In summary, burrs are a common occurrence in the process of shear cutting metal, and their size and shape affect the roughness of the sheared surface. A good choice of shear cutting parameters can minimize the size of burrs and reduce the roughness of the sheared surface.

7. Conclusions

A mathematical formulation of the thermomechanical problem of the shear cutting process is developed. Various flow stress and damage models are analyzed. Modified Johnson–Cook hardening and damage models are used to describe the mechanical behaviour of aluminium materials, taking into account the temperature field generated during the bar shear cutting process.

Experimental and numerical force–displacement curves of the shear cutting process are presented for both sheet and bar. By comparing the numerical and experimental results of shearing force and tool displacement during both sheet and bar shear cutting operations, it was found that the use of a thermomechanical model was crucial in accurately predicting the mechanical behaviour of the aluminium alloys during bar shear cutting. The study found that the thermomechanical model was able to accurately predict the temperature distribution and strain during the bar shear cutting process. In contrast, the sheet shear cutting process was found to be less sensitive to the use of a thermomechanical model. This is likely due to the fact that the deformation during sheet shear cutting is more uniform and less localized than during bar shear cutting.

In addition, numerical parametric studies are conducted in order to predict the influence of the shear clearance on the geometrical defects of bar workpiece. The evolution of burr and the quality of the sheared surface for different values of clearance are observed. Specifically, it is found that as the shear clearance increases, the burr height increases and the quality of the sheared surface decreases. This is because larger clearance values result in a larger deformation zone, which can lead to more severe deformations and greater surface defects.

Finally, the shearing process can also affect the surface finish and cleanliness of the bar. Surface defects can be carried over into the forging process, potentially leading to surface defects or other quality issues in the final product. In a forthcoming publication, the influence of the shearing process on the forging process may be studied in detail.

Author Contributions: L.B.S.: Conceptualization, Methodology, experimental investigation, Writing—Original draft preparation, Review and Editing. A.K.C.: Software, visualization, Data curation, investigation. M.W.: Supervision, Conceptualization, Methodology, Writing—Review and Editing. All authors have read and agreed to the published version of the manuscript.

Funding: This research received no external funding.

Institutional Review Board Statement: Not applicable.

Informed Consent Statement: Not applicable.

Data Availability Statement: Not applicable.

Conflicts of Interest: The authors declare no conflict of interest.

Appendix A. Special Discretization of Thermomechanical Problem

In this Appendix, we describe the special discretization of the thermomechanical problem used in the paper. The FEM is used to discretize both the thermal and mechanical domains. The temperature distribution within the workpiece is approximated by solving the heat transfer equation within each element, while the deformation of the workpiece can be approximated by solving the momentum balance equation within each element. Using the finite element method, the continuum mechanical problem (Equation (30)) is discretized, in which the total computation step is decomposed into a Δt time step. The displacement field $u_j^k(x, y, z, t)$ and its time derivatives of each node k of the element j are given by Equation (A1).

$$u_j = \sum_k \beta^k u_j^k \; ; \; \dot{u}_j = \sum_k \beta^k \dot{u}_j^k \; ; \; \ddot{u}_j = \sum_k \beta^k \ddot{u}_j^k$$
$$\delta \dot{u}_j = \sum_k \beta^k \delta \dot{u}_j^k \tag{A1}$$

where β^k is the shape function at the node k.

The relationship of the mechanical problem is given in Equation (A2).

$$\left(\left[M_j^{ki} \right] \ddot{u}_j^i - \left\{ G_j^k \right\} \right) \delta \dot{u}_j^k = 0 \tag{A2}$$

where $\left[M_j^{ki} \right]$ is the mass matrix of the element j, $\left\{ G_j^k \right\}$ is the resultant force's vector at the node k of the element j, and $\ddot{u}_j^i$ is the acceleration at the node i of the element j. We represent $[D_k]$ as a matrix, which relies the differential matrix developed in the thermomechanical problem with the shape function matrix. All vectors and matrices used for each element j of the mechanical equilibrium are given in Equation (A3).

$$\left\{ G_j^k \right\} = \int_{V_j} [D_k]^{tr} \underline{\sigma} \, dV + \int_{S_j/S_\tau} \left[\beta^k \right]^{tr} \tau \, dS + \int_{S_j/S_{fr}} \left[\beta^k \right]^{tr} F_{fr} \, dS$$
$$\left[M_j^{ki} \right] = \int_{V_j} \rho \left[\beta^k \right]^{tr} [\beta^i] dV \tag{A3}$$

In a cutting operation, the contact forces F_{fr} (Equation (21)) between tools, which are the punch and the die, and the workpiece are decomposed into normal and tangential components.

The normal force is responsible for holding the workpiece in place and preventing it from moving away from the shear cutting tool. The tangential force is responsible for actually shearing the metal bar.

Therefore, based on the virtual work formula for this formulation, we obtain

$$\left(\sum_{j=1}^n \left(\left[M_j^{ki} \right] \ddot{u}_j^i - \left(\int_{S_{fr}} \left[\beta^k \right]^{tr} F_{fr}^n \, dS + \int_{S_{fr}} \left[\beta^k \right]^{tr} F_{fr}^t \, dS + \int_{S_\tau} \left[\beta^k \right]^{tr} \tau \, dS \right) \right) \right) \delta \dot{u}^k$$
$$=$$
$$-\sum_j \int_V \left[D^k \right]^{tr} \underline{\sigma} dV \delta \dot{u}^k \tag{A4}$$

If the influence of temperature fields is taken account on the strain expression, the strain field becomes

$$\varepsilon = \varepsilon_{el} + \varepsilon_{pl} + \varepsilon_{th} \tag{A5}$$

Equation (A6) illustrates the temperature variable of each node, symbolized by k of the element j.

$$T_j = \sum_k \beta_T^k T_j^k \; ; \; \dot{T}_j = \sum_k \beta_T^k \dot{T}_j^k \tag{A6}$$

where β_T^k is the shape function related to temperature field at the node k. For each node k of the element j, the semi-discrete thermal energy balance is illustrated in Equation (A7). Here, the capacitance matrix is represented by $\left[C_j^{ki} \right]$. In the same equation, $\left[H_{j/\text{int}}^k \right]$ and $\left[H_{j/ext}^k \right]$ are the internal and external heat flux vectors, respectively.

$$\left(\left[C_j^{ki} \right] \dot{T}_j^i + \left[H_{j/\text{int}}^k \right] \right) \delta T_j^k = \left[H_{j/ext}^k \right] \delta T_j^k \tag{A7}$$

We obtain the system Equation (A8):

$$\left[C_j^{ki} \right] = \int_{V_j} \rho C_v \left[\beta_T^k \right]^{tr} [\beta_T^i] dV$$
$$\left[H_{j/\text{int}}^k \right] = \int_{V_j} [D_k]^{tr} k \, T[D_k] dV - \int_{V_j} \left[\beta^k \right]^{tr} \eta_{pl} \, \underline{\sigma} : \underline{\varepsilon} \, dV - \int_{S_f/S_j} \left[\beta^k \right]^{tr} Q_f \, dS \tag{A8}$$

For all elements, the thermal semi-discrete equilibrium equality is given by Equation (A9).

$$\sum_j \left[\left(\int_{V_j} \rho C_v \left[\beta_T^k \right]^{tr} \left[\beta_T^i \right] dV \right) \dot{T}_j^i \right] \delta T_j^k$$

$$+ \sum_j \left[\left(\int_{V_j} [B]^{tr} k\, T[B] dV - \int_{V_j} [\phi]^{tr} \eta_p\, \underline{\sigma} : \underline{\varepsilon}\, dV - \int_{S_f/S_j} [\phi]^{tr} Q_f dS \right) \right] \delta T_j^k \quad (A9)$$

$$= \sum_j \left[H_{j/ext}^k \right] \delta T_j^k$$

References

1. Calamaz, M.; Limido, J.; Nouari, M.; Espinosa, C.; Coupard, D.; Salaün, M.; Girot, F.; Chieragatti, R. Toward a better understanding of tool wear effect through a comparison between experiments and SPH numerical modelling of machining hard materials. *Int. J. Refract. Met. Hard Mater.* **2009**, *27*, 595–604. [CrossRef]
2. Ben Said, L.; Wali, M. Accuracy of Variational Formulation to Model the Thermomechanical Problem and to Predict Failure in Metallic Materials. *Mathematics* **2022**, *10*, 3555. [CrossRef]
3. Ben Said, L.; Allouch, M.; Wali, M.; Dammak, F. Numerical Formulation of Anisotropic Elastoplastic Behavior Coupled with Damage Model in Forming Processes. *Mathematics* **2023**, *11*, 204. [CrossRef]
4. Benzerga, A.A.; Leblond, J.B.; Needleman, A.; Tvergaard, V. Ductile failure modeling. *Int. J. Fract.* **2016**, *201*, 29–80. [CrossRef]
5. Oyane, M.; Sato, T.; Okimoto, K.; Shima, S. Criteria for ductile fracture and their applications. *J. Mech. Work. Technol.* **1980**, *4*, 65–81. [CrossRef]
6. Lemaitre, J. Local approach of fracture. *Eng. Fract. Mech.* **1986**, *25*, 523–537. [CrossRef]
7. Rice, J.R.; Tracey, D.M. On the ductile enlargement of voids in triaxial stress fields. *J. Mech. Phys. Solids* **1969**, *17*, 201–217. [CrossRef]
8. Gurson, A.L. Continuum Theory of Ductile Rupture by Void Nucleation and Growth: Part I-Yield Criteria and Flow Rules for Porous Ductile Media. *J. Eng. Mater. Technol.* **1977**, *99*, 2–15. [CrossRef]
9. Johnson, G.R.; Cook, W.H. A constitutive model and data for metals subjected to large strains, high strain rates and high temperatures. In Proceedings of the 7th International Symposium on Ballistics, The Hague, The Netherlands, 19–21 April 1983; pp. 541–547.
10. Johnson, G.R.; Cook, W.H. Fracture characteristics of three metals subjected to various strains, strain rates, temperatures and pressures. *Eng. Fract. Mech.* **1985**, *21*, 31–48. [CrossRef]
11. Shen, X.; Zhang, D.; Yao, C.; Tan, L.; Li, X. Research on parameter identification of Johnson–Cook constitutive model for TC17 titanium alloy cutting simulation. *Mater. Today Commun.* **2022**, *31*, 103772. [CrossRef]
12. No, T.; Gomez, M.; Karandikar, J.; Heigel, J.; Copenhaver, R.; Schmitz, T. Propagation of Johnson-Cook flow stress model uncertainty to milling force uncertainty using finite element analysis and time domain simulation. *Procedia Manuf.* **2021**, *53*, 223–235. [CrossRef]
13. Murugesan, M.; Jung, D.W. Johnson Cook Material and Failure Model Parameters Estimation of AISI-1045 Medium Carbon Steel for Metal Forming Applications. *Materials* **2019**, *12*, 609. [CrossRef]
14. Patil, S.P.; Prajapati, K.G.; Jenkouk, V.; Olivier, H.; Markert, B. Experimental and Numerical Studies of Sheet Metal Forming with Damage Using Gas Detonation Process. *Metals* **2017**, *7*, 556. [CrossRef]
15. Li, M. Micromechanisms of deformation and fracture in shearing aluminum alloy sheet. *Int. J. Mech. Sci.* **2000**, *42*, 907–923. [CrossRef]
16. Feistle, M.; Koslow, I.; Krinninger, M.; Golle, R.; Volk, W. Reduction of Burr Formation for Conventional Shear Cutting of Boron-alloyed Sheets through Focused Heat Treatment. *Procedia CIRP* **2017**, *63*, 493–498. [CrossRef]
17. Gotoh, M.; Yamashita, M. A study of high-rate shearing of commercially pure aluminum sheet. *J. Mater. Process. Technol.* **2001**, *110*, 253–264. [CrossRef]
18. Behrens, B.A.; Lippold, L.; Knigge, J. Investigations of the shear behaviour of aluminium alloys. *Prod. Eng.* **2013**, *7*, 319–328. [CrossRef]
19. Hu, C.L.; Chen, L.Q.; Zhao, Z.; Li, J.W.; Li, Z.M. Study on the pre-shearing cropping process of steel bars. *Int. J. Adv. Manuf. Technol.* **2018**, *97*, 783–793. [CrossRef]
20. Rachik, M.; Roelandt, J.M.; Maillard, A. Some phenomenological and computational aspects of sheet metal blanking simulation. *J. Mater. Process. Technol.* **2002**, *128*, 256–265. [CrossRef]
21. Mao, H.; Zhou, F.; Liu, Y.; Hua, L. Numerical and experimental investigation of the discontinuous dot indenter in the fine-blanking process. *J. Manuf. Process.* **2016**, *24*, 90–99. [CrossRef]
22. Liu, Y.; Tang, B.; Hua, L.; Mao, H. Investigation of a novel modified die design for fine-blanking process to reduce the die-roll size. *J. Mater. Process. Technol.* **2018**, *260*, 30–37. [CrossRef]

23. Sachnik, P.; Hoque, S.E.; Volk, W. Burr-free cutting edges by notch-shear cutting. *J. Mater. Process. Technol.* **2017**, *249*, 229–245. [CrossRef]
24. Bouhamed, A.; Mars, J.; Jrad, H.; Wali, M.; Dammak, F. Experimental and numerical methodology to characterize 5083-aluminium behavior considering non-associated plasticity model coupled with isotropic ductile damage. *Int. J. Solids Struct.* **2021**, *229*, 111–139. [CrossRef]
25. Škrlec, A.; Klemenc, J. Estimating the Strain-Rate-Dependent Parameters of the Johnson-Cook Material Model Using Optimisation Algorithms Combined with a Response Surface. *Mathematics* **2020**, *8*, 1105. [CrossRef]
26. Hollomon, J.H. Tensile deformation. *Trans. Metall. Soc. AIME* **1945**, *162*, 268–290.
27. Palaparti, D.P.R.; Choudhary, B.K.; Samuel, E.I.; Srinivasan, V.S.; Mathew, M.D. Influence of strain rate and temperature on tensile stress–strain and work hardening behaviour of 9Cr–1Mo ferritic steel. *Mater. Sci. Eng. A* **2012**, *538*, 110–117. [CrossRef]
28. Ludwigson, D.C. Modified stress-strain relation for FCC metals and alloys. *Metall. Trans.* **1971**, *2*, 2825–2828. [CrossRef]
29. Samuel, K.G. Limitations of Hollomon and Ludwigson stress-strain relations in assessing the strain hardening parameters. *J. Phys. D Appl. Phys.* **2006**, *39*, 203–212. [CrossRef]
30. Swift, H.W. Plastic instability under plane stress. *J. Mech. Phys. Solids* **1952**, *1*, 1–18. [CrossRef]
31. Priest, J.; Ghadbeigi, H.; Ayvar-Soberanis, S.; Liljerehn, A.; Way, M. A modified Johnson-Cook constitutive model for improved thermal softening prediction of machining simulations in C45 steel. *Procedia CIRP* **2022**, *108*, 106–111. [CrossRef]
32. Hooputra, H.; Gese, H.; Dell, H.; Werner, H. A comprehensive failure model for crashworthiness simulation of aluminium extrusions. *Int. J. Crashworthiness* **2004**, *9*, 449–464. [CrossRef]
33. Sohail, A.; Syed Husain, I.; Jaffery, M.K.; Muhammad, F.; Aamir, M.; Liaqat, A. Numerical and experimental investigation of Johnson–Cook material models for aluminum (Al 6061-T6) alloy using orthogonal machining approach. *Adv. Mech. Eng.* **2018**, *10*, 1–14.

Disclaimer/Publisher's Note: The statements, opinions and data contained in all publications are solely those of the individual author(s) and contributor(s) and not of MDPI and/or the editor(s). MDPI and/or the editor(s) disclaim responsibility for any injury to people or property resulting from any ideas, methods, instructions or products referred to in the content.

Article

Oversampling Application of Identifying 3D Selective Laser Sintering Yield by Hybrid Mathematical Classification Models

You-Shyang Chen [1], Jieh-Ren Chang [2,*], Ying-Hsun Hung [3,*] and Jia-Hsien Lai [2]

[1] College of Management, National Chin-Yi University of Technology, Taichung 411030, Taiwan; yschen@ncut.edu.tw
[2] Department of Electronic Engineering, National Ilan University, Yilan City 26047, Taiwan; vernon.lai@luxvisions-inno.com
[3] Department of Finance, Chaoyang University of Technology, Taichung 413310, Taiwan
* Correspondence: jrchang@niu.edu.tw (J.-R.C.); t2010102@cyut.edu.tw (Y.-H.H.)

Citation: Chen, Y.-S.; Chang, J.-R.; Hung, Y.-H.; Lai, J.-H. Oversampling Application of Identifying 3D Selective Laser Sintering Yield by Hybrid Mathematical Classification Models. *Mathematics* **2023**, *11*, 3204. https://doi.org/10.3390/math11143204

Academic Editor: Aleksey I. Shinkevich

Received: 15 June 2023
Revised: 17 July 2023
Accepted: 18 July 2023
Published: 21 July 2023

Copyright: © 2023 by the authors. Licensee MDPI, Basel, Switzerland. This article is an open access article distributed under the terms and conditions of the Creative Commons Attribution (CC BY) license (https://creativecommons.org/licenses/by/4.0/).

Abstract: Selective laser sintering (SLS) is one of the most popular 3D molding technologies; however, the manufacturing steps of SLS machines are cumbersome, and the most important step is focused on molding testing because it requires a lot of direct labor and material costs. This research establishes advanced hybrid mathematical classification models, including random forest (RF), support vector machine (SVM), and artificial neural network (ANN), for effectively identifying the SLS yield of the sintering results from three sintered objects (boxes, cylinders, and flats) to achieve the key purpose of reducing the number of model verification and machine parameter adjustments, thereby saving a lot of manufacturing time and costs. In the experimental process, performance evaluation indicators, such as classification accuracy (CA), area under the ROC curve (AUC), and F1-score, are used to measure the proposed models' experience with practical industry data. In the experimental results, the ANN gets the highest 0.6168 of CA, and it is found that each machine reduces the average sintering time by four hours when compared with the original manufacturing process. Moreover, we employ an oversampling method to expand the sample data to overcome the existing problems of class imbalance in the dataset collected. An important finding is that the RF algorithm is more suitable for predicting the sintering failure of objects, and its average sintering times per machine are 1.7, which is lower than the 1.95 times of ANN and 2.25 times of SVM. Conclusively, this research yields some valuable empirical conclusions and core research findings. In terms of research contributions, the research results can be provided to relevant academic circles and industry requirements for referential use in follow-up studies or industrial applications.

Keywords: selective laser sintering; random forest; support vector machine; artificial neural network; oversampling method

MSC: 03C13; 18B05

1. Introduction

In this section, we introduce why selective laser sintering (SLS) is studied and describe the important problems encountered in the manufacturing process of SLS machines. Then, we illustrate the relevant industrial application research of SLS and machine learning (ML) techniques, and we also explain the purpose of the relevant research.

1.1. Research Problems and Research Motivation

With the progress of the times, ordinary 2D printers can no longer meet customers' needs for storing memories or data, and even 3D additive manufacturing (3D-AM) can improve people's quality of life significantly. The inventor of the first 3D molding machine focused on using this excellent device to shorten the time for product design; at that time, it took about 5 to 8 weeks from plastic mold opening to plastic injection for the traditional manufacturing process, but now it could be shortened to several hours through the 3D-AM printing device and we could know instantly whether the product design was successful and available. With the advent of the information technology era, a variety of 3D-AM technologies have surfaced, from the simplest fused deposition modeling (FDM) to stereolithography (SLA), SLS, and finally direct metal laser sintering (DMLS) techniques. These technologies have their own advantages and difficulties; in particular, SLS becomes an excellent technology among them at this stage. The justified reason is that SLS has a variety of materials to choose from, and each material has different characteristics. These characteristics are highly dependent on the sintering temperature, and thus the temperature has become one of the many factors that need to be overcome in the SLS manufacturing process. However, the application use of SLS is very wide, particularly in pharmaceutical manufacturing [1]; there will be different usages according to the properties of different materials [2]. Interestingly, in order to make SLS with more industrial applications, there is even a study [3] that points out the coloring research of extra functions for SLS to increase the multi-application of SLS.

The so-called SLS [4,5] has the function of using laser and Galvo scanning systems (GSS) to draw the outline of objects (e.g., boxes, cylinders, and flats) on specific materials [6], and it is stacked layer by layer; following that, the noodles need to be heated through a heating system and accurately maintained at an appropriate temperature. The temperature setting needs to adjust different temperature values according to the different properties of materials. Based on their different natures, some materials require lower temperatures but have stronger toughness, and some materials require higher temperatures but have stronger hardness. However, there have been some fatal problems for research. First, this technique must build a heating system on the basis of a laser, and the laser system is very sensitive to heat, which may cause the deflection of the GSS meter [7], resulting in dimensional size errors of the molded object and in turn affecting the result of sintering. Second, in the SLS technique, the accuracy of the motor, the scanning accuracy of the laser and GSS, and the size of the laser power will deeply affect the sintering result or sintering quality [8,9]. SLS is melted at high temperatures, which means that it will pollute the natural environment [10], and thus it is an important issue for the difficulty addressed in how to recycle the powder after high temperatures and to measure the strength of sintering after using the recycled powder [11]. These are the SLS industry's major problems that must be faced at present. From an industrial perspective, if the use of these powder materials cannot be avoided now, reducing unnecessary testing procedures by using an effective binary classification model or technique will be an important issue. An accurate testing process can not only reduce the use of manpower but also reduce the pollution generated during the testing process. Thus, to construct such an effective classification technique motivates and rationalizes this research.

Regarding binary classification models, some techniques from data mining and deep learning [12,13] have been highly and widely used in various industrial application fields with good performance. In particular, further data analysis can be done for the collected industrial data to find more clues, and the importance of advanced models to industrial applications and data analysis is thus, further inspired. Based on the meaningful descriptions mentioned above, this research has the interest of designing advanced binary models to address the data analysis of industry applications. The accelerated triggering of the research is highlighted in developing an effective prediction system for driving the research's model for identifying manufacturing processes in the SLS industry.

1.2. Relevant Research Purposes

In the research related to 3D printing and deep learning techniques, some of them construct an identification mechanism to detect bed defects in powders through convolutional neural networks (CNN) [14]. In this study, the related data of the sintering process is collected and then put into the training mechanism of the CNN; after this training, it is identified whether the sintered object is formed smoothly and successfully. In the study [15], a semi-supervised learning method is used to predict whether the model is suitable for selective laser melting; the cases collected after actual sintering are thrown into the training network. Different types of data are generated by a generative adversarial network (GAN) to be evaluated due to the difficulty of actual sintering and the high cost of materials, thereby resulting in a small number of experimental samples obtained for the available data. In the study of Stathatos et al. [16], the laser power, speed, or energy during sintering is trained with ML techniques, and then the trajectory and energy of each laser sintering have an active optimization adjustment; finally, verification is performed after all 3D objects are formed. In the study of Shen et al. [17], the energy density of the object is estimated by sintering parameters such as laser intensity, scanning speed, scanning interval, and layer thickness, so that the results of strength and scalability for the sintered object can be predicted by supervised learning methods.

Through the above descriptions, this research takes the finished product from the SLS machine as the research object and provides a comparison of the difference between the old and new SLS production processes by analyzing the characteristic data for process improvement. Thus, this research is based on the hybrid mathematical models [18,19] with the following research purposes: (1) The research proposes a hybrid mathematical binary classification model, including random forest (RF) [20], support vector machine (SVM) [21], and artificial neural network (ANN) [21], due to their past superior performance, combined with an oversampling method for the data used due to the problem of class imbalance. (2) The method of cross-validation and the evaluation index of these algorithms are used for the industry data application of identifying SLS production processes. (3) By the predictive model, the sintering results are obtained in advance before the actual sintering, and the machine parameters are adjusted in advance for the SLS equipment; it is a key point that the actual sintering is not performed until it is predicted to be successful. (4) With this research, the number of sintering times, the number of adjustments during sintering, and the time and cost spent verifying the machine are reduced. (5) This research provides an applicable contribution with practical industry value.

The structure of this research is divided into six sections, as follows: The Section 1 is the introduction, which explores the research background and the prior industry applications as the research base. The Section 2 is the technical background applications, including reviews of the SLS techniques, the three well-known classification algorithms, the cross-validation method, and the evaluation standard. The Section 3 is the step-by-step algorithm of the hybrid mathematical binary classification model constructed in this research. The content focuses on the introduction of the experimental process and explains how to obtain data, build models, use an oversampling method, and compare sintering and adjustment times. The Section 4 is the empirical results of the effectiveness analysis and evaluation measurement after the demonstration; the Section 5 addresses research findings and research limitations. Finally, the Section 6 is about the study's contribution and future prospects.

2. Related Technical Works

This section reviews and explores the relevant technical background of identifying SLS, three classification algorithms, the cross-validation method, and evaluation indicators.

2.1. SLS Technology with Its Applications

The SLS [22] is to use a laser to select the area to be formed, while the unformed area should be in powder form. For the SLS applications, some core features (factors) have been determined. If the temperature [23] controlled by the heater is too high, the unsintered area agglomerates, and this increases the difficulty of picking up items. If the temperature is controlled too low, the temperature of the area to be formed is pulled due to the contrast with the air temperature in the sintering chamber, causing the object to bend; in a slight case, the size of the formed object is inconsistent and wrong, and in a serious case, the object is unable to form [24]. However, if during the sintering process of an object [25], high temperatures and low temperatures appear alternately, or even if the temperature distribution is uneven during the sintering process on the same plane, it causes some problems, such as insufficient strength of the object, inaccurate size of the object, and even failure to form the object. Thus, the layout and control of the heater are very important. Furthermore, each material has a different temperature range. Some materials have a high temperature and a small operating range, but they have high strength after molding; conversely, some materials have a low temperature and a large operating range, but they have strong toughness after molding. Under such circumstances, it becomes a very important issue to ensure that each material can be controlled within the range of its properties [26]. In summary, it is better that the smaller the temperature change, the smaller the range of temperature distribution [27]. Except for the above influences, it is also a factor that the laser is not powerful enough to penetrate the powder, which causes sintering defects. Importantly, there are three research directions defined. (1) The energy definitely affects the shape of the object, so we can use the instrument to collect the intensity of the laser energy as a very useful feature, which is used to dig out the relationship between the laser energy and the sintering result. (2) Another factor that affects the sintering result is the spot size of the laser. When the spot size is larger and the path overlap is higher, the energy density is stronger and the sintering speed is faster. Conversely, the smaller the spot size, the more compact the path is planned, so the sintering speed is slower but the sintered objects are finer. Thus, we identify the spot size as one of the features to predict the sintering result. (3) The galvanometer system often has pin distortion and barrel distortion, which affect the size of a single plane of the object, and the error of the single size is continuously amplified throughout the sintering process, which causes dimensional (size) errors of the overall object. Thus, we also collect the error amount as a feature to judge the sintering result.

For the manufacturing process of SLS [28,29], two key processes are identified. First, the target temperature must be set at the beginning of the process, and the temperature of the sintering chamber is raised and stably controlled at the target temperature through the controller to control the heater; this process is called preheating. Second, accordingly, wait for the temperature to reach a certain point and then start sintering. During the sintering process, powder needs to be supplied to the powder surface structure, and then reheating and laser scanning are performed; this process is called sintering. After the graphics on each layer hit the powder surface through the laser, the temperature needs to be lowered. Since the difference between the sintering temperature and the room temperature is too large, if it is taken out directly, the object is directly cooled and deformed, so it takes a long time for natural cooling to cool it. Figure 1 shows the entire SLS process flow. By sintering these objects, it is possible to know whether the molding is successful or not. Thus, we use the following three directions to identify it: (1) Measure the size of the sintered cube; the horizontal (X) axis and the vertical (Y) axis are both 30 mm ± 0.3 mm, and it is a sintered benchmark for success within this size range. (2) Observe whether the lines are completely connected and whether the lines are broken. If there is no break, the test is passed. (3) Observe the sintered gap. If the gap cannot be clearly seen, it means that the details of the gap cannot be clearly displayed, which means that the sintering has failed.

With the above sintering process and application of SLS [30,31], it is clear that SLS is a specific technology that requires long-term, precise control to complete. If the number of sintering times is reduced in the verification process, the verification cost is greatly reduced. We collect the sintering data as featured attributes for training to judge the sintering results, and we conduct a repair process on samples that have failed sintering.

2.2. Classification Algorithms

This section reviews the three mathematical classification algorithm models: RF, SVM, and ANN for supervised training to predict the SLS result, respectively.

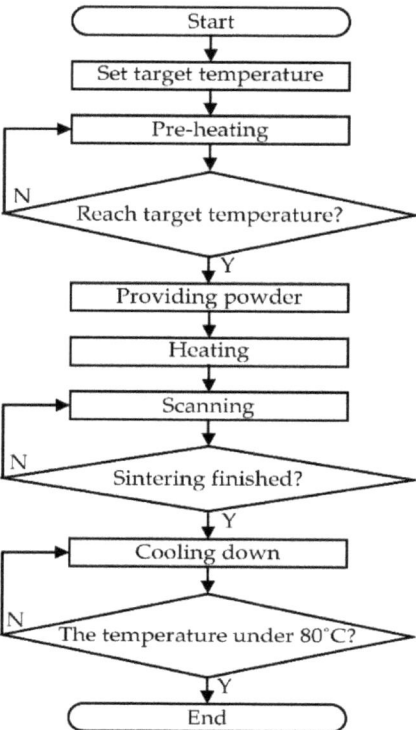

Figure 1. Sintering process flow of SLS.

2.2.1. Random Forest

In the field of classification applications, RF belongs to the Bagging training method. The Bagging concept is to randomly select training samples from the training data and put them back after selection, which means that there is a chance to draw out the same sample again next time, and even the selection of features during growth is random. This training method determines the diversity of the RF, and the combined results are more accurate. After the features are selected, a decision tree is built one by one, and finally, after a series of feature selection (FS) and tree growth, the result is a lot of trees, which are the so-called RFs model. RF is a combination of multiple decision trees, but there is no connection between different decision trees; decision trees determine the correct features by choosing the degree of disorder or entropy and determine the direction of tree growth, and the complexity or entropy must converge to grow. Every time a node is passed, it is in the messiest state at the beginning, and the messiness gets smaller and smaller. Importantly, RF can solve the overfitting problem that other classification methods have [32]. The overfitting problem is to closely match a specific data set so that it cannot be well adapted to other data, resulting in the original correct result being classified in the wrong category. If the RF wants to avoid overfitting, it needs to meet two conditions: one is that the trunk of the tree must be larger and must reflect the law of the big tree, and the other is that the randomness must be sufficient. Otherwise, if the sampling is biased towards a certain feature, trees of different properties cannot be obtained, and an overfitting problem occurs.

Moreover, due to the wide range of industrial applications for RF classifiers, some researchers had used RFs to predict real-life problems faced in different fields, such as the analysis of the surface roughness and mechanical properties of 316L samples produced by SLS [18], the ML prediction of SLS-AM part density [33], and the prediction for the 3D printability of SLS formulations [34]. In the study of Jaime et al. [35], the user is guided to choose which classification method is more suitable for different types of data sets, and how many samples do a RF need? Interestingly, the research results of Oshiro et al. [36] just illustrated and verified this application issue. In the study of Peng et al. [37], various types of in situ monitoring and defect detection methods (e.g., RFs) and their applications are reviewed for the SLS processes.

This research chooses RF as one of the training algorithms first based on the fact that it can avoid overfitting problems. The second reasonable reason is that there is not enough training data, and RF can process it with good performance. It is evidence that the characteristics of multiple trees for RFs can be established through the "big tree rule" to strengthen the training data.

2.2.2. Support Vector Machine

SVM is a very popular classification method with a wide range of applications. SVM can be used to detect network attack traffic [38]; particularly, the enhanced SVM method is used to classify porosity defects during the SLS process [39]. SVM is a supervised learning method based on the linear classification method; it can add support vectors to increase the tolerance of misclassification, and it adds kernel functions to solve nonlinear classification problems that linear classification methods cannot solve. SVMs have a place in ML by virtue of their ability to calculate linearly separable dichotomies, solve linearly inseparable kernel functions, and develop robust and rigorous mathematical theories. The importance and process of SVM are highlighted as follows:

(1) SVM is mainly divided into two types of hard cutting and soft cutting. Although both methods hope that the farther the boundary distance between them is the better, hard cutting does not allow other support vectors to appear between the support vectors, which will easily cause the problem of overfitting.

(2) When encountering linear inseparability, it is necessary to increase the dimension by one level through the kernel function; thus, the two-dimensional feature space is mapped into a three-dimensional feature space through the kernel function, then the support vector is found, and further, the hyperplane is found for processing the classification of features. So far, many calculation methods for kernel function algorithms have been announced, such as linear kernel function, polynomial kernel function, and Gaussian kernel function, which are studied and explored, and each kernel function has its corresponding parameters and suitable application occasions.

(3) We know that when all data is mixed together, it is impossible to distinguish them in a straight line from the perspective of a real-life situation. Accordingly, the SVM maps the feature space from the original dimension to a higher-dimensional feature space through the kernel function, and after mapping to a higher-dimensional space, we use different angles to observe the distribution of each feature [40].

Since SLS is a nonlinear system, this research expects to predict the yield of SLS by using the characteristics of SVM and kernel function to obtain good classification results, and the use of SVM is based on its past outstanding performance.

2.2.3. Artificial Neural Network

A neural network is an algorithm developed by simulating the nerves of a living being. With the advancement of the times, research on various types of ANNs has begun to grow exponentially; ANN has become synonymous with artificial intelligence. The application examples and uses of ANNs have been quite extensive, such as using ANNs to model solar energy systems [41], using ANNs to solve second-order boundary value problems [42], illustrating the recent application of ANNs in the study of Oludare et al. [43], and re-examining the similarity of ANN representations in the study of Kornblith et al. [44]. In particular, Stathatos and Vosniakos used ANNs for arbitrary long tracks in the laser-based AM of the SLS process [16]. In the related field of studying ANNs, there are many derived ANN models used for specific purposes in industry applications. CNN is used for visual recognition of images; especially, the study of Westphal and Seitz [45] based on CNN and ML methods offers an alternative approach for addressing non-destructive quality assurance and manufacturing files with good performance during part manufacturing of SLS. Yuan et al. [46] also used CNNs to well recognize desired quality metrics from videos in the SLS dataset.

The ANN consists of three routings, including an input layer, a hidden layer, and an output layer, and the connecting line between each layer represents a weight. When the weight is output by the activation function and reaches the threshold, it means that the neuron is activated and the data is transmitted to the next level. As to the activation function, it has many kinds of nonlinear functions, such as sigmoid and tanh, while the linear function has ReLU. From reviewing the literature, most studies confirmed that the linear activation function effectively solved the problems of gradient disappearance and gradient explosion. If we modify the weight value to achieve the effect of learning, backward propagation transfer is an important mechanism. In the process of supervised learning, the system randomly gives each neuron a weight, and the ANN uses these weights to calculate the first output value. However, the output value may be a messy value, in which case we calculate the cost value through the output value. The cost value is the squared difference between the predicted result and the actual result, and the smaller the squared difference, the higher the accuracy rate. In each backward pass, it modifies the weight value between each neuron from the back to the front based on the cost function, then repeatedly executes the output result, calculates the cost value, and passes the back-propagation network until the cost function is close to or equal to 0, and the complete neural model is finished. Figure 2 shows a schematic diagram of backward transmission.

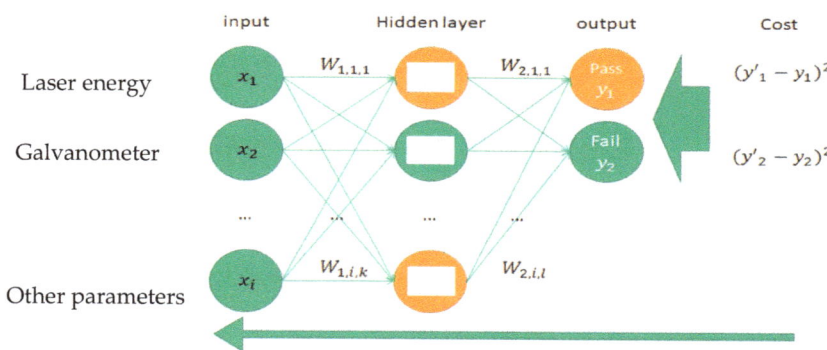

Figure 2. Schematic diagram of backward propagation transfer.

Due to the power and versatility of the ANN, if we need to modify the model used, it is only necessary to remove or add neurons. This advantage makes the application of the ANN much higher than other algorithms; thus, this research organizes the ANN model to identify SLS results to get good research results with supportability.

2.3. Cross-Validation Method

The commonly used cross-validation methods are quite extensive. We study the reliable accuracy estimation of K-fold cross-validation [47], optimize the cross-validation method and apply it to time series data with the ANN model [48], use genetic algorithm (GA) to optimize the SVM and K-means algorithms plus the K-fold crossover verification method for the mapping of mineral perspectivity [49], and employ ANN, SVM, and RF with hyperparameter tuning by GA optimization for the prediction of landslide susceptibility [50], etc. They are all verified through the cross-validation method to verify real-life issues. There are many effective types of cross-validation, including random example validation, leave-one-out cross validation, test on training data, K-fold cross validation, etc. They have attracted much concern about influencing performance from many researchers.

2.4. Evaluation Indicators of Verification

Evaluation indicators are used for the main function of judging the quality of the classifier. Commonly used indicators include area under ROC (AUC), classification accuracy (CA), F1-score, precision rate (PR), and recall rate (RR) used to measure the classification model for further verification [45,51]. For these indicators, confusion matrix is a core role and very versatile for different application fields, such as a CNN based on ML techniques widely used to classify good and defective image data recorded for AM parts [45], altering a SVM model with the FS method compared to those of the classical soft margin model through the confusion matrix [52], and based on the confusion matrix by different metrics for comparing two SVM models for AM [53]. They are described in detail as follows:

(1) Confusion matrix: it has four different prediction results, including true positive (TP_C), true negative (TN_C), false positive (FP_F), and false negative (FN_F).

(2) CA: the main purpose of the CA rate is to evaluate the performance of the model with a high value, but it cannot distinguish which category is the accuracy rate. Thus, if there is no special requirement for a certain category, we use this indicator to judge the model. The mathematical Formula (1) of the CA rate is formatted as:

$$CA = \frac{TP\_C + TN\_C}{TP\_C + TN\_C + FP\_F + FN\_F} \quad (1)$$

(3) PR and RR: it is a key purpose that the PR and RR provide a more accurate analysis of the samples for the binary of success or failure classes, respectively, which is helpful to describe the model for the practical application of product production. The following Formulas (2) and (3) are formatted for the PR and RR, respectively:

$$PR = \frac{TP\_C}{TP\_C + FP\_F} \text{ or } \frac{TN\_C}{TN\_C + FN\_F} \quad (2)$$

$$RR = \frac{TP\_C}{TP\_C + FN\_F} \text{ or } \frac{TN\_C}{TN\_C + FP\_F} \quad (3)$$

(4) F1-score: the F1-score reflects the weight and average of the PR and RR, and it reflects the most balanced value of the PR and RR when neither of them get the best score. The following mathematical Formula (4) of the F1-score is formatted. If the difference between the two values of PR and RR is too large, this value will tend to be smaller.

$$F1 - Score = \frac{PR \times RR}{PR + RR} \quad (4)$$

(5) Receiver operator characteristic (ROC) and AUC: ROC represents the change in decision threshold between the TP_C rate and the FP_F rate. An important purpose of calculating the ROC curve is to derive the AUC value. AUC is a probability, which means that when randomly given a sample of successful cases, the classifier correctly judging the value of a success is higher than judging the value of a failure. The related research on AUC has focused on (1) using AUC to classify the performance of unbalanced data for risk prediction of Chronic Obstructive Pulmonary Disease [54], (2) performance metrics of AUC to identify these intrinsic properties of AM-focused alloy design [55], and (3) using time-dependent AUC to address mortality or readmission prediction for hospitalized heart failure patients [56]. The AUC has three evaluation results: (a) AUC = 1: it represents the perfect classification of the sample data by this classifier; (b) 1 > AUC > 0.5: this represents better than random guessing; and (c) AUC $\leq$ 0.5: it means that the sample data is not suitable for this classifier.

This research mainly uses the above-mentioned excellent evaluation indicators to evaluate the model built and measure the analytical result after the cross-validation method to determine whether these classifiers are suitable for the SLS production process.

3. Materials and Methods

In this section, the research proposes a model to address the study topic used in materials and methods, and the proposed model has the following four main stages: (1) data collection stage: collect data through corresponding instruments and divide the given data into training data and testing data; (2) model building stage: build a model through training data with a cross-validation method and observe the real results of the validation; (3) oversampling method stage: carry out an oversampling method on the data to establish a classification model again and compare with the model results without processing the oversampling technique; and (4) process improvement stage: through the prediction results of the testing data, compare the sintering times and machine adjustment times of the new and old processes to judge how much labor time is saved. Thus, the proposed model has: data collection → model building → oversampling method → process improvement. Accordingly, the four stages are described in the following four subsections, respectively.

3.1. Data Collection Stage

Data is an important part of AI, and data mining is an important technique of data analysis. It can obtain information related to the target from some irregular data. We introduce the data collection stage by experiencing this research object in the case of the manufacturing process for the SLS industry, and thus the data acquisition and processing flow are divided into the following core data features for defining the data collection:

(1) Core features for data collection are first identified: we first identify the core features, such as the moving amount and inclination degree of the motor on the X and Y axes of the construction platform, the power energy of the laser system at 50%, the spot size of the laser, the scanning error of the galvanometer system, etc. We use the analysis method for the above feature data to predict the success rate of product molding in advance during the manufacturing process. Measure the movement of the vertical motor through the dial gauge. When the platform moves down once, the distance measured by the dial gauge should be 0.1 mm, and this value is recorded as a core feature (factor) to be used as the basis for the classification model.

(2) Collect all data for a successful sintering module when the laser energy is 50%: laser system measurements require specific and expensive instrumentation. We put the light beam into the laser power meter, measured it through the probe, and converted it into an electrical signal. The power meter integrates the read value and the converted value and records the value on the connected computer through a USB port. This value is measured when adjusting the laser galvanometer control system. In the test production phase, since the energy distribution obtained by each laser with the same energy is different, it is tested to see how much power the laser will output when the laser energy is 50%. In the case of simulated maintenance, the measured energy distribution is regarded as a set of modules to simulate the replacement of the laser module, and the successful sintering module is replaced by the sintering failure machine to observe the simulation result after repairing.

(3) Data on spot size is also collected: regarding the spot size of the laser, we use a beam analyzer to measure the size of the laser beam. Each different type of beam analyzer has a different measurement wavelength and energy range. Therefore, we must first know the required laser specifications and then select the correct measuring instrument; otherwise, the instrument itself is damaged. The size of the spot affects the degree of detail when the object is formed. Generally speaking, the smaller the size, the more delicate the object is formed, but the molding time is longer, and vice versa. Importantly, the specification range of the spot size set by the machine is 500 um~600 nm. The scanning error of the galvanometer system brings about information about the error of the plane size. Due to the principle of the galvanometer system, the system has a distortion problem, which affects the horizontal dimension error of the sintered object. However, the method of measuring the error can use

the weakest energy to print a dot every one centimeter on the white paper, fill the preset scanning range, and calculate the distance between the dots through image recognition. Then, record the values of the maximum error and the average error.

(4) The type data of boxes, cylinders, and flats and the total result are defined: judge whether the sintering is a successful product by each sintered object, and the basis or key point for judging is to measure whether the sizes of the box meet the specifications, check whether the lines of the cylinder are complete, and whether the gap between the flats is clear. Importantly, when one of the objects is marked as a failure, the total result is marked and classified as a failure; otherwise, it is marked as a pass product. After that, follow-up supervised learning models are used for this data.

(5) All data is collected and used: in this research object, Figure 3 shows the relationship diagram for all the data. In this part, 10 copies of all data are made. In Figure 3, six samples are randomly selected from each of these 10 copies as testing samples, and the rest are used as training data. The training data is used to build a model, and the cross-validation is used to obtain the verification evaluation index after the model is built. The testing data is used to verify the prediction results of the models.

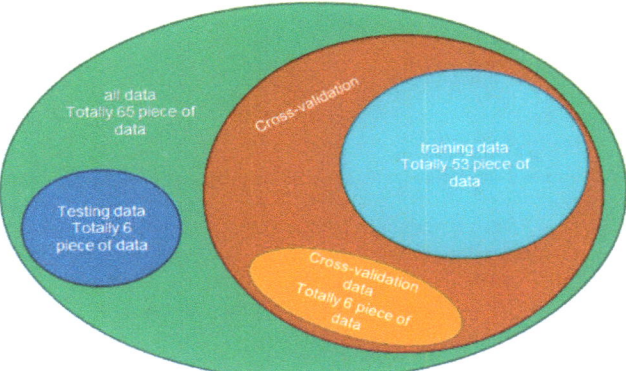

Figure 3. Relationship diagram of research data.

3.2. Model Building Stage

This research uses Orange software to test the data and then verify the predictions. Figure 4 shows the architecture diagram of the proposed model. In Figure 4, we see all the processes and the main components of the prediction model structure. The main components or results are training data (input elements), testing data, oversampling methods, RF, SVM, ANN, cross-validation methods, and prediction results. The operation flow of this model building stage is described in detail as follows: (1) The training data is inputted first, and the form of the parameter is set, which determines whether the role of the value is a feature or the marking result of each sintered object. (2) After these sample data are inputted and transmitted into four components: the cross-validation method, RF, SVM, and ANN. The set of parameters is also passed into the cross-validation method. (3) Take the training data into RF, SVM, and ANN to build a classification model and directly output these three algorithm parameters to the cross-validation method. (4) The cross-validation method is set as a 10-fold, and AUC, CA, and F1-scores are achieved after this calculation of these evaluation indexes is completed in order to preliminarily evaluate the superiority of the classification model.

3.3. An Oversampling Method Stage

In the data of asymmetric categories (or classes), the CA rate is often high, but there are some unrealistic situations, such as the class imbalance problem (resulting in an illusion of high accuracy rates). To avoid this serious problem, an oversampling method to expand the experimental data is a feasible method for processing and addressing it. Oversampling methods mean expanding the asymmetric data of the minority category to the same amount of data as the majority category, so that the classification model is strengthened and the prediction results are more reliable and feasible.

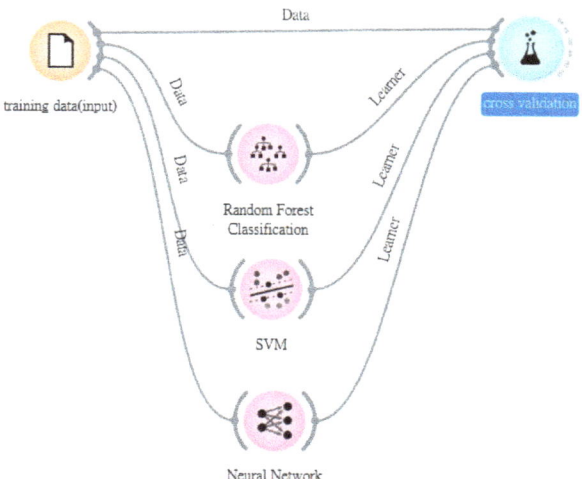

Figure 4. Architecture diagram of the proposed model with cross-validation method.

After implementing this stage for an oversampling method for the expansion, we understand that the experimental data becomes larger, which is conducive to subsequent implementation and good use of the three classifiers of RF, SVM, and ANN to establish a classification model again and use relevant test data for prediction.

3.4. Process Improvement Stage

Accordingly, after achieving the testing results of the previous step, the number of sintering times and the number of adjustments are identified and compared. In this process improvement stage, we have the following three main directions to address:

(1) Original verification process: Figure 5 shows the original verification process before the prediction model is established. In Figure 5, after the machine is assembled, it directly carries out sintering and directly observes the sintering result. If the sintering result is a failure, it is repaired and adjusted directly. After the repair, the above process continues to be repeated until the sintering result is successful. Thus, we find that the minimum number of sintering is to start the sintering process after the machine is assembled, and if the first sintering is successful, the verification is completed promptly. However, if the result of the first sintering is a failure product, it means that the second sintering process is required, and if the second sintering is successful, the verification job is completed in two sintering processes. Interestingly, the main goal of this research is to ensure that the verification is completed after the first sintering, so as to avoid the waste of time and cost of the second sintering.

(2) Improved verification process: Figure 6 shows the improved process to solve the above problems. The improved verification process is to first pass the prediction results and then decide whether adjustments are required. In Figure 6, after the machine is assembled, the sintering result is predicted first, and the parameters are adjusted when the prediction is a sintering failure. The sintering is performed when the sintering is predicted to be successful. The advantage of this approach is that only the practical sintering failure occurs, in that only the predicted sintering is successful. On the contrary, if it is predicted that the sintering process is a failure, it is adjusted in

advance at the time of prediction; thus, the number of sintering times is reduced and the probability of success in the first sintering is increased.

(3) Comparison results before and after process improvement: we use the following methods to count the possible sintering times of the test data: First, we must optimize the original verification process.

  (a) Assume that the second sintering is definitely sintered successfully, and there are six test samples in each test data set, of which three are sintered successfully and three are sintered unsuccessfully. Thus, through the original verification process in Figure 5, it is calculated that a total of nine sinterings were required in the original process.

  (b) In the new verification process in Figure 6, the rules for defining the number of sintering times are set and presented as follows:

   (i) Rule 1: The actual sintering success is also predicted as the sintering success, only needing once sintering;
   (ii) Rule 2: The actual sintering failure is also predicted as a sintering failure, only needing sintering once (because the first sintering failure has been predicted in advance);
   (iii) Rule 3: The actual sintering is successful, but the predicted sintering is a failure, requiring twice as much sintering;
   (iv) Rule 4: The actual sintering failure is predicted to be a sintering success, needing twice as much sintering.

  (c) Judge the sintering times according to the above rules, and compare the sintering times of the original process and the improved process. Accordingly, we need to determine the number to adjust the parameters. Figure 7 shows the flow of determining the number of parameters to adjust. When the predicted or actual sintering fails, we perform adjustments according to the process shown in Figure 7. Since no more actual sintering is done, we use some more objective methods to measure it. In practice, for sintered objects, there are probably shapes, such as boxes, cylinders, and flats, that are used to judge the results of sintered objects. The main judgment process is described in the following three directions: First, adjust according to the predicted sintering failure. If it is a box object, in addition to adjusting the error of the galvanometer, it is necessary to adjust the movement of the construction slot motor. Second, when the box object is judged to have failed, two adjustments are required. Third, both cylinder and flat objects only need to be adjusted once and then summed up for each object, which becomes the total number of adjustments in the classification model. The fewer the total number of adjustments, the higher the prediction accuracy.

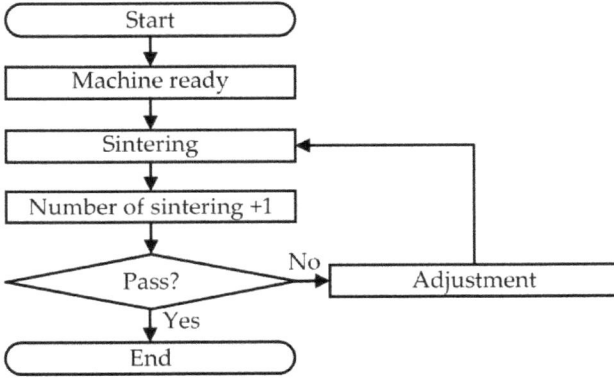

Figure 5. Original verification process.

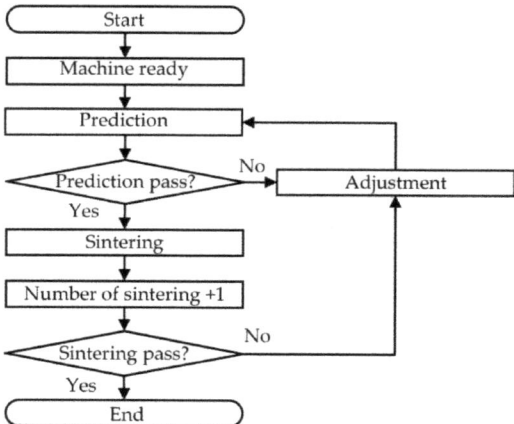

Figure 6. Improved verification process.

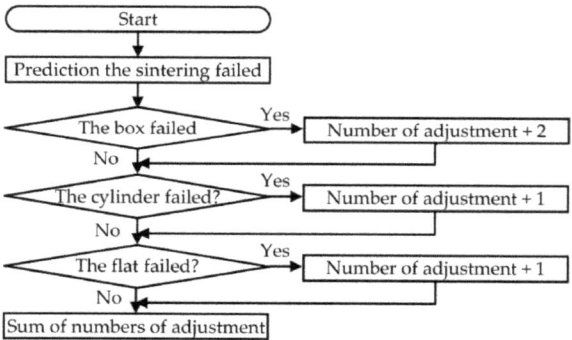

Figure 7. The process of judging the number of parameter adjustments.

4. Empirical Results and Data Analysis Results for a Real Case Study

This section mainly explains the experimental results of random distribution data collected, the cross-validation results of classifiers for each sintered object, the prediction results of classifiers with/without an oversampling method for the given data, and comparison results for the number of sintering and adjustment times for the original verification process and the improved verification process for the purpose of performance evaluation and data analysis. Lastly, the empirical summary from all the experiments and some discussions are further addressed.

4.1. Collection Results of Sample Data

In this section, after the first stage of data collection in Section 3, all 65-sample data with nine features is analyzed, and the detailed information of all samples of feature data is displayed as Appendix A, Table A1. From Appendix A, Table A1, it is found that the box objects have 25 failure cases and 40 successful cases they have 17 failure cases and 48 successful cases for cylinder objects; they have 18 failure cases and 47 successful cases for flat objects; and for total-result objects, they have 37 failure cases and 28 successful cases. Next, Table 1 shows the 10 samples of testing data performed each time with six data points; the testing data is randomly and fairly selected from six of the 65 record samples from the targeted data set each time, and the rest is used for training data. Importantly, it is not guaranteed that the proportion of sintering failure and sintering success for each selected object must be the same.

Table 1. 10 testing samples for each validation with six data.

	1st Data No.	2nd Data No.	3rd Data No.	4th Data No.	5th Data No.	6th Data No.
1st test sample	4	12	23	43	48	57
2nd test sample	13	23	37	41	56	65
3rd test sample	12	24	34	47	52	64
4th test sample	9	18	33	38	43	56
5th test sample	5	22	30	43	55	63
6th test sample	14	21	34	41	48	58
7th test sample	6	11	26	40	55	58
8th test sample	1	24	36	41	53	62
9th test sample	4	8	9	39	44	63
10th test sample	3	10	35	44	46	50

4.2. Implementing Results of Cross-Validation Method

For the cross-validation results of the case study, we illustrate it with four research objects: box, cylinder, flat, and the total-result into the following four parts, respectively.

(1) Results for box objects: Figure 8 shows the scores of various indicators in the cross-validation method for the box objects. From Figure 8, it is observed that among the three classification algorithms, the ANN (0.5777) and the RF (0.5761) have obtained the top two higher CA rates, and the ANN (0.6016) is better than random guessing in the evaluation of AUC (i.e., 1 > AUC > 0.5). Especially in the comparison of the F1-score, it is obvious that among the three algorithms, the accuracy rate of predicting sintering success is higher than the rate of predicting sintering failure.

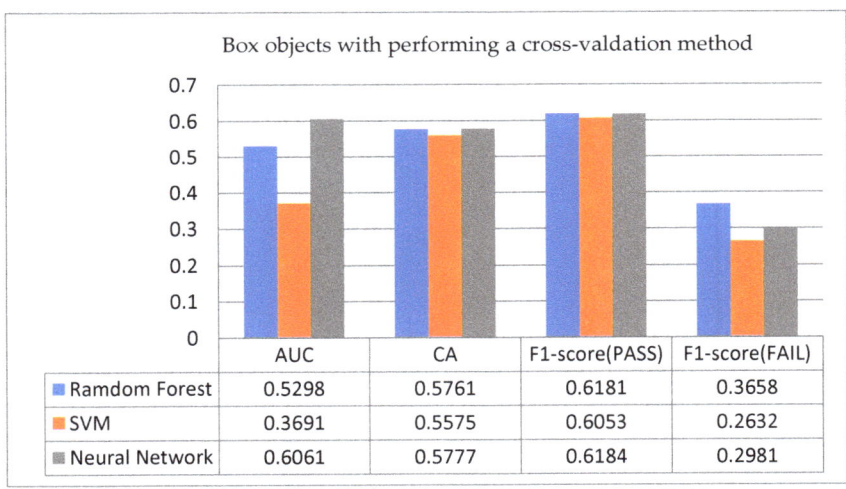

Figure 8. Cross-validation results for box objects.

(2) Results for cylinder objects: Figure 9 shows the results for the cross-validation index score of three algorithms used on the cylindrical objects. From Figure 9, we observe that in this cylindrical object, the three algorithms have achieved a CA rate higher than 0.65, the RF is as high as 0.712, and the performance of RF and SVM is better than random guessing (i.e., 0.5). However, the AUC part of the ANN is lower than random guessing for this cylindrical object. This situation is worthy of further research by subsequent scholars. Moreover, what is more serious when compared with box objects in Figure 8 is that the F1-score results of a sintering failure obtained by these three algorithms are all lower than those obtained by boxes, and the possible reason is also worthy of further investigation in the future.

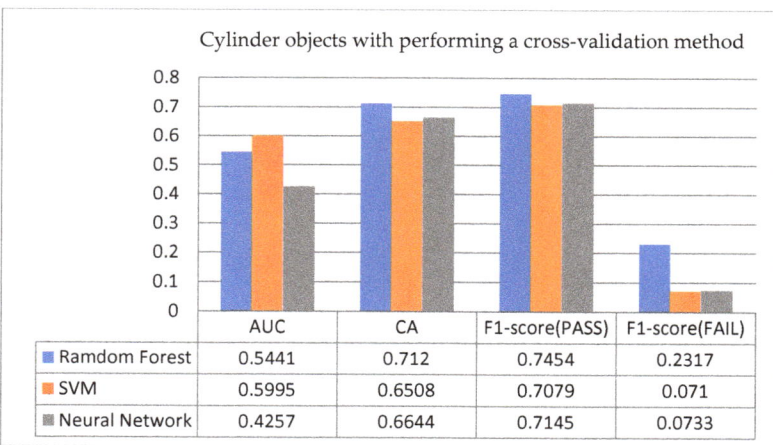

Figure 9. Cross-validation results for cylinder objects.

(3) Results for flat objects: The cross-validation results with score indicators for three algorithms used in the flat objects, are shown in Figure 10. In terms of AUC, the three algorithms are similar to random guessing, and in terms of CA rate, the ANN has the highest accuracy rate of 0.6712; but in terms of F1-score, it is found that the F1-score of a sintering failure for these three algorithms is close to 0, and even the ANN is 0, which means that in this confusion matrix, the number of samples successfully predicted as a sintering failure is 0.

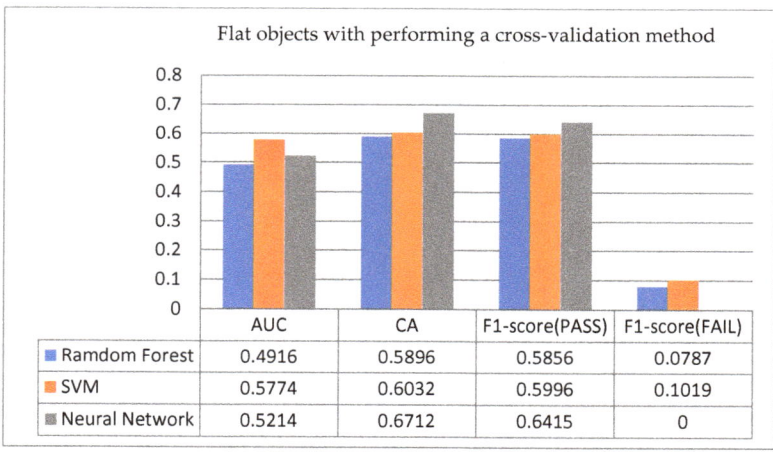

Figure 10. Cross-validation results for flat objects.

(4) Results for total-result objects: As for the results of the total-result objects, Figure 11 shows their cross-validation results. In the AUC part, the ANN shows better performance than random guessing; as for the CA rate, the ANN has the highest accuracy rate, reaching nearly 0.6, which is higher than the classification performance of the other two classifiers. After observing the F1-score, it is found that the results obtained for this object are different from those obtained for the other three objects. In the other three objects, the probability of sintering success is much higher than that of sintering failure. However, it has the opposite case in this total-result object. That is, a sintering failure is higher than a sintering success, but the gap in rate between a sintering failure and a sintering success is not large.

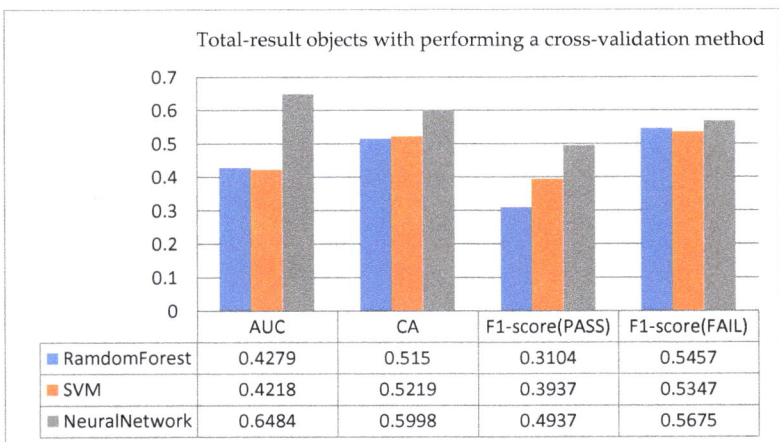

Figure 11. Cross-validation results for total-result of all objects.

Summarizing the above four results, we get the important results of implementing the cross-validation method, and there are fewer objects on the sintering failure of cylinders (17) and flats (18), so that the cross-validation results may directly be classified as successful sintering. Although such results can get a relatively high accuracy rate, they cannot faithfully present the real situation; thus, we need to perform an oversampling operation for the given data on each sintered object to solve the imbalance problem for two classes (fail and pass), and then compare the difference between each verification index with/without an oversampling method. The comparison results are shown in the next section.

4.3. Oversampling Results for Sintering Objects

For the empirical results of testing sintering objects, we still differentiate four different object purposes by identifying and illustrating their performance with/without an oversampling technique for the given data, respectively.

(1) Box objects: Provide the testing data to the established model and experiment operations, and observe the experimental results. Figure 12 shows a comparison of testing results with/without using an oversampling technique for box objects. Figure 12 (above) is the result obtained by verifying the no-oversampling data of samples for the box objects. In particular, from Figure 12 (above), there are three key points identified. (a) The accuracy rates of the three classification algorithms used are all above 0.6, and the highest are the SVM (0.6334) and the ANN (0.6333); (b) Moreover, the scores of the F1-score are all around 0.6. (c) In terms of AUC, the ANN is the highest, followed by the RF, and finally the SVM, and the SVM is even worse when compared to random guessing. To identify the difference between with/without using an oversampling method, this experiment adds the oversampling technique. Figure 12 (below) presents the empirical results with a data oversampling method; as a result, there are some key points identified from it. (a) The accuracy of the SVM and the ANN is improved to 0.6501 and 0.6668, respectively; from the CA results, it is found that the data processed by the oversampling technique is more helpful to the ANN in this box object. On the contrary, it is the least effective for RFs, and the accuracy rate does not increase but decreases. With this interesting result, it is a valuable issue to further explore in the future. (b) As an AUC indicator, the ranking is SVM ➔ ANN ➔ RF, just conversely without using an oversampling technique, and the three algorithms are better than random guessing. (c) On the F1-score, the ANN and SVM have improved, from 0.598 to 0.6644 and from 0.6085 to 0.6482, respectively. Finally, summarizing the empirical results on this box object from Figure 12, there are better testing results using an oversampling technique to conclude that the classification performance has been significantly improved.

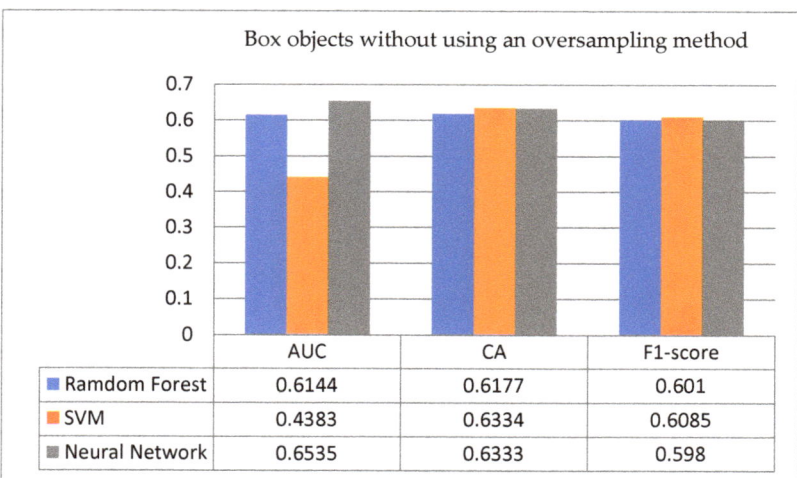

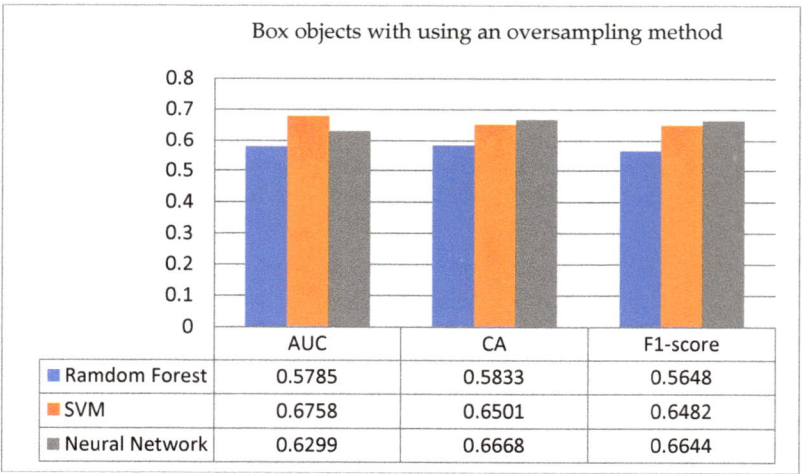

Figure 12. Testing results with/without using an oversampling technique for box objects.

Furthermore, Table 2 shows the classification results of box objects with/without an oversampling technique for the sample sets that are successfully sintered. From the comparison of statistical quantities, it is known that both the ANN and the SVM have one case of data that directly predicts the result of the sample set as sintering success when the 10 sample sets are not oversampled, while the RF has two cases of data. However, in the prediction after the oversampling technique, none of the sample sets are predicted as successful sintering, and the accuracy of the ANN is improved, which means that the accuracy of the prediction of a sintering failure is improved.

Table 2. The information whose classification results are all successfully entered in the box sample set.

	ANN	RF	SVM
Un-oversampled	1	2	1
Oversampled	0	0	0

(2) Cylindrical objects: Figure 13 shows the comparison with/without using an oversampling technique for testing the results of cylindrical objects. As shown in Figure 13

(above), the accuracy rates of these three classification algorithms are all higher than 0.7, among which the highest CA rate is 0.7499 for RF, 0.7167 for ANN, and 0.70 for SVM. In terms of the AUC evaluator, it is found that only the SVM is better than random guessing; however, in the F1-score indicator, the ranking of the three classification algorithms is the same as that of the CA rate. That is RF ➔ ANN ➔ SVM, and all the scores are above 0.63. From Figure 13 (below), there are two key directions identified. (a) After implementing the oversampling technique, it is found that only the performance of the RF is improved, while both the performances of the SVM and the ANN are reduced; this special case represents that when the model is changed, there may be an overfitting problem with the prediction data. (b) Among them, there exists one special thing: the accuracy of the RF remains unchanged, but the F1-score and AUC show a decline in terms of most performances. This interesting point is also worth further exploring the possible reasons in the future.

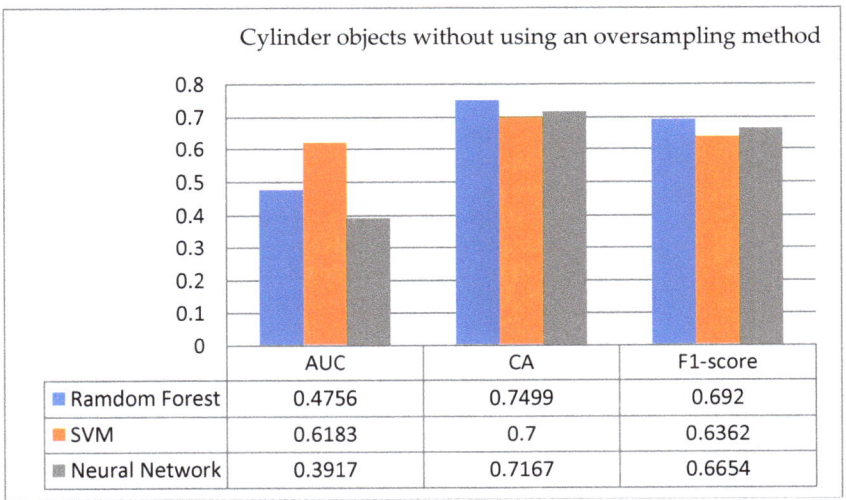

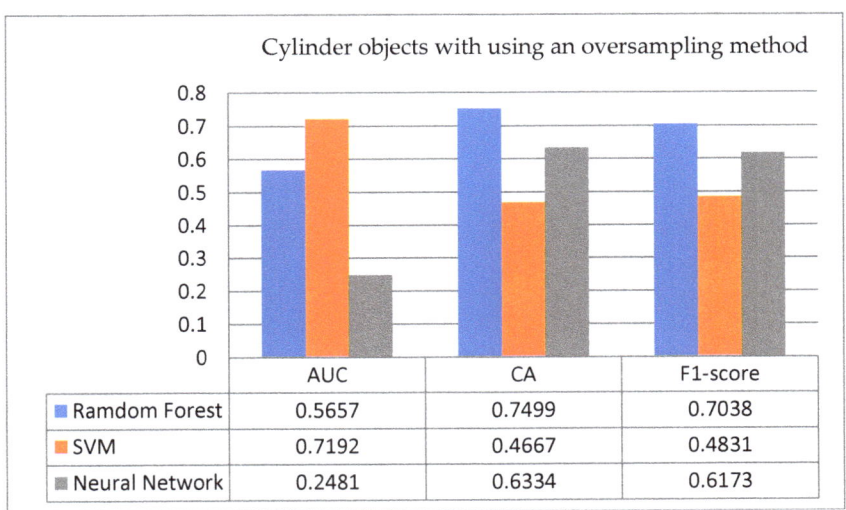

Figure 13. Testing results for cylindrical objects with/without an oversampling method.

Furthermore, Table 3 shows the classification results with/without an oversampling technique of successful sintering for cylindrical objects in the sample set. From its statistical outcome, in the 10 sample sets that have not been oversampled, both the ANN and the RF have six cases that directly predict a successful sintering case of the sample set, while there are five cases in the RF. However, in the prediction work after the oversampling technique, the number of sample data points that were originally classified as successful sintering has decreased significantly. In particular, the CA rate in the RF remains unchanged; this interesting phenomenon represents that this classification model is good, and the empirical result is more in line with the real situation and closer to the status quo.

Table 3. The information whose classification results are all successful sintering in the cylindrical sample set.

	ANN	RF	SVM
Un-oversampled	6	6	5
Oversampled	2	4	0

(3) Flat objects: Figure 14 shows the comparison of testing results for the flat objects with/without treatment using an oversampling technique. From Figure 14 (above), the accuracy rate and F1-score in the ANN without using an oversampling technique are higher than those of the other two classification models; however, only in the AUC indicator is it lower than the SVM, and it is inferior to random guessing. In exploring the possible reasons, it is possible that due to the unbalanced categories of the original training data, all classifiers predict the sintering result as successful, resulting in higher accuracy. However, in practice, the expected results cannot be achieved, which is compared and seen from the cross-validation method of flat objects. In Figure 14 (below), after using the oversampling technique, it is strange that the accuracy rates of the ANN and the SVM are greatly reduced to 0.4499 and 0.4334, respectively; however, the RF is just the opposite, and its accuracy rate has slightly improved from 0.6333 to 0.6499. Both the F1-score and AUC have also increased slightly to 0.6262 and 0.5163, respectively. Moreover, from the above empirical results, we discover a very interesting fact: on flat objects, when the data classes are more unbalanced and after implementing the oversampling technique of data, the RF gets a relatively good classification performance.

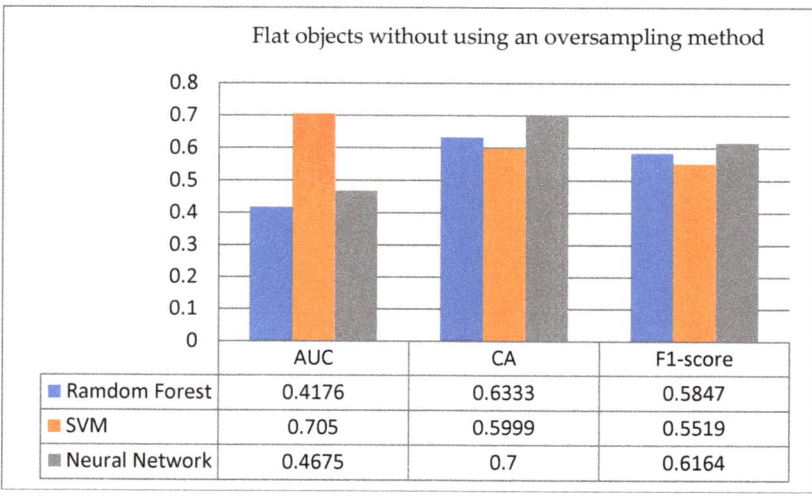

Figure 14. *Cont.*

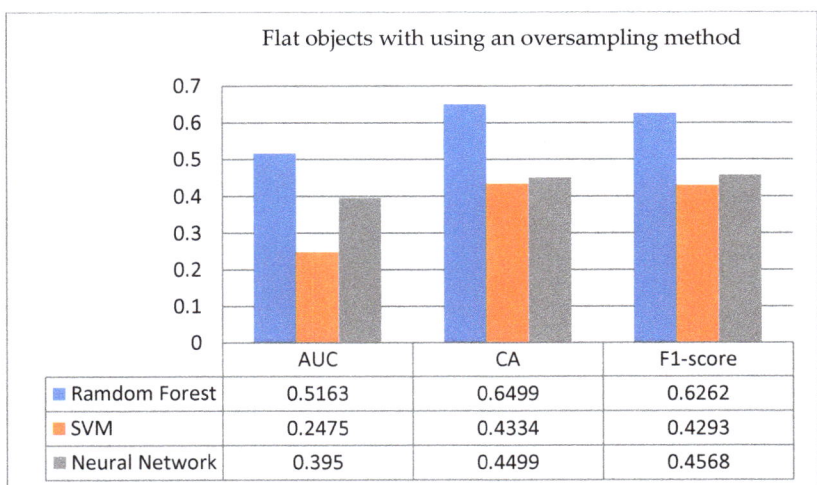

Figure 14. Testing results for flat objects with/without using an oversampling technique.

Accordingly, Table 4 shows the classification results of sample sets for flat objects with/without using an oversampling method with successful sintering. From Table 4, we count that among the 10 un-oversampled sample sets, the results of eight, four, and six sample sets of the ANN, RF, and SVM are directly predicted as successful sintering, respectively. However, in the prediction, after implementing the oversampling technique, the number of sample data points that are all classified as successful sintering is reduced. In this flat object, the accuracy rate of the RF has increased, and this special case means that the accuracy rate of predicting a sintering failure has increased, which implies that the classification model is more in line with the reality of 3D-SLS for the case company.

Table 4. The information whose classification results are all successfully sintered in the flat sample set.

	ANN	RF	SVM
Un-oversampled	8	4	6
Oversampled	0	2	2

(4) Total result of summarized objects: In yield prediction for SLS on the total result of sintered objects, Figure 15 shows the comparison of testing results for summarized objects with/without sample augmentation. Through Figure 15 (above), it is observed that when there is no processing sample augmentation, the ANN performance is higher than the other two listed models regardless of indicators of AUC, CA rate, and F1-score; therefore, the prediction ability of the ANN model is the best performer. However, in Figure 15 (below), the CA rate of the ANN after implementing the sample data augmentation method has dropped to 0.5668, the F1-score has dropped to 0.525, and the AUC has dropped to 0.5556. On the contrary, the indicators of AUC, CA rate, and F1-score for the RF are increased to 0.5777, 0.5834, and 0.5468, respectively; similarly, all the performances of the SVM are also improved. However, since there is no serious class unbalance problem in the total result of summarizing objects, the function of an oversampling technique is not performed; the data is directly expanded to more than 200 items. Unfortunately, such an approach may lead to overfitting problems in these models; in this total result of the cross-validation method, the ANN has also achieved the best result in this research. Thus, we can clearly express that in this model, the ANN can still be used as a predictive model, and in the overall result, the best performance result is the ANN model.

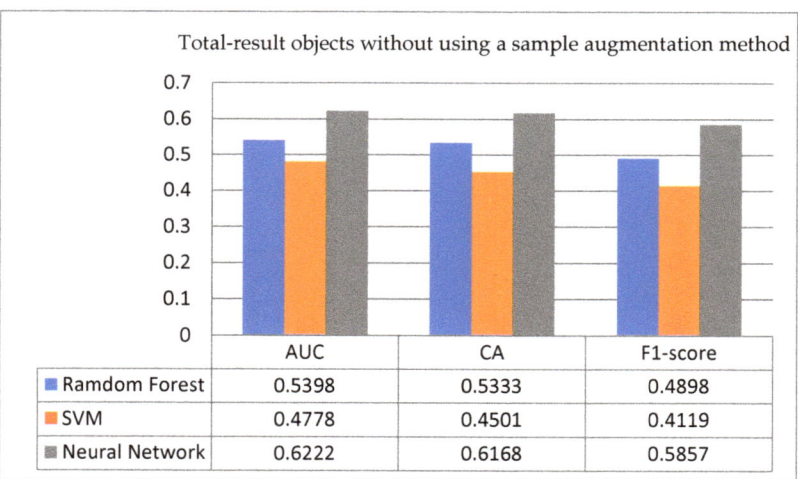

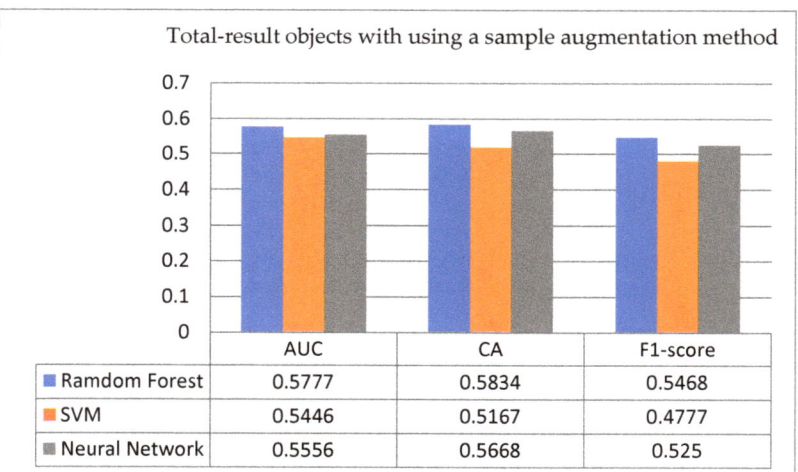

Figure 15. Test results for objects summary processed with/without sample data augmentation.

Subsequently, Table 5 shows the classification results of the total-result object sample sets with/without sample data expansion for a successful sintering. From Table 5, no matter whether sample data has been expanded or not, there is no sample of the sintering results, which is classified into the sample set of a successful sintering. After data expansion, the CA rate of the ANN has decreased significantly, while the accuracy of the RF and SVM has increased, however, they are not higher than the un-augmented ANN.

Table 5. The information in which the classification results are all successfully sintered in the total-result sample set.

	ANN	RF	SVM
Un-oversampled	0	0	0
Oversampled	0	0	0

More importantly, this research thus concludes with two core directions for the overall results. (1) It is unnecessary for the total-result objects to perform data expansion processing.

(2) However, in the prediction results for box, cylinder, and flat objects, it is absolutely necessary to perform data processing using an oversampling technique because it can reduce the case that the sintering results are all predicted as successful sintering, and it can make the predicted results closer to the actual situation of SLS and increase the plasticity and credibility of these classification models.

4.4. Comparison Results for Sintering Times and Adjustment Times before and after the Modification of Verification Process

Consequently, this research first calculates the comparison of sintering times for the proposed model. To facilitate the follow-up comparison operation, we assume that the sintering will be successful in the second sintering, then count the number of sintering times based on the predicted results, and further compare the number of sintering times obtained before and after the modification of the verification process. By the previous testing sample data in Table 1, we know that there are six testing samples each time; in the data set of the total-result objects, there are three samples of failed sintering and three samples of successfully sintered. Looking at this combination again, the verification process before modification needs to be sintered nine times ($3 + 3 \times 2$) before the six samples are successfully verified. As a result, Figure 16 shows the statistical results of sintering times for each data set after the modification.

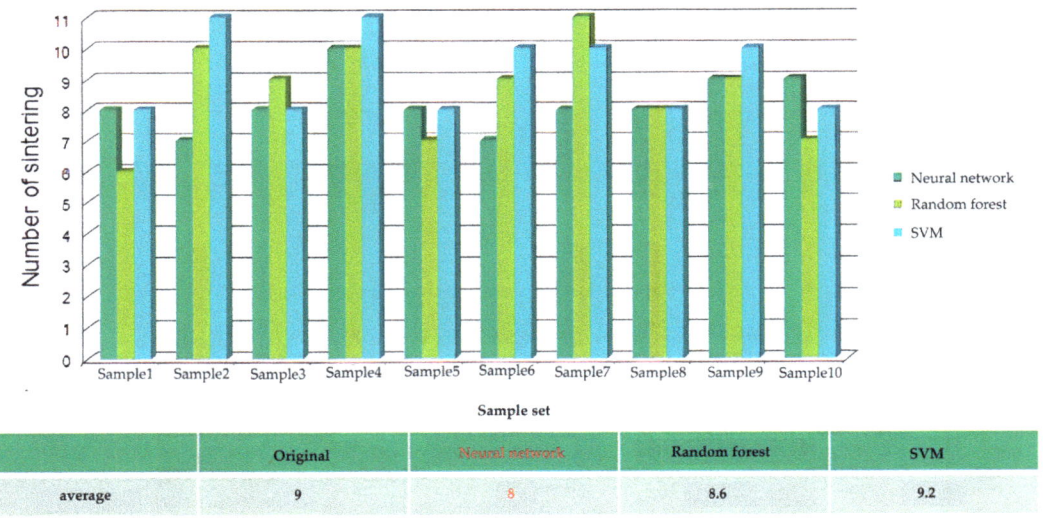

Figure 16. Statistical results of sintering times for the modified verification process for each sample data set.

From Figure 16, we get the number of sintering times for each classification model. Interestingly, the number of sintering times for the ANN is reduced by one time (i.e., eight times) on average in each sample set; especially in the first and second sample sets, the sintering times of the verification process before and after the modification are the same, except the seventh sample set is sintered once more after the modification than the verification process before the modification, and the sintering times of other sample sets are the same. Thus, it is less than nine times, so the average number of sintering times is calculated as eight times for the ANN model. The average sintering times for the modified verification process of the ANN outperform the verification process before the modification and that of other classification models: RF and SVM. Especially, SVM (9.2 times) is even worse than the original verification process (9.0 times) before the modification, and the potential reason is also worthy of further exploration in the future.

Subsequently, in the comparison of the number of adjustment times after quantifying the oversampled data results, Figure 17 shows the number of prediction adjustment times for the three classifiers on each testing data set. By observing Figure 17, we know that among the 10 sample sets, the average number of adjustments for the RF is the least, and each test sample set has an average adjustment of 10.7 times, while the average adjustment times of the ANN and SVM are 11.7 times and 13.5 times, respectively. In terms of the number of adjustment times, it is found that the RF model yields fewer adjustments than the other two models; thus, RFs perform the best in terms of the number of adjustment times for this research case.

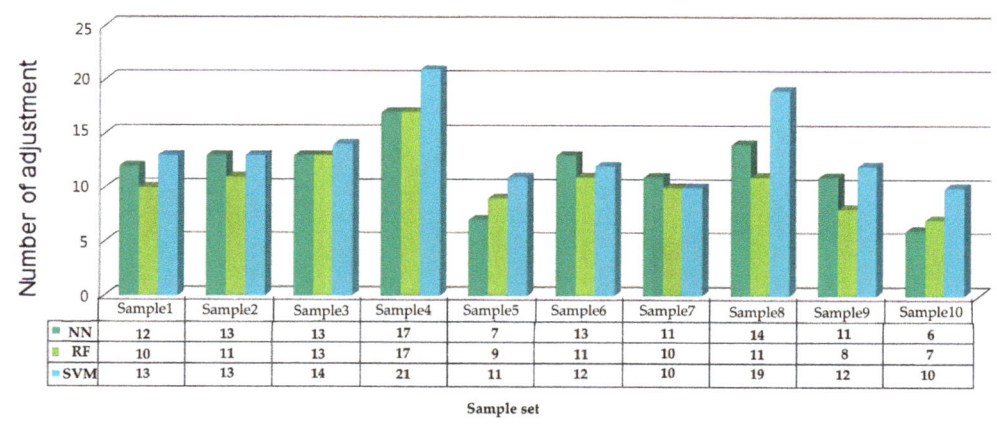

Figure 17. Information on adjustment times for the three classifiers in each testing data set.

More importantly, through the above empirical results, the following key points are sorted out: (1) It is found that the best verification process is to use the ANN that has not been processed by the oversampling technique to forecast the total-result objects. (2) Use the RF model obtained after an oversampling method to predict the sintering results for each sintered object and to train out the parameters of the best model. (3) After doing the above operations, the study models proposed are used to effectively carry out the best verification process with the least number of sintering times and the least number of adjustment times, which is one of the major contributions of this research for experiencing industrial data analysis and application.

4.5. Empirical Summary of All Results for the Experiments with Discussions

Totally, we use five directions to uniformly illustrate the primary outcome of the empirical summary with some meaningful discussions and values after executing all the experiments in this research, as follows:

(1) Key experimental results of objects: in the mathematical experiment operations based on the cross-validation method, we have identified and summarized the following four main points: (a) On the box objects: the evaluation indicators of the ANN are the best, and the results of three indicators are AUC 0.50, CA rate 0.57, and F1-scores of a sintering success of 0.61 and a sintering failure of 0.30. (b) On the cylindrical objects: the evaluation indicators of RF are the best, and the three indicators are described as AUC 0.54, CA rate 0.71, and F1-score of a sintering success of 0.74 and a sintering failure of 0.23. (c) On the flat objects: ANNs have the best performance results, and the evaluation indicators are AUC 0.52, CA rate 0.67, and F1-score of a sintering success

of 0.64 and a sintering failure of 0. (d) On the total-result objects: the performance results are the same as those of flat objects, and the experimental results of the ANNs model are also the best. The evaluation indicators are identified as AUC 0.65, CA rate 0.60, and F1-scores of a sintering success of 0.50 and a sintering failure of 0.56.

(2) Gaps of the cross-validation method: regarding the cross-validation method, the result for the gap of the F1-score between the sintering success and the sintering failure for the three objects is too large, which means that most mathematical binary classification models are still more inclined to classify the data as sintering success.

(3) Differences with/without using an oversampling technique: we obtain the following four core values for the gaps with/without the oversampling technique: (a) In the case of box objects: the best CA is to use the ANN model; after using the oversampling technique, its CA is increased from 0.6333 to 0.6668, and the F1-score is increased from the original 0.587 to 0.6644. (b) In the case of cylindrical objects: the highest CA is 0.7499 in the RF, its AUC is increased from 0.4756 to 0.5657, and its F1-score is increased from 0.6920 to 0.7038. (c) In the case of flat objects: the best CA is the ANN when the samples have un-oversampled data. However, after implementing the oversampling technique, the CA of ANN is not rising but falling, and even lower than 0.5; interestingly, the RF has achieved the highest CA from 0.6333 to 0.6499, the highest F1-score from 0.5847 to 0.6262, and the lowest AUC from less than 0.5 to 0.5163. (e) In the case of total-result objects: the ANN model without sample data expansion has the highest CA of 0.6168, AUC of 0.6222, and F1-score of 0.5857. However, after expanding the sample data, the highest CA for the total-result objects is the RF model, which has increased from 0.5333 to 0.5834; the F1-score has increased from 0.4898 to 0.5468; and the AUC indicator has also increased from 0.5389 to 0.5777.

(4) Reduction of time and times: After integrating the experiment results and comparing them with the original manufacturing process time, it is found that each machine reduces the sintering time by an average of four hours. Moreover, if the sampling of the data used is expanded, it is more suitable to use the RF algorithm when predicting the sintering failure of the objects, and its average number of sintering times per machine is 1.70 times, which is better than 1.95 times for the ANN and 2.25 times for the SVM.

(5) Results of sample data expansion: the result of the cross-validation method for the total-result objects does not have the serious problem of class imbalance; thus, using the sample data expansion method instead of the oversampling method is suitable. Especially in this case, there are two core concerns identified. (a) This research confirms that in each given data set, the ANN without sample expansion can reduce the sintering verification by one time. (b) After processing the sample expansion method, the RF for the failure prediction of objects gets a minimum of 10.7 times of adjustments, which is lower than the 11.7 and 13.5 of the ANN and SVM, respectively.

5. Research Findings and Research Limitations

It is necessary to identify two types of research concerns for further aggregating the study results mentioned above, including research findings and research limitations, in order to benefit from and highlight the study issue of the SLS manufacturing process, as follows.

5.1. Important Research Findings

In summarizing the empirical study results of this research in the field of industrial data analysis, the following key research findings have been defined, and these findings can provide a useful reference for relevant industry applications and academic circles.

(1) As a total result of object prediction, this research finds that it is not absolutely necessary to carry out data expansion processing on samples. However, in the mathematical prediction of experiment results for box, cylinder, and flat objects, it is necessary to perform an oversampling technique because this technique can solve the problem that

the sintering results are all predicted to be sintering successes, making the prediction results more accurate and real. The closeness to the factual situation can increase the plasticity and credibility of the mathematical classification model.

(2) In terms of the number of adjustment times in this research case, it is found that the performance of the RF model is the best. Thus, it is recommended that follow-up operators simulate and use the constructed RF model if they are more focused on reducing the number of adjustment times for identifying the SLS yield.

(3) In the empirical results, it is found that the best verification process is to use the ANN model that has not been processed by the oversampling technique as the prediction of the total result for the objects sintered.

(4) In the CA for the modified verification process, it is found that the average performance of the ANN is better than that before the modification, and its verification process of the binary classification model is better than the other listed models, followed by the RF, and finally the SVM; that is, in the ranking of ANN ➔ RF ➔ SVM.

(5) If the sample data is processed by an oversampling technique, it is found that the RF model in this research is the best to optimize the parameters used to predict the sintering failure of each sintered object. After performing the above operations, the proposed mathematical binary classification model effectively carries out and appropriately obtains the best verification process with the least number of sintering times and the least number of machine parameter adjustments for interested parties.

5.2. Research Limitations

The focus of this research is the SLS manufacturing process, and there are three potential research limitations identified.

(1) Due to many shortcomings in sintering the SLS products, such as the high unit price of machine equipment, the high construction cost of the sintering environment, and the high sintering cost, these major defects result in a limited application value: the sales volume of the machine (already a niche market) has shrunk even more, and even this makes companies daunting. Due to the high costs of purchasing this equipment, general business is discouraged. This special situation causes the sample data to be relatively scarce; thus, the small amount of raw sample data has also become the first main research limitation for this research.

(2) For manufacturers of SLS machines, the verification results of machine output are a huge expense; thus, the data of each verification record is an expensive and valuable experience. Given this reason, general SLS manufacturers mainly hope to reduce the number of sintering times in order to lower the high verification cost of the machine output. Thus, enhancing the one-time sintering greatly lowers the operating burden on the manufacturer. The high verification cost creates a bottleneck problem in data collection, and this problem is serious and is the second research limitation.

(3) The third research limitation is that the example of the research objects is only from a certain SLS company, which may result in a lack of diversity of sample data and an inference limitation of research results.

6. Conclusions and Future Research

To overcome the serious problems when forming the sintering of a standard SLS object, this research has constructed a mathematical prediction system to reduce the time and cost of sintering verification. The following two sections give the core highlights of empirical conclusions with contributions and future prospects, respectively.

6.1. Empirical Conclusions with Industrial Contribution

After all the experiments, we have concluded that the following two key contributions were integrated into the study conclusions:

(1) Industrial contribution: this research is mainly aimed at realizing an effective prediction framework for identifying SLS yield, which is mainly used to reduce the sintering

time cost and direct material cost of the verification process. The ability of proposed mathematical binary classification models for each object is evaluated through the cross-validation method, and their accuracy is verified by actual data collected from a case study for industrial applications. Thus, through the above empirical results, the number of sintering times is reduced. Importantly, although this research has not provided an innovative technique, such a binary model constructed is rarely seen in the SLS industry for 3D-AM issues, and it has made a great industrial contribution by effectively reducing the verification cost of the SLS manufacturing process in practice.

(2) Applicable values: the proposed mathematical binary models in this research make the prediction of the SLS yield more accurate to reduce the situation that the prediction results are all predicted to be sintering success, and to be closed to the real case of industries, it is proved that the mathematical binary model has the superiority of its application performance in industrial manufacturing processes. Thus, it also has significant applicable values based on the empirical results of industrial data analysis.

6.2. Future Research

Although the experimental performance of this research has research advantages and benefits and the empirical results are remarkable, there are still some rooms for improvement in the future, and these improvements can provide references for subsequent directions to interested researchers or industry requirements, as follows:

(1) The first improvement is about the diversity of molding materials; these materials have different material properties, molding parameters, and shrinkage rates. Since the main material of this research is PA12 (Polyamide 12 powder for SLS printing material) [10,30], subsequent researchers can use materials different from PA12, and the new material may not be able to adapt to the optimized parameters of the proposed binary classification model. Therefore, we suggest that new types of materials are added into the proposed models as new features (factors), and after collecting sample data, data retraining and data retesting are conducted to further measure the classification performance and efficiency of the binary classification model.

(2) In the practical sintering application, since the sintering result is not only determined by the dimensional size accuracy but also requires other measurements of unique characteristics of different materials, such as the range of strength and toughness or the density detection of the objects, these results directly or indirectly lead to molding whether the object is successful. Thus, it is suggested that subsequent researchers can collect the above different data, add it to the proposed models, and then re-predict the forming results of the SLS manufacturing process.

(3) The biggest problem in this research is that the amount of SLS practical sample data is insufficient, causing insufficient training data, which directly affects the prediction results. Thus, it is recommended to collect more raw samples of data to retrain the mathematical binary classification model and address future directions.

(4) In some large machine tools, it is a common problem that obtaining the sample data is difficult; thus, it is suggested that the models of how to predict with a small amount of data should be further focused in the future. It is a feasible alternative to use the GAN method to create more fake sample data of a sintering failure to increase the sample number for sufficiently training the binary model and improving its performance.

(5) For the RF algorithm, it also has a feature importance score, which can help gain insight into which features are important. Thus, the RF can be used for the technique of FS to reduce the dimensionality of data to select the best features [57]. For this reason, the RF can be added to the proposed model to further remove irrelative features, facilitate experiment operations, and measure its model performance in the future.

(6) Finally, this research is still committed to constructing a set of classification frameworks to judge sintering result strategies in a process-based structure of automatic and intelligent methods. The purpose is that researchers can regard the proposed

models as a basis to develop their future models for comprehensive comparison with more techniques of the state of the art, such as Xgboost or K shot. Moreover, the establishment of the maintenance strategy for sintering enables the adjustment of machine parameters to be more automatic and intelligent, with effective and efficient effects.

Author Contributions: Conceptualization, J.-R.C. and Y.-S.C.; Methodology, J.-R.C. and Y.-S.C.; Software, J.-H.L. and Y.-H.H.; Visualization, J.-R.C., Y.-S.C. and Y.-H.H.; Writing—original draft, J.-H.L., J.-R.C. and Y.-S.C.; Writing—review and editing, Y.-S.C. and Y.-H.H. All authors have read and agreed to the published version of the manuscript.

Funding: This research was partially supported by the National Science and Technology Council of Taiwan for grant number NSTC 111-2221-E-167-036-MY2.

Data Availability Statement: Not applicable.

Conflicts of Interest: The authors declare no conflict of interest.

Appendix A

Table A1. Information of 65 records of raw data.

Serial No.	Z at 239.9 mm Accuracy	Spot Size (um)	The Max. Error of the X-Axis Galvanometer	The Max. Error of the Y-Axis Galvanometer	Laser Energy 50%	Box	Cylinder	Flat	Total-Result
1	0.09	525	0.22	0.31	23.35	fail	pass	fail	fail
2	0.09	515	0.33	0.27	22.26	fail	fail	fail	fail
3	0.11	555	0.28	0.28	20.72	pass	pass	fail	fail
4	0.12	545	0.18	0.22	21.38	pass	pass	fail	fail
5	0.10	545	0.27	0.31	22.79	pass	pass	fail	fail
6	0.10	575	0.30	0.35	20.79	fail	pass	fail	fail
7	0.10	555	0.23	0.24	18.02	pass	fail	fail	fail
8	0.11	565	0.31	0.23	20.93	fail	pass	pass	fail
9	0.10	545	0.24	0.31	21.46	fail	fail	pass	fail
10	0.10	575	0.31	0.22	18.29	fail	pass	pass	fail
11	0.10	565	0.19	0.26	21.62	fail	pass	pass	fail
12	0.11	545	0.33	0.20	20.74	fail	pass	fail	fail
13	0.09	535	0.25	0.31	20.47	fail	pass	fail	fail
14	0.11	525	0.33	0.28	22.99	fail	pass	pass	fail
15	0.11	505	0.25	0.26	22.20	pass	pass	fail	fail
16	0.11	515	0.26	0.22	23.67	fail	pass	pass	fail
17	0.12	535	0.34	0.33	22.23	fail	fail	fail	fail
18	0.09	555	0.21	0.26	18.66	fail	fail	fail	fail
19	0.11	555	0.23	0.20	22.09	fail	pass	pass	fail
20	0.12	515	0.21	0.18	21.75	fail	pass	fail	fail
21	0.11	535	0.27	0.29	21.88	fail	fail	pass	fail
22	0.10	545	0.32	0.21	22.52	fail	pass	fail	fail
23	0.08	555	0.24	0.32	20.25	fail	pass	pass	fail
24	0.11	555	0.33	0.33	24.33	fail	fail	pass	fail
25	0.10	525	0.27	0.24	22.18	fail	pass	pass	fail
26	0.10	515	0.22	0.26	23.49	pass	fail	fail	fail
27	0.10	545	0.33	0.28	23.18	pass	fail	fail	fail
28	0.12	535	0.25	0.31	19.58	fail	pass	pass	fail
29	0.10	535	0.28	0.27	21.52	fail	pass	pass	fail
30	0.12	515	0.21	0.25	23.36	pass	fail	pass	fail
31	0.11	545	0.18	0.14	22.23	pass	fail	pass	fail
32	0.11	525	0.26	0.22	20.89	pass	fail	pass	fail
33	0.09	535	0.26	0.20	22.45	fail	fail	fail	fail
34	0.10	565	0.23	0.30	23.32	pass	fail	fail	fail
35	0.10	545	0.18	0.15	22.41	pass	fail	fail	fail
36	0.09	515	0.21	0.33	23.75	fail	fail	pass	fail

Table A1. Cont.

Serial No.	Z at 239.9 mm Accuracy	Spot Size (um)	The Max. Error of the X-Axis Galvanometer	The Max. Error of the Y-Axis Galvanometer	Laser Energy 50%	Box	Cylinder	Flat	Total-Result
37	0.10	545	0.20	0.18	25.86	fail	fail	pass	fail
38	0.10	535	0.32	0.26	20.52	pass	pass	pass	pass
39	0.10	525	0.32	0.21	21.03	pass	pass	pass	pass
40	0.10	555	0.27	0.26	19.90	pass	pass	pass	pass
41	0.10	525	0.28	0.32	21.56	pass	pass	pass	pass
42	0.11	525	0.18	0.27	22.19	pass	pass	pass	pass
43	0.09	545	0.30	0.31	21.13	pass	pass	pass	pass
44	0.10	535	0.26	0.23	22.50	pass	pass	pass	pass
45	0.10	545	0.21	0.23	22.30	pass	pass	pass	pass
46	0.12	555	0.27	0.255	21.13	pass	pass	pass	pass
47	0.11	525	0.24	0.24	22.08	pass	pass	pass	pass
48	0.10	555	0.18	0.24	25.09	pass	pass	pass	pass
49	0.11	575	0.28	0.20	22.80	pass	pass	pass	pass
50	0.11	615	0.25	0.28	24.72	pass	pass	pass	pass
51	0.11	535	0.26	0.26	22.97	pass	pass	pass	pass
52	0.10	525	0.24	0.28	26.70	pass	pass	pass	pass
53	0.12	515	0.30	0.26	24.54	pass	pass	pass	pass
54	0.11	545	0.26	0.21	22.87	pass	pass	pass	pass
55	0.10	545	0.17	0.24	23.65	pass	pass	pass	pass
56	0.11	515	0.22	0.23	22.34	pass	pass	pass	pass
57	0.10	575	0.24	0.26	23.81	pass	pass	pass	pass
58	0.11	555	0.26	0.32	22.07	pass	pass	pass	pass
59	0.11	515	0.30	0.30	21.83	pass	pass	pass	pass
60	0.10	565	0.27	0.25	21.88	pass	pass	pass	pass
61	0.11	545	0.18	0.26	21.60	pass	pass	pass	pass
62	0.09	525	0.15	0.26	21.27	pass	pass	pass	pass
63	0.11	595	0.23	0.26	21.68	pass	pass	pass	pass
64	0.10	595	0.27	0.32	22.61	pass	pass	pass	pass
65	0.10	535	0.20	0.20	23.67	pass	pass	pass	pass

References

1. Fina, F.; Goyanes, A.; Gaisford, S.; Basit, A.W. Selective laser sintering (SLS) 3D printing of medicines. *Int. J. Pharm.* **2017**, *529*, 285–293. [CrossRef] [PubMed]
2. Schmid, M.; Amado, A.; Wegener, K. Polymer Powders for Selective Laser Sintering (SLS). In *AIP Conference Proceedings, Cleveland, OH, USA, 6–12 June 2014*; AIP Publishing LLC: New York, NY, USA, 2015; Volume 1664, p. 160009. [CrossRef]
3. Wai Ming, L.; Gibson, I. Possibility of colouring SLS prototypes using the ink-jet method. *Rapid Prototyp. J.* **1999**, *5*, 152–154. [CrossRef]
4. Kruth, J.P.; Wang, X.; Laoui, T.; Froyen, L. Lasers and materials in selective laser sintering. *Assem. Autom.* **2003**, *23*, 357–371. [CrossRef]
5. Kumar, S. Selective laser sintering: A qualitative and objective approach. *JOM* **2003**, *55*, 43–47. [CrossRef]
6. Gibson, I.; Shi, D. Material properties and fabrication parameters in selective laser sintering process. *Rapid Prototyp. J.* **1997**, *3*, 129–136. [CrossRef]
7. Wang, X. Calibration of shrinkage and beam offset in SLS process. *Rapid Prototyp. J.* **1999**, *5*, 129–133. [CrossRef]
8. Reddy, T.J.; Kumar, Y.R.; Rao, C.S.P. Determination of Optimum Process Parameters Using Taguchi's Approach to Improve the Quality of SLS Parts. In Proceedings of the 17th IASTED International Conference on Modelling and Simulation (MS'06), Montreal, QC, Canada, 24–26 May 2006; pp. 228–233.
9. Shi, Y.; Li, Z.; Sun, H.; Huang, S.; Zeng, F. Effect of the properties of the polymer materials on the quality of selective laser sintering parts. *Proc. Inst. Mech. Eng. L J. Mater. Des. Appl.* **2004**, *218*, 247–252. [CrossRef]
10. Muhamad Damanhuri, A.A.; Md Fauadi, M.H.F.; Hariri, A.; Alkahari, M.R.; Omar, M.R. Emission of selected Environmental Exposure from Selective Laser Sintering (SLS) Polyamide Nylon (PA12) 3D printing Process. *J. Saf. Health Ergon.* **2019**, *1*, 1–6. Available online: http://fazpublishing.com/jshe/index.php/jshe/article/view/1/5 (accessed on 11 October 2022).
11. Lopes, A.C.; Sampaio, Á.M.; Silva, C.S.; Pontes, A.J. Prediction of SLS parts properties using reprocessing powder. *Rapid Prototyp. J.* **2021**, *27*, 496–506. [CrossRef]
12. Atluri, G.; Karpatne, A.; Kumar, V. Spatio-temporal data mining: A survey of problems and methods. *ACM Comput. Surv.* **2018**, *51*, 1–41. [CrossRef]

13. Wang, S.; Cao, J.; Philip, S.Y. Deep learning for spatio-temporal data mining: A survey. *IEEE Trans. Knowl. Data Eng.* **2020**, *34*, 3681–3700. [CrossRef]
14. Xiao, L.; Lu, M.; Huang, H. Detection of powder bed defects in selective laser sintering using convolutional neural network. *Int. J. Adv. Manuf. Technol.* **2020**, *107*, 2485–2496. [CrossRef]
15. Guo, Y.; Lu, W.F.; Fuh, J.Y.H. Semi-supervised deep learning based framework for assessing manufacturability of cellular structures in direct metal laser sintering process. *J. Intell. Manuf.* **2021**, *32*, 347–359. [CrossRef]
16. Stathatos, E.; Vosniakos, G.C. Real-time simulation for long paths in laser-based additive manufacturing: A machine learning approach. *Int. J. Adv. Manuf. Technol.* **2019**, *104*, 1967–1984. [CrossRef]
17. Shen, X.; Yao, J.; Wang, Y.; Yang, J. Density Prediction of Selective Laser Sintering Parts Based on Artificial Neural Network. In Proceedings of the ISNN 2004: International Symposium on Neural Networks Part II 1, Dalian, China, 19–21 August 2004; Yin, F.L., Wang, J., Guo, C., Eds.; Advances in Neural Networks; Springer: Berlin/Heidelberg, Germany; Volume 3174, pp. 832–840. [CrossRef]
18. La Fé-Perdomo, I.; Ramos-Grez, J.A.; Jeria, I.; Guerra, C.; Barrionuevo, G.O. Comparative analysis and experimental validation of statistical and machine learning-based regressors for modeling the surface roughness and mechanical properties of 316L stainless steel specimens produced by selective laser melting. *J. Manuf. Process.* **2022**, *80*, 666–682. [CrossRef]
19. Sharifani, K.; Amini, M. Machine learning and deep learning: A review of methods and applications. *World Inf. Technol. Eng. J.* **2023**, *10*, 3897–3904.
20. Zhu, M.; Yang, Y.; Feng, X.; Du, Z.; Yang, J. Robust modeling method for thermal error of CNC machine tools based on random forest algorithm. *J. Intell. Manuf.* **2023**, *34*, 2013–2026. [CrossRef]
21. Kurani, A.; Doshi, P.; Vakharia, A.; Shah, M. A comprehensive comparative study of artificial neural network (ANN) and support vector machines (SVM) on stock forecasting. *Ann. Data Sci.* **2023**, *10*, 183–208. [CrossRef]
22. Yan, C.; Shi, Y.; Hao, L. Investigation into the differences in the selective laser sintering between amorphous and semi-crystalline polymers. *Int. Polym. Process.* **2011**, *26*, 416–423. [CrossRef]
23. Chen, P.; Cai, H.; Li, Z.; Li, M.; Wu, H.; Su, J.; Wen, S.; Zhou, Y.; Liu, J.; Wang, C.; et al. Crystallization kinetics of polyetheretherketone during high temperature-selective laser sintering. *Addit. Manuf.* **2020**, *36*, 101615. [CrossRef]
24. Hassan, M.S.; Billah, K.M.M.; Hall, S.E.; Sepulveda, S.; Regis, J.E.; Marquez, C.; Cordova, S.; Whitaker, J.; Robison, T.; Keating, J.; et al. Selective laser sintering of high-temperature thermoset polymer. *J. Compos. Sci.* **2022**, *6*, 41. [CrossRef]
25. Mojaddarasil, M.; Kiani, A.; Tavakoli, M.R.; Badrossamay, M. A parametric study of powder bed temperature distribution in selective laser sintering process. *J. Mater. Eng. Perform.* **2023**, *32*, 3348–3367. [CrossRef]
26. Sharma, V.; Singh, J.; Sharma, V.S.; Sachdeva, A.; Gupta, M.K.; Singh, S. Investigations on mechanical properties of polyamide parts fabricated by selective laser sintering process. *J. Mater. Eng. Perform.* **2022**, *31*, 5767–5781. [CrossRef]
27. Chavez, L.A.; Ibave, P.; Hassan, M.S.; Hall-Sanchez, S.E.; Billah, K.M.M.; Leyva, A.; Marquez, C.; Espalin, D.; Torres, S.; Robison, T.; et al. Low-temperature selective laser sintering 3D printing of PEEK-Nylon blends: Impact of thermal post-processing on mechanical properties and thermal stability. *J. Appl. Polym. Sci.* **2022**, *139*, 52290. [CrossRef]
28. Lupo, M.; Ajabshir, S.Z.; Sofia, D.; Barletta, D.; Poletto, M. Experimental metrics of the powder layer quality in the selective laser sintering process. *Powder Technol.* **2023**, *419*, 118346. [CrossRef]
29. Lupone, F.; Padovano, E.; Pietroluongo, M.; Giudice, S.; Ostrovskaya, O.; Badini, C. Optimization of selective laser sintering process conditions using stable sintering region approach. *Express Polym. Lett.* **2021**, *15*, 177–192. [CrossRef]
30. Xu, Z.; Wang, Y.; Wu, D.; Ananth, K.P.; Bai, J. The process and performance comparison of polyamide 12 manufactured by multi jet fusion and selective laser sintering. *J. Manuf. Process.* **2019**, *47*, 419–426. [CrossRef]
31. Lupone, F.; Padovano, E.; Casamento, F.; Badini, C. Process phenomena and material properties in selective laser sintering of polymers: A review. *Materials* **2021**, *15*, 183. [CrossRef] [PubMed]
32. Li, J.; Yang, Z.; Qian, G.; Berto, F. Machine learning based very-high-cycle fatigue life prediction of Ti-6Al-4V alloy fabricated by selective laser melting. *Int. J. Fatigue* **2022**, *158*, 106764. [CrossRef]
33. Li, B.; Zhang, W.; Xuan, F. Machine-learning prediction of selective laser melting additively manufactured part density by feature-dimension-ascended Bayesian network model for process optimisation. *Int. J. Adv. Manuf. Technol.* **2022**, *121*, 4023–4038. [CrossRef]
34. Abdalla, Y.; Elbadawi, M.; Ji, M.; Alkahtani, M.; Awad, A.; Orlu, M.; Gaisford, S.; Basit, A.W. Machine learning using multi-modal data predicts the production of selective laser sintered 3D printed drug products. *Int. J. Pharm.* **2023**, *633*, 122628. [CrossRef] [PubMed]
35. Speiser, J.L.; Miller, M.E.; Tooze, J.; Ip, E. A comparison of random forest variable selection methods for classification prediction modeling. *Expert Syst. Appl.* **2019**, *134*, 93–101. [CrossRef] [PubMed]
36. Oshiro, T.M.; Perez, P.S.; Baranauskas, J.A. How Many Trees in a Random Forest? In Proceedings of the 8th International Conference of Machine Learning and Data Mining in Pattern Recognition, Berlin, Germany, 13–20 July 2012; Perner, P., Ed.; Springer: Berlin/Heidelberg, Germany; Volume 7376, pp. 154–168. [CrossRef]
37. Peng, X.; Kong, L.; An, H.; Dong, G. A review of in situ defect detection and monitoring technologies in selective laser melting. *3D Print. Addit. Manuf.* **2023**, *10*, 438–466. [CrossRef] [PubMed]
38. Sahoo, K.S.; Tripathy, B.K.; Naik, K.; Ramasubbareddy, S.; Balusamy, B.; Khari, M.; Burgos, D. An evolutionary SVM model for DDOS attack detection in software defined networks. *IEEE Access* **2020**, *8*, 132502–132513. [CrossRef]

39. Li, J.; Cao, L.; Xu, J.; Wang, S.; Zhou, Q. In situ porosity intelligent classification of selective laser melting based on coaxial monitoring and image processing. *Measurement* **2022**, *187*, 110232. [CrossRef]
40. Pande, C.B.; Kushwaha, N.L.; Orimoloye, I.R.; Kumar, R.; Abdo, H.G.; Tolche, A.D.; Elbeltagi, A. Comparative assessment of improved SVM method under different kernel functions for predicting multi-scale drought index. *Water Resour. Manag.* **2023**, *37*, 1367–1399. [CrossRef]
41. Elsheikh, A.H.; Sharshir, S.W.; Abd Elaziz, M.; Kabeel, A.E.; Guilan, W.; Haiou, Z. Modeling of solar energy systems using artificial neural network: A comprehensive review. *Sol. Energy* **2019**, *180*, 622–639. [CrossRef]
42. Anitescu, C.; Atroshchenko, E.; Alajlan, N.; Rabczuk, T. Artificial neural network methods for the solution of second order boundary value problems. *Comput. Mater. Contin.* **2019**, *59*, 345–359. [CrossRef]
43. Abiodun, O.I.; Jantan, A.; Omolara, A.E.; Dada, K.V.; Mohamed, N.A.; Arshad, H. State-of-the-art in artificial neural network applications: A survey. *Heliyon* **2018**, *4*, e00938. [CrossRef]
44. Kornblith, S.; Norouzi, M.; Lee, H.; Hinton, G. Similarity of Neural Network Representations Revisited. In Proceedings of the 36th International Conference on Machine Learning, Long Beach, CA, USA, 10–15 June 2019; Volume 97, pp. 3519–3529. Available online: http://proceedings.mlr.press/v97/kornblith19a.html (accessed on 11 October 2022).
45. Westphal, E.; Seitz, H. A machine learning method for defect detection and visualization in selective laser sintering based on convolutional neural networks. *Addit. Manuf.* **2021**, *41*, 101965. [CrossRef]
46. Yuan, B.; Giera, B.; Guss, G.; Matthews, I.; Mcmains, S. Semi-Supervised Convolutional Neural Networks for In-Situ Video Monitoring of Selective Laser Melting. In Proceedings of the 2019 IEEE Winter Conference on Applications of Computer Vision (WACV), Waikoloa, HI, USA, 7–11 January 2019; pp. 744–753.
47. Wong, T.T.; Yeh, P.Y. Reliable accuracy estimates from k-fold cross validation. *IEEE Trans. Knowl. Data Eng.* **2019**, *32*, 1586–1594. [CrossRef]
48. Sathe, A.M.; Upadhye, N.S.; Wyłomańska, A. Forecasting of symmetric $\alpha-$ stable autoregressive models by time series approach supported by artificial neural networks. *J. Comput. Appl. Math.* **2023**, *425*, 115051. [CrossRef]
49. Ghezelbash, R.; Maghsoudi, A.; Shamekhi, M.; Pradhan, B.; Daviran, M. Genetic algorithm to optimize the SVM and K-means algorithms for mapping of mineral prospectivity. *Neural. Comput. Appl.* **2023**, *35*, 719–733. [CrossRef]
50. Daviran, M.; Shamekhi, M.; Ghezelbash, R.; Maghsoudi, A. Landslide susceptibility prediction using artificial neural networks, SVMs and random forest: Hyperparameters tuning by genetic optimization algorithm. *Int. J. Environ. Sci. Technol.* **2023**, *20*, 259–276. [CrossRef]
51. Vij, R.; Arora, S. A novel deep transfer learning based computerized diagnostic systems for multi-class imbalanced diabetic retinopathy severity classification. *Multimed. Tools. Appl.* **2023**, 1–38. [CrossRef]
52. Valero-Carreras, D.; Alcaraz, J.; Landete, M. Comparing two SVM models through different metrics based on the confusion matrix. *Comput. Oper. Res.* **2023**, *152*, 106131. [CrossRef]
53. Amini, M.; Rahmani, A. Machine learning process evaluating damage classification of composites. *Int. J. Adv. Sci. Technol.* **2023**, *9*, 240–250.
54. Wang, X.; Ren, H.; Ren, J.; Song, W.; Qiao, Y.; Ren, Z.; Zhao, Y.; Linghu, L.; Cui, Y.; Zhao, Z.; et al. Machine learning-enabled risk prediction of Chronic Obstructive Pulmonary Disease with unbalanced data. *Comput. Methods Prog. Biomed.* **2023**, *230*, 107340. [CrossRef]
55. Vela, B.; Mehalic, S.; Sheikh, S.; Elwany, A.; Karaman, I.; Arróyave, R. Evaluating the intrinsic resistance to balling of alloys: A high-throughput physics-informed and data-enabled approach. *Addit. Manuf. Lett.* **2022**, *3*, 100085. [CrossRef]
56. Tong, R.; Zhu, Z.; Ling, J. Comparison of linear and non-linear machine learning models for time-dependent readmission or mortality prediction among hospitalized heart failure patients. *Heliyon* **2023**, *9*, e16068. [CrossRef]
57. Hua, L.; Zhang, C.; Sun, W.; Li, Y.; Xiong, J.; Nazir, M.S. An evolutionary deep learning soft sensor model based on random forest feature selection technique for penicillin fermentation process. *ISA Trans.* **2023**, *136*, 139–151. [CrossRef] [PubMed]

Disclaimer/Publisher's Note: The statements, opinions and data contained in all publications are solely those of the individual author(s) and contributor(s) and not of MDPI and/or the editor(s). MDPI and/or the editor(s) disclaim responsibility for any injury to people or property resulting from any ideas, methods, instructions or products referred to in the content.

Review

Application of Mass Service Theory to Economic Systems Optimization Problems—A Review

Farida F. Galimulina and Naira V. Barsegyan *

Logistics and Management Department, Kazan National Research Technological University, 420015 Kazan, Russia; galimulinaff@corp.knrtu.ru
* Correspondence: n.v.barsegyan@yandex.ru or barsegyannv@corp.knrtu.ru

Abstract: An interdisciplinary approach to management allows for the integration of knowledge and tools of different fields of science into a unified methodology in order to improve the efficiency of resource management of different kinds of systems. In the conditions of global transformations, it is economic systems that have been significantly affected by external destabilizing factors. This determines the focus of attention on the need to develop tools for the modeling and optimization of economic systems, both in terms of organizational structure and in the context of resource management. The purpose of this review study is to identify the current gaps (shortcomings) in the scientific literature devoted to the issues of the modeling and optimization of economic systems using the tools of mass service theory. This article presents a critical analysis of approaches for the formulation of provisions on mass service systems in the context of resource management. On the one hand, modern works are characterized by the inclusion of an extensive number of random factors that determine the performance and efficiency of economic systems: the probability of delays and interruptions in mobile networks; the integration of order, inventory, and production management processes; the cost estimation of multi-server system operation; and randomness factors, customer activity, and resource constraints, among others. On the other hand, controversial points are identified. The analytical study carried out allows us to state that the prevailing majority of mass service models applied in relation to economic systems and resource supply optimization are devoted to Markov chain modeling. In terms of the chronology of the problems studied, there is a marked transition from modeling simple systems to complex mass service networks. In addition, we conclude that the complex architecture of modern economic systems opens up a wide research field for finding a methodology for assessing the dependence of the enterprise performance on the effect of optimization provided by using the provisions of mass service theory. This statement can be the basis for future research.

Keywords: modeling; productivity and efficiency of economic systems; mass service theory; resource supply; complex networks; optimization; organizational structure

MSC: 37N40; 60K20; 90B22

Citation: Galimulina, F.F.; Barsegyan, N.V. Application of Mass Service Theory to Economic Systems Optimization Problems—A Review. Mathematics 2024, 12, 403. https://doi.org/10.3390/math12030403

Academic Editor: Manuel Alberto M. Ferreira

Received: 13 December 2023
Revised: 22 January 2024
Accepted: 23 January 2024
Published: 26 January 2024

Copyright: © 2024 by the authors. Licensee MDPI, Basel, Switzerland. This article is an open access article distributed under the terms and conditions of the Creative Commons Attribution (CC BY) license (https://creativecommons.org/licenses/by/4.0/).

1. Introduction

Modeling is generally recognized as an effective tool for making managerial decisions and realizing the hidden potential of the management object. According to the theory of decision making, the basis for the justified choice of the best alternative for solving a problem situation is the use of mathematical tools; the situation itself is considered as the object of research. Managerial decisions are performed on the scale of economic, organizational, technical, and other types of systems. An interdisciplinary approach to management allows for the integration of the knowledge and tools of different fields of science into a unified methodology in order to improve the efficiency of resource management of different types of systems. In the context of global transformations, the focus is economic systems that have been significantly affected by external destabilizing factors. The importance of optimizing flows in global supply chains has increased significantly. The Russian economy is at the stage of the radical revision of import routes, which is accompanied by changes in the load on border crossing points. As a consequence, queues are inevitable due to the large traffic flow. Similar problems are characteristic not only for macroeconomic systems, but also for meso- (region, industrial complex) and micro-level systems (business entity).

The abovementioned factors determine the focus of attention on the need to develop tools for the modeling and optimization of economic systems, both in terms of organizational structure and in the context of resource management.

Modern economic systems are a complex structure, a set of interrelated elements united by flows of resources and information, processes, and operations. The key problem of the functioning of economic systems is limited resources, which determines the emergence of «bottlenecks» and queues. As a consequence, it affects the efficiency of the whole system and its competitiveness.

There is a wide variety of mathematical methods used in economics to forecast processes, operations, and indicators, such as statistical models and dynamic models (linear and nonlinear) [1]. The methods that provide the search for optimal solutions include the following: linear or nonlinear programming problems, combinatorial problems, production functions, mass service systems, and others. However, there are disadvantages that are compensated by the theory of mass service. The main difference of the latter is the ability to effectively manage the flow (of information, customers, orders, etc.), while other methods focus on optimizing the functioning of individual links. An alternative modeling method can be the problem of optimizing the distribution of requests for servicing the flow of container cargoes by time slots (a time slot is a time window for receiving and servicing requests). However, this method ignores the definition of probabilities (denial of service, system downtime, queue formation), which allows us to judge the leveling by the theory of mass service on the drawbacks of other methods of optimization.

Summarizing the above, we emphasize that the study of the provisions of the mass service theory and the study of practicing its application in modeling economic systems of different levels (macro-, meso- and microsystems) is a topical issue. However, under the conditions of the complexity increasing in economic systems structures, the intensive development of technologies, as well as the transition to Industry 5.0, the interest in flexible complex automated solutions is growing. Such solutions can be built on the basis of combined (covering several constraints, including resource constraints) and network (combined systems of several processes) mass service systems. It is necessary to study scientific approaches of the application of provisions adapted for mass service theory in the management of complex organized systems and their optimization. Therefore, the purpose of this review study is to identify the current gaps (shortcomings) in the scientific literature devoted to the issues of the modeling and optimization of economic systems using the tools of mass service theory.

2. Materials and Methods

The main method of this research was the content analysis of scientific papers devoted to the problem under study. The international bibliographic platforms Scopus, Web of Science, Science Direct, Springer journals, as well as the official website of MDPI publishing house served as the knowledge base.

The research algorithm covers three key steps:
1. Searching for and studying scientific papers;
2. The systematization of approaches to the application of mass service theory in the context of the optimization of economic systems through the prism:
    - Resourcing of processes and operations;
    - Of the organizational structure of management;
3. The formulation of identified gaps, whose filling is planned to be realized by the authors in future research.

A more detailed outline of the research work is reflected in the Figure 1.

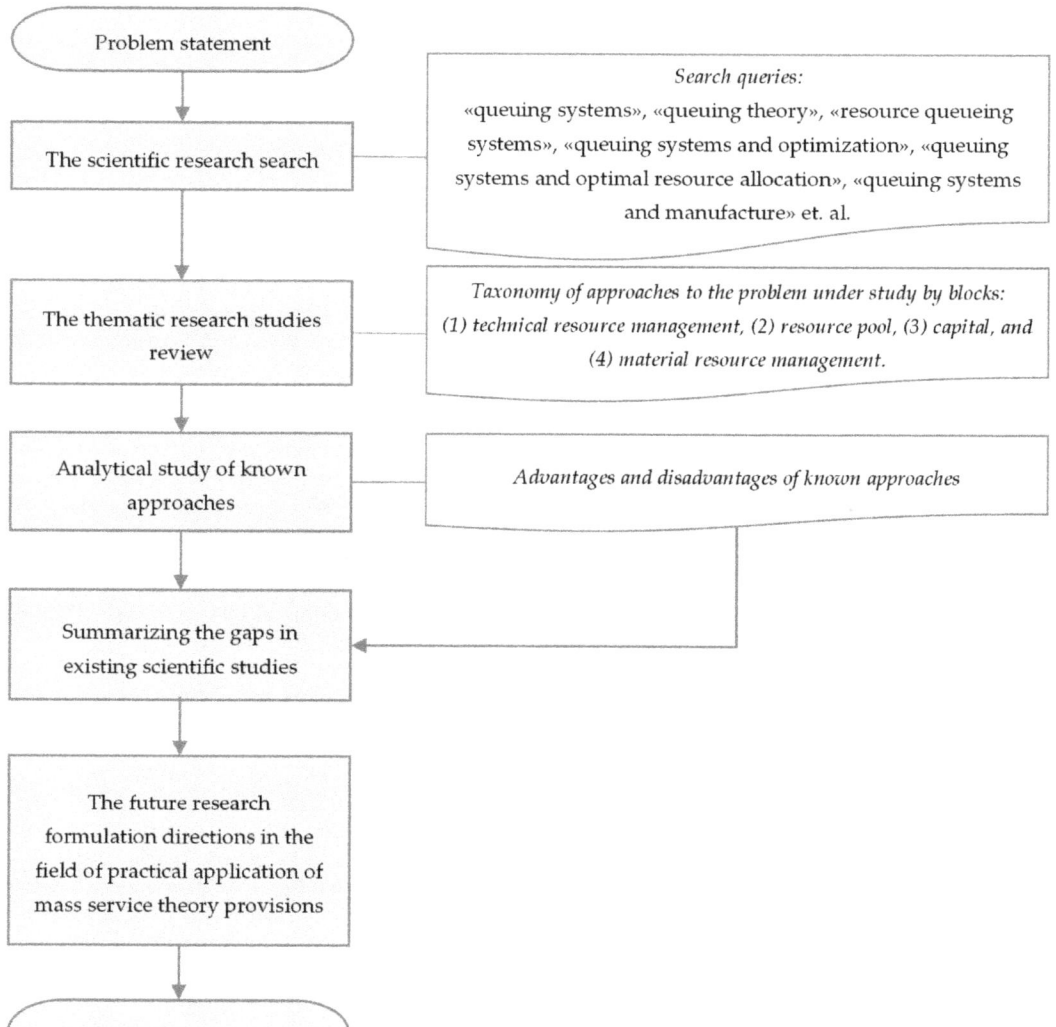

Figure 1. The flowchart of the survey study.

3. An Analytical Review of the Current State of Scientific Research

Mass service systems are present in various fields of activity and can project production systems, computing systems, order and sales management systems, purchasing, warehouses, transport, organizational structures, border points, etc. The key categories of mass service theory are requests for service and service channels, while the parameters of evaluation are the intensity of the flow of lost or served requests, the probability of one or another system state (denial of service, queuing, system idle time), and the duration of service.

The fundamentals of mass service theory were outlined by Erlang in his work «Sandsynlighedsregning og Telefonsamtaler», and the probability of hitting x events in a time interval a (probability Sx) is usually defined as follows [2]:

$$S_x = \frac{(na)^x}{x!} \cdot e^{-na} \quad (1)$$

where n is the flow intensity (average number of calls during the device operation time); a is the specified time interval; and x is the number of events.

Subsequent adaptation of the theory of mass service to various spheres of activity represents modifications aimed at optimizing the distribution of resources (personnel, stocks, production capacity, transport, etc.), etc.

3.1. Resource Management Based on a Mass Maintenance System

The functioning of the economic system relies on the use of a wide range of resources, the combination of which is determined by the level of management and industry specifics. In our study, we focus on types of resources such as:

- Personnel;
- Material;
- Technical (devices, servers, appliances);
- Capital (buildings, structures, machinery, equipment).

The mass service system is considered at the microeconomic level and refers to manufacturing, warehousing, transport, service, or other types of economic systems. In each of these areas, queues occur. It is necessary to distinguish three types of models: (1) the maintenance of excess capacities provides immediate customer service (no queue is formed, supply exceeds demand); (2) the capacities (resources) for customer service are loaded almost completely and used more efficiently, but a queue is formed due to available prices (demand is higher than supply); (3) the capacities (resources) are idle, and a queue is formed (high fluctuations of demand during the day, week, seasons). On this basis, the mass service system is applicable to the models of the second and third types.

From the point of view of the management object, all known approaches are proposed to be classified into four categories: management of technical resources, resource pool, capital, and material resources. A further review of the scientific literature within this section is differentiated by the four blocks.

3.1.1. Optimization of Technical Resources

An extensive body of scientific research focuses directly on technical devices, devices, servers, and information-computing systems. These are the key resources in mass service models describing the behavior of the economic system in the conditions of improving business processes and queuing. Mobile networks, order management systems (in warehousing, production, catering), the resource capacity of nodes in service channels, banking systems, the operation of post offices, and other aspects are the subject area of the research. The listed systems are mostly discrete in nature, i.e., the system parameters change only in case of customer arrival (incoming request). It is reasonable to classify all resource capacity management models into two types: single-server and multi-server.

Single-server mass service models (model notation—M/M/1) are simple with a single service unit, a Poisson flow of incoming requests, and an exponential distribution of service times [3–6]. The advantage of building the simplest models is the ability to conduct preliminary studies before proceeding to modeling complex multi-server systems.

However, modern economic systems focused on high productivity, high level of service quality, and profit maximization are not limited to a single service channel; on the contrary, they are complex multi-channel systems. In this regard, multi-server service models are more popular. Next, let us focus on the coverage of this type of system in the literature.

The theory of mass service finds application in the field of mobile communication system optimization, which is caused by mass flows of requests for information transfer requiring organization. In this case, the input flow is described by a Markov process. Modeling the user service of mobile networks has been the subject of research [7–9]. Thus, the system model of Makeeva et al. is characterized by taking into account the probability of delays and interruptions in the operation of the 5G network as well as the retransmission of data. The system of repeated calls in the categories of mass service theory, according to the authors' idea, is described by a Markov chain with a continuous process [7]:

$$X(t) = (N_m(t), N_u(t), Q_1(t), Q_2(t)), t \geq 0,$$
$$\chi = \{(n_m, n_u, q_1, q_2): n_m \geq 0, n_u \geq 0, 0 \leq q_1 \leq C_1, 0 \leq q_2 \leq C_2, bn_m + n_u \leq C, n_m + q_2 \leq N\}, \quad (2)$$

where χ is the state space; $N_m(t)$ is the number of active extended mobile broadband sessions; $N_u(t)$ is the number of active URLLC (ultra-reliable low-latency communication) sessions; $Q_1(t)$ is the number of pending extended mobile broadband sessions; $Q_2(t)$ is the number of interrupted sessions; C_i is the capacity of buffer 1 (for storing pending sessions) and buffer 2 (for storing interrupted sessions); and N is the number of resource blocks.

Multi-server models find applications in order and production inventory management. In the work of Shajin et al., the optimization of the number of required servers is based on the total cost minimization function [10]. The advantage of the author's solution, in our opinion, is the consideration of the causal relationship between orders, inventories, and the production process. Researchers have determined that when the probability of fulfilling a customer order is 50%, the optimal number of servers stabilizes, and the cost of the order management system decreases. In this case, the system is described by a continuous Markov chain [10]:

$$\Omega = \{(N(t), I(t), C(t), J(t), t \geq 0\}, \quad (3)$$

where $N(t)$ is the number of customers in the system; $I(t)$ is the number of goods in stock; $J(t)$ is the production phase (production on/off); and $C(t)$ is a component taking the value «0» when production is «off» and the value «1» when production is «on».

A number of multi-server customer service systems are based on setting aside time for maintenance and upgrades to ensure uninterrupted operation of the system («vacation»—a period of time during which the server is unavailable for maintenance) [11–14]. Jeganathan et al. consider a mass service system with server holidays with respect to warehouse order management [13]. According to the study, the server independently determines the necessity of going on holiday (when insufficient number of customers is detected) independently of other servers. The practical value of the authors' research results is due to the cost estimation of the functioning of a multi-server system with an adjustable number of servers. Also, the team of scientists led by Jeganathan developed a model of mass service based on a two-level service system: junior and senior servers. Such a model takes place when the junior servers do not have the data to solve the problem and they turn to the senior server [15].

The problems of optimal server resource allocation are widespread. In the work of R. Yang et al., the authors study three cases with a characteristic optimal level of resources: in the first case, the studied service centers are independent of each other; in the second case, there is a distribution of resources between service centers (when launching a new task); and in the third case, resources are redistributed during the execution of operations. Scientists have revealed the following regularity: the optimal number of server resources has the highest value for the first case and the lowest for the third model [16]. In the example of heterogeneous resource-based mass service systems, Pankratova et al. offer a method for determining the optimal level of resource provision for the k-th channel of the system [17]:

$$V_k^{opt} = a_k + r\sqrt{K_{kk}}, \quad (4)$$

where a is the mathematical expectation; r is the radius of the hyperellipsoid due to the probability of losing customers; and K_k is the state of the Markov chain.

At the same time, the authors propose a solution for mass service systems with an unlimited number of servers. However, the question remains open as to how cybersecure and capital- and energy-intensive such a solution is for large industrial enterprises. After all, an industrial system is a set of interconnected elements and processes united by commodities, energy, information, and financial and service flows that contribute to the production of industrial products.

Modern catering businesses are also mass service systems that integrate combinations of online and offline ordering. Zhan et al. determined the optimal throughput of an industry enterprise for different service channels [18].

Methods of mass service theory are widely used in the banking sector, as the bank system is built on the management of incoming requests, i.e., customer service through N channels (bank specialists). With the application of mass service models, the problems of managing the requests of multiple classes of customers [19], stability of the mass service network [20], and reengineering of business processes in order to eliminate «bottlenecks» [21] are solved. In the latter case, Hao and Yifei, relying on the classical provisions of the theory of mass service, offer a model for optimizing the number of servers based on simulation. The key criteria of optimization are the growth of the customer satisfaction level and reduction of waiting time. It is noteworthy that the authors based their study on the assumption that it is economically inexpedient to open a large number of servers.

Another area of service subject to the provisions of mass service theory is the operation of post offices. The processes in such systems are described by their stochastic nature, infinite queues, and the need to optimize the number of service counters. An example of optimizing the operation of post offices is the simulation modeling of a mass service system [22]. The ambiguity of the author's approach is that the result is based on finding the optimal number of service counters «manually». The imperfection of this method lies in the risk of missing the true optimal value in a set of search iterations.

The principles of mass service theory are also realized in the sphere of medical services. The research and modeling of this category of systems are covered in the works of [23,24].

Summarizing the highlighted points, we summarize the numerical superiority of manuscripts devoted to multi-server mass service models. The complex architecture of such systems opens a wide research field but at the same time requires taking into account many different factors that determine a high level of entropy in service systems.

3.1.2. The Object of the Mass Service Model Is a Pool of Resources

This group of scientific works includes studies of universal character, which do not focus on a specific type of resource, but are not limited to the sphere of application of mass service models. A special place in the literature devoted to the practical application of mass service theory is occupied by the works of Naumov and Samouylov. In the work of [25], the scientists, in the context of resource management, discuss the occurrence of negative resources; these occur in the case of excess demand over supply, but the total amount of resources should not be negative and should correspond to the established threshold level. In another study [26], the authors propose a method for analyzing mass service systems that provides accurate convolution power calculations and is based on the detection of the pattern of approximation error from the level of resource load. As a consequence, the authors conclude that the accuracy of calculations increases with increasing resource load. Summarizing the ideas of Naumov and Samouylov, it should be emphasized that the accuracy of calculations increases with increasing resource load. For Samouylov, it should be emphasized that the factors of randomness, client activity, and resource constraints are taken into account.

Kim and Yeun, in terms of a sharing economy, justified the mass service model of the $G/M/1$ type on the example of a technological (online) platform. The key task of this model is to find a balance of interests of the key participants of the model—resource owners and consumers. The authors take into account the term of the contract and distinguish two types of contracts: individual (one-time) and permanent. The peculiarity of the mass service system examined by the authors is as follows: the first subsystem is aimed at checking suppliers and estimating the time between their arrival in a single-channel queue; the second subsystem—customer (consumer) service—is built on Markovian service time [27]. The advantage of the model proposed by the authors is its universal character and its applicability to the management of any type of resource.

3.1.3. Focus of Mass Maintenance Models on Capital Resources

The optimization of capital resource management is less represented in the global scientific literature than the modeling of server resources. However, the published works are undoubtedly practically significant and cover an extensive sphere of economic systems. Such works include the ANFIS model for the optimization of a queuing system in warehouses [28], a model of railway stations [29,30], an analytical study of the capacity of Cairo International Airport [31], etc.

A separate niche in the section of research devoted to the study of fixed assets and their management is occupied by works focused on modeling logistics systems. A logistics system is a set of harmoniously interacting subsystems oriented towards the management of material and service flows with an optimal level of costs and maximum customer satisfaction. As a consequence, a logistics system is a set of mass service systems, the efficiency of which is conditioned by rational management of queues of transport units, passenger flow, and material flow.

Stojčić et al. propose a model for managing the time component in the context of logistics system optimization: the arrival time of vehicles and the service time of logistics operations (loading and unloading) [28]. The authors conclude that the time spent in the system determines the total vehicle dwell time in the warehouse, total logistics costs, and efficiency of the microeconomic system as a whole. Servers are associated with loading zones where queuing is possible, and the modeled warehouse system includes two such servers. The peculiarity of the solution proposed by the authors is the combination of the principles of mass service theory and artificial neural networks (adaptive neuro-fuzzy inference system, ANFIS). The input variables are: (1) time between vehicle arrivals; (2) total dwell time; and (3) service time. The output variable is the time spent in the system. The advantages of the model include: the ability to take into account the uncertainty factor in the management of logistics processes; and adaptability, which is achieved in the process of training neural networks.

In the example of railway stations, the theory of mass service is disclosed in the papers by Bychkov et al. [29] and Kazakov et al. [30]. The station operation system covers four subsystems (arrival, accumulation, loading, departure), each of which represents a separate mass service system [29]. A special merit of the authors lies in the development of a model of mass service networks serving as a basis for routing within the logistics system. The solution makes it possible to optimize the service channels (number of service crews, locomotives) and contribute to the reduction of service time. The mathematical apparatus is based on the BMAP (batch Markovian arrival process) model and allows for the control of the intensity of request processing, which is described as follows [29]:

$$(D_0)_{v,v} = -\lambda_v, v = \overline{0,W}, (D_0)_{v,v'} = \lambda_v p_0(v,v'), v,v' = \overline{0,W}, (D_k)_{v,v'} = \lambda_v p_k(v,v'), v,v' = \overline{0,W}, k \geq 1 \quad (5)$$

where v_t is a Markov chain with continuous time and state $\{0, 1,\ldots, W\}$; λ_v is the query intensity; and $p_k(v, v')$ is the probability that the chain transitions to state v'.

The problem of modeling the airport service system has been reflected in a few scientific studies [31–36]. The classical mass service system for the example of the infrastructure of Cairo International Airport was studied by Abdulaziz Alnowibet et al. [31]. In the work of the scientists, it is emphasized that check-in counters are an extremely limited resource, the irrational management of which leads to an increase in the time of passenger flow service. The authors described the notations (Kendall) of mass service systems, differentiated for different links of passenger flow passage:

- "Check-in" subsystem—model M/M/s/GD/N/N/N;
- "Security Check" subsystem—M/G/s/FCFS//∞∞;
- "Immigration" subsystem—M/G/s/GD/N/∞;
- "Boarding" subsystem—M/G/s/GD/N/N/N.

This approach can provide the flexibility of an automated system for managing scarce airport resources but ignores the baggage service channels that are an integral part of the flight service process.

A related area of economic systems research is the modeling of taxi operation. The service device in such a mass service system is a taxi itself, and a taxi call is a request. The taxi service is a model with an unlimited queue, an example of a Markov process. In this case, the system is characterized by non-uniformity and randomness of flow (unlike an airport, where the schedule of aircraft departures and arrivals is known in advance). Accordingly, the main purpose of solving taxi service optimization problems is the modeling of dynamic queues [37,38]. Yang et al. see the solution of this problem as considering random factors such as the coincidence of passenger flow and free taxis, the pattern of passenger arrival (taxis on the airport territory), etc. [39].

In addition to logistic systems, the block of capital resource research includes production processes. A technological system as a set of machines and production equipment with the flow of products and the probability of equipment failure (in case of failure) can serve as a mass service system. Scientists have developed a number of solutions to improve the efficiency of the production system: the method of identifying «bottlenecks» in the technological process in the conditions of Industry 4.0 [40], a model for the accurate forecasting of queue length [41], a model of a repairable mass service system [42], etc.

Martyn et al. rightly point out that the productivity of a technological process is determined by the productivity of its weakest link, and they also determine the optima intensity of material feeding based on the following methodology [40]:

$$p = \lambda/\mu,$$
$$\psi(n) = p/n, \qquad (6)$$

where p—loading intensity of the production line (channel); λ—average processing time; μ—intensity of material processing in the channel; and $\psi(n)$—intensity of material supply for n channels.

Complex production systems are characterized by the type of production (continuous, direct flow) and intensity of material flow. From the point of view of mass service theory, material flow is a queue that is characterized by unstable size (length). Scientists see the solution to the problem of queue management as optimizing its length. So, May et al., in the example of semiconductor production using machine learning tools, offer the following heuristic approach [41]:

$$Queue\ (j,t_1) = Queue\ (j,t_0) - LeavingJobs + ArrivingJobs, \qquad (7)$$

where t_0 is the time before the material arrives in the system (on the machine); t_1 is the time after machining is completed on this machine; and *LeavingJobs*, *ArrivingJobs* are outgoing and incoming machining jobs.

However, the statements formulated by May et al. are only based on machine learning and require comparative analysis with alternative methods of mass service system prediction.

In general, approaches to capital resource management require consideration of a greater number of random factors, which is firstly due to the dynamism of the development of new technologies and secondly due to the high degree of uncertainty of external factors.

3.1.4. Optimization of Material Flow Based on Mass Service Models

The theory of mass service considers the material flow as a flow of requirements (orders, stocks, material resources, finished products, etc.), and the efficiency of the management of queues of requirements determines the level (quality) of service of the system.

The stock level optimization problem is a classical problem in logistics systems management. From the perspective of a mass service system, the problem is to determine the inventory level (and the number of customers) such that the server will self-regulate going on and off holiday. This approach ensures that it is possible to pre-process information about the product that is booked during the holiday [5].

Various studies of the inventory management system are presented in the works of Melikov. These works cover the modeling of the system with the formation of stock shortages due to production delays [10]; the problems of stock shortage and the search for the optimal threshold level of stocks [43]; a warehouse system with catastrophes (in the form of two-dimensional Markov chains) and the optimization of the reorder point [44]; and systems with flows of primary customers, repeat sales customers, repeat service customers, and destructive customers (customers who do not purchase an item but destroy stock, after which stock is reduced by one) [45], among others. The models proposed by the author represent a Markov chain based on random factors and are aimed at minimizing expected total costs and improving the efficiency of the inventory management system. The random variables are order fulfilment time, inventory volume, and customer flow.

The time for processing orders, stocks, and delivery of the order to the distributor is also considered as a random variable in the works of Jeganathan et al. (using the example of asynchronous holidays in a multi-server system) [13], Baek and Moon (the independence of the level of production stocks and queue length is proven) [46], Alnowibet et al. (mass service system with impatient customers leaving the queue for various reasons) [47], Dissa and Ushakumari (in modeling the flows of perishable products with random lifetime) [48], and other works. Random demands on the stock of manufactured products are considered in the model of Chang and Lu; the researchers optimize the base stock level in a hybrid production system for standard and ad hoc needs [49].

Limitations—Earlier, we noted that a modern economic system is a rather complex structure that combines many subsystems and requires simultaneous consideration of a wide range of random factors. Scientists have presented serious attempts to develop hybrid models that integrate mass service models with machine learning or neuro-fuzzy models, which are able to jointly solve control and optimization problems. At the same time, digitalization of business processes requires capacious capacities for collecting, storing, and processing big data. And the economic system is a set of connected mass service models that regulate the functioning of the individual links of the system. To service such a volume of information flows requires significant energy resources and capacity, which entails significant costs. A number of authors address the issues of the total costs of the functioning of the subsystems under study [10,13,16,22,43]. However, the numerical measurement of the dependence of enterprise performance (including profitability) on the optimization effect (achieved through simulation) is poorly represented in the literature and represents a promising area of research.

3.2. Optimization of Organizational Structure on the Basis of Mass Service Systems

The practices in recent decades have shown that the Russian industry is facing the acute task of increasing competitiveness and efficiency. It is possible to achieve these tasks only on the basis of innovative transformations of both the production system itself and its structural elements.

The organizational structure of management is one of the tools for improving the management system, the units of which are subject to constant changes and adjustments—creation, reduction, division, and unification of links—as enterprises develop and grow. Consequently, there is a need for an evaluation to identify a more effective and optimal organizational structure, which requires the development of appropriate techniques or a set of them.

The design methods, their essence, and the approaches that are used in each method are summarized and shown in Table 1.

Table 1. Methods of designing organizational management structures (summarized by the authors).

Methods of Designing Organizational Management Structures	Approaches/Models/Stages	Characterization
Analogies Method [50–55]	Building an organizational management structure based on best practices	Use of best practices for enterprises with similar parameters; recommendations to enterprises based on typical organizational structures
	Development of model organizational management structures	
Expert-analytical method [50–55]	Quantitative and qualitative evaluation methods, questionnaires	Identification by experts and managers of the peculiarities and failures in the functioning of organizational structures and development of measures to improve the methods of their management
Structurization purposes method [54–58]	Developing a goal tree	Analyzing management organizational structures in terms of whether the functional mix is fit for the purpose
	Expert analysis of structured objectives	
	Development of key performance indicators to achieve objectives	
Organizational modeling method [57–61]	Mathematical and cybernetic models	Designing organizational management structures based on the use of mathematical, graphical, and machine models for the purpose of the optimal distribution of functional powers
	Graphoanalytical models	
	Natural models	
	Mathematical and statistical models	

The application of a set of these methods makes it possible to evaluate management organizational structures in order to determine their efficiency and identify weak links in the structure that need to be improved and changed. However, it is necessary to adapt these methods for the management organizational structures of petrochemical enterprises focused on saving resources.

An analysis of their advantages and disadvantages should be carried out to determine the methodology that will enable the design of the optimal organizational management structure (Figure 2).

The analysis allows us to conclude that for the design of flexible organizational management structures, it is not enough to use one method. It is necessary to use a set of methods, focusing on the positive characteristics of each of them. To verify the correctness of the selected methods of the design and development of organizational structures, it is also necessary to determine the methods of evaluation, conducting their comparative analyses (Figure 3).

One of the important indicators for assessing the effectiveness of the management hierarchy in the chain «supervisor—subordinates» is the norm of controllability.

In the theory of personnel management, the norms of manageability for management levels have been derived. Numerous empirical studies and the law of rational range of management derived by the American scientist Graicunas, presented in the research Calvo and Wellisz [62], were the basis for the development of management norms. This law states that the number of unit, direct, group, and cross relations in an organization is in geometric progression and obeys Formula (8):

$$N = n\,[2^{n-1} + (n-1)], \tag{8}$$

where N is the number of possible interrelationships of the unit's employees, units; and n is the number of subordinates of the manager, people.

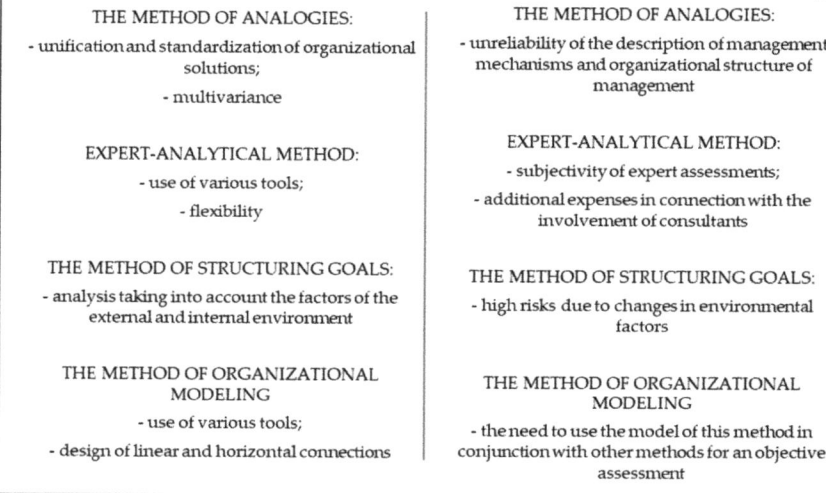

Figure 2. Advantages and disadvantages of methods of designing organizational management structures (summarized by the authors).

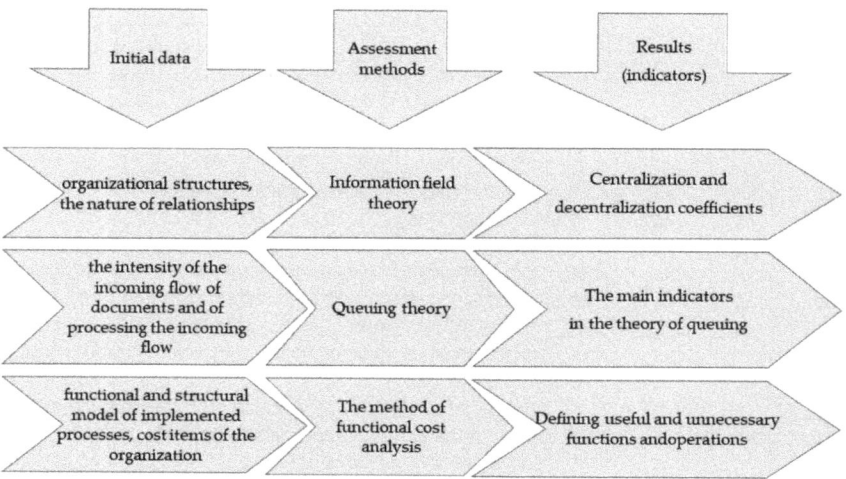

Figure 3. Outlying parameters and performance indicators of methods for assessing organizational management structures (summarized by the authors).

It is very difficult to represent this dependence graphically, but we provide the estimated number of possible relationships according to the Graicunas formula for 10 subordinate employees (the index at the bottom is the number of subordinates).

$N_1 = 1$; $N_2 = 6$; $N_3 = 18$; $N_4 = 44$; $N_5 = 100$; $N_6 = 182$; $N_7 = 504$; $N_8 = 1080$; $N_9 = 2306$; $N_{10} = 5210$.

The calculation shows that with 5 subordinates, the number of links is 100, and with 10 subordinates, the number of links is 5210, i.e., when the number of subordinates is doubled, the number of links increases more than 50 times.

The design of optimal organizational structures characterizes the efficiency of management and the speed of processes within each enterprise. In this regard, it is very important to determine the speed of the processes running within each unit and evaluate their efficiency.

One method of analyzing organizational structure, as already presented in Figure 3, is to represent structures in the form of mass service networks. The use of a method based on the mass service theory makes it possible to perform an evaluation using indicators such as the average number of operations performed by an employee, the average time to perform an operation, the average number of operations waiting to be performed, and the average waiting time to perform an operation, which makes it possible to find problem areas in the management structure and in individual departments.

Often, the assessment is carried out by integrated indicators; for example, the ratio of management costs per one manager and the share of the number of management employees in the stock output and stock capacity is calculated. However, such calculations do not allow for characterization of the organizational structure itself and the processes that take place in it.

The use of a method based on the theory of mass service provides an opportunity to estimate the speed of information passage in the control system of petrochemical enterprises.

The representation of the organizational structure in the form of a mass service system model is justified by the fact that org structures are affected by the multitude of tasks that the system must solve given the requirements placed on the system (Figure 4).

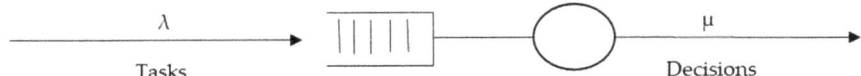

Figure 4. Organizational structure model in the form of a mass service system [50].

In Figure 4, λ characterizes the average speed of arrival of tasks to be performed, adapting it to the management org structure of a petrochemical enterprise; it is an indicator that characterizes the requirements of petrochemical consumers. μ is the average speed of operations per unit of time, i.e., the satisfaction of needs. Individual structures of the control system can be represented as a mass service network.

In the case of a lean strategy of petrochemical enterprises development and a development strategy aimed at the development of new petrochemical products, divisional and project types of organizational management structures are recommended. In this regard, let us present these structures in the form of mass service networks (Figure 5a,b).

In the presented schemes, the general director of the enterprise, line and functional managers, and the project manager are single-channel mass service systems, and the other units of the organizational structure are multi-channel systems. Each employee is a part of a multi-channel system. And it should be noted that the organizational structure of management is a mass service network without queue limitation, which means that the incoming request to the enterprise will be fulfilled sooner or later.

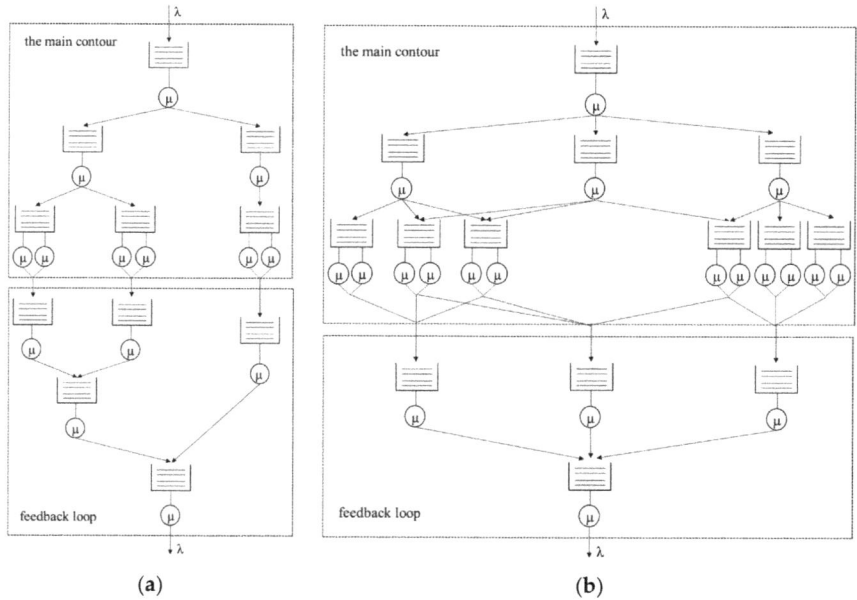

Figure 5. Modeling of the organizational structure of management in the form of a mass service network: (**a**) mass service network of the divisional organizational structure of management of a petrochemical enterprise; (**b**) mass service network of the project organizational structure of management of a petrochemical enterprise (proposed by the authors).

The main characteristics of a classical mass service system, like any mass service system, are the following numerical characteristics of it:

- Probability of waiting;
- Average number of claims under service (related to the service unit utilization rate);
- Average queue length;
- Average number of requirements in the system;
- Average length of the real queue.

For single-channel mass service systems, the calculation of the main indicators can be presented in the form of the following formulas, which are specified in the work of Prof. Kirpichnikov [63].

Waiting probability, i.e., the probability that an incoming demand will be in the queue (find the serving device busy):

$$p_{\exp} = \sum_{k=1}^{\infty} p_k = \sum_{k=0}^{\infty} p_k - p_0 = 1 - (1 - \rho) = \rho \tag{9}$$

where $p_{\exp}$—the probability of waiting for the application to be completed; p_0—the maximum probability that the system is free; and p_k—the maximum probability that the system is busy servicing existing applications.

Respectively, the probability of immediate servicing of the request received in the system:

$$p_{ser} = 1 - p_{\exp} = 1 - \rho = p_0 \tag{10}$$

where p_{ser}—the probability of maintenance.

The average number of demands simultaneously under service (in this case, i.e., for the single-channel model, which coincides with the load factor) is obvious:

$$l.f. = \overline{m} = 0 \cdot p_0 + 1 \cdot p_1 + 1 \cdot p_2 + \ldots = 1 - p_0 = \rho \tag{11}$$

where *l.f.*—load factor.

The variance of this value is:

$$\sigma_m^2 = 0^2 p_0 + 1^2(p_1 + p_2 + \ldots) - \overline{m}^2 = 1 - p_0 - \rho^2 = \rho - \rho^2 \tag{12}$$

Further, if the service flow is a Poisson flow, then the probability $B_k(t)$ that k requests are served by the system at time t is defined by Formula (1).

The average number of claims in the queue (actual average queue length) is:

$$\overline{l} = 0 \cdot p_0 + 0 \cdot p_1 + 1 \cdot p_2 + 2 \cdot p_3 + 3 \cdot p_4 + \ldots = \sum_{k=1}^{\infty}(k-1)p_k \tag{13}$$

The average number of demands in the mass service system as a whole (both in queue and under service) is:

$$\overline{k} = \sum_{k=0}^{\infty} k p_k = \frac{\rho}{1-\rho} \tag{14}$$

The waiting probability in a multi-channel mass service system, i.e., the probability that an incoming demand finds all channels occupied, is obviously given by the formula:

$$p_{\exp} = \sum_{k=m}^{\infty} p_k = \frac{p_0}{m!} \sum_{k=m}^{\infty} \frac{\rho^k}{m^{k-m}} = \frac{\rho^m p_0}{m!}\left(1 + \frac{\rho}{m} + \frac{\rho^2}{m^2} + \ldots\right) = \frac{\rho^m p_0}{(m-1)!(m-\rho)} \tag{15}$$

This formula in the USA is called the Erlang C formula and is denoted as $C(m,\rho)$, while in Europe it has a different designation—$E_{2,m}(\rho)$, where it is called Erlang's second formula.

To carry out the assessment of organizational management structures of industrial enterprises, which are complex systems, it is necessary to apply these methods comprehensively, taking into account different criteria and indicators. And it should be noted that the organizational structure of management is a mass service network without queue limitation, which means that the incoming request to the enterprise will be fulfilled sooner or later.

4. Discussion

The conducted analytical study allows us to state that the prevailing majority of mass service models applied in relation to economic systems and resource supply optimization are devoted to the modeling of Markov chains. In terms of the chronology of the problems studied, there is a noticeable transition from modeling simple systems to the creation of complex mass service networks.

At the same time, certain peculiarities of approaches to the formulation of provisions on mass service systems in the context of resource management have been found. On the one hand, modern works are characterized by the inclusion of a large number of random factors that determine the performance and efficiency of economic systems: probabilities of delays and interruptions of mobile networks [7]; the integration of order, inventory and production management processes [10]; cost estimation of multi-server system performance [13]; and randomness, customer activity, and resource constraints [25,26], among others. On the other hand, controversial points have been identified. For example, there is a contradiction in the approaches of some authors: E. Pankratova et al. propose a mass service model with an unlimited number of servers [17], and Hao and Yifei are based on the idea that it is economically inexpedient to open a large number of servers [21]; in optimization issues, scientists rely on the development of alternative hypotheses and models [22], which is not always able to reflect the single best solution; and in the context of forecasting, a number of alternative prediction methods should be applied rather than limiting to comparing only two different models, as was conducted in May et al. [41].

As a consequence, the literature review revealed the need for a systematic consideration of a number of optimal criteria: profit, costs (energy, material, and labor costs), production capacity, and others. Only such a multi-criteria approach can overcome the difficulties of the effective application of the provisions of the theory of mass service in the optimization of economic systems. The solution of this problem can help to increase the efficiency of business process automation and form a highly efficient digital corporate platform.

In modern conditions of the transformation of the production structure of economic management, deployment of the Fourth Industrial Revolution, technological modernization of the industrial complex, and new approaches to the organization of resource-saving production systems are required. One of the tools for solving such an important problem is the design of organizational structures for managing resource-saving production systems in the conditions of digitalization of industry, as well as the development of approaches assessing their effectiveness. An effective method of designing optimal organizational structures, which characterizes the efficiency of management and the speed of processes within each enterprise, has been proposed to represent management structures in the form of mass service networks. This method makes it possible to perform evaluations using indicators such as the average number of operations performed by an employee, the average time to perform an operation, the average number of operations waiting to be performed, and the average waiting time to perform an operation, which makes it possible to find problem areas in the management structure and in individual departments.

Implementation of the policy of resource-saving production technologies finds practical application in all sectors of industry, which predetermines the importance and relevance of their use to achieve sustainable development and improve the competitiveness of industrial enterprises. At present, it is impossible to ignore the fact of the complex nature of this issue, which involves competitiveness management, the development of product and process innovations, networking models, and ensuring the sustainable development of industry. It is not possible to achieve a solution to these problems without a proper assessment of existing organizational structures and their optimization, if necessary.

5. Conclusions

Thus, the following gaps in the research of mass service systems have been revealed: the principles of system analysis (unity of elements, connectivity, hierarchy, etc.) are often ignored when modeling functional subsystems interconnected within the contour of an economic system (for example, an industrial enterprise); calculations of the optimal level of resource consumption should be based on the analysis of the maximum number of solutions (search iterations) within the modeled mass service system and should not be limited to alternative ones; causal relationships between the eco-economic effect of the practical implementation of the provisions of the theory of mass service (in the context of processes) and the level of competitiveness of organizations are insufficiently presented and substantiated; and studies devoted to the construction of an effective organizational structure on the basis of the mass service system are poorly presented.

Regarding digital platforms, which are flexible and scalable, it becomes possible to plan the production of new goods. The organizational structure of management is one of the tools to improve the management system, the units of which are subject to constant changes and adjustments—the creation, reduction, division, and unification of links—in the process of the development and growth of enterprises. Each type of organizational structure has its advantages and disadvantages and can be formed in accordance with a particular strategy of enterprise development. The identification of a more effective and optimal organizational structure requires the development of appropriate methods or a set of them. Each employee is a part of a multi-caliber system. In this regard, the systematized toolkit of industrial production efficiency management based on the methodology of mass service system, the technology of designing the organizational structure of management, and the formed indicators for assessing its effectiveness allows us to improve the performance of the existing organizational structure of the enterprise as a whole. The organizational structure of management is a network of mass service without queue limitation, which means that the incoming request to the enterprise will be fulfilled sooner or later. The main characteristics of a classical mass service system are its numerical characteristics: the waiting probability; average number of requirements under service (related to the load factor of the servicing unit); average queue length; average number of requirements in the system; and average length of the real queue, which requires further testing as data are accumulated. For correct management decision making and evaluation of the efficiency of the management system, we propose to take into account, for example, the following criteria: the coefficient of manageability; the share of personnel involved in innovative management projects; the coefficient of the labor efficiency of the staff; the coefficient of the economic efficiency of managerial activity; the output of the target product; and the cost of production, among others.

In addition, we conclude that the complex architecture of modern economic systems opens a wide research field for finding a methodology for assessing the dependence of enterprise performance on the effect of optimization provided by using the provisions of the theory of mass service. The application of this theory to resource and organizational-structural components seems to be a promising direction of research. This statement can be used as the basis for future research aimed at formalizing the mathematical dependence of the effective indicators of the organization's functioning (profit, profitability, etc.) on the optimization effect (reducing customer service costs, order management, process and operation management, organizational structure rationalization, etc.).

Author Contributions: Conceptualization, N.V.B.; methodology, F.F.G.; formal analysis, F.F.G. and N.V.B.; investigation, F.F.G. and N.V.B.; writing—original draft preparation, F.F.G. and N.V.B.; writing—review and editing, F.F.G. and N.V.B. All authors have read and agreed to the published version of the manuscript.

Funding: This research was carried out within the framework of the grant of the President of the Russian Federation for state support of leading scientific schools of the Russian Federation, project number NSh-1886.2022.2, agreement 075-15-2022-836.

Data Availability Statement: No new data were created or analyzed in this study. Data sharing is not applicable to this article.

Conflicts of Interest: The authors declare no conflicts of interest.

References

1. Budzko, V.; Ereshko, F.; Gorelov, M. Mathematical models of control in Digital Economy platforms. *Procedia Comput. Sci.* **2021**, *190*, 115–121. [CrossRef]
2. Erlang, A.K. Sandsynlighedsregning og Telefonsamtaler. *Nyt Tidsskr. Mat.* **1909**, *20*, 33–39.
3. Civelek, I.; Biller, B.; Scheller-Wolf, A. Impact of dependence on single-server queueing systems. *Eur. J. Oper. Res.* **2021**, *290*, 1031–1045. [CrossRef]
4. Kondrashova, E. Optimization of Controlled Queueing Systems: The Case of Car Wash Services. *Transp. Res. Procedia* **2021**, *54*, 662–671. [CrossRef]
5. Krishnamoorthy, A.; Joshua, A.N.; Kozyrev, D. Analysis of a Batch Arrival, Batch Service Queuing-Inventory System with Processing of Inventory While on Vacation. *Mathematics* **2021**, *9*, 419. [CrossRef]
6. Singh, S.K.; Acharya, S.K.; Cruz, F.R.B.; Quinino, R.C. Estimation of traffic intensity from queue length data in a deterministic single server queueing system. *J. Comput. Appl. Math.* **2021**, *398*, 113693. [CrossRef]
7. Makeeva, E.; Kochetkova, I.; Alkanhel, R. Retrial Queueing System for Analyzing Impact of Priority Ultra-Reliable Low-Latency Communication Transmission on Enhanced Mobile Broadband Quality of Service Degradation in 5G Networks. *Mathematics* **2023**, *11*, 3925. [CrossRef]
8. Al-Begain, K.; Dudin, A.; Kazimirsky, A.; Yerima, S. Investigation of the M2/G2/1/∞, N queue with restricted admission of priority customers and its application to HSDPA mobile systems. *Comput. Netw.* **2009**, *53*, 1186–1201. [CrossRef]
9. Van Do, T. A new computational algorithm for retrial queues to cellular mobile systems with guard channels. *Comput. Ind. Eng.* **2010**, *59*, 865–872. [CrossRef]

10. Shajin, D.; Krishnamoorthy, A.; Melikov, A.Z.; Sztrik, J. Multi-Server Queuing Production Inventory System with Emergency Replenishment. *Mathematics* **2022**, *10*, 3839. [CrossRef]
11. Fiems, D.; Bruneel, H. Discrete-time queueing systems with Markovian preemptive vacations. *Math. Comput. Model.* **2013**, *57*, 782–792. [CrossRef]
12. Palmer, G.I.; Harper, P.R.; Knight, V.A. Modelling deadlock in open restricted queueing networks. *Eur. J. Oper. Res.* **2018**, *266*, 609–621. [CrossRef]
13. Jeganathan, K.; Harikrishnan, T.; Prasanna Lakshmi, K.; Nagarajan, D. A multi-server retrial queueing-inventory system with asynchronous multiple vacations. *Decis. Anal. J.* **2023**, *9*, 100333. [CrossRef]
14. Saravanan, V.; Poongothai, V.; Godhandaraman, P. Performance analysis of a multi server retrial queueing system with unreliable server, discouragement and vacation model. *Math. Comput. Simul.* **2023**, *214*, 204–226. [CrossRef]
15. Jeganathan, K.; Harikrishnan, T.; Lakshmanan, K.; Melikov, A.; Sztrik, J. Modeling of Junior Servers Approaching a Senior Server in the Retrial Queuing-Inventory System. *Mathematics* **2023**, *11*, 4581. [CrossRef]
16. Yang, R.; Bhulai, S.; van der Mei, R. Optimal resource allocation for multiqueue systems with a shared server pool. *Queueing Syst.* **2011**, *68*, 133–163. [CrossRef]
17. Pankratova, E.; Moiseeva, S.; Farkhadov, M. Infinite-Server Resource Queueing Systems with Different Types of Markov-Modulated Poisson Process and Renewal Arrivals. *Mathematics* **2022**, *10*, 2962. [CrossRef]
18. Zhan, W.; Jiang, M.; Wang, X. Optimal Capacity Decision-Making of Omnichannel Catering Merchants Considering the Service Environment Based on Queuing Theory. *Systems* **2022**, *10*, 144. [CrossRef]
19. Filipowicz, B.; Bieda, B. Application of Queuing Systems with Many Classes of Customers for Structural Optimization of Banks. *IFAC Proc. Vol.* **1997**, *30*, 149–154. [CrossRef]
20. Zhang, H.; Akuamoah, S.W.; Apeanti, W.O.; Harvim, P.; Yaro, D.; Georgescu, P. The Stability Analysis of a Double-X Queuing Network Occurring in the Banking Sector. *Mathematics* **2021**, *9*, 1957. [CrossRef]
21. Hao, T.; Yifei, T. Study on Queuing System Optimization of Bank Based on BPR. *Procedia Environ. Sci.* **2011**, *10 Pt A*, 640–646. [CrossRef]
22. Ďutková, S.; Achimský, K.; Hoštáková, D. Simulation of Queuing System of Post Office. *Transp. Res. Procedia* **2019**, *40*, 1037–1044. [CrossRef]
23. Zychlinski, N. Applications of fluid models in service operations management. *Queueing Syst.* **2023**, *103*, 161–185. [CrossRef]
24. Majlesinasab, N.; Maleki, M.; Nikbakhsh, E. Performance evaluation of an EMS system using queuing theory and location analysis: A case study. *Am. J. Emerg. Med.* **2022**, *51*, 32–45. [CrossRef] [PubMed]
25. Naumov, V.; Samouylov, K. Product-form markovian queueing systems with multiple resources. *Probab. Eng. Informational Sci.* **2021**, *35*, 180–188. [CrossRef]
26. Naumov, V.A.; Gaidamaka, Y.V.; Samouylov, K.E. Computing the Stationary Distribution of Queueing Systems with Random Resource Requirements via Fast Fourier Transform. *Mathematics* **2020**, *8*, 772. [CrossRef]
27. Kim, S.-K.; Yeun, C.Y. A Versatile Queuing System for Sharing Economy Platform Operations. *Mathematics* **2019**, *7*, 1005. [CrossRef]
28. Stojčić, M.; Pamučar, D.; Mahmutagić, E.; Stević, Ž. Development of an ANFIS Model for the Optimization of a Queuing System in Warehouses. *Information* **2018**, *9*, 240. [CrossRef]
29. Bychkov, I.; Kazakov, A.; Lempert, A.; Zharkov, M. Modeling of Railway Stations Based on Queuing Networks. *Appl. Sci.* **2021**, *11*, 2425. [CrossRef]
30. Kazakov, A.; Lempert, A.; Zharkov, M. An approach to railway network sections modelling based on queuing networks. *J. Rail Transp. Plan. Manag.* **2023**, *27*, 100404. [CrossRef]
31. Abdulaziz Alnowibet, K.; Khireldin, A.; Abdelawwad, M.; Mohamed, A.W. Airport terminal building capacity evaluation us- ing queuing system. *Alex. Eng. J.* **2022**, *61*, 10109–10118. [CrossRef]
32. Selvi, A.; Rosenshine, M. A queueing system for airport buses. *Transp. Res. Part B Methodol.* **1983**, *17*, 427–434. [CrossRef]
33. Shone, R.; Glazebrook, K.; Zografos, K.G. Resource allocation in congested queueing systems with time-varying demand: An application to airport operations. *Eur. J. Oper. Res.* **2019**, *276*, 566–581. [CrossRef]
34. Itoh, E.; Mitici, M. Analyzing tactical control strategies for aircraft arrivals at an airport using a queuing model. *J. Air Transp. Manag.* **2020**, *89*, 101938. [CrossRef]
35. Rodríguez-Sanz, Á.; Fernández de Marcos, A.; Pérez-Castán, J.A.; Comendador, F.G.; Arnaldo Valdés, R.; París Loreiro, Á. Queue behavioural patterns for passengers at airport terminals: A machine learning approach. *J. Air Transp. Manag.* **2021**, *90*, 101940. [CrossRef]
36. Zhao, X.; Wang, Y.; Li, L.; Delahaye, D. A Queuing Network Model of a Multi-Airport System Based on Point-Wise Stationary Approximation. *Aerospace* **2022**, *9*, 390. [CrossRef]
37. Jia, W.; Huang, Y.-l.; Zhao, Q.; Qi, Y. Modelling taxi drivers' decisions at airport based on queueing theory. *Res. Transp. Econ.* **2022**, *92*, 101093. [CrossRef]
38. Yang, Q.; Qiao, Z.; Yang, B.; Shi, Z. Modelling and uncovering the passenger-taxi dynamic queues at taxi station with multiple boarding points using a Markovian environment. *Phys. A Stat. Mech. Its Appl.* **2021**, *572*, 125870. [CrossRef]
39. Yang, Q.; Yang, B.; Qiao, Z.; Tang, M.; Gao, F. Impact of possible random factors on queue behaviours of passengers and taxis at taxi stand of transport hubs. *Phys. A Stat. Mech. Its Appl.* **2021**, *580*, 126131. [CrossRef]

40. Martyn, Y.; Liaskovska, S.; Gregus, M.; Izonin, I.; Velyka, O. Optimization of Technological's Processes Industry 4.0 Parameters for Details Manufacturing via Stamping: Rules of Queuing Systems. *Procedia Comput. Sci.* **2021**, *191*, 290–295. [CrossRef]
41. May, M.C.; Albers, A.; Fischer, M.D.; Mayerhofer, F.; Schäfer, L.; Lanza, G. Queue Length Forecasting in Complex Manufacturing Job Shops. *Forecasting* **2021**, *3*, 322–338. [CrossRef]
42. Chiacchio, F.; Oliveri, L.; Khodayee, S.M.; D'Urso, D. Performance Analysis of a Repairable Production Line Using a Hybrid Dependability Queueing Model Based on Monte Carlo Simulation. *Appl. Sci.* **2023**, *13*, 271. [CrossRef]
43. Melikov, A.Z.; Mirzayev, R.R.; Nair, S.S. Numerical Study of a Queuing-Inventory System with Two Supply Sources and Destructive Customers. *J. Comput. Syst. Sci. Int.* **2022**, *61*, 581–598. [CrossRef]
44. Melikov, A.; Poladova, L.; Edayapurath, S.; Sztrik, J. Single-Server Queuing-Inventory Systems with Negative Customers and Catastrophes in the Warehouse. *Mathematics* **2023**, *11*, 2380. [CrossRef]
45. Melikov, A.; Aliyeva, S.; Nair, S.S.; Kumar, B.K. Retrial Queuing-Inventory Systems with Delayed Feedback and Instantaneous Damaging of Items. *Axioms* **2022**, *11*, 241. [CrossRef]
46. Baek, J.W.; Moon, S.K. A production-inventory system with a Markovian service queue and lost sales. *J. Korean Stat. Soc.* **2016**, *45*, 14–24. [CrossRef]
47. Alnowibet, K.A.; Alrasheedi, A.F.; Alqahtani, F.S. Queuing Models for Analyzing the Steady-State Distribution of Stochastic Inventory Systems with Random Lead Time and Impatient Customers. *Processes* **2022**, *10*, 624. [CrossRef]
48. Dissa, S.; Ushakumari, P.V. Two commodity queueing inventory system with random common lifetime, two demand classes and pool of customers. *Heliyon* **2023**, *9*, e21478. [CrossRef] [PubMed]
49. Chang, K.-H.; Lu, Y.-S. Queueing analysis on a single-station make-to-stock/make-to-order inventory-production system. *Appl. Math. Model.* **2010**, *34*, 978–991. [CrossRef]
50. Barsegyan, N.V.; Shinkevich, A.I. Optimization of the organizational structure of enterprise management using the theory of queuing. *Mod. High-Tech Technol.* **2020**, *9*, 9–15. [CrossRef]
51. Christopher, O.A.; Akindele, J. Re-design of Organisational Structure of a Manufacturing Firm. In *Advancing Industrial Engineering in Nigeria through Teaching, Research and Innovation*; Department of Industrial and Production Engineering, University of Ibadan: Oyo, Nigeria, 2020; pp. 549–589.
52. Dopson, S.; Stewart, R. Information Technology, Organizational Restructuring and the Future of Middle Management. *New Technol. Work. Employ.* **2007**, *8*, 10–20. [CrossRef]
53. Hague, D.C.; Drucker, P. Management: Tasks, Responsibilities, Practices. *Econ. J.* **1975**, *85*, 195. [CrossRef]
54. Trzcieliński, S.; Pawłowski, E.; Kałkowska, J. *Management Systems. Methods and Structures*; Publishing House of Poznan University of Technology: Poznań, Poland, 2009; Volume 123. [CrossRef]
55. Alyokhina, O.I. Choosing the optimal organizational structure: Market, hierarchical structures and hybrid forms. *Strateg. Manag.* **2012**, *3*, 212–220. (In Russian)
56. Brom, A.E.; Belonosov, K.Y. Development of an approach to the implementation of a lean production system based on the hierarchy analysis method. *Bull. Mosc. State Reg. Univ. Ser. Econ.* **2017**, *2*, 46–53. (In Russian)
57. Mintzberg, H. *The Structuring of Organization: A Synthesis of the Research*; Printice Hall: Englewood Cliffs, NJ, USA, 1979; pp. 481–496.
58. Gritans, Y.M. Organizational design and restructuring (reengineering) of enterprises and holdings. In *Economic, Managerial and Legal Aspects*; Wolters Kluwer Russia: Moscow, Russia, 2006; Volume 205. (In Russian)
59. Milgrom, P.; Roberts, J. Economics of modern manufacturing: Technology, strategy, and organization. *Am. Econ. Rev.* **2013**, *80*, 511–528.
60. Serbin, V.V.; Zhanalinova, A.A. Management of the process of designing multi-stream business processes. *Bull. Almaty Univ. Energy Commun.* **2023**, *1*, 163–172. [CrossRef]
61. Vostroknutov, A.E. Development of a new concept, notation of the representation of the organizational structure and models of their assessment using the theory of queuing. *Polythematic Online Electron. Sci. J. KubGAU* **2017**, *130*, 1087–1121. (In Russian)
62. Calvo, G.; Wellisz, S. Hierarchy, Ability and Income Distribution. *J. Political Econ.* **1979**, *87*, 991–1010. [CrossRef]
63. Kirpichnikov, A.P.; Titovtsev, A.S. Practical Recommendations on the Application of Markov Queuing Models with a Restricted Queue. In Proceedings of the 2019 3rd School on Dynamics of Complex Networks and Their Application in Intellectual Robotics (DCNAIR), Innopolis, Russia, 9–11 September 2019; pp. 81–82. [CrossRef]

Disclaimer/Publisher's Note: The statements, opinions and data contained in all publications are solely those of the individual author(s) and contributor(s) and not of MDPI and/or the editor(s). MDPI and/or the editor(s) disclaim responsibility for any injury to people or property resulting from any ideas, methods, instructions or products referred to in the content.

MDPI
St. Alban-Anlage 66
4052 Basel
Switzerland
www.mdpi.com

Mathematics Editorial Office
E-mail: mathematics@mdpi.com
www.mdpi.com/journal/mathematics

Disclaimer/Publisher's Note: The statements, opinions and data contained in all publications are solely those of the individual author(s) and contributor(s) and not of MDPI and/or the editor(s). MDPI and/or the editor(s) disclaim responsibility for any injury to people or property resulting from any ideas, methods, instructions or products referred to in the content.

www.ingramcontent.com/pod-product-compliance
Lightning Source LLC
LaVergne TN
LVHW070729100526
838202LV00013B/1196